the Seamless Bible

COMPILED BY
CHARLES ROLLER WITH CAROL MERSCH

the Seamless Bible

THE STORY OF CHRIST

THE EVENTS OF THE NEW TESTAMENT
IN CHRONOLOGICAL ORDER

Cover Design by WGroup, Tulsa, OK

The Seamless Bible
ISBN 0-7684-2231-0

1 2 3 4 5 6 7 8 9 10 / 09 08 07 06 05 04

For a U.S. bookstore nearest you, call
1-800-722-6774
For information on foreign distributors, call
717-532-3040
Or reach us on the Internet:
www.destinyimage.com

*Dedicated to those with an interest
in the journey toward Christ*

Acknowledgements

I feel deeply grateful to the people who, throughout my life, freely gave me substance and support in the formation and fulfillment of my dream.

Heartfelt thanks go to the following:

- My mother, Maurine, for passing on to me the seed of talent; for teaching me about courage, patience, and sharing; and for giving me my independent spirit. Her memory, her goodness, and her love will always be in my heart.

I also want to thank the special people from whom I learned the meaning of selfless support and boundless wisdom, and through whom this book project gained clear focus and gathered great spiritual strength:

- Carol Mersch, for the help she provided in giving birth to the project; for transforming my early efforts from the possible to the practical; for sharing her talent, treasure, and spiritual outlook; for the faithful friendship quietly given throughout the years; and for exemplifying the silent power of Providence in all that she beholds.
- Rev. Danny Lynchard, for joining with Carol in providing encouragement; for applying able ministerial guidance; and for thoughtful insights vital to the book project.
- Gail Runnels, for the quiet guidance and rare wisdom of a superior mind; for the special talent of advising the right thing at the right time for the right reason; and for giving the book project the vision of the widest appeal to the most readers.

Also, special thanks to two people who devoted their talents to the project with spiritual and technical expertise in order to form and fashion the book's unity and appeal:

- Timothy L. Disney, for applying his enormous will and skill in programming as he alone could, taking one systematic step after another to provide an electronic framework that could transform the book's concepts into reality; for the endless hours he gave to this labor of love, with a standard of excellence and dedication defying description; and for being a faithful friend for over a decade.

- Sherry Jackson, for being more than an editor; for sharing her intangible way of making just the right suggestion; for her spiritual integrity and personal goodness; and for granting her friendship.

Endorsements

"The compilation of these New Testament stories, put in chronological order, is very well done. I trust that people who never pick up a Bible will read *The Seamless Bible* for a better understanding and be blessed."

Oral Roberts, *B.A., M.Div, LL.D*
Founder, Oral Roberts University
Oral Roberts Evangelistic Association

"The greatest possession in life is wisdom. Wisdom is the ability to apply knowledge effectively. However, it is impossible to apply what you don't or can't understand. Therefore, understanding is the key to wisdom. It is said that in all your getting, get understanding. *The Seamless Bible* has taken a great leap in presenting the most important body of knowledge and truth in a people-friendly form. This is going to be a classic and will open the world of biblical revelation to a world in desperate need of it."

Myles Munroe
BFM International, Nassau, Bahamas

"The truth of God's Word sets people free. To have the Word of God presented in a sequential order is helpful in understanding the events and therefore grasping the true meaning of the scriptures. I pray the Holy Spirit will give you revelation in the knowledge of Jesus."

Billy Joe Daugherty
Pastor, Victory Christian Center, Tulsa, OK

"*The Seamless Bible* is a flowing narrative of the most important story ever told. It is the King James Bible of old arranged in such a way that a grandparent can captivate the imagination and attention of even a young child as the good news of Jesus Christ is warmly shared. I found myself reading *The Seamless Bible* as I would a modern novel, but the time I spent reading it will be measured not in hours, but in eternity. I highly commend *The Seamless Bible*."

Wade Burleson
President, Baptist General Convention of Oklahoma

⁓

"The life of Jesus can be difficult to follow because His story is told in four Gospels. When we read the New Testament like any other book, it can seem like we're going in circles. The aim of *The Seamless Bible* is to sequence the life of Jesus in an easier-to-read fashion. This approach can be very helpful to those who are being introduced to Jesus."

Dr. Tom Harrison
Senior Pastor, Asbury United Methodist Church, Tulsa, OK

⁓

"*The Seamless Bible* is an incredible scripture text that has allowed us an opportunity to see scripture come alive. There are a number of Bibles that are open to us for reading, for application, for inspiration and devotion. But when a reader turns to the Bible, he is looking for a connection from one text to the other. *The Seamless Bible* has made this connection in a way that causes the scripture to come to life."

Emil Hawkins, *BPS, ThB, MA*
Senior Pastor, Liberty World Outreach Church

⁓

"The innovative presentation of *The Seamless Bible* preserves all the integrity and richness of the King James Version, at the same time bringing the message of the gospel to 21st century seekers in a creative and meaningful way."

Rev. Penelope A. Black and Canon Elizabeth St. C. Stewart
Anglican Church of Canada, Diocese of British Columbia

⁓

"*The Seamless Bible* is a unique presentation of the New Testament. It is easy to read and an accurate rendering of the King James Version. I recommend it."

Warren Hultgren
Former Senior Pastor, First Baptist Church, Tulsa, OK
Theological Reference, New King James Bible

⁓

"A great and scholarly job of bringing chronological order into the work."

Dr. Edgar D. Mitchell
Apollo 14 Lunar Module Pilot
Founder, Institute of Noetic Sciences
Author, "The Way of the Explorer" and "Psychic Exploration"

⁓

"Thank God we live in a day when a person, moved by God's Spirit, may freely bring to the eyes of the people something that will stir the heart!"

Danny Lynchard
Pastor, Fisher Baptist Church, Sand Springs, OK
Executive Director, Tulsa Police/Fire Chaplaincy Corps

"Now I get it…."

Jay Cronley
Journalist, Novelist, and Screenwriter
Author, "Let it Ride," "Funny Farm," and "Quick Change"

Table of Contents

THE JOURNEY OF CHRIST

THE JOURNEY OF THE APOSTLES

To the Reader

The collection of lessons witnessed and recorded by the disciples as they walked with Jesus may well be the single most valuable guidepost to living that we have today. You have in your hands a powerful new presentation of the life of Christ, drawn from the original King James New Testament and recast in a refreshing narrative format that weaves all of the accounts of Jesus' life into one seamless story.

Over twenty-five years in the making, *The Seamless Bible* presents the entire King James New Testament arranged in sequential order, with special care given to preserve and blend the original King James text into one continuous flow of events without translation or interpretation. The King James Version of the Bible, first published in 1611 and revised in 1769, was chosen as the basis of the work, as it remains the most beautiful and widely accepted translation of the Bible in the world today.

From this translation the Books of the New Testament are used to create a biblical biography of unique simplicity that details the life of Jesus. In the first section, "The Journey of Christ," the text of the Gospel authors—Matthew, Mark, Luke, and John—are woven together into one complete narrative of the life of Jesus in a consistent flow of time from His birth to His resurrection. The time-sequenced events of the second section, "The Journey of the Apostles," is taken from Acts and the Letters and follows the apostles and disciples as they took up the teachings of their Master and continued His work after His death. Eleven Letters are inserted in Acts at the time they were written, and the other eleven Letters follow to conclude the New Testament.

The result is a unique presentation of the most time-honored Book in all literature, meticulously arranged in order of time and true in every detail to the original King James text. Every available reference was researched and studied in the compilation of this book, including other versions of the Bible, Bible reference, and related scriptural texts.

17

The most memorable phrases of Jesus are inset in the margins and all text quotations from the Old Testament are noted in italics. Outdated words in the original version were carefully researched and replaced with their modern-day equivalents so that the lessons given by Jesus so many years ago can be clearly applied to our lives today.

The column of paragraph numbers in the margin of each page serves a unique purpose. As you study this book you may find it useful to refer to your favorite passages quickly by chapter and paragraph number.

The reader will realize that *The Seamless Bible* does not contain the traditional chapter and verse. *The Seamless Bible* is the New Testament arranged in chronological order, without chapter and verse as in the original text, to allow a more undistracted reading of the Word. The cross-reference index in the back of the book can be used to trace a specific chapter and verse to its location in the associated chapter and paragraph.

Included in this narrative are some of the most respected words that exist in print—an endless stream of Jesus' experiences, words, and deeds that reveal God's love and provide spiritual guidance for every hungry heart.

Thus, following in the footsteps of time, page by page, *The Seamless Bible* leads you alongside Jesus and His disciples in a journey through the greatest story ever told. Its sole aim is to carry the story forward in a more inspiring, vital, and meaningful manner so that you, the reader, might apprehend and apply its message more fully in the world today.

We search the world for truth; we cull

the good, the pure, the beautiful,

from graven stone and written scroll,

from all old flower-fields of the soul;

and, weary seekers of the best,

we come back laden from our quest,

to find that all the sages said

is in the Book our mothers read.

John Greenleaf Whittier, excerpt from "Miriam"

The Journey of Christ

PART 1

Birth and Childhood

The birth of Jesus was foretold long before He made His appearance on earth. His coming was revealed to many people in many ways hundreds of years before His birth. Throughout time, angels were the messengers sent by God to deliver His word to those chosen to do His calling. It is important, therefore, that we start at the true beginning of the story—with the prophecy of angels.

> THE ANGEL GABRIEL WAS SENT FROM GOD
> UNTO A CITY OF GALILEE, NAMED NAZARETH, TO
> A VIRGIN PLEDGED TO BE MARRIED TO A MAN
> WHOSE NAME WAS JOSEPH, OF THE HOUSE OF
> DAVID; AND THE VIRGIN'S NAME WAS MARY.
>
> (LUKE 1:26-27)

CHAPTER 1

THE GREAT ANNOUNCEMENT

The Proclamation
Luke 1:1-4

1   Inasmuch as many have taken in hand to set forth in order a declaration of those things which are most surely believed among us, even as they delivered them unto us, which from the beginning were eyewitnesses, and ministers of the word; it seemed good to me also, having had perfect understanding of all things from the very first, to write unto you in order that you might know the certainty of those things wherein you have been instructed.

Birth of John Foretold
Luke 1:5-25

2   There was in the days of Herod, the king of Judea, a certain priest named Zacharias, of the division of Abijah: and his wife was of the daughters of Aaron, and her name was Elizabeth. And they were both righteous before God, walking in all the commandments and ordinances of the Lord blameless. And they had no child, because Elizabeth was barren, and they both were now well advanced in years.

3   And it came to pass, that while he executed the priest's office before God in the order of his division, according to the custom of the priest's office, his lot was to burn incense when he went into the temple of the Lord. And the whole multitude of the people were praying outside at the time of incense.

4   And there appeared unto him an angel of the Lord standing on the right side of the altar of incense. And when Zacharias saw him, he was troubled, and fear fell upon him. But the angel said unto him, "Fear not, Zacharias: for your prayer is heard; and your wife Elizabeth shall bear you a son, and you shall call his name John.

"And you shall have joy and gladness; and many shall rejoice at his 5 birth. For he shall be great in the sight of the Lord, and shall drink neither wine nor strong drink; and he shall be filled with the Holy Ghost, even from his mother's womb. And many of the children of Israel shall he turn to the Lord their God. And he shall go before him in the spirit and power of Elijah, '*to turn the hearts of the fathers to the children*,' and the disobedient to the wisdom of the just; to make ready a people prepared for the Lord."

And Zacharias said unto the angel, "How shall I know this? for I am 6 an old man, and my wife well advanced in years." And the angel answering said unto him, "I am Gabriel, that stands in the presence of God; and am sent to speak unto you, and to show you these glad tidings. And, behold, you shall be mute, and not able to speak, until the day that these things shall be performed, because you believe not my words, which shall be fulfilled in their season."

And the people waited for Zacharias, and marveled that he tarried so 7 long in the temple. And when he came out, he could not speak unto them: and they perceived that he had seen a vision in the temple: for he beckoned unto them, and remained speechless.

And it came to pass, that, as soon as the days of his service were 8 accomplished, he departed to his own house. And after those days his wife Elizabeth conceived, and hid herself five months, saying, "Thus has the Lord dealt with me in the days wherein he looked on me, to take away my disgrace among men."

Birth of Jesus Foretold
Luke 1:26-38

And in the sixth month the angel Gabriel was sent from God unto a 9 city of Galilee, named Nazareth, to a virgin pledged to be married to a man whose name was Joseph, of the house of David; and the virgin's name was Mary.

And the angel came in unto her, and said, "Hail, you that are highly 10 favored, the Lord is with you: blessed are you among women." And when she saw him, she was troubled at his saying, and cast in her mind what manner of greeting this should be.

> "FEAR NOT, MARY: FOR YOU HAVE FOUND FAVOR WITH GOD."

And the angel said unto her, "Fear not, Mary: for you have found favor 11 with God. And, behold, you shall conceive in your womb, and bring forth a son, and shall call his name Jesus. He shall be great, and shall be called the Son of the Highest: and the Lord God shall give unto him the throne of his father David: and he shall reign over the house of Jacob for ever; and of his kingdom there shall be no end."

Then said Mary unto the angel, "How shall this be, seeing I have no 12 union with a man?" And the angel answered and said unto her, "The Holy

12 Ghost shall come upon you, and the power of the Highest shall overshadow you: therefore also that holy thing which shall be born of you shall be called the Son of God. And, behold, your relative Elizabeth, she has also conceived a son in her old age: and this is the sixth month with her, who was called barren. For with God nothing shall be impossible."

13 And Mary said, "Behold the handmaid of the Lord; be it unto me according to your word." And the angel departed from her.

Mary's Visit With Elizabeth
Luke 1:39-45

14 And Mary arose in those days, and went into the hill country with haste, into a city of Judah; and entered into the house of Zacharias, and greeted Elizabeth.

15 And it came to pass, that, when Elizabeth heard the greeting of Mary, the baby leaped in her womb; and Elizabeth was filled with the Holy Ghost: and she spoke out with a loud voice, and said, "Blessed are you among women, and blessed is the fruit of your womb. And what is this to me, that the mother of my Lord should come to me? For, lo, as soon as the voice of your greeting sounded in my ears, the baby leaped in my womb for joy. And blessed is she that believed: for there shall be a performance of those things which were told her from the Lord."

Mary's Praise of God
Luke 1:46-56

16 And Mary said, "My soul does magnify the Lord, and my spirit has rejoiced in God my Savior. For he has regarded the low status of his hand-maiden: for, behold, from henceforth all generations shall call me blessed. For he that is mighty has done to me great things; and holy is his name. And his mercy is on them that fear him from generation to generation.

17 "He has showed strength with his arm; he has scattered the proud in the imagination of their hearts. He has put down the mighty from their seats, and exalted them of low degree. He has filled the hungry with good things; and the rich he has sent empty away. He has helped his servant Israel, in remembrance of his mercy; as he spoke to our fathers, to Abraham, and to his seed for ever."

18 And Mary stayed with her about three months, and returned to her own house.

Birth of John the Baptist
Luke 1:57-66

19 Now Elizabeth's full time came that she should be delivered; and she brought forth a son. And her neighbors and her relatives heard how the Lord had showed great mercy upon her; and they rejoiced with her.

20 And it came to pass, that on the eighth day they came to circumcise the child; and they called him Zacharias, after the name of his father. And

his mother answered and said, "Not so; but he shall be called John." And 20 they said unto her, "There is none of your family that is called by this name."

And they made signs to his father, how he would have him called. And 21 he asked for a writing tablet, and wrote, saying, "His name is John." And they all marveled. And his mouth was opened immediately, and his tongue loosed, and he spoke, and praised God.

And fear came on all that dwelt round about them: and all these say- 22 ings were talked about throughout all the hill country of Judea. And all they that heard them laid them up in their hearts, saying, "What manner of child shall this be!" And the hand of the Lord was with him.

Zacharias Prophesies John's Destiny
Luke 1:67-80

And his father Zacharias was filled with the Holy Ghost, and prophe- 23 sied, saying, "Blessed be the Lord God of Israel; for he has visited and redeemed his people, and has raised up a horn of salvation for us in the house of his servant David; as he spoke by the mouth of his holy prophets, which have been since the world began: that we should be saved from our enemies, and from the hand of all that hate us; to perform the mercy prom- ised to our fathers, and to remember his holy covenant; the oath which he swore to our father Abraham, that he would grant unto us, that we being delivered out of the hand of our enemies might serve him without fear, in holiness and righteousness before him, all the days of our life.

"And you, child, shall be called the prophet of the Highest: for you 24 shall go before the face of the Lord to prepare his ways; to give knowledge of salvation unto his people by the remission of their sins, through the ten- der mercy of our God; by which the dayspring from on high has visited us, to give light to them that sit in darkness and in the shadow of death, to guide our feet into the way of peace."

And the child grew, and became strong in spirit, and was in the deserts 25 till the day of his showing unto Israel.

CHAPTER 2

THE PROMISE FULFILLED

Birth of Jesus Christ
Matthew 1:18-25; Luke 2:1-7

1   Now the birth of Jesus Christ was in this way: When as his mother Mary was pledged to be married to Joseph, before they came together, she was found with child of the Holy Ghost. Then Joseph her husband, being a just man, and not willing to make her a public example, was minded to put her away secretly.

2   But while he thought on these things, behold, the angel of the Lord appeared unto him in a dream, saying, "Joseph, son of David, fear not to take unto you Mary your wife: for that which is conceived in her is of the Holy Ghost. And she shall bring forth a son, and you shall call his name Jesus: for he shall save his people from their sins."

3   Now all this was done, that it might be fulfilled which was spoken of the Lord by the prophet, saying, *"Behold, a virgin shall be with child, and shall bring forth a son, and they shall call his name Emmanuel,"* which being interpreted is, *"God with us."*

4   Then Joseph being raised from sleep did as the angel of the Lord had commanded him, and took unto him his wife: and had no union with her till she had brought forth her firstborn son: and he called his name Jesus.

5   And it came to pass in those days, that there went out a decree from Caesar Augustus, that all the world should be taxed. (And this taxing was first made when Cyrenius was governor of Syria.)

6   And all went to be taxed, everyone into his own city. And Joseph also went up from Galilee, out of the city of Nazareth, into Judea, unto the city of David, which is called Bethlehem; (because he was of the house and lineage of David): to be taxed with Mary his pledged wife, being great with child.

7   And so it was, that, while they were there, the days were accomplished that she should be delivered. And she brought forth her firstborn son, and wrapped him in swaddling clothes, and laid him in a manger; because there was no room for them in the inn.

Shepherds Receive Good Tidings
Luke 2:8-20

And there were in the same country shepherds abiding in the field, 8 keeping watch over their flock by night.

And, lo, the angel of the Lord came upon them, and the glory of the 9 Lord shone round about them: and they were very afraid. And the angel said unto them, "Fear not: for, behold, I bring you good tidings of great joy, which shall be to all people. For unto you is born this day in the city of David a Savior, which is Christ the Lord. And this shall be a sign unto you: You shall find the baby wrapped in swaddling clothes, lying in a manger."

> "FEAR NOT: FOR, BEHOLD, I BRING YOU GOOD TIDINGS OF GREAT JOY."

And suddenly there was with the angel a multitude of the heavenly 10 host praising God, and saying, "Glory to God in the highest, and on earth peace, goodwill toward men."

And it came to pass, as the angels were gone away from them into 11 heaven, the shepherds said one to another, "Let us now go even unto Bethlehem, and see this thing which is come to pass, which the Lord has made known unto us." And they came with haste, and found Mary, and Joseph, and the baby lying in a manger.

And when they had seen it, they made known abroad the saying which 12 was told them concerning this child. And all they that heard it wondered at those things which were told them by the shepherds.

But Mary kept all these things, and pondered them in her heart. And 13 the shepherds returned, glorifying and praising God for all the things that they had heard and seen, as it was told unto them.

His Name Is Jesus
Luke 2:21

And when eight days were accomplished for the circumcision of the 14 child, his name was called Jesus, which was so named of the angel before he was conceived in the womb.

Jesus Is Presented to the Lord
Luke 2:22-24

And when the days of her purification according to the law of Moses 15 were accomplished, they brought him to Jerusalem, to present him to the Lord; (as it is written in the law of the Lord, *"Every male that opens the womb shall be called holy to the Lord);"* and to offer a sacrifice according to that which is said in the law of the Lord, *"A pair of turtledoves, or two young pigeons."*

Simeon's Prophecy About Jesus
Luke 2:25-35

And, behold, there was a man in Jerusalem, whose name was Simeon; 16 and the same man was just and devout, waiting for the consolation of Israel:

16 and the Holy Ghost was upon him. And it was revealed unto him by the Holy Ghost, that he should not see death, before he had seen the Lord's Christ. And he came by the Spirit into the temple: and when the parents brought in the child Jesus, to do for him after the custom of the law, then he took him up in his arms, and blessed God, and said, "Lord, now let your servant depart in peace, according to your word: for my eyes have seen your salvation, which you have prepared before the face of all people; a light to enlighten the Gentiles, and the glory of your people Israel."

17   And Joseph and his mother marveled at those things which were spoken of him. And Simeon blessed them, and said unto Mary his mother, "Behold, this child is set for the fall and rising again of many in Israel; and for a sign which shall be spoken against; (yes, a sword shall pierce through your own soul also), that the thoughts of many hearts may be revealed."

Anna Testifies of the Savior
Luke 2:36-39

18   And there was one Anna, a prophetess, the daughter of Phanuel, of the tribe of Asher: she was of a great age, and had lived with a husband seven years from her virginity; and she was a widow of about eighty and four years of age, which departed not from the temple, but served God with fastings and prayers night and day. And she coming in that instant gave thanks likewise unto the Lord, and spoke of him to all them that looked for redemption in Jerusalem.

19   And when they had performed all things according to the law of the Lord, they returned into Galilee, to their own city Nazareth.

CHAPTER 3

··THE PROTECTED CHILDHOOD ··

Wise Men From the East
Matthew 2:1-12

Now when Jesus was born in Bethlehem of Judea in the days of Herod 1
the king, behold, there came wise men from the east to Jerusalem, saying,
"Where is he that is born King of the Jews? for we have seen his star in the
east, and are come to worship him."

When Herod the king had heard these things, he was troubled, and 2
all Jerusalem with him. And when he had gathered all the chief priests
and scribes of the people together, he inquired of them where Christ
should be born. And they said unto him, "In Bethlehem of Judea: for thus
it is written by the prophet, *'And you Bethlehem, in the land of Judah, are
not the least among the princes of Judah: for out of you shall come a Governor, that shall rule my people Israel.'"*

Then Herod, when he had secretly called the wise men, inquired of 3
them diligently what time the star appeared. And he sent them to Bethlehem, and said, "Go and search diligently for the young child; and when you
have found him, bring me word again, that I may come and worship him
also."

When they had heard the king, they departed; and, lo, the star, which 4
they saw in the east, went before them, till it came and stood over where the
young child was. When they saw the star, they rejoiced with exceedingly
great joy.

And when they were come into the house, they saw the young child 5
with Mary his mother, and fell down, and worshiped him: and when they
had opened their treasures, they presented unto him gifts; gold, and frankincense, and myrrh.

And being warned of God in a dream that they should not return to 6
Herod, they departed into their own country another way.

Flight Into Egypt With Jesus
Matthew 2:13-18

7   And when they were departed, behold, the angel of the Lord appeared to Joseph in a dream, saying, "Arise, and take the young child and his mother, and flee into Egypt, and be there until I bring you word: for Herod will seek the young child to destroy him." When he arose, he took the young child and his mother by night, and departed into Egypt: and was there until the death of Herod: that it might be fulfilled which was spoken of the Lord by the prophet, saying, *"Out of Egypt have I called my son."*

8   Then Herod, when he saw that he was mocked of the wise men, was exceedingly angry, and sent forth, and slew all the male children that were in Bethlehem, and in all the regions thereof, from two years old and under, according to the time which he had diligently inquired of the wise men. Then was fulfilled that which was spoken by Jeremiah the prophet, saying, *"In Ramah was there a voice heard, lamentation, and weeping, and great mourning, Rachel weeping for her children, and would not be comforted, because they are no more."*

The Family's Return to Nazareth
Matthew 2:19-23; Luke 2:40

9   But when Herod was dead, behold, an angel of the Lord appeared in a dream to Joseph in Egypt, saying, "Arise, and take the young child and his mother, and go into the land of Israel: for they are dead which sought the young child's life."

10   And he arose, and took the young child and his mother, and came into the land of Israel. But when he heard that Archelaus (Herod) did reign in Judea in the succession of his father Herod, he was afraid to go there: nevertheless, being warned of God in a dream, he turned aside into the parts of Galilee: and he came and dwelt in a city called Nazareth: that it might be fulfilled which was spoken by the prophets, "He shall be called a Nazarene."

11   And the child grew, and became strong in spirit, filled with wisdom: and the grace of God was upon him.

Young Jesus in the Temple
Luke 2:41-50

12   Now his parents went to Jerusalem every year at the feast of the passover. And when he was twelve years old, they went up to Jerusalem after the custom of the feast. And when they had fulfilled the days, as they returned, the child Jesus tarried behind in Jerusalem; and Joseph and his mother knew not of it. But they, supposing him to have been in the company, went a day's journey; and they sought him among their relatives and acquaintances. And when they did not find him, they turned back again to Jerusalem, seeking him.

13   And it came to pass, that after three days they found him in the temple, sitting in the midst of the teachers, both hearing them, and asking them

questions. And all that heard him were astonished at his understanding and 13
answers.

And when they saw him, they were amazed: and his mother said unto 14
him, "Son, why have you thus dealt
with us? behold, your father and I have
sought you sorrowing." And he said
unto them, "How is it that you sought

> "I MUST BE ABOUT MY FATHER'S BUSINESS."

me? knew you not that I must be about my Father's business?" And they did
not understand the saying which he spoke unto them.

Jesus Increases in Wisdom
Luke 2:51-52

And he went down with them, and came to Nazareth, and was subject 15
unto them: but his mother kept all these sayings in her heart.

And Jesus increased in wisdom and stature, and in favor with God 16
and man.

PART 2

PUBLIC PREPARATION

In conscious awareness of His divine purpose, Jesus accepted baptism by John the Baptist and prepared to fulfill the mission for which He was sent. It was John's hope that this baptism would serve to enforce the conviction that Jesus was indeed the Christ, the Son of God, and that life would come through belief in Him. In patient obedience to a patient God, Jesus affirmed His destiny by His works, purging the temple of moneychangers, turning the wedding water into wine, and rebuking the temptations of the devil. His mission was clear; the Word was with Him.

> THE WORD WAS WITH GOD, AND THE WORD
> WAS GOD....IN HIM WAS LIFE; AND THE LIFE WAS
> THE LIGHT OF MEN. AND THE LIGHT SHINES IN
> DARKNESS. (JOHN 1:1, 4-5)

CHAPTER 4

THE GREAT BEGINNING

Prologue: The Word Made Flesh
John 1:1-5, 10-14, 16-18

In the beginning was the Word, and the Word was with God, and the 1
Word was God. The same was in the beginning with God. All things were
made by him; and without him was not anything made that was made. In
him was life; and the life was the light of men. And the light shines in darkness; and the darkness comprehended it not.

He was in the world, and the world was made by him, and the world 2
knew him not. He came unto his own, and his own received him not. But as
many as received him, to them he gave authority to become the sons of God,
even to them that believe on his name: which were born, not of blood, nor
of the will of the flesh, nor of the will of man, but of God.

And the Word was made flesh, and dwelt among us, (and we beheld 3
his glory, the glory as of the only begotten of the Father), full of grace and
truth. And of his fulness have we all received, and grace for grace. For the
law was given by Moses, but grace and truth came by Jesus Christ. No man
has seen God at any time; the only begotten Son, which is in the bosom of
the Father, he has declared him.

Prologue: The Witness Sent
John 1:6-9

There was a man sent from God, whose name was John. The same came 4
for a witness, to bear witness of the Light, that all men through him might
believe. He was not that Light, but was sent to bear witness of that Light. That
was the true Light, which lights every man that comes into the world.

John the Baptist Prepares the Way
Matthew 3:1-12; Mark 1:1-8; Luke 3:1-18; John 1:15

Now in the fifteenth year of the reign of Tiberius Caesar, Pontius 5
Pilate being governor of Judea, and Herod (Antipas) being tetrarch (ruler)

5 of Galilee, and his brother Philip tetrarch (ruler) of Iturea and of the region of Trachonitis, and Lysanias the tetrarch (ruler) of Abilene, Annas and Caiaphas being the high priests, the word of God came unto John the son of Zacharias in the wilderness.

6 The beginning of the gospel of Jesus Christ, the Son of God; as it is written in the prophets, *"Behold, I send my messenger before your face, which shall prepare your way before you."* In those days came John the Baptist, preaching in the wilderness of Judea, and saying, "Repent: for the kingdom of heaven is at hand."

7 And he came into all the country about Jordan, preaching the baptism of repentance for the remission of sins; as it is written in the book of the words of Isaiah the prophet, saying, *"The voice of one crying in the wilderness, 'Prepare the way of the Lord, make his paths straight. Every valley shall be filled, and every mountain and hill shall be brought low; and the crooked shall be made straight, and the rough ways shall be made smooth; and all flesh shall see the salvation of God.'"* John did baptize in the wilderness, and preach the baptism of repentance for the remission of sins.

8 And the same John had his clothing of camel's hair, and a leather belt of a skin about his waist; and his food was locusts and wild honey. And there went out unto him all the land of Judea, and all the region round about Jordan, and they of Jerusalem, and were all baptized of him in the river of Jordan, confessing their sins. But when he saw many of the Pharisees and Sadducees come to his baptism, he said unto them, to the multitude that came forth to be baptized of him, "O generation of vipers, who has warned you to flee from the wrath to come?

9 "Bring forth therefore fruits worthy of repentance: and begin not to say within yourselves, 'We have Abraham to our father:' for I say unto you that God is able of these stones to raise up children unto Abraham. And now also the ax is laid unto the root of the trees: therefore every tree which brings not forth good fruit is cut down, and cast into the fire."

10 And the people asked him, saying, "What shall we do then?" He answered and said unto them, "He that has two coats, let him impart to him that has none; and he that has food, let him do likewise."

11 Then came also tax collectors to be baptized, and said unto him, "Teacher, what shall we do?" And he said unto them, "Exact no more than that which is appointed you."

12 And the soldiers likewise asked of him, saying, "And what shall we do?" And he said unto them, "Do violence to no man, neither accuse any falsely; and be content with your wages."

13 And as the people were in expectation, and all men mused in their hearts of John, whether he were the Christ, or not; John answered, saying unto them all, "I indeed baptize you with water unto repentance; but one mightier than I comes after me, whose shoes I am not worthy to bear, the strap of whose shoes I am not worthy to stoop down and loose: he shall baptize you with the Holy Ghost and with fire: whose fan is in his hand, and he

will thoroughly purge his floor, and will gather the wheat into his store- 14
house; but the chaff he will burn with fire unquenchable."

John bore witness of him, and cried, saying, "This was he of whom I 15
spoke. He that comes after me is preferred before me: for he was before
me." And many other things in his message he preached unto the people.

John Baptizes Jesus
Matthew 3:13-17; Mark 1:9-11; Luke 3:21-22

And Jesus himself began to be about thirty years of age. And it came 16
to pass in those days, that Jesus came from Nazareth of Galilee to Jordan
unto John, to be baptized of him. But John forbade him, saying, "I have
need to be baptized of you, and you come to me?" And Jesus answering said
unto him, "Allow it to be so now: for thus it becomes us to fulfill all righteousness." Then he allowed him.

Now when all the people were baptized, it came to pass, that Jesus also 17
being baptized, and praying, went up straightway out of the water: and, lo,
the heavens were opened unto him, and he saw the Spirit of God descending in a bodily form, like a dove, and lighting upon him: and lo a voice from
heaven, saying, "This is my beloved Son, in whom I am well pleased."

Jesus Tempted of the Devil
Matthew 4:1-11; Mark 1:12-13; Luke 4:1-13

And Jesus being full of the Holy Ghost immediately returned from 18
Jordan, and the Spirit drove him into the wilderness to be tempted of the
devil. And in those days he did eat nothing: and when he had fasted forty
days and forty nights, and they were ended, he afterward was hungry.

And when the tempter came to him, the devil said unto him, "If you 19
be the Son of God, command that these stones be made bread." And Jesus
answered him saying, "It is written, *Man shall not live by bread alone, but
by every word that proceeds out of the mouth of God.*"

Then the devil took him up into the holy city, Jerusalem, and set him 20
on a pinnacle of the temple, and said unto him, "If you be the Son of God,
cast yourself down from here: for it is written, *He shall give his angels
charge over you, to keep you: and in their hands they shall bear you up, lest
at any time you dash your foot against a stone.'*" And Jesus answering said
unto him, "It is written again, *You shall not tempt the Lord your God.'* "

Again, the devil took him up into an exceedingly high mountain, and 21
showed him all the kingdoms of the world in a moment of time, and the glory
of them; and said unto him, "All this authority will I give you, and the glory of
them: for that is delivered unto me; and to whomsoever I will I give it. If you
therefore will fall down and worship me, all these things shall be yours." And
Jesus answered and said unto him, "Get you behind me, Satan: for it is written, *You shall worship the Lord your God, and him only shall you serve.'* "

And when the devil had ended all the temptation, he departed from 22
him for a season. And he was there in the wilderness forty days, tempted of
Satan; and was with the wild beasts; and, behold, the angels came and ministered unto him.

CHAPTER 5

THE FIRST FOLLOWERS

John the Baptist's Testimony
John 1:19-28

1   And this is the testimony of John, when the Jews sent priests and Levites from Jerusalem to ask him, "Who are you?" And he confessed, and denied not; but confessed, "I am not the Christ."

2   And they asked him, "What then? Are you Elijah?" And he said, "I am not." "Are you that prophet?" And he answered, "No."

3   Then they said unto him, "Who are you? that we may give an answer to them that sent us. What do you say of yourself?" He said, "I am *'the voice of one crying in the wilderness, "Make straight the way of the Lord," '* as said the prophet Isaiah."

4   And they which were sent were of the Pharisees. And they asked him, and said unto him, "Why do you baptize then, if you be not that Christ, nor Elijah, neither that prophet?" John answered them, saying, "I baptize with water: but there stands one among you, whom you know not; he it is, who coming after me is preferred before me, whose shoe's strap I am not worthy to loose."

5   These things were done in Bethany beyond Jordan, where John was baptizing.

"Behold the Lamb of God"
John 1:29-34

6   The next day John saw Jesus coming unto him, and said, "Behold the Lamb of God, which takes away the sin of the world. This is he of whom I said, 'After me comes a man which is preferred before me: for he was before me.' And I knew him not: but that he should be made manifest to Israel, therefore I am come baptizing with water."

7   And John bore witness, saying, "I saw the Spirit descending from heaven like a dove, and it rested upon him. And I knew him not: but he that

sent me to baptize with water, the same said unto me, 'Upon whom you 7 shall see the Spirit descending, and remaining on him, the same is he which baptizes with the Holy Ghost.' And I saw, and bore witness that this is the Son of God."

First Three Disciples Join Jesus
John 1:35-42

Again the next day after John stood, and two of his disciples; and look- 8 ing upon Jesus as he walked, he said, "Behold the Lamb of God!" And the two disciples heard him speak, and they followed Jesus.

Then Jesus turned, and saw them following, and said unto them, 9 "What do you seek?" They said unto him, "Rabbi," (which is to say, being interpreted, Teacher), "where do you dwell?" He said unto them, "Come and see." They came and saw where he dwelt, and stayed with him that day: for it was about the tenth hour.

One of the two which heard John speak, and followed him, was 10 Andrew, Simon Peter's brother. He first found his own brother Simon, and said unto him, "We have found the Messiah," which is, being interpreted, the Christ.

And he brought him to Jesus. And when Jesus beheld him, he said, 11 "You are Simon the son of Jonah: you shall be called Cephas," which is by interpretation, A stone.

Jesus Summons Two More Disciples
John 1:43-51

The following day Jesus went forth into Galilee, and found Philip, and 12 said unto him, "Follow me." Now Philip was of Bethsaida, the city of Andrew and Peter. Philip found Nathanael, and said unto him, "We have found him, of whom Moses in the law, and the prophets, did write, Jesus of Nazareth, the son of Joseph." And Nathanael said unto him, "Can there any good thing come out of Nazareth?" Philip said unto him, "Come and see."

Jesus saw Nathanael coming to him, and said of him, "Behold an 13 Israelite indeed, in whom is no deceit!" Nathanael said unto him, "How do you know me?" Jesus answered and said unto him, "Before Philip called you, when you were under the fig tree, I saw you." Nathanael answered and said unto him, "Rabbi, you are the Son of God; you are the King of Israel."

Jesus answered and said unto him, "Because I said unto you, 'I saw you 14 under the fig tree,' do you believe? you shall see greater things than these." And he said unto him, "Truly, truly, I say unto you, Hereafter you shall see heaven open, and the angels of God ascending and descending upon the Son of man."

First Miracle: Water Made Into Wine
John 2:1-12

And the third day there was a marriage in Cana of Galilee; and the 15 mother of Jesus was there: and both Jesus was called, and his disciples, to the marriage.

16   And when they lacked wine, the mother of Jesus said unto him, "They have no wine." Jesus said unto her, "Woman, what have I to do with you? my hour is not yet come." His mother said unto the servants, "Whatsoever he says unto you, do it."

17   And there were set there six waterpots of stone, after the manner of the purification of the Jews, containing twenty or thirty gallons apiece. Jesus said unto them, "Fill the waterpots with water." And they filled them up to the brim. And he said unto them, "Draw out now, and bear unto the steward of the feast." And they bore it.

18   When the steward of the feast had tasted the water that was made wine, and did not know from where it was: (but the servants which drew the water knew); the steward of the feast called the bridegroom, and said unto him, "Every man at the beginning does set forth good wine; and when men have drunk freely, then that which is worse: but you have kept the good wine until now."

19   This beginning of miracles Jesus did in Cana of Galilee, and manifested forth his glory; and his disciples believed on him.

20   After this he went down to Capernaum, he, and his mother, and his brethren, and his disciples: and they continued there not many days.

CHAPTER 6

FIRST MINISTRY AT JERUSALEM

Jesus Clears the Temple
John 2:13-25

And the Jews' passover was at hand, and Jesus went up to Jerusalem, 1
and found in the temple those that sold oxen and sheep and doves, and the
changers of money sitting: and when he had made a scourge of small cords,
he drove them all out of the temple, and the sheep, and the oxen; and poured
out the changers' money, and overturned the tables; and said unto them that
sold doves, "Take these things from here; make not my Father's house a
house of merchandise." And his disciples remembered that it was written,
"The zeal of your house has eaten me up."

Then answered the Jews and said unto him, "What sign do you show 2
unto us, seeing that you do these things?" Jesus answered and said unto
them, "Destroy this temple, and in three days I will raise it up." Then said the
Jews, "Forty and six years was this temple in building, and will you raise it
up in three days?" But he spoke of the temple of his body. When therefore he
was risen from the dead, his disciples remembered that he had said this unto
them; and they believed the scripture, and the word which Jesus had said.

Now when he was in Jerusalem at the passover, in the feast day, many 3
believed in his name, when they saw the miracles which he did. But Jesus
did not commit himself unto them, because he knew all men, and needed
not that any should testify of man: for he knew what was in man.

Jesus Enlightens Nicodemus
John 3:1-21

There was a man of the Pharisees, named Nicodemus, a ruler of the 4
Jews: the same came to Jesus by night, and said unto him, "Rabbi, we know
that you are a teacher come from God: for no man can do these miracles
that you do, except God be with him." Jesus answered and said unto him,

4 "Truly, truly, I say unto you, Except a man be born again, he cannot see the kingdom of God."

5 Nicodemus said unto him, "How can a man be born when he is old? can he enter the second time into his mother's womb, and be born?" Jesus answered, "Truly, truly, I say unto you, Except a man be born of water and of the Spirit, he cannot enter into the kingdom of God. That which is born of the flesh is flesh; and that which is born of the Spirit is spirit. Marvel not that I said unto you, 'You must be born again.' The wind blows where it wishes, and you hear the sound thereof, but cannot tell from where it comes, and where it goes: so is everyone that is born of the Spirit."

> "YOU MUST BE BORN AGAIN."

6 Nicodemus answered and said unto him, "How can these things be?" Jesus answered and said unto him, "Are you a teacher of Israel, and know not these things? Truly, truly, I say unto you, We speak that we do know, and testify that we have seen; and you do not receive our witness. If I have told you earthly things, and you do not believe, how shall you believe, if I tell you of heavenly things?

7 "And no man has ascended up to heaven, but he that came down from heaven, even the Son of man which is in heaven. And as Moses lifted up the serpent in the wilderness, even so must the Son of man be lifted up: that whosoever believes in him should not perish, but have eternal life.

8 "For God so loved the world, that he gave his only begotten Son, that whosoever believes in him should not perish, but have everlasting life. For God did not send his Son into the world to condemn the world; but that the world through him might be saved. He that believes on him is not condemned: but he that believes not is condemned already, because he has not believed in the name of the only begotten Son of God.

> "FOR GOD SO LOVED THE WORLD, THAT HE GAVE HIS ONLY BEGOTTEN SON, THAT WHOSOEVER BELIEVES IN HIM SHOULD NOT PERISH, BUT HAVE EVERLASTING LIFE."

9 "And this is the condemnation, that light is come into the world, and men loved darkness rather than light, because their deeds were evil. For everyone that does evil hates the light, neither comes to the light, lest his deeds should be exposed. But he that does truth comes to the light, that his deeds may be made manifest, that they are wrought in God."

John's Final Witness of Christ
John 3:22-36

10 After these things Jesus came and his disciples into the land of Judea; and there he tarried with them, and baptized. And John also was baptizing in Aenon near to Salim, because there was much water there: and they came, and were baptized. For John was not yet cast into prison.

Then there arose a question between some of John's disciples and the 11 Jews about purification. And they came unto John, and said unto him, "Rabbi, he that was with you beyond Jordan, to whom you bore witness, behold, the same baptizes, and all men come to him."

John answered and said, "A man can receive nothing, except it be 12 given him from heaven. You yourselves bear me witness, that I said, 'I am not the Christ,' but that 'I am sent before him.' He that has the bride is the bridegroom: but the friend of the bridegroom, which stands and hears him, rejoices greatly because of the bridegroom's voice: this my joy therefore is fulfilled. He must increase, but I must decrease.

> "A MAN CAN RECEIVE NOTHING, EXCEPT IT BE GIVEN HIM FROM HEAVEN."

"He that comes from above is above all: he that is of the earth is 13 earthly, and speaks of the earth: he that comes from heaven is above all. And what he has seen and heard, that he testifies; and no man receives his testimony. He that has received his testimony has certified that God is true. For he whom God has sent speaks the words of God: for God does not give the Spirit by measure unto him.

"The Father loves the Son, and has given all things into his hand. He 14 that believes on the Son has everlasting life: and he that does not believe the Son shall not see life; but the wrath of God remains on him."

CHAPTER 7

THE FIRST BELIEVERS

John's Imprisonment
Luke 3:19-20; John 4:1-4

1   But Herod the tetrarch (ruler), being exposed by him for Herodias his brother Philip's wife, and for all the evils which Herod had done, added yet this above all, that he shut up John in prison.

2   When therefore the Lord knew how the Pharisees had heard that Jesus made and baptized more disciples than John, (though Jesus himself did not baptize, but his disciples), he left Judea, and departed again into Galilee. And he must of necessity go through Samaria.

The Woman at the Well
John 4:5-26

3   Then he came to a city of Samaria, which is called Sychar, near to the parcel of ground that Jacob gave to his son Joseph. Now Jacob's well was there. Jesus therefore, being wearied with his journey, sat thus on the well: and it was about the sixth hour.

4   There came a woman of Samaria to draw water: Jesus said unto her, "Give me to drink." (For his disciples were gone away unto the city to buy food.) Then said the woman of Samaria unto him, "How is it that you, being a Jew, ask drink of me, which am a woman of Samaria? for the Jews have no dealings with the Samaritans."

5   Jesus answered and said unto her, "If you knew the gift of God, and who it is that says to you, 'Give me to drink;' you would have asked of him, and he would have given you living water." The woman said unto him, "Sir, you have nothing to draw with, and the well is deep: from where then have you that living water? Are you greater than our father Jacob, which gave us the well, and drank thereof himself, and his children, and his cattle?"

6   Jesus answered and said unto her, "Whosoever drinks of this water shall thirst again: but whosoever drinks of the water that I shall give him

shall never thirst; but the water that I shall give him shall be in him a well 6 of water springing up into everlasting life." The woman said unto him, "Sir, give me this water, that I thirst not, neither come here to draw."

Jesus said unto her, "Go, call your husband, and come here." The 7 woman answered and said, "I have no husband." Jesus said unto her, "You have well said, 'I have no husband:' for you have had five husbands; and he whom you now have is not your husband: in that said you truly."

The woman said unto him, "Sir, I perceive that you are a prophet. Our 8 fathers worshiped in this mountain; and you say, that in Jerusalem is the place where men ought to worship." Jesus said unto her, "Woman, believe me, the hour comes, when you shall neither in this mountain, nor at Jerusalem, worship the Father. You worship you know not what: we know

> "GOD IS A SPIRIT: AND THEY THAT WORSHIP HIM MUST WORSHIP HIM IN SPIRIT AND IN TRUTH."

what we worship: for salvation is of the Jews. But the hour comes, and now is, when the true worshipers shall worship the Father in spirit and in truth: for the Father seeks such to worship him. God is a Spirit: and they that worship him must worship him in spirit and in truth."

The woman said unto him, "I know that Messiah comes, which is 9 called Christ: when he is come, he will tell us all things." Jesus said unto her, "I that speak unto you am he."

"One Sows and Another Reaps"
John 4:27-38

And upon this came his disciples, and marveled that he talked with the 10 woman: yet no man said, "What do you seek?" or, "Why do you talk with her?" The woman then left her waterpot, and went her way into the city, and said to the men, "Come, see a man, which told me all things that ever I did: is not this the Christ?" Then they went out of the city, and came unto him.

In the meanwhile his disciples asked him, saying, "Rabbi, eat." But he 11 said unto them, "I have food to eat that you know not of." Therefore said the disciples one to another, "Has any man brought him anything to eat?" Jesus said unto them, "My food is to do the will of him that sent me, and to finish his work.

"Do you not say, 'There are yet four months, and then comes harvest'? 12 behold, I say unto you, Lift up your eyes, and look on the fields; for they are white already to harvest. And he that reaps receives wages, and gathers fruit unto life eternal: that both he that sows and he that reaps may rejoice together. And herein is that saying true, 'One sows, and another reaps.' I

> "LIFT UP YOUR EYES, AND LOOK ON THE FIELDS; FOR THEY ARE WHITE ALREADY TO HARVEST."

sent you to reap that whereon you bestowed no labor: other men labored, and you are entered into their labors."

This Is the Savior of the World
John 4:39-42

13   And many of the Samaritans of that city believed on him for the saying of the woman, which testified, "He told me all that ever I did." So when the Samaritans were come unto him, they pleaded with him that he would tarry with them: and he stayed there two days. And many more believed because of his own word; and said unto the woman, "Now we believe, not because of your saying: for we have heard him ourselves, and know that this is indeed the Christ, the Savior of the world."

PART 3

Miracles in Galilee

With news of His works spreading throughout the region, Jesus set out on His journey to perform the works His Father had sent Him to do. The doctrines He taught and the healings He brought were far removed from those the people were accustomed to accepting. His purpose was to reveal God and to demonstrate the power of His kingdom. In this He had little regard for man-made rules. To this also, the authorities would take great exception.

> JESUS RETURNED IN THE POWER OF THE SPIRIT INTO GALILEE, PREACHING THE GOSPEL OF THE KINGDOM OF GOD....AND THERE WENT OUT A REPORT OF HIM THROUGH ALL THE REGION ROUND ABOUT. (LUKE 4:14)

CHAPTER 8

JESUS BEGINS HIS MINISTRY

In the Power of the Spirit
Mark 1:14-15; Luke 4:14-15; John 4:43-45

1   Now after two days he departed from there and went into Galilee. For Jesus himself testified, that a prophet has no honor in his own country. And Jesus returned in the power of the Spirit into Galilee, preaching the gospel of the kingdom of God, and saying, "The time is fulfilled, and the kingdom of God is at hand: repent, and believe the gospel." Then the Galileans received him, having seen all the things that he did at Jerusalem at the feast: for they also went unto the feast. And there went out a report of him through all the region round about. And he taught in their synagogues, being glorified of all.

Jesus Heals a Nobleman's Dying Son
John 4:46-54

2   So Jesus came again into Cana of Galilee, where he made the water wine. And there was a certain nobleman, whose son was sick at Capernaum. When he heard that Jesus was come out of Judea into Galilee, he went unto him, and pleaded with him that he would come down, and heal his son: for he was at the point of death.

3   Then Jesus said unto him, "Except you see signs and wonders, you will not believe." The nobleman said unto him, "Sir, come down before my child dies." Jesus said unto him, "Go your way; your son lives." And the man believed the word that Jesus had spoken unto him, and he went his way.

4   And as he was now going down, his servants met him, and told him, saying, "Your son lives." Then he inquired of them the hour when he began to get better. And they said unto him, "Yesterday at the seventh hour the fever left him." So the father knew that it was at the same hour, in which Jesus said unto him, "Your son lives": and he believed, and his whole household.

This is again the second miracle that Jesus did, when he was come out 5 of Judea into Galilee.

"This Scripture Fulfilled"
Luke 4:16-32

And he came to Nazareth, where he had been brought up: and, as his 6 custom was, he went into the synagogue on the sabbath day, and stood up to read. And there was delivered unto him the book of the prophet Isaiah. And when he had opened the book, he found the place where it was written, "*The Spirit of the Lord is upon me, because he has anointed me to preach the gospel to the poor; he has sent me to heal the brokenhearted, to proclaim deliverance to the captives, and recovery of sight to the blind, to set at liberty them that are oppressed, to proclaim the acceptable year of the Lord.*"

And he closed the book, and he gave it again to the attendant, and sat 7 down. And the eyes of all them that were in the synagogue were fastened on him. And he began to say unto them, "This day is this scripture fulfilled in your ears."

And all bore him witness, and wondered at the gracious words which 8 proceeded out of his mouth. And they said, "Is not this Joseph's son?" And he said unto them, "You will surely say unto me this proverb, 'Physician, heal yourself: whatsoever we have heard done in Capernaum, do also here in your country.'"

And he said, "Truly I say unto you, No prophet is accepted in his own 9 country. But I tell you of a truth, many widows were in Israel in the days of Elijah, when the heaven was shut up three years and six months, when great famine was throughout all the land; but unto none of them was Elijah sent, except unto Zarephath, a city of Sidon, unto a woman that was a widow. And many lepers were in Israel in the time of Elisha the prophet; and none of them was cleansed, but only Naaman the Syrian."

And all they in the synagogue, when they heard these things, were 10 filled with wrath, and rose up, and thrust him out of the city, and led him unto the brow of the hill whereon their city was built, that they might cast him down headlong. But he passing through the midst of them went his way, and came down to Capernaum, a city of Galilee, and taught them on the sabbath days. And they were astonished at his doctrine: for his word was with authority.

His Home Is at Capernaum
Matthew 4:12-17

Now when Jesus had heard that John was cast into prison, he departed 11 into Galilee; and leaving Nazareth, he came and dwelt in Capernaum, which is upon the seacoast, in the borders of Zebulun and Naphtali: that it might be fulfilled which was spoken by Isaiah

"REPENT: FOR THE KINGDOM OF HEAVEN IS AT HAND."

the prophet, saying, "*The land of Zebulun, and the land of Naphtali, by the way of the sea, beyond Jordan, Galilee of the Gentiles; the people which sat*

11   *in darkness saw great light; and to them which sat in the region and shadow of death light is sprung up."* From that time Jesus began to preach, and to say, "Repent: for the kingdom of heaven is at hand."

Jesus Calls Four Fishermen
Matthew 4:18-22; Mark 1:16-20; Luke 5:1-11

12   And Jesus, walking by the sea of Galilee, saw two brethren, Simon called Peter, and Andrew his brother, casting a net into the sea: for they were fishers.

13   And it came to pass, that, as the people crowded upon him to hear the word of God, he stood by the sea of Galilee, and saw two ships standing by the sea: but the fishermen were gone out of them, and were washing their nets. And he entered into one of the ships, which was Simon's, and asked him that he would thrust out a little from the land. And he sat down, and taught the people out of the ship.

14   Now when he had left speaking, he said unto Simon, "Launch out into the deep, and let down your nets for a catch." And Simon answering said unto him, "Master, we have toiled all the night, and have taken nothing: nevertheless at your word I will let down the net." And when they had this done, they caught a great multitude of fishes: and their net broke. And they beckoned unto their partners, which were in the other ship, that they should come and help them. And they came, and filled both the ships, so that they began to sink.

15   When Simon Peter saw it, he fell down at Jesus' knees, saying, "Depart from me; for I am a sinful man, O Lord." For he was astonished, and all that were with him, at the catch of the fishes which they had taken:

> "FOLLOW ME, AND I WILL MAKE YOU FISHERS OF MEN."

and so was also James, and John, the sons of Zebedee, which were partners with Simon. And Jesus said unto Simon, "Fear not; from henceforth you shall catch men." And Jesus said unto them, "Follow me, and I will make you fishers of men." And when they had brought their ships to land, they forsook all, and followed him.

16   And going on from there, he saw two other brethren, James the son of Zebedee, and John his brother, in a ship with Zebedee their father, mending their nets. And straightway he called them: and they immediately left their father Zebedee in the ship with the hired servants, and followed him.

Jesus Casts Out Unclean Spirits
Mark 1:21-28; Luke 4:33-37

17   And they went into Capernaum; and straightway on the sabbath day he entered into the synagogue, and taught. And they were astonished at his doctrine: for he taught them as one that had authority, and not as the scribes.

18   And there was in their synagogue a man with an unclean spirit; and it cried out with a loud voice, saying, "Let us alone; what have we to do with you, Jesus of Nazareth? are you come to destroy us? I know who you are; the Holy

One of God." And Jesus rebuked it, saying, "Hold your peace, and come out 18 of him." And when the unclean spirit had convulsed him, and thrown him in the midst, and cried with a loud voice, it came out of him, and did not hurt him.

And they were all amazed, insomuch that they questioned among 19 themselves, saying, "What thing is this? what new doctrine is this?" and spoke among themselves, saying, "What a word is this! for with authority and power he commands even the unclean spirits, and they do obey him, and they come out." And immediately his fame spread abroad throughout all the region round about Galilee.

Healing Peter's Mother-in-Law
Matthew 8:14-15; Mark 1:29-31; Luke 4:38-39

And immediately, when they were come out of the synagogue, they 20 entered into the house of Simon and Andrew, with James and John. But Simon's wife's mother lay sick of a great fever, and at once they told him about her. And he came and stood over her, and rebuked the fever; and took her by the hand, and lifted her up; and immediately the fever left her: and immediately she arose and ministered unto them.

Healing All Who Come to Him
Matthew 8:16-17; Mark 1:32-34; Luke 4:40-41

Now when the sun was setting, all they that had any sick with various 21 diseases brought them unto him; and he laid his hands on every one of them, and healed them. And all the city was gathered together at the door. And they brought unto him many that were possessed with demons: and he cast out the spirits with his word: that it might be fulfilled which was spoken by Isaiah the prophet, saying, *"He took our infirmities, and bore our sicknesses."* And demons also came out of many, crying out, and saying, "You are Christ the Son of God." And he rebuking them did not allow them to speak: for they knew that he was Christ.

CHAPTER 9

MINISTRY IN NEARBY TOWNS
"For This Purpose Am I Sent"
Mark 1:35-39; Luke 4:42-44

1   And in the morning, rising up a great while before daylight, he went out, and departed into a solitary place, and there prayed. And Simon and they that were with him followed after him. And when they had found him, they said unto him, "All men seek for you." And he said unto them, "Let us go into the next towns, that I may preach there also: for this purpose I came forth."

2   And when it was day, the people sought him, and came unto him, and detained him, that he should not depart from them. And he said unto them, "I must preach the kingdom of God to other cities also: for this purpose am I sent." And he preached in their synagogues throughout all Galilee, and cast out demons.

Jesus Cleanses a Man of Leprosy
Matthew 8:2-4; Mark 1:40-45; Luke 5:12-16

3   And it came to pass, when he was in a certain city, behold a man full of leprosy: who seeing Jesus fell on his face and worshiped him, and pleaded with him, saying, "Lord, if you will, you can make me clean." And Jesus, moved with compassion, put forth his hand, and touched him, saying, "I will: be clean." And as soon as he had spoken, immediately the leprosy departed from him, and he was cleansed.

4   And he strictly charged him, and immediately sent him away; and said unto him, "See you say nothing to any man: but go your way, show yourself to the priest, and offer for your cleansing those things which Moses commanded, for a testimony unto them."

5   But he went out, and began to publish it much, and to spread abroad the matter, insomuch that Jesus could no more openly enter into the city, but was outside in desert places: and they came to him from every direction. But so much the more went there a report abroad of him: and great multitudes

came together to hear, and to be healed by him of their infirmities. And he withdrew himself into the wilderness, and prayed. 5

A Paralytic Man Walks!
Matthew 9:2-8; Mark 2:1-12; Luke 5:17-26

And again he entered into Capernaum after some days; and it was rumored that he in the house. And straightway many were gathered together, insomuch that there was no room to receive them, no, not so much as about the door: and he preached the word unto them. And it came to pass on a certain day, as he was teaching, that there were Pharisees and teachers of the law sitting by, which were come out of every town of Galilee, and Judea, and Jerusalem: and the power of the Lord was present to heal them. 6

And, behold, men brought in a bed a man which was taken with a paralysis, which was carried by four: and they sought means to bring him in, and to lay him before him. And when they could not find by what way they might bring him in because of the multitude, they went upon the housetop, and they uncovered the roof where he was: and when they had broken it up, they let him down through the tiling with his couch into the midst before Jesus. When Jesus saw their faith, he said unto the sick of the paralysis, "Son, be of good cheer; your sins be forgiven you." 7

But, behold, there were certain of the scribes sitting there, and reasoning in their hearts, "Why does this man thus speak blasphemies? who can forgive sins but God only?" And immediately when Jesus perceived in his spirit that they so reasoned within themselves, said unto them, "Why do you reason these things in your hearts? Which is it easier to say to the sick of the paralysis, 'Your sins be forgiven you;' or to say, 'Arise, and take up your bed, and walk?' But that you may know that the Son of man has authority on earth to forgive sins, (he said to the sick of the paralysis), I say unto you, Arise, and take up your bed, and go your way into your house." 8

> "THE SON OF MAN HAS AUTHORITY ON EARTH TO FORGIVE SINS."

And immediately he rose up before them all, and took up the bed whereon he lay, and departed to his own house, glorifying God. But when the multitudes saw it, they marveled, and glorified God, which had given such authority unto men. And they were all amazed, and were filled with fear, saying, "We never saw it like this fashion. We have seen strange things today." 9

Matthew Obeys Jesus' Call
Matthew 9:9; Mark 2:13-14; Luke 5:27-28

And he went forth again by the seaside; and all the multitude came unto him, and he taught them. And after these things as Jesus passed forth from there, he saw a tax collector, a man named Matthew, Levi the son of Alphaeus, sitting at the receipt of custom: and said unto him, "Follow me." And he left all, rose up, and followed him. 10

Eating With Sinners
Matthew 9:10-13; Mark 2:15-17; Luke 5:29-32

11   And Levi made him a great feast in his own house: and there was a great company of tax collectors and of others. And it came to pass, as Jesus sat at the table in the house, many tax collectors and sinners came and sat together with Jesus and his disciples: for there were many, and they followed him. But when their scribes and Pharisees saw him eat with tax collectors and sinners, they said unto his disciples, "How is it that he eats and drinks with tax collectors and sinners?"

12   When Jesus heard that, he said unto them, "They that are whole have no need of the physician, but they that are sick: I came not to call the righteous, but sinners to repentance. But go and learn what that means, '*I will have mercy, and not sacrifice.*'"

First Parable Concerns Fasting
Matthew 9:14-17; Mark 2:18-22; Luke 5:33-39

13   Then came to him the disciples of John, saying, "Why do we and the Pharisees fast often, but your disciples do not fast?" And likewise the disciples of the Pharisees came and said unto him, "Why do the disciples of John and of the Pharisees fast, and make prayers, but your disciples eat and drink?" And Jesus said unto them, "Can the friends of the bridegroom fast, while the bridegroom is with them? as long as they have the bridegroom with them, they cannot fast. But the days will come, when the bridegroom shall be taken away from them, and then shall they fast in those days."

14   And he spoke also a parable unto them; "No man sews a piece of a new cloth on an old garment: else the new piece that filled it up takes away from the old; if otherwise, then both the new makes a tear, and the piece that was taken out of the new does not match with the old, and the tear is made worse.

15   "And no man puts new wine into old wineskins: else the new wine will burst the wineskins, and the wine is spilled, and the wineskins shall perish. But new wine must be put into new wineskins; and both are preserved. No man also having drunk old wine straightway desires new: for he says, 'The old is better.'"

CHAPTER 10

·.· SECOND MINISTRY AT JERUSALEM ·.·

Sabbath Healing of a Man at the Pool
John 5:1-13

After this there was a feast of the Jews; and Jesus went up to Jerusalem. 1
Now there is at Jerusalem by the sheep gate a pool, which is called in the
Hebrew tongue Bethesda, having five porches. In these lay a great multitude
of paralyzed folks, of blind, lame, withered, waiting for the moving of the
water. For an angel went down at a certain season into the pool, and stirred
the water: whosoever then first after the stirring of the water stepped in was
made whole of whatsoever disease he had.

And a certain man was there, which had an infirmity thirty and eight 2
years. When Jesus saw him lying there, and knew that he had been now a
long time in that condition, he said unto him, "Will you be made whole?"
The paralyzed man answered him, "Sir, I have no man, when the water is
stirred, to put me into the pool: but while I am coming, another steps down
before me." Jesus said unto him, "Rise, take up your bed, and walk." And
immediately the man was made whole, and took up his bed, and walked:
and on the same day was the sabbath.

The Jews therefore said unto him that was cured, "It is the sabbath 3
day: it is not lawful for you to carry your bed." He answered them, "He that
made me whole, the same said unto me, 'Take up your bed, and walk.' "
Then they asked him, "What man is that which said unto you, 'Take up your
bed, and walk?'" And he that was healed knew not who it was: for Jesus had
taken himself away, a multitude being in that place.

Sabbath Healing and the Law
John 5:14-18

Afterward Jesus found him in the temple, and said unto him, "Behold, 4
you are made whole: sin no more, lest a worse thing come unto you." The
man departed, and told the Jews that it was Jesus, which had made him

4 whole. And therefore did the Jews persecute Jesus, and sought to slay him, because he had done these things on the sabbath day.

5 But Jesus answered them, "My Father works until now, and I work." Therefore the Jews sought the more to kill him, because he not only had broken the sabbath, but said also that God was his Father, making himself equal with God.

"The Resurrection of Life"
John 5:19-29

6 Then Jesus answered and said unto them, "Truly, truly, I say unto you, The Son can do nothing of himself, but what he sees the Father do: for whatsoever things he does, these also does the Son likewise. For the Father loves the Son, and shows him all things that he himself does: and he will show him greater works than these, that you may marvel. For as the Father raises up the dead, and quickens them; even so the Son quickens whom he will.

7 "For the Father judges no man, but has committed all judgment unto the Son: that all men should honor the Son, even as they honor the Father. He that does not honor the Son does not honor the Father which has sent him. Truly, truly, I say unto you, He that hears my word, and believes on him that sent me, has everlasting life, and shall not come into condemnation; but is passed from death unto life.

> "HE THAT HEARS MY WORD, AND BELIEVES ON HIM THAT SENT ME, HAS EVERLASTING LIFE."

8 "Truly, truly, I say unto you, The hour is coming, and now is, when the dead shall hear the voice of the Son of God: and they that hear shall live. For as the Father has life in himself; so has he given to the Son to have life in himself; and has given him authority to execute judgment also, because he is the Son of man.

9 "Marvel not at this: for the hour is coming, in which all that are in the graves shall hear his voice, and shall come forth; they that have done good, unto the resurrection of life; and they that have done evil, unto the resurrection of condemnation."

"In My Father's Name"
John 5:30-47

10 "I can of my own self do nothing: as I hear, I judge: and my judgment is just; because I seek not my own will, but the will of the Father which has sent me. If I bear witness of myself, my witness is not true. There is another that bears witness of me; and I know that the witness which he witnesses of me is true.

> "I SEEK NOT MY OWN WILL, BUT THE WILL OF THE FATHER WHICH HAS SENT ME."

11 "You sent unto John, and he bore witness unto the truth. But I do not receive testimony from man: but these things I say, that you might be saved.

He was a burning and a shining light: and you were willing for a season to 11
rejoice in his light. But I have greater witness than that of John: for the
works which the Father has given me to finish, the same works that I do,
bear witness of me, that the Father has sent me.

"And the Father himself, which has sent me, has borne witness of 12
me. You have neither heard his voice
at any time, nor seen his form. And
you have not his word dwelling in
you: for whom he has sent, him you
do not believe. Search the scriptures;
for in them you think you have eter-

> "SEARCH THE SCRIPTURES; FOR
> IN THEM YOU THINK YOU HAVE
> ETERNAL LIFE: AND THEY ARE
> THEY WHICH TESTIFY OF ME."

nal life: and they are they which testify of me. And you will not come to
me, that you might have life.

"I do not receive honor from men. But I know you, that you have not 13
the love of God in you. I am come in my Father's name, and you do not
receive me: if another shall come in his own name, him you will receive.
How can you believe, which receive honor one of another, and seek not the
honor that comes from God only? Do not think that I will accuse you to the
Father: there is one that accuses you, even Moses, in whom you trust. For
had you believed Moses, you would have believed me: for he wrote of me.
But if you do not believe his writings, how shall you believe my words?"

CHAPTER 11

MINISTRY AT CAPERNAUM

Sabbath Harvest and the Law
Matthew 12:1-8; Mark 2:23-28; Luke 6:1-5

1   And it came to pass on the second sabbath after the first, that Jesus went through the grainfields; and his disciples were hungry, and plucked the heads of grain, and did eat, rubbing them in their hands. But when the Pharisees saw it, they said unto him, "Behold, why do your disciples do that which is not lawful to do on the sabbath days?"

2   And Jesus answering them said, "Have you never read what David did, when he had need, and was hungry, he, and they that were with him? How he went into the house of God in the days of Abiathar the high priest, and did eat the showbread, which is not lawful to eat but for the priests alone, and gave also to them which were with him? Or have you not read in the law, how that on the sabbath days the priests in the temple profane the sabbath, and are blameless?

3   "But I say unto you, That in this place is one greater than the temple. But if you had known what this means, 'I will have mercy, and not sacrifice,' you would not have condemned the guiltless." And he said unto them, "The sabbath was made for man, and not man for the sabbath: therefore the Son of man is Lord also of the sabbath."

Sabbath Healing of a Withered Hand
Matthew 12:9-14; Mark 3:1-6; Luke 6:6-11

4   And it came to pass also on another sabbath, that he entered into the synagogue and taught: and, behold, there was a man whose right hand was withered. And the scribes and Pharisees watched him, whether he would heal on the sabbath day; that they might find an accusation against him. And they asked him, saying, "Is it lawful to heal on the sabbath days?" that they might accuse him.

And he said unto them, "What man shall there be among you, that 5 shall have one sheep, and if it falls into a pit on the sabbath day, will he not lay hold on it, and lift it out? How much then is a man better than a sheep? Therefore it is lawful to do well on the sabbath days."

But he knew their thoughts, and said to the man which had the with- 6 ered hand, "Rise up, and stand forth in the midst." And he arose and stood forth. Then said Jesus unto them, "I will ask you one thing; Is it lawful on the sabbath days to do good, or to do evil? to save life, or to destroy it?" But they held their peace. And when he had looked round about on them with anger, being grieved for the hardness of their hearts, he said unto the man, "Stretch forth your hand." And he did so: and his hand was restored whole as the other.

Then they were filled with fury; and discussed one with another what 7 they might do to Jesus. And straightway the Pharisees went forth, plotted with the Herodians against him, how they might destroy him.

Multitudes Seek Jesus' Healing
Matthew 4:23-25; 12:15-21; Mark 3:7-12

But when Jesus knew it, he withdrew himself with his disciples to the 8 sea: and a great multitude from Galilee followed him, and from Judea, and from Jerusalem, and from Idumaea, and from beyond Jordan; and they about Tyre and Sidon, a great multitude, when they had heard what great things he did, came unto him. And he healed them all; and charged them that they should not make him known: that it might be fulfilled which was spoken by Isaiah the prophet, saying, *"Behold my servant, whom I have chosen; my beloved, in whom my soul is well pleased: I will put my spirit upon him, and he shall show judgment to the Gentiles. He shall not quarrel, nor cry; neither shall any man hear his voice in the streets. A bruised reed shall he not break, and smoking wick shall he not quench, till he sends forth judgment unto victory. And in his name shall the Gentiles trust."*

And he spoke to his disciples, that a small ship should wait on him 9 because of the multitude, lest they should trample him. For he had healed many; insomuch that they crowded upon him to touch him, as many as had afflictions.

And unclean spirits, when they saw him, fell down before him, and 10 cried, saying, "You are the Son of God." And he strictly charged them that they should not make him known.

And Jesus went about all Galilee, teaching in their synagogues, and 11 preaching the gospel of the kingdom, and healing all manner of sickness and all manner of disease among the people. And his fame went throughout all Syria: and they brought unto him all sick people that were taken with various diseases and torments, and those which were possessed with demons, and those which were lunatic, and those that had the paralysis; and he healed them. And there followed him great multitudes of people from

11 Galilee, and from Decapolis, and from Jerusalem, and from Judea, and from beyond Jordan.

Twelve Ordained as the Apostles
Mark 3:13-19; Luke 6:12-16

12 And it came to pass in those days, that he went out into a mountain to pray, and continued all night in prayer to God. And when it was day, he called unto him his disciples whom he would: and they came unto him. And of them he ordained twelve, that they should be with him, and that he might send them forth to preach, and to have authority to heal sicknesses, and to cast out demons: whom also he named apostles; Simon, (whom he also named Peter), and Andrew his brother; James the son of Zebedee, and John the brother of James; and he surnamed them Boanerges, which is, "The sons of thunder": Philip and Bartholomew, Matthew and Thomas, James the son of Alphaeus, and Simon the Canaanite called Zelotes, and Judas the brother of James (whose surname was Thaddaeus), and Judas Iscariot, which also was the traitor, which also betrayed him.

To Hear and Be Healed
Luke 6:17-19

13 And he came down with them, and stood in the plain, and the company of his disciples, and a great multitude of people out of all Judea and Jerusalem, and from the sea coast of Tyre and Sidon, which came to hear him, and to be healed of their diseases; and they that were tormented with unclean spirits: and they were healed. And the whole multitude sought to touch him: for there went power out of him, and healed them all.

PART 4

THE SERMON ON THE MOUNT

Seeking to be understood, Jesus withdrew from the multitudes and, gathering His disciples together, delivered to them one of the purest guides for Christian living found in the Scriptures. The life-giving truths in these Beatitudes were intended not merely as instructions for the disciples, but as enduring guideposts to blessings for all those who seek to build their lives on the firm foundation of Truth.

"IF YOU FORGIVE MEN THEIR TRESPASSES, YOUR
HEAVENLY FATHER WILL ALSO FORGIVE YOU."
(MATTHEW 6:14)

CHAPTER 12

BLESSINGS OF THE NEW LIFE

Blessings
Matthew 5:1-12; Luke 6:22-23

1   And seeing the multitudes, he went up into a mountain: and when he was seated, his disciples came unto him: and he opened his mouth, and taught them, saying, "Blessed are the poor in spirit: for theirs is the kingdom of heaven. Blessed are they that mourn: for they shall be comforted. Blessed are the meek: for they shall inherit the earth. Blessed are they which do hunger and thirst after righteousness: for they shall be filled. Blessed are the merciful: for they shall obtain mercy. Blessed are the pure in heart: for they shall see God. Blessed are the peacemakers: for they shall be called the children of God. Blessed are they which are persecuted for righteousness' sake: for theirs is the kingdom of heaven.

2   "Blessed are you, when men shall hate you, and when they shall separate you from their company, and shall reproach you, and persecute you, and shall say all manner of evil against you falsely, for the Son of man's sake.

3   "Rejoice in that day, and leap for joy, and be exceedingly glad: for, behold, great is your reward in heaven: for in the like manner they persecuted the prophets which were before you."

Woes
Luke 6:20-21; 24-26

4   And he lifted up his eyes on his disciples, and said, "Blessed be you poor: for yours is the kingdom of God. Blessed are you that hunger now: for you shall be filled. Blessed are you that weep now: for you shall laugh. But woe unto you that are rich! for you have received your consolation. Woe unto you that are full! for you shall hunger. Woe unto you that laugh now! for you shall mourn and weep. Woe unto you, when all men shall speak well of you! for so did their fathers to the false prophets."

The Salt of the Earth
Matthew 5:13

"You are the salt of the earth: but if the salt has lost its savor, with what   5
shall it be salted? it is thereafter good for nothing, but to be cast out, and to
be trampled underfoot of men."

The Light of the World
Matthew 5:14-16

"You are the light of the world. A city that is set on a hill cannot be   6
hidden. Neither do men light a lamp, and put it under a tub, but on a lampstand; and it gives light unto all that are in the house. Let your light so shine
before men, that they may see your good works, and glorify your Father
which is in heaven."

The Law Fulfilled
Matthew 5:17-20

"Think not that I am come to destroy the law, or the prophets: I am not   7
come to destroy, but to fulfill. For truly I say unto you, Till heaven and earth
pass, one letter or one little stroke shall in no way pass from the law, till all
be fulfilled.

"Whosoever therefore shall break one of these least command-   8
ments, and shall teach men so, he shall be called the least in the kingdom
of heaven: but whosoever shall do and teach them, the same shall be
called great in the kingdom of heaven. For I say unto you, That except
your righteousness shall exceed the righteousness of the scribes and
Pharisees, you shall in no way enter into the kingdom of heaven."

Anger
Matthew 5:21-22

"You have heard that it was said by them of old time, '*You shall not*   9
kill; and whosoever shall kill shall be in danger of the judgment:' but I say
unto you, That whosoever is angry with his brother without a cause shall be
in danger of the judgment: and whosoever shall say to his brother, 'Raca'
(Fool), shall be in danger of the council: but whosoever shall say, 'You fool,'
shall be in danger of hell fire."

Reconciliation
Matthew 5:23-26

"Therefore if you bring your gift to the altar, and there remember   10
that your brother has anything
against you; leave there your gift | "FIRST BE RECONCILED TO
before the altar, and go your way; | YOUR BROTHER, AND THEN
first be reconciled to your brother, | COME AND OFFER YOUR GIFT."
and then come and offer your gift.

"Agree with your adversary quickly, while you are on the way with   11
him; lest at any time the adversary deliver you to the judge, and the judge

11 deliver you to the officer, and you be cast into prison. Truly I say unto you, You shall by no means come out from there, till you have paid the uttermost copper coin."

Adultery
Matthew 5:27-30

12   "You have heard that it was said by them of old time, '*You shall not commit adultery*:' but I say unto you, That whosoever looks on a woman to lust after her has committed adultery with her already in his heart.

13   "And if your right eye causes you to sin, pluck it out, and cast it from you: for it is profitable for you that one of your members should perish, and not that your whole body should be cast into hell.

14   "And if your right hand causes you to sin, cut it off, and cast it from you: for it is profitable for you that one of your members should perish, and not that your whole body should be cast into hell."

Divorce
Matthew 5:31-32

"It has been said, '*Whosoever shall put away his wife, let him give her* 15 *a writing of divorcement*:' but I say unto you, That whosoever shall put away his wife, except for the cause of fornication, causes her to commit adultery: and whosoever shall marry her that is divorced commits adultery."

Oaths
Matthew 5:33-37

16   "Again, you have heard that it has been said by them of old time, '*You shall not falsely swear yourself, but shall perform unto the Lord your oaths*:' but I say unto you, Swear not at all; neither by heaven; for it is God's throne: nor by the earth; for it is his footstool: neither by Jerusalem; for it is the city of the great King. Neither shall you swear by your head, because you cannot make one hair white or black. But let your communication be, Yes, yes; No, no: for whatsoever is more than these comes of evil."

Retaliation
Matthew 5:38-42; Luke 6:29-30

17   "You have heard that it has been said, '*An eye for an eye, and a tooth for a tooth*:' but I say unto you, That you resist not evil: but whosoever shall strike you on your right cheek, turn to him the other also. And unto him that takes away your cloak do not forbid to take your tunic also.

18   "And if any man will sue you at the law, and take away your tunic, let him have your cloak also. And whosoever shall compel you to go a mile, go with him two.

19   "Give to every man that asks you, and from him that would borrow of you do not turn you away; and of him that takes away your goods do not ask for them back."

Enemies
Matthew 5:43-48; Luke 6:27-28; 32-36

"You have heard that it has been said, '*You shall love your neighbor*, 20 and hate your enemy.' But I say unto you which hear, Love your enemies, bless them that curse you, do good to them that hate you, and pray for them which despitefully use you, and persecute you; that you may be the children of your Father which is in heaven: for he makes his sun to rise on the evil and on the good, and sends rain on the just and on the unjust.

> "LOVE YOUR ENEMIES, BLESS THEM THAT CURSE YOU, DO GOOD TO THEM THAT HATE YOU, AND PRAY FOR THEM WHICH DESPITEFULLY USE YOU."

"For if you love them which love you, what reward do you have? do 21 not even the tax collectors the same? for sinners also love those that love them. And if you greet your brethren only, what do you more than others? do not even the tax collectors so? And if you do good to them which do good to you, what thanks do you have? for sinners also do even the same. And if you lend to them of whom you hope to receive, what thanks do you have? for sinners also lend to sinners, to receive as much in return.

"But love your enemies, and do good, and lend, hoping for nothing in 22 return; and your reward shall be great, and you shall be the children of the Highest: for he is kind unto the unthankful and to the evil. Be therefore merciful, as your Father also is merciful.

"Be therefore perfect, even as your Father which is in heaven is perfect." 23

CHAPTER 13

BLESSINGS OF GOD

Charity
Matthew 6:1-4

1   "Take heed that you do not do your righteousness before men, to be seen of them: otherwise you have no reward of your Father which is in heaven.

2   "Therefore when you do your charitable deeds, do not sound a trumpet before you, as the hypocrites do in the synagogues and in the streets, that they may have glory of men. Truly I say unto you, They have their reward.

3   "But when you do charitable deeds, let not your left hand know what your right hand does: that your charitable deeds may be in secret: and your Father which sees in secret himself shall reward you openly."

Prayer
Matthew 6:5-15

4   "And when you pray, you shall not be as the hypocrites are: for they love to pray standing in the synagogues and in the corners of the streets, that they may be seen of men. Truly I say unto you, They have their reward.

5   "But you, when you pray, enter into your inner room, and when you have shut your door, pray to your Father which is in secret; and your Father which sees in secret shall reward you openly. But when you pray, use not vain repetitions, as the heathen do: for they think that they shall be heard for their many words. Be not therefore like them: for your Father knows what things you have need of, before you ask him.

6   "After this manner therefore pray: Our Father which are in heaven, Hallowed be your name. Your kingdom come. Your will be done on earth, as it is in heaven. Give us this day our daily bread. And forgive us our debts, as we forgive our debtors. And lead us not into temptation, but deliver us from evil: For yours is the kingdom, and the power, and the glory, for ever. Amen. For if you forgive men their trespasses, your heavenly Father will

also forgive you: but if you forgive not men their trespasses, neither will 6 your Father forgive your trespasses."

Fasting
Matthew 6:16-18

"Moreover when you fast, be not, as the hypocrites, of a sad counte- 7 nance: for they disfigure their faces, that they may appear unto men to fast. Truly I say unto you, They have their reward.

"But you, when you fast, anoint your head, and wash your face; that 8 you do not appear unto men to fast, but unto your Father which is in secret: and your Father, which sees in secret, shall reward you openly."

Treasures
Matthew 6:19-21

"Do not lay up for yourselves treasures upon earth, where moth and 9 rust does corrupt, and where thieves break in and steal: but lay up for yourselves treasures in heaven, where neither moth nor rust does

> "LAY UP FOR YOURSELVES TREASURES IN HEAVEN."

corrupt, and where thieves do not break in nor steal: for where your treasure is, there will your heart be also."

Light of the Body
Matthew 6:22-23

"The light of the body is the eye: if therefore your eye be single, your 10 whole body shall be full of light. But if your eye be evil, your whole body shall be full of darkness. If therefore the light that is in you be darkness, how great is that darkness!"

Consider This
Matthew 6:24-34

"No man can serve two masters: for either he will hate the one, and 11 love the other; or else he will hold to the one, and despise the other. You cannot serve God and money.

"Therefore I say unto you, Be not anxious for your life, what you shall 12 eat, or what you shall drink; nor for your body, what you shall put on. Is not the life more than food, and the body than clothing? Behold the birds of the air: for they sow not, neither do they reap, nor gather into barns; yet your heavenly Father feeds them. Are you not much better than they? Which of you by worrying can add one cubit unto his stature?

"And why do you worry for clothing? Consider the lilies of the field, 13 how they grow; they toil not, neither do they spin: and yet I say unto you, That even Solomon in all his glory was not arrayed like one of these. For,

> "CONSIDER THE LILIES OF THE FIELD, HOW THEY GROW."

if God so clothe the grass of the field, which today is, and tomorrow is cast into the oven, shall he not much more clothe you, O you of little faith?

14   "Therefore be not anxious, saying, 'What shall we eat?' or, 'What shall we drink?' or, 'With what shall we be clothed?' (For after all these things do the Gentiles seek): for your heavenly Father knows that you have need of all these things.

15   "But seek first the kingdom of God, and his righteousness; and all these things shall be added unto you. Therefore be not anxious for tomorrow: for tomorrow shall take care for the things of itself. Sufficient unto the day is the evil thereof."

> "SEEK FIRST THE KINGDOM OF GOD."

CHAPTER 14

BLESSINGS OF WISDOM

Judgment
Matthew 7:1-6; Luke 6:37-42

"Judge not, and you shall not be judged: condemn not, and you shall 1 not be condemned: forgive, and you shall be forgiven. Give, and it shall be given unto you; good measure, pressed down, and shaken together, and running over, shall men give into your bosom. For with what judgment you judge, you shall be judged: and with what measure you measure, it shall be measured to you again."

And he spoke a parable unto them, "Can the blind lead the blind? shall 2 they not both fall into the ditch? The disciple is not above his teacher: but everyone that is perfect shall be as his teacher.

"And why do you behold the speck that is in your brother's eye, but do 3 not consider the log that is in your own eye? Or how can you say to your brother, 'Brother, let me pull out the speck that is in your eye,' when you yourself do not behold the log that is in your own eye? You hypocrite, cast out first the log out of your own eye, and then shall you see clearly to pull out the speck that is in your brother's eye.

"Give not that which is holy unto the dogs, neither cast your pearls 4 before swine, lest they trample them under their feet, and turn again and tear you."

The Golden Rule
Matthew 7:7-12; Luke 6:31

"Ask, and it shall be given you; seek, and you shall find; knock, and it 5 shall be opened unto you: for everyone that asks receives; and he that seeks finds; and to him that knocks it shall be opened.

"Or what man is there of you, whom if his son asks for bread, will he 6 give him a stone? Or if he asks for a fish, will he give him a serpent? If you

6 then, being evil, know how to give good gifts unto your children, how much more shall your Father which is in heaven give good things to them that ask him? Therefore all things whatsoever you would that men should do to you, do you even so to them: for this is the law and the prophets."

Narrow Gate
Matthew 7:13-14

7 "Enter in at the strait gate: for wide is the gate, and broad is the way, that leads to destruction, and many there be which go in thereat: because strait is the gate, and narrow is the way, which leads unto life, and few there be that find it."

False Prophets
Matthew 7:15-20; Luke 6:43-45

8 "Beware of false prophets, which come to you in sheep's clothing, but inwardly they are ravenous wolves. You shall know them by their fruits. Do men gather grapes of bramble bushes, or figs of thornbushes?

9 "Even so every good tree brings forth good fruit; but a corrupt tree brings forth evil fruit. A good tree cannot bring forth evil fruit, neither can a corrupt tree bring forth good fruit. Every tree that does not bring forth good fruit is cut down, and cast into the fire.

10 "For every tree is known by its own fruit. For of thornbushes men do not gather figs, nor of a bramble bush do they gather grapes. A good man out of the good treasure of his heart brings forth that which is good; and an evil man out of the evil treasure of his heart brings forth that which is evil: for of the abundance of the heart his mouth speaks.

> "A GOOD MAN OUT OF THE GOOD TREASURE OF HIS HEART BRINGS FORTH THAT WHICH IS GOOD."

11 "For by their fruits you shall know them."

Kingdom of Heaven
Matthew 7:21-23; Luke 6:46

12 "Not everyone that says unto me, 'Lord, Lord,' shall enter into the kingdom of heaven; but he that does the will of my Father which is in heaven. Many will say to me in that day, 'Lord, Lord, have we not prophesied in your name? and in your name have cast out demons? and in your name done many wonderful works?'

13 "And then will I profess unto them, 'I never knew you: depart from me, you that work iniquity.' And why do you call me, 'Lord, Lord,' and do not the things which I say?"

Wise and Foolish Builders
Matthew 7:24-27; Luke 6:47-49

14 "Therefore whosoever comes to me, and hears these sayings of mine, and does them, I will liken him unto a wise man, which dug deep, and laid

the foundation on a rock: which built his house upon a rock: and the rain 14
descended, and the floods came, and the stream beat violently upon that
house, and could not shake it; and the winds blew, and beat upon that house,
and it did not fall: for it was founded upon a rock.

"But everyone that hears these sayings of mine, and does not do them, 15
shall be likened unto a foolish man, that without a foundation built his
house upon the sand: and the rain descended, and the floods came; against
which the stream did beat violently; and the winds blew, and beat upon that
house; and immediately it fell: and great was the fall of it; and the ruin of
that house was great."

The People's Response
Matthew 7:28-29

And it came to pass, when Jesus had ended these sayings, the people 16
were astonished at his doctrine: for he taught them as one having authority,
and not as the scribes.

PART 5

PURPOSE AND PARABLES

As the fame of Jesus grew and word of His marvelous works became widely known among the people, great multitudes followed Him, seeking healing. Through the many miracles and ministries He performed, the spiritual power of this holy man of God revealed to others who God is and what a right understanding of God can do for man. The grace and wisdom He demonstrated in answering admirers and adversaries alike were lesson to all.

HE WENT THROUGHOUT EVERY CITY AND VIL-
LAGE, PREACHING: AND THE TWELVE WERE WITH
HIM, AND CERTAIN WOMEN, MARY CALLED
MAGDALENE...AND JOANNA...AND SUSANNA,
AND MANY OTHERS, WHICH MINISTERED UNTO
HIM OF THEIR SUBSTANCE.   (LUKE 8:1-3)

CHAPTER 15

JESUS AND JOHN THE BAPTIST

Jesus Heals the Centurion's Servant
Matthew 8:1, 5-13; Luke 7:1-10

Now when he had ended all his sayings in the audience of the people, 1
when he was come down from the mountain, great multitudes followed him
into Capernaum.

And when Jesus was entered into Capernaum, a certain centurion's 2
servant, who was dear unto him, was sick, and about to die. And when he
heard of Jesus, he sent unto him the elders of the Jews, pleading with him
that he would come and heal his servant, and saying, "Lord, my servant lies
at home sick of the paralysis, grievously tormented." And when they came
to Jesus, they pleaded with him earnestly, saying, "That he was worthy for
whom he should do this: for he loves our nation, and he has built us a synagogue." And Jesus said, "I will come and heal him."

Then Jesus went with them. And when he was now not far from the 3
house, the centurion sent friends to him, saying unto him, "Lord, do not
trouble yourself: for I am not worthy that you should enter under my roof:
therefore neither thought I myself worthy to come unto you: but say in a
word, and my servant shall be healed. For I also am a man set under authority, having under me soldiers, and I say unto one, 'Go,' and he goes; and to
another, 'Come,' and he comes; and to my servant, 'Do this,' and he does it."

When Jesus heard these things, he marveled at him, and turned him- 4
self about, and said to them that followed him, "Truly I say unto you, I have
not found so great a faith, no, not in Israel. And I say unto you, That many
shall come from the east and west, and shall sit down with Abraham, and
Isaac, and Jacob, in the kingdom of heaven. But the children of the kingdom shall be cast out into outer darkness: there shall be weeping and gnashing of teeth."

5   And Jesus said unto the centurion, "Go your way; and as you have believed, so be it done unto you." And his servant was healed in the self-same hour. And they that were sent, returning to the house, found the servant whole that had been sick.

Restoring Life to a Widow's Son
Luke 7:11-17

6   And it came to pass the day after, that he went into a city called Nain; and many of his disciples went with him, and many people. Now when he came near to the gate of the city, behold, there was a dead man carried out, the only son of his mother, and she was a widow: and many people of the city were with her. And when the Lord saw her, he had compassion on her, and said unto her, "Weep not."

7   And he came and touched the coffin: and they that bore him stood still. And he said, "Young man, I say unto you, Arise." And he that was dead sat up, and began to speak. And he delivered him to his mother. And there came a fear on all: and they glorified God, saying, "That a great prophet is risen up among us;" and, "That God has visited his people." And this rumor of him went forth throughout all Judea, and throughout all the region round about.

John the Baptist's Message to Jesus
Matthew 11:2-6; Luke 7:18-23

8   And the disciples of John showed him of all these things. Now when John had heard in the prison the works of Christ, John calling unto him two of his disciples sent them to Jesus, saying, "Are you he that should come? or do we look for another?"

9   When the men were come unto him, they said, "John the Baptist has sent us unto you, saying, 'Are you he that should come? or do we look for another?' " And in that same hour he cured many of their diseases and afflictions, and of evil spirits; and unto many that were blind he gave sight.

10   Then Jesus answering said unto them, "Go your way, and tell John again what things you have seen and heard; how the blind receive their sight, and the lame walk, the lepers are cleansed, and the deaf hear, the dead are raised up, and the poor have the gospel preached to them. And blessed is he, whosoever shall not fall away because of me."

John Is Much More Than a Prophet
Matthew 11:7-19; Luke 7:24-35

11   And as they departed, Jesus began to say unto the multitudes concerning John, "What went you out into the wilderness to see? A reed shaken with the wind? But what went you out to see? A man clothed in soft clothing? Behold, they which are gorgeously appareled, and live in luxury, are in kings' courts. But what went you out to see? A prophet? yes, I say unto you, and much more than a prophet. For this is he, of whom it is written, '*Behold, I send my messenger before your face, which shall prepare your way before you.*'

12   "Truly I say unto you, Among those that are born of women there is not a greater prophet than John the Baptist: but he that is least in the kingdom

of God is greater than he. And from the days of John the Baptist until now 12 the kingdom of heaven suffers violence, and the violent take it by force. For all the prophets and the law prophesied until John. And if you will receive it, this is Elijah, which was to come. He that has ears to hear, let him hear."

And all the people that heard him, and the tax collectors, justified God, 13 being baptized with the baptism of John. But the Pharisees and lawyers rejected the purpose of God for themselves, being not baptized of him.

And the Lord said, "To what then shall I liken the men of this genera- 14 tion? and to what are they like? They are like children sitting in the marketplace, and calling one to another, and saying, 'We have piped unto you, and you have not danced; we have mourned unto you, and you have not lamented.' For John the Baptist came neither eating bread nor drinking wine; and you say, 'He has a demon.' The Son of man is come eating and drinking; and you say, 'Behold a gluttonous man, and a winebibber, a friend of tax collectors and sinners!' But wisdom is justified of all her children."

A Sinful Woman Is Forgiven
Luke 7:36-50

And one of the Pharisees desired him that he would eat with him. And 15 he went into the Pharisee's house, and sat down to eat. And, behold, a woman in the city, which was a sinner, when she knew that Jesus sat at the table in the Pharisee's house, brought an alabaster jar of ointment, and stood at his feet behind him weeping, and began to wash his feet with tears, and did wipe them with the hairs of her head, and kissed his feet, and anointed them with the ointment.

Now when the Pharisee which had invited him saw it, he spoke within 16 himself, saying, "This man, if he were a prophet, would have known who and what manner of woman this is that touches him: for she is a sinner." And Jesus answering said unto him, "Simon, I have something to say unto you." And he said, "Teacher, say on."

"There was a certain creditor which had two debtors: the one owed 17 five hundred silver coins, and the other fifty. And when they had nothing to pay, he freely forgave them both. Tell me therefore, which of them will love him more?" Simon answered and said, "I suppose that he, to whom he forgave more." And he said unto him, "You have rightly judged."

And he turned to the woman, and said unto Simon, "Do you see this 18 woman? I entered into your house, you gave me no water for my feet: but she has washed my feet with tears, and wiped them with the hairs of her head. You gave me no kiss: but this woman since the time I came in has not ceased to kiss my feet. My head with oil you did not anoint: but this woman has anointed my feet with ointment. Therefore I say unto you, Her sins, which are many, are forgiven; for she loved much: but to whom little is forgiven, the same loves little."

And he said unto her, "Your sins are forgiven." And they that sat at the 19 table with him began to say within themselves, "Who is this that forgives sins also?" And he said to the woman, "Your faith has saved you; go in peace."

CHAPTER 16

..KINGDOM OF GOD VS. KINGDOM OF DARKNESS..

Women Minister Unto Jesus
Luke 8:1-3

1   And it came to pass afterward, that he went throughout every city and village, preaching and showing the glad tidings of the kingdom of God: and the twelve were with him, and certain women, which had been healed of evil spirits and infirmities, Mary called Magdalene, out of whom went seven demons, and Joanna the wife of Chuza Herod's steward, and Susanna, and many others, which ministered unto him of their substance.

Jesus Is Not Beelzebub
Matthew 12:22-30; Mark 3:20-27

2   And they went into a house. And the multitude came together again, so that they could not so much as eat bread. And when his friends heard of it, they went out to lay hold on him: for they said, "He is gone mad."

3   Then was brought unto him one possessed with a demon, blind, and mute: and he healed him, insomuch that the blind and mute both spoke and saw. And all the people were amazed, and said, "Is not this the son of David?" But when the Pharisees heard it, said, "This fellow does not cast out demons, but by Beelzebub the prince of the demons." And the scribes which came down from Jerusalem said, "He has Beelzebub, and by the prince of the demons casts he out demons."

4   And Jesus knew their thoughts, and he called them unto him, and said unto them in parables, "How can Satan cast out Satan? Every kingdom divided against itself is brought to desolation. And every city divided against itself shall not stand. And if a house be divided against itself, that house cannot stand. And if Satan rises up against himself, and be divided, he cannot stand, but has an end.

5   "And if I by Beelzebub cast out demons, by whom do your children cast them out? therefore they shall be your judges. But if I cast out demons

by the Spirit of God, then the kingdom of God is come unto you. Or else 5
how can one enter into a strong man's house, and steal his goods, except he
first binds the strong man? and then he will rob his house. He that is not
with me is against me; and he that gathers not with me scatters abroad."

The One Unforgiven Sin
Matthew 12:31-32; Mark 3:28-30

"Truly I say unto you, All manner of sin and blasphemy shall be for- 6
given unto men: but the blasphemy against the Holy Ghost shall not be forgiven unto men. And whosoever speaks a word against the Son of man, it
shall be forgiven him: but whosoever speaks against the Holy Ghost, it shall
not be forgiven him, neither in this world, neither in the world to come, but
is in danger of eternal condemnation: because they said, He has an unclean
spirit."

Judged by Your Words
Matthew 12:33-37

"Either make the tree good, and its fruit good; or else make the tree 7
corrupt, and its fruit corrupt: for the
tree is known by its fruit. O generation

> "OUT OF THE ABUNDANCE OF THE HEART THE MOUTH SPEAKS."

of vipers, how can you, being evil,
speak good things? for out of the
abundance of the heart the mouth
speaks. A good man out of the good treasure of the heart brings forth good
things: and an evil man out of the evil treasure brings forth evil things.

"But I say unto you, That every idle word that men shall speak, they 8
shall give account thereof in the day of judgment. For by your words you
shall be justified, and by your words you shall be condemned."

Seeking a Sign
Matthew 12:38-42

Then certain of the scribes and of the Pharisees answered, saying, 9
"Teacher, we would see a sign from you." But he answered and said unto
them, "An evil and adulterous generation seeks after a sign; and there shall
no sign be given to it, but the sign of the prophet Jonah: for as Jonah was
three days and three nights in the whale's belly; so shall the Son of man be
three days and three nights in the heart of the earth. The men of Nineveh
shall rise in judgment with this generation, and shall condemn it: because
they repented at the preaching of Jonah; and, behold, one greater than Jonah
is here.

"The queen of the south shall rise up in the judgment with this gener- 10
ation, and shall condemn it: for she came from the uttermost parts of the
earth to hear the wisdom of Solomon; and, behold, one greater than
Solomon is here."

Unclean Spirits
Matthew 12:43-45

11   "When the unclean spirit is gone out of a man, it walks through dry places, seeking rest, and finds none. Then it says, 'I will return into my house from which I came out;' and when it is come, it finds it empty, swept, and put in order. Then it goes, and takes with itself seven other spirits more wicked than itself, and they enter in and dwell there: and the last state of that man is worse than the first. Even so shall it be also unto this wicked generation."

Jesus' Mother and Brethren
Matthew 12:46-50; Mark 3:31-35; Luke 8:19-21

12   There came then to him his mother and his brethren, and could not come at him for the crowd, and, standing outside, sent unto him, calling him. While he yet talked to the people, and the multitude sat about him, one said unto him, "Behold, your mother and your brethren stand outside, desiring to speak with you." But he answered and said unto him that told him, "Who is my mother? and who are my brethren?"

13

> "WHOSOEVER SHALL DO THE WILL OF MY FATHER WHICH IS IN HEAVEN, THE SAME IS MY BROTHER, AND SISTER, AND MOTHER."

And he looked round about on them which sat about him, and he stretched forth his hand toward his disciples, and said, "Behold my mother and my brethren! My mother and my brethren are these which hear the word of God, and do it. For whosoever shall do the will of my Father which is in heaven, the same is my brother, and sister, and mother."

CHAPTER 17

PARABLES BY THE SEA

Parable of the Sower
Matthew 13:1-9; Mark 4:1-9; Luke 8:4-8

The same day went Jesus out of the house, and sat by the seaside. And 1 he began again to teach by the seaside: and there was gathered unto him a great multitude out of every city, so that he entered into a ship, and sat in the sea; and the whole multitude stood on the shore by the sea. And he taught them many things by parables, and said unto them in his doctrine, by a parable: "Hearken; Behold, there went out a sower to sow his seed: and it came to pass, as he sowed, some fell by the wayside; and was trampled down, and the birds of the air came and devoured them up.

"And some fell on stony ground, where it had not much earth; and 2 immediately it sprang up, because it had no depth of earth: but when the sun was up, it was scorched; and because it had no root, it withered away, because it lacked moisture.

"And some fell among thorns; and the thorns sprang up with it, and 3 the thorns grew up, and choked it, and it yielded no fruit.

"And others fell on good ground, and did yield fruit that sprang up and 4 increased; and brought forth fruit, some a hundredfold, some sixtyfold, some thirtyfold." And when he had said these things, he cried, "He that has ears to hear, let him hear."

The Divine Purpose of Parables
Matthew 13:10-17; Mark 4:10-12; Luke 8:9-10

And the disciples came, and said unto him, "Why do you speak unto 5 them in parables?" He answered and said unto them, "Because it is given unto you to know the mysteries of the kingdom of heaven, but to them it is not given. For whosoever has, to him shall be given, and he shall have more abundance: but whosoever has not, from him shall be taken away even that

5 he has. Therefore I speak to them in parables: because they seeing see not; and hearing they hear not, neither do they understand."

6 And when he was alone, they that were about him with the twelve asked of him the parable, saying, "What might this parable be?" And he said unto them, "Unto you it is given to know the mystery of the kingdom of God: but unto them that are outside, all these things are done in parables. And in them is fulfilled the prophecy of Isaiah, which says, *'By hearing you shall hear, and shall not understand; and seeing you shall see, and shall not perceive: for this people's heart is grown coarse, and their ears are dull of hearing, and their eyes they have closed; lest at any time they should see with their eyes, and hear with their ears, and should understand with their hearts, and should be converted, and I should heal them,'* and their sins should be forgiven them.

7 "But blessed are your eyes, for they see: and your ears, for they hear. For truly I say unto you, That many prophets and righteous men have desired to see those things which you see, and have not seen them; and to hear those things which you hear, and have not heard them."

Parable of the Sower Explained
Matthew 13:18-23; Mark 4:13-20; Luke 8:11-15

8 And he said unto them, "Do you not know this parable? and how then will you know all parables? Hear therefore the parable of the sower.

9 "Now the parable of the sower is this: The seed is the word of God. The sower sows the word. And these are they by the wayside, where the word of the kingdom is sown. When anyone hears the word of the kingdom, and does not understand it, then comes the wicked one. But when they have heard, Satan comes immediately, and takes away the word that was sown in their hearts, lest they should believe and be saved.

10 "And these are they likewise which are sown on stony ground; who, when they have heard the word, immediately receive it with gladness; and these have no root in themselves, which for a while believe, and so endure but for a time: afterward, when affliction or persecution arises for the word's sake, immediately they are fallen away, and in time of temptation fall away.

11 "And these are they which are sown among thorns; such as hear the word, which, when they have heard, go forth, and are choked with cares of this world, and the deceitfulness of riches, and pleasures of this life, and the lusts of other things entering in, choke the word, and bring no fruit to maturity.

12 "And these are they which are sown on good ground; which in an honest and good heart, having heard the word, receive it, and keep it, and bring forth fruit with patience, some thirtyfold, some sixty, and some a hundred."

Parable of the Lamp
Mark 4:21-25; Luke 8:16-18

13 And he said unto them, "Is a lamp brought to be put under a tub, or under a bed? and not to be set on a lampstand? No man, when he has

lit a lamp, covers it with a vessel, or puts it under a bed; but sets it on 13
a lampstand, that they which enter in may see the light. For nothing is
secret, that shall not be made manifest; neither anything hidden, that
shall not be known and come to light. If any man has ears to hear, let
him hear."

And he said unto them, "Take heed what you hear: with what meas- 14
ure you measure, it shall be measured
to you: and unto you that hear shall

> "WITH WHAT MEASURE YOU
> MEASURE, IT SHALL BE MEAS-
> URED TO YOU."

more be given. Take heed therefore
how you hear: for whosoever has, to
him shall be given; and whosoever
has not, from him shall be taken even that which he seems to have."

Parable of the Weeds
Matthew 13:24-30

Another parable he put forth unto them, saying, "The kingdom of 15
heaven is likened unto a man which sowed good seed in his field: but while
men slept, his enemy came and sowed weeds among the wheat, and went his
way. But when the blade was sprung up, and brought forth fruit, then
appeared the weeds also.

"So the servants of the landowner came and said unto him, 'Sir, did 16
not you sow good seed in your field? from where then has it weeds?' He
said unto them, 'An enemy has done this.' The servants said unto him, 'Will
you then that we go and gather them up?' But he said, 'No; lest while you
gather up the weeds, you root up also the wheat with them. Let both grow
together until the harvest: and in the time of harvest I will say to the reapers,
"Gather together first the weeds, and bind them in bundles to burn them:
but gather the wheat into my barn." ' "

Parable of the Growth of Seed
Mark 4:26-29

And he said, "So is the kingdom of God, as if a man should cast seed 17
into the ground; and should sleep, and rise night and day, and the seed should
sprout and grow up, he knows not how. For the earth brings forth fruit of
itself; first the blade, then the head, after that the full grain in the head. But
when the fruit is brought forth, immediately he puts in the sickle, because
the harvest is come."

Parable of the Mustard Seed
Matthew 13:31-32; Mark 4:30-32

Another parable he put forth unto them, saying, "To what shall we 18
liken the kingdom of God? or with what comparison shall we compare it?
The kingdom of heaven is like a grain of mustard seed, which a man took,
and sowed in his field: which, when it is sown in the earth, is less than all
the seeds that be in the earth: but when it is sown, it grows up, and becomes
greater than all herbs, and becomes a tree, and shoots out great branches; so

18 that the birds of the air come and lodge in the branches thereof; so may lodge under the shadow of it."

Parable of the Leaven
Matthew 13:33

19   Another parable he spoke unto them; "The kingdom of heaven is like unto leaven, which a woman took, and hid in three measures of meal, till the whole was leavened."

Parables Fulfill Prophecy
Matthew 13:34-35; Mark 4:33-34

20   All these things spoke Jesus unto the multitude in parables: that it might be fulfilled which was spoken by the prophet, saying, "*I will open my mouth in parables; I will utter things which have been kept secret from the foundation of the world.*" And with many such parables he spoke the word unto them, as they were able to hear it. But without a parable he spoke not unto them: and when they were alone, he explained all things to his disciples.

Parable of the Weeds Explained
Matthew 13:36-43

21   Then Jesus sent the multitude away, and went into the house: and his disciples came unto him, saying, "Explain unto us the parable of the weeds of the field." He answered and said unto them, "He that sows the good seeds is the Son of man; the field is the world; the good seeds are the children of the kingdom; but the weeds are the children of the wicked one; the enemy that sowed them is the devil; the harvest is the end of the world; and the reapers are the angels.

22   "THEN SHALL THE RIGHTEOUS SHINE FORTH AS THE SUN IN THE KINGDOM OF THEIR FATHER."

"As therefore the weeds are gathered and burned in the fire; so shall it be in the end of this world. The Son of man shall send forth his angels, and they shall gather out of his kingdom all things that cause sin, and them which do iniquity; and shall cast them into a furnace of fire: there shall be wailing and gnashing of teeth. Then shall the righteous shine forth as the sun in the kingdom of their Father. Who has ears to hear, let him hear."

Parable of the Hidden Treasure
Matthew 13:44

23   "Again, the kingdom of heaven is like treasure hidden in a field; which when a man has found, he hides, and for joy thereof goes and sells all that he has, and buys that field."

Parable of the Pearl of Great Price
Matthew 13:45-46

24   "Again, the kingdom of heaven is like a merchant, seeking beautiful pearls: who, when he had found one pearl of great price, went and sold all that he had, and bought it."

Parable of the Net
Matthew 13:47-50

"Again, the kingdom of heaven is like unto a net, that was cast into the 25 sea, and gathered of every kind: which, when it was full, they drew to shore, and sat down, and gathered the good into vessels, but cast the bad away.

"So shall it be at the end of the world: the angels shall come forth, and 26 sever the wicked from among the just, and shall cast them into the furnace of fire: there shall be wailing and gnashing of teeth."

Parable of the Home Owner
Matthew 13:51-53

Jesus said unto them, "Have you understood all these things?" They 27 said unto him, "Yes, Lord."

Then he said unto them, "Therefore every scribe which is instructed 28 unto the kingdom of heaven is like a man that is a home owner, which brings forth out of his treasure things new and old."

And it came to pass, that when Jesus had finished these parables, he 29 departed from there.

CHAPTER 18

MIRACLES BY THE SEA

Jesus Calms the Winds and Sea
Matthew 8:18, 23-27; Mark 4:35-41; Luke 8:22-25

1   Now it came to pass on the same day, when the evening was come, when Jesus saw great multitudes about him, he said unto them, "Let us go over unto the other side of the sea." And when he was entered into a ship, his disciples followed him. And when they had sent away the multitude, they took him even as he was in the ship. And there were also with him other little ships. And they launched forth.

2   But as they sailed he fell asleep: and, behold, there arose a great tempest in the sea, and the waves beat into the ship, insomuch that the ship was covered with the waves; and they were filled with water, and were in jeopardy. And he was in the rear part of the ship, asleep on a pillow: and his disciples came to him, and awoke him, saying, "Teacher, teacher, we perish, save us: do you not care that we perish?" And he said unto them, "Why are you fearful, O you of little faith?" Then he arose, and rebuked the wind and the raging of the water: and said unto the sea, "Peace, be still." And the wind ceased, and there was a great calm.

3   And he said unto them, "Why are you so fearful? how is it that you have no faith? Where is your faith?" And they being afraid wondered, saying one to another, "What manner of man is this! for he commands even the winds and water, and they obey him."

Delivering the Demon-Possessed
Matthew 8:28-34; Mark 5:1-20; Luke 8:26-39

4   And when he was come to the other side of the sea into the country of the Gadarenes, which is opposite Galilee, there met him two possessed with demons, coming out of the tombs, exceedingly fierce, so that no man might pass by that way.

And when he was come out of the ship, immediately there met him out 5 of the city a certain man with an unclean spirit, and wore no clothes, neither lived in any house, who had his dwelling among the tombs. And no man could bind him, no, not with chains: because he had been often bound with fetters and chains, and the chains had been pulled apart by him, and the fetters broken in pieces: neither could any man tame him. And always, night and day, he was in the mountains, and in the tombs, crying, and cutting himself with stones.

But when he saw Jesus afar off, he ran and fell down before him and 6 worshiped him, and cried out with a loud voice, and said, "What have I to do with you, Jesus, Son of the most high God? I beg you, I command you by God, that you torment me not." For he had commanded the unclean spirit, "Come out of the man, you unclean spirit." (For many times it had caught him: and he was kept bound with chains and in fetters; and he broke the bands, and was driven of the demon into the wilderness.)

And Jesus asked him, saying, "What is your name?" And he answered, 7 saying, "My name is Legion: for we are many:" because many demons were entered into him. And he begged him much that he would not send them away out of the country. And they begged him that he would not command them to go out into the deep.

Now there was there a good way off from them near unto the moun- 8 tains a great herd of swine feeding on the mountain. So all the demons begged him, saying, "If you cast us out, permit us to go away into the herd of swine." And immediately Jesus gave them permission. And he said unto them, "Go." And when they were come out of the man, they went into the herd of swine: and, behold, the whole herd of swine ran violently down a steep place into the sea, (they were about two thousand); and perished in the waters.

When they saw what was done, they that fed the swine fled, and went 9 their ways into the city, and in the country, and told everything, and what was befallen to the possessed of the demons. Then they went out to see what was done; and came to Jesus, and found the man, that was possessed with the demon, and had the legion, out of whom the demons were departed, sitting at the feet of Jesus, clothed, and in his right mind: and they were afraid. They also which saw it told them by what means he that was possessed of the demons was healed, and also concerning the swine.

And, behold, the whole city came out to meet Jesus: then the whole 10 multitude of the country of the Gadarenes round about, when they saw him, asked him to depart from them; for they were taken with great fear: and he went up into the ship, and returned back again.

And when he was come into the ship, the man out of whom the 11 demons were departed begged him that he might be with him: but Jesus sent him away, saying, "Go home to your friends, and tell them how great things the Lord has done for you, and has had compassion on you." And he went

11   his way, and began to publish in Decapolis, and published throughout the whole city how great things Jesus had done unto him: and all men did marvel.

Restoring Life and Healing a Woman
Matthew 9:1, 18-26; Mark 5:21-43; Luke 8:40-56

12   And when Jesus was crossed over again by ship unto the other side, and came into his own city, many people gathered unto him: and he was near unto the sea. And it came to pass, that, the people gladly received him: for they were all waiting for him.

13   And, behold, there came one of the rulers of the synagogue, Jairus by name; and when he saw him, he fell down at Jesus' feet, and pleaded with him greatly that he would come into his house, saying, "My little daughter lies at the point of death: I appeal to you, come and lay your hands on her, that she may be healed; and she shall live." For he had one only daughter, about twelve years of age, and she lay dying. And Jesus arose, and followed him, and so did his disciples. But as he went the people thronged him.

14   And, behold, a woman, which was diseased with a flow of blood twelve years, and had suffered many things of many physicians, and had spent all that she had upon physicians, and was nothing bettered, but rather grew worse, when she had heard of Jesus, came in the crowd behind him, and touched the hem of his garment: for she said within herself, "If I may but touch his garment, I shall be whole." And immediately her flow of blood was dried up; and she felt in her body that she was healed of that affliction. And Jesus, immediately knowing in himself that power had gone out of him, turned himself around in the crowd, and said, "Who touched my clothes?" When all denied, Peter and they that were with him said, "Master, the multitudes throng you and crowd you, and you say, 'Who touched me?'" And Jesus said, "Somebody has touched me: for I perceive that power is gone out of me." And he looked round about to see her that had done this thing.

15   But Jesus turned himself about, and when the woman saw that she was not hidden, she came fearing and trembling, and falling down before him, she told him all the truth,

> "BE OF GOOD CHEER: YOUR FAITH HAS MADE YOU WHOLE."

declared unto him before all the people for what cause she had touched him, and how she was healed immediately. And he said unto her, "Daughter, be of good cheer: your faith has made you whole; go in peace, and be whole of your affliction." And the woman was made whole from that hour.

16   While he yet spoke, there came one from the ruler of the synagogue's house, saying to him, "Your daughter is dead: why do you trouble the Teacher any further?" As soon as Jesus heard the word that was spoken, he said unto the ruler of the synagogue, "Be not afraid, only believe, and she shall be made whole." And he allowed no man to follow him, except Peter, and James, and John the brother of James.

And he came to the house of the ruler of the synagogue, and saw 17
the tumult and the flute players and the people making a noise, and
them that wept and wailed greatly. And when Jesus came into the ruler's
house, he allowed no man to go in, except Peter, and James, and John,
and the father and the mother of the
little girl. And all wept, and
bewailed her: but he said, "Give
room: weep not; she is not dead, but

> AND THEY LAUGHED HIM TO
> SCORN.

sleeps." And they laughed him to scorn, knowing that she was dead. But
when he had put them all out, he took the father and the mother of the
little girl, and them that were with him, and entered in where the little
girl was lying.

And he took the little girl by the hand, and said unto her, "Talitha 18
cumi;" which is, being interpreted, "Little girl, I say unto you, arise." And
her spirit came again, and straightway the little girl arose, and walked; for
she was of the age of twelve years. And her parents were overcome with a
great astonishment: but he charged them strictly that they should tell no
man what was done; and commanded that something should be given her to
eat. And the report hereof went abroad into all that land.

Jesus Heals Two Blind Men
Matthew 9:27-31

And when Jesus departed from there, two blind men followed him, 19
crying, and saying, "Son of David, have mercy on us." And when he was
come into the house, the blind men came to him: and Jesus said unto them,
"Do you believe that I am able to do this?" They said unto him, "Yes, Lord."

Then touched he their eyes, saying, "According to your faith be it unto 20
you." And their eyes were opened; and Jesus strictly charged them, saying,
"See that no man knows it." But they, when they were departed, spread
abroad his fame in all that country.

A Mute Man Speaks
Matthew 9:32-34

As they went out, behold, they brought to him a mute man possessed 21
with a demon. And when the demon was cast out, the mute spoke: and the
multitudes marveled, saying, "It was never so seen in Israel."

But the Pharisees said, "He casts out demons through the prince of the 22
demons."

CHAPTER 19

AUTHORITY GIVEN TO THE APOSTLES

Second Rejection at Nazareth
Matthew 13:54-58; Mark 6:1-6

1   And he went out from there, and came into his own country, and his disciples followed him. And when the sabbath day was come, he began to teach in their synagogue: and many hearing him were astonished, saying, "From where has this man these things? and what wisdom is this which is given unto him, that even such mighty works are wrought by his hands?

2   "Is not this the carpenter? is not this the carpenter's son? is not his mother called Mary? and his brethren, James, and Joses, and Simon, and Jude? And his sisters, are they not all with us? From where then has this man all these things?" And they were offended at him. But Jesus said unto them, "A prophet is not without honor, except in his own country, and among his own relatives, and in his own house."

3   And he could there do no mighty work, except that he laid his hands upon a few sick folks, and healed them. And he marveled because of their unbelief. And he did not many mighty works there because of their unbelief. And he went round about the villages, teaching.

Laborers Are Few
Matthew 9:35-38

4   And Jesus went about all the cities and villages, teaching in their synagogues, and preaching the gospel of the kingdom, and healing every sickness and every disease among the people.

5   But when he saw the multitudes, he was moved with compassion on them, because they were discouraged, and were scattered abroad, as sheep having no shepherd. Then he said unto his disciples, "The harvest truly is plentiful, but the laborers are few; pray you therefore the Lord of the harvest, that he will send forth laborers into his harvest."

Authority: Sending Forth Apostles
Matthew 10:1-15; Mark 6:7-11; Luke 9:1-5

And when he had called unto him his twelve disciples, he gave them 6 power and authority over all unclean spirits, to cast them out, and to heal all manner of sickness and all manner of disease. Now the names of the twelve apostles are these; The first, Simon, who is called Peter, and Andrew his brother; James the son of Zebedee, and John his brother; Philip, and Bartholomew; Thomas, and Matthew the tax collector; James the son of Alphaeus, and Lebbaeus, whose surname was Thaddaeus; Simon the Canaanite, and Judas Iscariot, who also betrayed him. These twelve Jesus began to send forth by two and two, and commanded them, saying, "Go not into the land of the Gentiles, and into any city of the Samaritans do not you enter: but go rather to the lost sheep of the house of Israel. And as you go, preach, saying, 'The kingdom of heaven is at hand.' Heal the sick, cleanse the lepers, raise the dead, cast out demons: freely you have received, freely give."

And he said unto them, "Take nothing for your journey, neither staves, 7 nor bag, neither bread; neither have two tunics apiece. Provide neither gold, nor silver, nor copper coins in your purses: for the workman is worthy of his food." And he commanded them that they should take nothing for their journey, except a staff only; but be shod with sandals.

"And into whatsoever city or town you shall enter, inquire who in it is 8 worthy; and there stay till you go from there. And when you come into a house, greet it. And if the house be worthy, let your peace come upon it: but if it be not worthy, let your peace return to you. And whatsoever house you enter into, there stay till you depart from that place.

"And whosoever shall not receive you, nor hear your words, when you 9 depart out of that house or when you go out of that city, shake off the very dust from under your feet for a testimony against them. Truly I say unto you, It shall be more tolerable for the land of Sodom and Gomorrah in the day of judgment, than for that city."

Authority: Coming Persecutions
Matthew 10:16-26

"Behold, I send you forth as sheep in the midst of wolves: be therefore 10 wise as serpents, and harmless as doves. But beware of men: for they will deliver you up to the councils, and they will scourge you in their synagogues; and you shall be brought before governors and kings for my sake, for a testimony against them and the Gentiles.

> "BE THEREFORE WISE AS SERPENTS, AND HARMLESS AS DOVES."

But when they deliver you up, do not worry how or what you shall speak: for it shall be given you in that same hour what you shall speak. For it is not you that speak, but the Spirit of your Father which speaks in you.

11   "And the brother shall deliver up the brother to death, and the father the child: and the children shall rise up against their parents, and cause them to be put to death. And you shall be hated of all men for my name's sake: but he that endures to the end shall be saved. But when they persecute you in this city, flee into another: for truly I say unto you, You shall not have gone over the cities of Israel, till the Son of man is come.

12   "The disciple is not above his teacher, nor the servant above his master. It is enough for the disciple that he be as his teacher, and the servant as his master. If they have called the master of the house Beelzebub, how much more shall they call them of his household? Do not fear them therefore: for there is nothing covered, that shall not be revealed; and hidden, that shall not be known."

> "THERE IS NOTHING COVERED, THAT SHALL NOT BE REVEALED; AND HIDDEN, THAT SHALL NOT BE KNOWN."

Authority: Proclaiming Boldly
Matthew 10:27-31

13   "What I tell you in darkness, that speak in light: and what you hear in the ear, that preach upon the housetops. And fear not them which kill the body, but are not able to kill the soul: but rather fear him which is able to destroy both soul and body in hell. Are not two sparrows sold for a copper coin? and one of them shall not fall on the ground without your Father. But the very hairs of your head are all numbered. Fear not therefore, you are of more value than many sparrows."

Authority: Confessing Christ
Matthew 10:32-39

14   "Whosoever therefore shall confess me before men, him will I confess also before my Father which is in heaven. But whosoever shall deny me before men, him will I also deny before my Father which is in heaven.

15   "Think not that I am come to send peace on earth: I came not to send peace, but a sword. For I am come to *set a man at variance against his father, and the daughter against her mother, and the daughter-in-law against her mother-in-law.* And *a man's foes shall be they of his own household.*

16   "He that loves father or mother more than me is not worthy of me: and he that loves son or daughter more than me is not worthy of me. And he that takes not his cross, and follows after me, is not worthy of me. He that finds his life shall lose it: and he that loses his life for my sake shall find it."

Authority: Receiving Rewards
Matthew 10:40-42

17   "He that receives you receives me, and he that receives me receives him that sent me. He that receives a prophet in the name of a prophet shall receive a prophet's reward; and he that receives a righteous man in the name

of a righteous man shall receive a righteous man's reward. And whosoever 17
shall give to drink unto one of these little ones a cup of cold water only in
the name of a disciple, truly I say unto you, he shall in no way lose his
reward."

The Twelve Apostles Go Forth
Matthew 11:1; Mark 6:12-13; Luke 9:6

And they departed, and went through the towns, preaching the gospel 18
that men should repent. And they cast out many demons, and anointed with
oil many that were sick, and healed them, and healing everywhere. And it
came to pass, when Jesus had made an end of commanding his twelve disciples, he departed from there to teach and to preach in their cities.

John the Baptist Is Beheaded
Matthew 14:1-12; Mark 6:14-29; Luke 9:7-9

Now Herod (Antipas) the tetrarch (ruler) heard of the fame of Jesus, 19
of all that was done by him: and he was perplexed, because it was said of
some, that John was risen from the dead; and of some, that Elijah had
appeared; and of others, that one of the old prophets was risen again. At that
time Herod said unto his servants, "This is John the Baptist; he is risen from
the dead; and therefore mighty works do show forth themselves in him."
And Herod said, "John have I beheaded: but who is this, of whom I hear
such things?" And he desired to see him.

For Herod himself had sent forth and laid hold upon John, and bound 20
him in prison for Herodias' sake, his brother Philip's wife: for he had married her. For John had said unto Herod, "It is not lawful for you to have your
brother's wife." And when he would have put him to death, he feared the
multitude, because they counted him as a prophet. Therefore Herodias had
a quarrel against him, and would have killed him; but she could not: for
Herod feared John, knowing that he was a just man and holy, and protected
him; and when he heard him, he did many things, and heard him gladly.

And when the opportune day was come, that Herod on his birthday 21
made a supper to his officials, high captains, and leading men of Galilee;
and when the daughter of the said Herodias came in, and danced, and
pleased Herod and them that sat with him, the king said unto the girl, "Ask
of me whatsoever you will, and I will give it you." And he swore unto her,
"Whatsoever you shall ask of me, I will give it you, unto the half of my
kingdom." And she went forth, and said unto her mother, "What shall I
ask?" And she said, "The head of John the Baptist." And she came in
straightway with haste unto the king, and asked, saying, "Give me here the
head of John the Baptist in a platter."

And the king was exceedingly sorry; yet for his oath's sake, and for 22
their sakes which sat with him at the table, he would not reject her. And
immediately the king sent an executioner, and commanded his head to be

22 brought: and he went and beheaded him in the prison, and brought his head in a platter, and gave it to the girl: and the girl gave it to her mother.

23   And when his disciples heard of it, they came and took up the body, and laid it in a tomb, and went and told Jesus.

CHAPTER 20

TRAINING THE APOSTLES

The Twelve Apostles Return
Matthew 14:13-14; Mark 6:30-34; Luke 9:10-11; John 6:1-3

When Jesus heard of it, he departed from there by ship into a deserted 1
place apart: and when the people had heard thereof, they followed him on
foot out of the cities. And the apostles, when they were returned, gathered
themselves together unto Jesus, and told him all things, both what they had
done, and what they had taught. And he said unto them, "Come you yourselves apart into a deserted place, and rest a while:" for there were many
coming and going, and they had no leisure so much as to eat.

And they departed into a deserted place belonging to the city called 2
Bethsaida by ship privately. And the people saw them departing, and many
knew him, and ran on foot there out of all cities, and ahead of them, and
came together unto him: and he received them, and spoke unto them of the
kingdom of God, and healed them that had need of healing.

After these things Jesus went over the sea of Galilee, which is the sea 3
of Tiberias. And a great multitude followed him, because they saw his miracles which he did on them that were diseased. And Jesus went up into a
mountain, and there he sat with his disciples. And Jesus, when he came out,
saw many people, and was moved with compassion toward them, because
they were as sheep not having a shepherd: and he began to teach them many
things, and he healed their sick.

Feeding the Five Thousand
Matthew 14:15-21; Mark 6:35-44; Luke 9:12-17; John 6:4-13

And the passover, a feast of the Jews, was near. And when the day 4
began to wear away, the twelve came to him, saying, "This is a deserted
place, and the time is now past; send the multitude away, that they may go
into the villages and country round about, and lodge, and buy themselves
food: for they have nothing to eat." But Jesus said unto them, "They need

4 not depart; give them to eat." And they said unto him, "Shall we go and buy two hundred silver coins worth of bread, and give them to eat?"

5 When Jesus then lifted up his eyes, and saw a great company come unto him, he said unto Philip, "Where shall we buy bread, that these may eat?" And this he said to test him: for he himself knew what he would do. Philip answered him, "Two hundred silver coins worth of bread is not sufficient for them, that every one of them may take a little."

6 He said unto them, "How many loaves do you have? go and see." One of his disciples, Andrew, Simon Peter's brother, said unto him, "There is a lad here, which has five barley loaves, and two small fishes: but what are they among so many?" And when they knew, they said unto him, "We have here but five loaves, and two fishes." But he said unto them, "Give them to eat." And they said, "We have no more but five loaves and two fishes; except we should go and buy food for all these people." Jesus said, "Bring them here to me."

7 Now there was much grass in the place. And Jesus said, to his disciples, "Make them sit down by fifties in a company." And they did so, and made them all sit down upon the green grass in ranks, by hundreds, and by fifties. So the men sat down, in number about five thousand. Then he took the five loaves and the two fishes, and looking up to heaven, he blessed them, and broke the loaves, and gave to the disciples to set before the multitude that were seated; and the two fishes he divided among them all.

8 And they did all eat, and were filled. When they were filled, he said unto his disciples, "Gather up the fragments that remain, that nothing be lost." Therefore they gathered them together, and filled twelve baskets with the fragments of the five barley loaves, which remained over and above unto them that had eaten. And they that had eaten were about five thousand men, besides women and children.

Jesus Goes Apart to Pray Alone
Matthew 14:22-23; Mark 6:45-46; John 6:14-15

9 And straightway Jesus persuaded his disciples to get into a ship, and to go before him unto the other side unto Bethsaida, while he sent the multitudes away.

10 Then those men, when they had seen the miracle that Jesus did, said, "This is of a truth that prophet that should come into the world." When Jesus therefore perceived that they would come and take him by force, to make him a king, he sent them away, and he went up again into a mountain apart to pray: and when the evening was come, he was there alone.

> "THIS IS OF A TRUTH THAT PROPHET THAT SHOULD COME INTO THE WORLD."

Jesus Walks on the Water
Matthew 14:24-33; Mark 6:47-52; John 6:16-21

11 And when evening was now come, his disciples went down unto the sea, and entered into a ship, and went over the sea toward Capernaum. And

it was now dark, and Jesus was not come to them, and he alone on the land. 11 And the sea arose by reason of a great wind that blew. But the ship was now in the midst of the sea, tossed with waves: for the wind was contrary.

And he saw them toiling in rowing; for the wind was contrary unto 12 them: and about the fourth watch of the night he came unto them, walking upon the sea, and would have passed by them. So when they had rowed about three or four miles, they saw Jesus walking on the sea, and drawing near unto the ship: and the disciples were troubled, saying, "It is a spirit;" and they cried out for fear. But immediately Jesus talked with them, and said unto them, "Be of good cheer: it is I; be not afraid."

And Peter answered him and said, "Lord, if it be you, tell me come 13 unto you on the water." And he said, "Come." And when Peter was come down out of the ship, he walked on the water, to go to Jesus. But when he saw the wind boisterous, he was afraid; and beginning to sink, he cried, saying, "Lord, save me." And immediately Jesus stretched forth his hand, and caught him, and said unto him, "O you of little faith, why did you doubt?"

And when they were come into the ship, the wind ceased: and they 14 were very amazed in themselves beyond measure, and wondered. For they had not understood the miracle of the loaves: for their heart was hardened. Then they willingly received him into the ship: and immediately the ship was

> "OF A TRUTH YOU ARE THE SON OF GOD."

at the land where they were heading. Then they that were in the ship came and worshiped him, saying, "Of a truth you are the Son of God."

Healed by Touching Jesus' Garment
Matthew 14:34-36; Mark 6:53-56

And when they had crossed over, they came into the land of Gennesaret, and drew to the shore. 15

And when they were come out of the ship, straightway the men of that place had knowledge of him, they sent out into all that country round about, 16 and ran through that whole region round about, and began to carry about in beds those that were sick, where they heard he was, and brought unto him all that were diseased; and begged him that they might only touch the hem of his garment: and as many as touched were made perfectly whole.

And wherever he entered, into villages, or cities, or country, they laid the sick in the marketplaces, and begged him that they might touch if it were but 17 the border of his garment: and as many as touched him were made whole.

CHAPTER 21

Teaching the Apostles
"True Bread From Heaven"
John 6:22-40

1   The following day, when the people which stood on the other side of the sea saw that there was no other boat there, except that one whereinto his disciples were entered, and that Jesus went not with his disciples into the boat, but that his disciples were gone away alone; (howbeit there came other boats from Tiberias near unto the place where they did eat bread, after that the Lord had given thanks): when the people therefore saw that Jesus was not there, neither his disciples, they also took boats, and came to Capernaum, seeking for Jesus.

2   And when they had found him on the other side of the sea, they said unto him, "Rabbi, when did you come here?" Jesus answered them and said, "Truly, truly, I say unto you, You seek me, not because you saw the miracles, but because you did eat of the loaves, and were filled. Labor not for the food which perishes, but for that food which endures unto everlasting life, which the Son of man shall give unto you: for him has God the Father sealed."

3   Then they said unto him, "What shall we do, that we might work the works of God?" Jesus answered and said unto them, "This is the work of God, that you believe on him whom he has sent."

4   They said therefore unto him, "What sign do you show then, that we may see, and believe you? what do you work? Our fathers did eat manna in the desert; as it is written, *'He gave them bread from heaven to eat.'*" Then Jesus said unto them, "Truly, truly, I say unto you, Moses did not give you that bread from heaven; but my Father gives you the true bread from heaven. For the bread of God is he which comes down from heaven, and gives life unto the world."

Then they said unto him, "Lord, evermore give us this bread." And 5
Jesus said unto them, "I am the bread of life: he that comes to me shall
never hunger; and he that believes on
me shall never thirst. But I said unto
you, That you also have seen me, and
do not believe. All that the Father
gives me shall come to me; and him

> "I AM THE BREAD OF LIFE: HE THAT COMES TO ME SHALL NEVER HUNGER."

that comes to me I will in no way cast out. For I came down from heaven,
not to do my own will, but the will of him that sent me.

"And this is the Father's will which has sent me, that of all which he 6
has given me I should lose nothing, but should raise it up again at the last
day. And this is the will of him that sent me, that everyone which sees the
Son, and believes on him, may have everlasting life: and I will raise him up
at the last day."

"I Am That Bread of Life"
John 6:41-59

The Jews then murmured at him, because he said, "I am the bread 7
which came down from heaven." And
they said, "Is not this Jesus, the son of
Joseph, whose father and mother we
know? how is it then that he says, 'I
came down from heaven?'" Jesus
therefore answered and said unto

> "NO MAN CAN COME TO ME, EXCEPT THE FATHER WHICH HAS SENT ME DRAWS HIM."

them, "Murmur not among yourselves. No man can come to me, except the
Father which has sent me draws him: and I will raise him up at the last day.

"It is written in the prophets, '*And they shall be all taught of God.*' 8
Every man therefore that has heard, and has learned of the Father, comes
unto me. Not that any man has seen the Father, except he which is of God,
he has seen the Father. Truly, truly, I say unto you, He that believes on me
has everlasting life. I am that bread of life.

"Your fathers did eat manna in the wilderness, and are dead. This is 9
the bread which comes down from heaven, that a man may eat thereof, and
not die. I am the living bread which came down from heaven: if any man
eats of this bread, he shall live for ever: and the bread that I will give is my
flesh, which I will give for the life of the world."

The Jews therefore quarreled among themselves, saying, "How can 10
this man give us his flesh to eat?" Then Jesus said unto them, "Truly, truly,
I say unto you, Except you eat the flesh of the Son of man, and drink his
blood, you have no life in you. Whoever eats my flesh, and drinks my blood,
has eternal life; and I will raise him up at the last day. For my flesh is food
indeed, and my blood is drink indeed. He that eats my flesh, and drinks my
blood, dwells in me, and I in him.

"As the living Father has sent me, and I live by the Father: so he that 11
eats me, even he shall live by me. This is that bread which came down from

11 heaven: not as your fathers did eat manna, and are dead: he that eats of this bread shall live for ever."

12 These things he said in the synagogue, as he taught in Capernaum.

"It Is the Spirit That Quickens"
John 6:60-65

13 Many therefore of his disciples, when they had heard this, said, "This is a hard saying; who can hear it?" When Jesus knew in himself that his disciples murmured at it, he said unto them, "Does this offend you? What and if you shall see the Son of man ascend up where he was before?

> "THE WORDS THAT I SPEAK UNTO YOU, THEY ARE SPIRIT, AND THEY ARE LIFE."

It is the spirit that quickens; the flesh profits nothing: the words that I speak unto you, they are spirit, and they are life. But there are some of you that do not believe." For Jesus knew from the beginning who they were that believed not, and who should betray him. And he said, "Therefore I said unto you, that no man can come unto me, except it were given unto him of my Father."

Peter's First Confession
John 6:66-71

14 From that time many of his disciples went back, and walked no more with him. Then said Jesus unto the twelve, "Will you also go away?" Then Simon Peter answered him, "Lord, to whom shall we go? you have the words of eternal life. And we believe and are sure that you are that Christ, the Son of the living God." Jesus answered them, "Have not I chosen you twelve, and one of you is a devil?" He spoke of Judas Iscariot the son of Simon: for he it was that should betray him, being one of the twelve.

Defilement: Teaching Man's Tradition
Matthew 15:1-9; Mark 7:1-13

15 Then came together unto him the Pharisees, and certain of the scribes, which came from Jerusalem. And when they saw some of his disciples eat bread with defiled, that is to say, with unwashed, hands, they found fault. For the Pharisees, and all the Jews, unless they wash their hands often, do not eat, holding the tradition of the elders. And when they come from the marketplace, unless they wash, they do not eat. And many other things there be, which they have received to hold, as the washing of cups, and pots, copper vessels, and of tables. Then the Pharisees and scribes asked him, "Why do your disciples transgress the tradition of the elders? for they do not wash their hands when they eat bread."

16 He answered and said unto them, "Well has Isaiah prophesied of you hypocrites, as it is written, '*This people draws near unto me with their mouth, and honors me with their lips; but their heart is far from me. Howbeit in vain do they worship me, teaching for doctrines the commandments of men.*' For laying aside the commandment of God, you hold the tradition

of men, as the washing of pots and cups: and many other such like things 16 you do."

And he said unto them, "Full well you reject the commandment of 17 God, that you may keep your own tradition. For Moses said, '*Honor your father and your mother;*' and, '*Whoever curses father or mother, let him die the death.*' But you say, 'If a man shall say to his father or his mother, "It is Corban," that is to say, a gift, by whatsoever you might be profited from me; and honors not his father or his mother, he shall be free.' And you permit him no longer to do anything for his father or his mother; making the word of God of no effect through your tradition, which you have delivered: and many such like things do you."

Defilement: Evil Comes From Within
Matthew 15:10-20; Mark 7:14-23

And when he had called all the people unto him, he said unto them, 18 "Hearken unto me every one of you, and understand: there is nothing from outside a man, that entering into the mouth can defile him: but the things which come out of the mouth, those are they that defile a man. If any man has ears to hear, let him hear."

Then came his disciples, and said unto him, "Do you know that the 19 Pharisees were offended, after they heard this saying?" But he answered and said, "Every plant, which my heavenly Father has not planted, shall be rooted up. Let them alone: they be blind leaders of the blind. And if the blind leads the blind, both shall fall into the ditch."

> "IF THE BLIND LEADS THE BLIND, BOTH SHALL FALL INTO THE DITCH."

And when he was entered into the house from the people, his disciples 20 asked him concerning the parable. Then Peter answered and said unto him, "Explain unto us this parable." And Jesus said unto them, "Are you so without understanding also? Do you not perceive, that whatsoever thing from outside enters into the man, it cannot defile him; because it enters not into his heart, but into the belly, and goes out into the elimination, purging all foods? But those things which proceed out of the mouth come forth from the heart; and they defile the man.

> "THOSE THINGS WHICH PRO-CEED OUT OF THE MOUTH COME FORTH FROM THE HEART."

"For from within, out of the heart of men, proceed evil thoughts, mur- 21 ders, adulteries, fornications, thefts, false witness, covetousness, wickedness, deceit, lewdness, an evil eye, blasphemy, conceit, foolishness: all these evil things come from within, and defile a man: but to eat with unwashed hands does not defile a man."

PART 6

EARLY REVELATIONS

Jesus was aware of His ultimate fate. Admonishing His disciples continually to turn from the limited laws of man to the infinite laws of God, He offered strict spiritual guidance to those who would follow in His ways, and revealed through His own testimony and transfiguration that He was indeed the Son of the living God. Jesus knew the manner of His impending death, but more importantly, He knew the manner of His resurrection that would inevitably follow.

> "THE SON OF MAN SHALL COME IN THE GLORY
> OF HIS FATHER WITH HIS ANGELS; AND THEN HE
> SHALL REWARD EVERY MAN ACCORDING TO HIS
> WORKS." (MATTHEW 16:27)

CHAPTER 22

WIDENING THE MINISTRY

Healing a Gentile Woman's Daughter
Matthew 15:21-28; Mark 7:24-30

And from there he arose, and went into the borders of Tyre and Sidon, and 1
entered into a house, and would have no man know it: but he could not be hidden. For behold, a woman of Canaan, whose young daughter had an unclean spirit, heard of him, came out of the same region, and cried unto him, saying, "Have mercy on me, O Lord, Son of David; my daughter is grievously possessed with a demon." But he answered her not a word. And his disciples came and urged him, saying, "Send her away; for she cries after us."

But he answered and said, "I am not sent except unto the lost sheep of 2
the house of Israel." Then came she and fell at his feet and worshiped him, saying, "Lord, help me." The woman was a Greek, a Syrophoenician by nation; and she pleaded with him that he would cast forth the demon out of her daughter.

But Jesus said unto her, "Let the children first be filled: for it is not 3
right to take the children's bread, and to cast it unto the little dogs." And she answered and said unto him, "Yes, Lord: yet the little dogs under the table eat of the children's crumbs which fall from their masters' table." Then Jesus answered and said unto her, "O woman, great is your faith: be it unto you even as you will." And her daughter was made whole from that very hour.

And he said unto her, "For this saying go your way; the demon is gone 4
out of your daughter." And when she was come to her house, she found the demon gone out, and her daughter lying upon the bed.

Healing a Deaf-Mute
Mark 7:31-37

And again, departing from the region of Tyre and Sidon, he came unto 5
the sea of Galilee, through the midst of the region of Decapolis.

6   And they brought unto him one that was deaf, and had an impediment in his speech; and they begged him to put his hand upon him. And he took him aside from the multitude, and put his fingers into his ears, and he spit, and touched his tongue; and looking up to heaven, he sighed, and said unto him, "Ephphatha," that is, "Be opened." And straightway his ears were opened, and the binding of his tongue was loosed, and he spoke plainly.

7   And he charged them that they should tell no man: but the more he charged them, so much the more a great deal they published it; and were beyond measure astonished, saying, "He has done all things well: he makes both the deaf to hear, and the mute to speak."

Healed to the Glory of God
Matthew 15:29-31

8   And Jesus departed from there, and came near unto the sea of Galilee; and went up into a mountain, and sat down there. And great multitudes came unto him, having with them those that were lame, blind, mute, maimed, and many others, and cast them down at Jesus' feet; and he healed them: insomuch that the multitude wondered, when they saw the mute to speak, the maimed to be whole, the lame to walk, and the blind to see: and they glorified the God of Israel.

Feeding the Four Thousand
Matthew 15:32-39; Mark 8:1-10

9   In those days the multitude being very great, and having nothing to eat, Jesus called his disciples unto him, and said unto them, "I have compassion on the multitude, because they have now been with me now three days, and have nothing to eat: and if I send them away fasting to their own houses, they will faint on the way: for many of them came from far away." And his disciples answered him, "From where should we have so much bread here in the wilderness, as to fill so great a multitude?" And Jesus asked them, "How many loaves have you?" And they said, "Seven, and a few little fishes."

10   And he commanded the multitude to sit down on the ground. And he took the seven loaves and the few small fishes, and gave thanks, and broke them, and gave to his disciples, and the disciples to the multitude.

11   And they did all eat, and were filled: and they took up of the broken food that was left seven baskets full. And they that had eaten were about four thousand men, besides women and children: and he sent the multitude away.

12   And straightway he entered into a ship with his disciples, and came into the region of Magdala and Dalmanutha.

"Discern the Signs of the Times"
Matthew 16:1-4; Mark 8:11-13

13   The Pharisees also with the Sadducees came forth, and began to question with him, seeking of him that he would show them a sign from heaven,

tempting him. He answered and said unto them, "When it is evening, you 13
say, 'It will be fair weather: for the sky is red.' And in the morning, 'It will
be foul weather today: for the sky is red and threatening.' O you hypocrites,
you can discern the face of the sky; but can you not discern the signs of the
times?"

And he sighed deeply in his spirit, and said, "Why does this wicked 14
and adulterous generation seek after a sign? truly I say unto you, There shall
no sign be given unto this generation, but the sign of the prophet Jonah."
And he left them, and entering into the ship again departed to the other side.

Beware of the Leaven of Man's Doctrine
Matthew 16:5-12; Mark 8:14-21

And when his disciples were come to the other side, they had forgot- 15
ten to take bread, neither had they in the ship with them more than one loaf.
And he charged them, saying, "Take heed, beware of the leaven of the Pharisees, and of the leaven of Herod." And they reasoned among themselves,
saying, "It is because we have taken no bread."

And when Jesus perceived it, he said unto them, "O you of little faith, 16
why do you reason among yourselves, because you have brought no bread?
Do you not yet understand, neither remember the five loaves of the five
thousand, and how many baskets you took up? Neither the seven loaves of
the four thousand, and how many baskets you took up? have you your heart
yet hardened?

"Having eyes, do you not see? and having ears, do you not hear? and 17
do you not remember? When I broke the five loaves among five thousand,
how many baskets full of fragments did you take up?" They said unto him,
"Twelve." "And when the seven among four thousand, how many baskets
full of fragments did you take up?" And they said, "Seven."

And he said unto them, "How is it that you do not understand that I 18
spoke it not to you concerning bread, that you should beware of the leaven
of the Pharisees and of the Sadducees?" Then they understood how that he
told them not beware of the leaven of bread, but of the doctrine of the Pharisees and of the Sadducees.

A Blind Man's Eyes Restored
Mark 8:22-26

And he came to Bethsaida; and they brought a blind man unto him, 19
and begged him to touch him. And he took the blind man by the hand, and
led him out of the town; and when he had spit on his eyes, and put his hands
upon him, he asked him if he saw anything. And he looked up, and said, "I
see men as trees, walking."

After that he put his hands again upon his eyes, and made him look up: 20
and he was restored, and saw every man clearly. And he sent him away to his
house, saying, "Neither go into the town, nor tell it to any in the town."

Peter's Second Confession
Matthew 16:13-20; Mark 8:27-30; Luke 9:18-22

21   And Jesus went out, and his disciples, into the towns of Caesarea Philippi: and on the road, it came to pass, as he was alone praying, his disciples were with him: and he asked them, saying, "Whom say the people that I the Son of man am?" And they answered, "Some say that you are John the Baptist: but some say, Elijah; and others, Jeremiah, or one of the prophets; and others say, that one of the old prophets is risen again." And he said unto them, "But whom do you say that I am?" And Simon Peter answered and said, "You are the Christ, the Son of the living God."

> "YOU ARE THE CHRIST, THE SON OF THE LIVING GOD."

22   And Jesus answered and said unto him, "Blessed are you, Simon Bar-Jonah: for flesh and blood has not revealed it unto you, but my Father which is in heaven. And I say also unto you, That you are Peter, and upon this rock I will build my church; and the gates of Hades shall not prevail against it. And I will give unto you the keys of the kingdom of heaven: and whatsoever you shall bind on earth shall be bound in heaven: and whatsoever you shall loose on earth shall be loosed in heaven."

> "I WILL GIVE UNTO YOU THE KEYS OF THE KINGDOM OF HEAVEN."

23   And he strictly charged and commanded his disciples that they should tell no man that he was Jesus the Christ; saying, "The Son of man must suffer many things, and be rejected of the elders and chief priests and scribes, and be slain, and be raised the third day."

CHAPTER 23

Mysteries of the Ministry

God's Plan for Redemption
Matthew 16:21-23; Mark 8:31-33

From that time forth Jesus began to show unto his disciples, how that 1
he must go unto Jerusalem, and the Son of man must suffer many things,
and be rejected of the elders, and of the chief priests, and scribes, and be
killed, and be raised again the third day.

And he spoke that saying openly. Then Peter took him, and began to 2
rebuke him, saying, "Far be it from you, Lord: this shall not be unto you."
But when he had turned about and looked on his disciples, he rebuked Peter,
saying, "Get you behind me, Satan: you are an offense unto me: for you set
your mind not the things that be of God, but the things that be of men."

Taking Up Our Own Crosses Daily
Matthew 16:24-28; Mark 8:34-38; 9:1; Luke 9:23-27

And when he had called the people unto him with his disciples also, 3
he said unto them all, "Whosoever will come after me, let him deny himself, and take up his cross daily, and follow me. For whosoever will save his
life shall lose it; but whosoever shall lose his life for my sake and the
gospel's, the same shall save it.

"For what shall it profit a man, if he shall gain the whole world, and 4
lose his own soul? Or what shall a man give in exchange for his soul? For
what is a man advantaged, if he gains the whole world, and loses himself,
or be cast away?

"Whosoever therefore shall be ashamed of me and of my words in this 5
adulterous and sinful generation; of him also shall the Son of man be
ashamed, when he shall come in his own glory, and in his Father's, and of the
holy angels. For the Son of man shall come in the glory of his Father with
his angels; and then he shall reward every man according to his works."

6   And he said unto them, "I tell you of a truth, there be some standing here, which shall not taste of death, till they see the kingdom of God come with power, till they see the Son of man coming in his kingdom."

The Transfiguration
Matthew 17:1-13; Mark 9:2-13; Luke 9:28-36

7   And it came to pass about eight days after these sayings, Jesus took with him Peter, James, and John his brother, and led them up into a high mountain apart by themselves to pray: and he was transfigured before them. And as he prayed, the fashion of his countenance was altered, and his face did shine as the sun, and his clothing was white as the light. And his clothing became shining, exceedingly white as snow and glistening; so as no bleacher on earth can whiten them.

8   And, behold, there appeared unto them two men talking with Jesus, which were Moses and Elijah: who appeared in glory, and spoke of his decease which he should accomplish at Jerusalem. But Peter and they that were with him were heavy with sleep: and when they were awake, they saw his glory, and the two men that stood with him.

9   And it came to pass, as they departed from him, Peter said unto Jesus, "Rabbi, it is good for us to be here: and let us make three tabernacles; one for you, and one for Moses, and one for Elijah:" not knowing what he said. For he knew not what to say; for they were very afraid.

10   While he yet spoke, behold, there came a bright cloud, and overshadowed them: and they feared as they entered into the cloud. And there came a voice out of the cloud, saying, "This is my beloved Son, in whom I am well pleased; hear him." And when the disciples heard it, they fell on their faces, and were very afraid. And when the voice was past, Jesus was found alone. And Jesus came and touched them, and said, "Arise, and be not afraid." And suddenly, when they had lifted up their eyes, and looked round about, they saw no man anymore, except Jesus only with themselves. And they kept it close, and told no man in those days any of those things which they had seen.

> THERE CAME A VOICE OUT OF THE CLOUD, SAYING, "THIS IS MY BELOVED SON."

11   And as they came down from the mountain, Jesus charged them, saying, "Tell the vision to no man, until the Son of man be risen again from the dead." And they kept that saying with themselves, questioning one with another what the rising from the dead should mean.

12   And his disciples asked him, saying, "Why then say the scribes that Elijah must first come?" And Jesus answered and said unto them, "Elijah truly shall first come, and restore all things. But I say unto you, That Elijah is come already, and they knew him not, but have done unto him whatsoever they wished, as it is written of him. Likewise it is written of the Son of man, that he must suffer many things, and be rejected." Then the disciples understood that he spoke unto them of John the Baptist.

Jesus Heals a Lunatic Son
Matthew 17:14-21; Mark 9:14-29; Luke 9:37-42

And it came to pass, that on the next day, when they were come down 13 from the mountain, many people met him. And when he came to his disciples, he saw a great multitude about them, and the scribes questioning with them. And straightway all the people, when they beheld him, were greatly amazed, and running to him greeted him. And he asked the scribes, "What do you question with them?"

And, behold, a man of the company cried out, saying, "Teacher, I beg 14 you, look upon my son: for he is my only child." And came to him, kneeling down to him, saying, "Lord, have mercy on my son: for he is lunatic, and very possessed. I have brought unto you my son, which has a mute spirit; and wheresoever it takes him, it convulses him: and he foams, and gnashes with his teeth, and withers away: and he suddenly cries out; and it convulses him that he foams again, and bruising him with difficulty departs from him. And I begged your disciples to cast it out; and they could not."

Then Jesus answered and said, "O faithless and perverse generation, 15 how long shall I be with you? how long shall I be patient with you? Bring your son here to me." And they brought him unto him: and when he saw him, straightway the spirit convulsed him; and he fell on the ground, and wallowed foaming. And he asked his father, "How long is it ago since this came unto him?" And he said, "Of a child. And many times it has cast him into the fire, and into the waters, to destroy him: but if you can do anything, have compassion on us, and help us."

Jesus said unto him, "If you can believe, all things are possible to him that believes." And straightway

> "ALL THINGS ARE POSSIBLE TO HIM THAT BELIEVES." 16

the father of the child cried out, and said with tears, "Lord, I believe; help my unbelief."

And as he was yet coming, the demon threw him down, and convulsed 17 him. When Jesus saw that the people came running together, he rebuked the unclean spirit, saying unto it, "You mute and deaf spirit, I command you, come out of him, and enter no more into him." And the spirit cried, and convulsed him greatly, and came out of him: and he was as one dead; insomuch that many said, "He is dead." But Jesus took him by the hand, and lifted him up; and he arose. And Jesus delivered him again to his father: and the child was cured from that very hour.

And when he was come into the house, his disciples asked him pri- 18 vately, "Why could not we cast it out?" And Jesus said unto them, "Because of your unbelief: for truly I say unto you, If you have faith as a grain of mustard seed, you shall say unto this mountain, 'Move from here to yonder place;' and it shall move; and nothing shall be impossible unto you. Howbeit this kind does not go out except by prayer and fasting."

CHAPTER 24

CHILDREN IN GOD'S KINGDOM

Jesus Again Predicts His Death
Matthew 17:22-23; Mark 9:30-32; Luke 9:43-45

1   And they were all amazed at the mighty power of God. But while they wondered every one at all things which Jesus did, he said unto his disciples, "Let these sayings sink down into your ears: for the Son of man shall be delivered into the hands of men."

2   And they departed from there, and passed through Galilee; and he would not that any man should know it. For while they stayed in Galilee, he taught his disciples, and said unto them, "The Son of man shall be betrayed into the hands of men: and they shall kill him, and the third day he shall be raised again." And they were exceedingly sorry.

3   But they did not understand this saying, and it was hidden from them, that they did not perceive it: and they feared to ask him of that saying.

Peter and Jesus Pay Taxes
Matthew 17:24-27

4   And when they were come to Capernaum, they that received tribute money came to Peter, and said, "Does not your Teacher pay tribute?" He said, "Yes." And when he was come into the house, Jesus preceded him, saying, "What do you think, Simon? of whom do the kings of the earth take custom or tribute? of their own children, or of strangers?" Peter said unto him, "Of strangers." Jesus said unto him, "Then are the children free.

5   "Notwithstanding, lest we should offend them, go to the sea, and cast a hook, and take up the fish that first comes up; and when you have opened its mouth, you shall find a piece of money: that take, and give unto them for me and you."

Children: Greatest in God's Kingdom
Matthew 18:1-5; Mark 9:33-37; Luke 9:46-48

6   And he came to Capernaum: and at the same time the disciples came unto Jesus, saying, "Who is the greatest in the kingdom of heaven?" And

being in the house he asked them, "What was it that you disputed among 6 yourselves on the road?" But they held their peace: for on the road they had disputed among themselves, who should be the greatest.

And he sat down, and called the twelve, and said unto them, "If any 7 man desires to be first, the same shall be last of all, and servant of all."

And Jesus, perceiving the thought of their heart, called a little child 8 unto him, and set him in the midst of them, and said, "Truly I say unto you, Except you be converted, and become as little children, you shall not enter into the kingdom of heaven. Whosoever therefore shall humble himself as this little child, the same is greatest in the kingdom of heaven."

> "EXCEPT YOU BE CONVERTED, AND BECOME AS LITTLE CHILDREN, YOU SHALL NOT ENTER INTO THE KINGDOM OF HEAVEN."

And when he had taken him in his arms, he said unto them, "Whosoever shall receive one of such children in my name, receives me: and 9 whosoever shall receive me, receives not me, but him that sent me: for he that is least among you all, the same shall be great."

Doing Good Is Rewarded
Mark 9:38-41; Luke 9:49-50

And John answered him, saying, "Teacher, we saw one casting out 10 demons in your name, and he does not follow us: and we forbade him, because he does not follow with us."

And Jesus said unto him, "Do not forbid him: for there is no man 11 which shall do a miracle in my name, that can lightly speak evil of me. For he that is not against us is for us. For whosoever shall give you a cup of water to drink in my name, because you belong to Christ, truly I say unto you, he shall not lose his reward."

Causing Sin Is Punished
Matthew 18:6-7; Mark 9:42

"But whosoever shall cause sin to one of these little ones that believe 12 in me, it is better for him that a millstone were hung about his neck, and he were cast into the sea, and that he were drowned in the depth of the sea.

"Woe unto the world because of causes to sin! for it must of neces- 13 sity be that causes to sin come; but woe to that man by whom the cause to sin comes!"

Keeping Yourself From Sin
Matthew 18:8-9; Mark 9:43-50

"And if your hand causes you to sin, cut it off: it is better for you to 14 enter into life maimed, than having two hands to go into hell, into the fire that never shall be quench: where *'their worm dies not, and the fire is not quenched.'* And if your foot causes you to sin, cut it off: it is better for you to enter lame into life, than having two feet toed be cast into hell, into the fire that never shall be quenched: *'where their worm dies not, and the fire is not quenched.'*

15   "And if your eye causes sin of you, pluck it out: it is better for you to enter into life with one eye, into the kingdom of God with one eye, than having two eyes to be cast into hell fire: where '*their worm dies not, and the fire is not quenched.*' For everyone shall be salted with fire, and every sacrifice shall be salted with salt.

16   "Salt is good: but if the salt has lost its flavor, with what will you season it? Have salt in yourselves, and have peace one with another."

Parable of the Lost Sheep
Matthew 18:10-14

17   "Take heed that you do not despise one of these little ones; for I say unto you, That in heaven their angels do always behold the face of my Father which is in heaven. For the Son of man is come to save that which was lost.

18   "How do you think? if a man has a hundred sheep, and one of them be gone astray, does he not leave the ninety and nine, and go into the mountains, and seek that which is gone astray? And if so be that he finds it, truly I say unto you, he rejoices more of that sheep, than of the ninety and nine which went not astray.

> "THE SON OF MAN IS COME TO SAVE THAT WHICH WAS LOST."

19   "Even so it is not the will of your Father which is in heaven, that one of these little ones should perish."

CHAPTER 25

⋅⋅⋅ COMING TOGETHER IN JESUS' NAME ⋅⋅⋅

Brotherly Correction and Unity
Matthew 18:15-20

"Moreover if your brother shall trespass against you, go and tell him 1
his fault between you and him alone: if he shall hear you, you have gained
your brother. But if he will not hear you, then take with you one or two
more, that '*in the mouth of two or three witnesses every word may be established.*' And if he shall neglect to hear them, tell it unto the church: but if
he neglects to hear the church, let him be unto you as a heathen man and a
tax collector.

"Truly I say unto you, Whatsoever you shall bind on earth shall be 2
bound in heaven: and whatsoever you shall loose on earth shall be loosed in
heaven.

"Again I say unto you, That if two of you shall agree on earth as con- 3
cerning anything that they shall ask, it shall be done for them of my Father
which is in heaven. For where two or three are gathered together in my
name, there am I in the midst of them."

Parable of the Wicked Servant
Matthew 18:21-35

Then Peter came to him, and said, "Lord, how often shall my brother 4
sin against me, and I forgive him? until seven times?" Jesus said unto him,
"I say not unto you, Until seven times: but, Until seventy times seven.

"Therefore is the kingdom of heaven likened unto a certain king, 5
which would take account of his servants. And when he had begun to take
account, one was brought unto him, which owed him ten thousand talents. But inasmuch as he had nothing to pay, his master commanded him
to be sold, and his wife, and children, and all that he had, and payment to
be made.

6   "The servant therefore fell down, and worshiped him, saying, 'Master, have patience with me, and I will pay you all.' Then the master of that servant was moved with compassion, and loosed him, and forgave him the debt.

7   "But the same servant went out, and found one of his fellow servants, which owed him a hundred silver coins: and he laid hands on him, and took him by the throat, saying, 'Pay me that you owe.'

8   "And his fellow servant fell down at his feet, and begged him, saying, 'Have patience with me, and I will pay you all.' And he would not: but went and cast him into prison, till he should pay the debt.

9   "So when his fellow servants saw what was done, they were very sorry, and came and told unto their master all that was done. Then his master, after he had called him, said unto him, 'O you wicked servant, I forgave you all that debt, because you appealed to me: should not you also have had compassion on your fellow servant, even as I had pity on you?' And his master was angry, and delivered him to the jailers, till he should pay all that was due unto him.

10   "So likewise shall my heavenly Father do also unto you, if you from your hearts do not forgive every one of you his brother their trespasses."

Jesus' Brethren Do Not Believe
John 7:1-9

11   After these things Jesus walked in Galilee: for he would not walk in Judea, because the Jews sought to kill him. Now the Jews' feast of tabernacles was at hand. His brethren therefore said unto him, "Depart from here, and go into Judea, that your disciples also may see the works that you do. For there is no man that does anything in secret, and he himself seeks to be known openly. If you do these things, show yourself to the world." For neither did his brethren believe in him.

12   Then Jesus said unto them, "My time is not yet come: but your time is always ready. The world cannot hate you; but me it hates, because I testify of it, that the works thereof are evil. You go up unto this feast: I do not go up yet unto this feast; for my time is not yet fully come." When he had said these words unto them, he stayed on in Galilee.

Samaritans Refuse Jesus' Messengers
Luke 9:51-56

13   And it came to pass, when the time was come that he should be received up, he steadfastly set his face to go to Jerusalem, and sent messengers before his face: and they went, and entered into a village of the Samaritans, to make ready for him. And they did not receive him, because his face was as though he would go to Jerusalem.

14   And when his disciples James and John saw this, they said, "Lord, will you that we command fire to come down from heaven, and consume them,

even as Elijah did?" But he turned, and rebuked them, and said, "You know 14 not what manner of spirit you are of. For the Son of man is not come to destroy men's lives, but to save them." And they went to another village.

The Cost of Following Jesus
Matthew 8:19-22; Luke 9:57-62

And it came to pass, that, as they went on the road, a certain scribe 15 came, and said unto him, "Teacher, I will follow you wherever you go." And Jesus said unto him, "The foxes have holes, and the birds of the air have nests; but the Son of man has nowhere to lay his head."

And he said unto another of his disciples, "Follow me." But he said, 16 "Lord, let me first to go and bury my father." But Jesus said unto him, "Let the dead bury their dead: but go you and preach the kingdom of God."

And another also said, "Lord, I will follow you; but let me first go bid 17 them farewell, which are at home at my house." And Jesus said unto him, "No man, having put his hand to the plow, and looking back, is fit for the kingdom of God."

PART 7

DOCTRINES OF TRUTH

Jesus spoke as one having authority. The doctrines He taught were from above, not from this world. His adversaries accused Him of transgressing the written Law of Moses and plotted to find fault with Him so that they could arrest Him. Yet Jesus confounded His opponents with answers of divine wisdom and moved through their company unseen. They ruled in darkness. He brought the Light.

"BLESSED ARE THE EYES WHICH SEE THE THINGS THAT YOU SEE: FOR I TELL YOU, THAT MANY PROPHETS AND KINGS HAVE DESIRED TO SEE THOSE THINGS WHICH YOU SEE, AND HAVE NOT SEEN THEM; AND TO HEAR THOSE THINGS WHICH YOU HEAR, AND HAVE NOT HEARD THEM." (LUKE 10:23-24)

CHAPTER 26

THIRD MINISTRY AT JERUSALEM

"My Doctrine Is Not Mine"
John 7:10-24

But when his brethren were gone up, then went he also up unto the 1 feast, not openly, but as it were in secret. Then the Jews sought him at the feast, and said, "Where is he?" And there was much murmuring among the people concerning him: for some said, "He is a good man:" others said, "No; but he deceives the people." Howbeit no man spoke openly of him for fear of the Jews.

Now about the middle of the feast Jesus went up into the temple, and 2 taught. And the Jews marveled, saying, "How does this man know letters, having never studied?" Jesus answered them, and said, "My doctrine is not mine, but his that sent me. If any man will do his will, he shall know of the doctrine, whether it be of God, or whether I speak of myself. He that speaks of himself seeks his own glory: but he that seeks his glory that sent him, the same is true, and no unrighteousness is in him.

"Did not Moses give you the law, and yet none of you keeps the law? 3 Why do you go about to kill me?" The people answered and said, "You have a demon: who goes about to kill you?" Jesus answered and said unto them, "I have done one work, and you all marvel. Moses therefore gave unto you circumcision; (not because it is of Moses, but of the fathers); and you on the sabbath day circumcise a man. If a man on the sabbath day receives circumcision, that the law of Moses should not be broken; are you angry at me, because I have made a man every bit whole on the sabbath day? Judge not according to the appearance, but judge righteous judgment."

"He That Sent Me Is True"
John 7:25-36

Then said some of them of Jerusalem, "Is not this he, whom they seek 4 to kill? But, lo, he speaks boldly, and they say nothing unto him. Do the

4   rulers know indeed that this is the very Christ? Howbeit we know this man from where he is: but when Christ comes, no man knows from where he is."

5   Then cried Jesus in the temple as he taught, saying, "You both know me, and you know from where I am: and I am not come of myself, but he that sent me is true, whom you know not. But I know him: for I am from him, and he has sent me."

6   Then they sought to take him: but no man laid hands on him, because his hour was not yet come. And many of the people believed on him, and said, "When Christ comes, will he do more miracles than these which this man has done?"

7   The Pharisees heard that the people murmured such things concerning him; and the Pharisees and the chief priests sent officers to take him. Then Jesus said unto them, "Yet a little while am I with you, and then I go unto him that sent me. You shall seek me, and shall not find me: and where I am, there you cannot come."

8   Then the Jews said among themselves, "Where will he go, that we shall not find him? will he go unto the dispersed among the Gentiles, and teach the Gentiles? What manner of saying is this that he said, 'You shall seek me, and shall not find me: and where I am, there you cannot come?'"

"Rivers of Living Water"
John 7:37-44

9   In the last day, that great day of the feast, Jesus stood and cried, saying, "If any man thirsts, let him come unto me, and drink. He that believes on me, as the scripture has said, out of his heart shall flow rivers of living water." (But this spoke he of the Spirit, which they that believe on him should receive: for the Holy Ghost was not yet given; because Jesus was not yet glorified.)

10   Many of the people therefore, when they heard this saying, said, "Of a truth this is the Prophet." Others said, "This is the Christ." But some said, "Shall Christ come out of Galilee? Has not the scripture said, That Christ comes of the seed of David, and out of the town of Bethlehem, where David was?" So there was a division among the people because of him. And some of them would have taken him; but no man laid hands on him.

Leaders Dispute Over Jesus
John 7:45-53

11   Then came the officers to the chief priests and Pharisees; and they said unto them, "Why have you not brought him?" The officers answered, "Never man spoke like this man." Then the Pharisees answered them, "Are you also deceived? Have any of the rulers or of the Pharisees believed on him? But these people who do not know the law are accursed."

> "NEVER MAN SPOKE LIKE THIS MAN."

Nicodemus said unto them, (he that came to Jesus by night, being one 12 of them), "Does our law judge any man, before it hears him, and knows what he does?" They answered and said unto him, "Are you also of Galilee? Search, and look: for out of Galilee arises no prophet." And every man went unto his own house.

An Adulterous Woman Is Forgiven
John 8:1-11

Jesus went unto the Mount of Olives. And early in the morning he 13 came again into the temple, and all the people came unto him; and he sat down, and taught them. And the scribes and Pharisees brought unto him a woman taken in adultery; and when they had set her in the midst, they said unto him, "Teacher, this woman was taken in adultery, in the very act."

"Now Moses in the law commanded us, that such should be stoned: 14 but what do you say?" This they said, tempting him, that they might have to accuse him. But Jesus stooped down, and with his finger wrote on the ground, as though he did not hear them.

So when they continued asking him, he lifted up himself, and said 15 unto them, "He that is without sin among you, let him first cast a stone at her." And again he stooped down, and wrote on the ground. And they which heard it, being convicted by their own conscience, went out one by one, beginning at the eldest, even unto the last: and Jesus was left alone, and the woman standing in the midst.

> "HE THAT IS WITHOUT SIN AMONG YOU, LET HIM FIRST CAST A STONE."

When Jesus had lifted up himself, and saw none but the woman, he 16 said unto her, "Woman, where are those your accusers? has no man condemned you?" She said, "No man, Lord." And Jesus said unto her, "Neither do I condemn you: go, and sin no more."

"I Am the Light of the World"
John 8:12-30

Then spoke Jesus again unto them, saying, "I am the light of the 17 world: he that follows me shall not walk in darkness, but shall have the light of life." The Pharisees therefore said unto him, "You bear witness of yourself; your witness is not true." Jesus answered and said unto them, "Though I bear witness of myself, yet my witness is true: for I know from where I came, and where I go; but you cannot know from where I come, and where I go. You judge after the flesh;

> "I AM THE LIGHT OF THE WORLD: HE THAT FOLLOWS ME SHALL NOT WALK IN DARKNESS, BUT SHALL HAVE LIGHT OF LIFE."

I judge no man. And yet if I judge, my judgment is true: for I am not alone, but I and the Father that sent me. It is also written in your law, that

17 the testimony of two men is true. I am one that bears witness of myself, and the Father that sent me bears witness of me."

18 Then they said unto him, "Where is your Father?" Jesus answered, "You neither know me, nor my Father: if you had known me, you should have known my Father also." These words Jesus spoke in the treasury, as he taught in the temple: and no man laid hands on him; for his hour was not yet come.

19 Then said Jesus again unto them, "I go my way, and you shall seek me, and shall die in your sins: where I go, you cannot come." Then the Jews said, "Will he kill himself? because he says, 'Where I go, you cannot come.'" And he said unto them, "You are from beneath; I am from above: you are of this world; I am not of this world. I said therefore unto you, that you shall die in your sins: for if you do not believe that I am he, you shall die in your sins."

20 Then they said unto him, "Who are you?" And Jesus said unto them, "Even the same that I said unto you from the beginning. I have many things to say and to judge of you: but he that sent me is true; and I speak to the world those things which I have heard of him." They did not understand that he spoke to them of the Father.

21 Then Jesus said unto them, "When you have lifted up the Son of man, then shall you know that I am he, and that I do nothing of myself; but as my Father has taught me, I speak these things. And he that sent me is with me: the Father has not left me alone; for I do always those things that please him." As he spoke these words, many believed on him.

"You Shall Know the Truth"
John 8:31-41

22 Then said Jesus to those Jews which believed on him, "If you continue in my word, then are you my disciples indeed; and you shall know the truth, and the truth shall make you free." They answered him, "We be Abraham's seed, and were never in bondage to any man: how do you say, 'You shall be made free?'"

> "YOU SHALL KNOW THE TRUTH, AND THE TRUTH SHALL MAKE YOU FREE."

23 Jesus answered them, "Truly, truly, I say unto you, Whosoever commits sin is the servant of sin. And the servant does not abide in the house for ever: but the Son abides ever. If the Son therefore shall make you free, you shall be free indeed. I know that you are Abraham's seed; but you seek to kill me, because my word has no place in you. I speak that which I have seen with my Father: and you do that which you have seen with your father."

> "WHOSOEVER COMMITS SIN IS THE SERVANT OF SIN."

24 They answered and said unto him, "Abraham is our father." Jesus said unto them, "If you were Abraham's children, you would do the works of Abraham. But now you seek to kill me, a man that has told you the truth,

which I have heard of God: this did not Abraham. You do the deeds of your 24 father." Then they said to him, "We be not born of fornication; we have one Father, even God."

"I Tell You the Truth"
John 8:42-47

Jesus said unto them, "If God were your Father, you would love me: 25 for I proceeded forth and came from God; neither came I of myself, but he sent me. Why do you not understand my speech? even because you cannot hear my word. You are of your father the devil, and the lusts of your father you will do. He was a murderer from the beginning, and dwelt not in the truth, because there is no truth in him. When he speaks a lie, he speaks of his own: for he is a liar, and the father of it. And because I tell you the truth, you do not believe me.

"Which of you convicts me of sin? And if I say the truth, why do you 26 not believe me? He that is of God hears God's words: you therefore do not hear them, because you are not of God."

"I Honor My Father"
John 8:48-59

Then answered the Jews, and said unto him, "Say we not rightly that 27 you are a Samaritan, and have a demon?" Jesus answered, "I have not a demon; but I honor my Father, and you do dishonor me. And I seek not my own glory: there is one that seeks and judges.

"Truly, truly, I say unto you, If a man keeps my saying, he shall 28 never see death." Then the Jews said unto him, "Now we know that you have a demon. Abraham is dead, and the prophets; and you say, 'If a man keeps my saying, he shall never taste of death.' Are you greater than our father Abraham, which is dead? and the prophets are dead: whom do you make yourself?"

> "IF A MAN KEEPS MY SAYING, HE SHALL NEVER SEE DEATH."

Jesus answered, "If I honor myself, my honor is nothing: it is my 29 Father that honors me; of whom you say, that he is your God: yet you have not known him; but I know him: and if I should say, I do not know him, I shall be a liar like you: but I know him, and keep his saying. Your father Abraham rejoiced to see my day: and he saw it, and was glad."

Then the Jews said unto him, "You are not yet fifty years old, and have 30 you seen Abraham?" Jesus said unto them, "Truly, truly, I say unto you, Before Abraham was, I am." Then they took up stones to cast at him: but Jesus hid himself, and went out of the temple, going through the midst of them, and so passed by.

> "BEFORE ABRAHAM WAS, I AM."

CHAPTER 27

MINISTERING IN JERUSALEM

Healing a Man Born Blind
John 9:1-12

1   And as Jesus passed by, he saw a man which was blind from his birth. And his disciples asked him, saying, "Rabbi, who did sin, this man, or his parents, that he was born blind?" Jesus answered, "Neither has this man sinned, nor his parents: but that the works of God should be made manifest in him. I must work the works of him that sent me, while it is day: the night comes, when no man can work. As long as I am in the world, I am the light of the world."

2   When he had thus spoken, he spit on the ground, and made clay of the saliva, and he anointed the eyes of the blind man with the clay, and said unto him, "Go, wash in the pool of Siloam," (which is by interpretation, Sent). He went his way therefore, and washed, and came seeing.

3   The neighbors therefore, and they which before had seen him that he was blind, said, "Is not this he that sat and begged?" Some said, "This is he:" others said, "He is like him:" but he said, "I am he."

4   Therefore they said unto him, "How were your eyes opened?" He answered and said, "A man that is called Jesus made clay, and anointed my eyes, and said unto me, 'Go to the pool of Siloam, and wash:' and I went and washed, and I received sight." Then they said unto him, "Where is he?" He said, "I know not."

Pharisees Reject Healed Man
John 9:13-34

5   They brought to the Pharisees him that before was blind. And it was the sabbath day when Jesus made the clay, and opened his eyes. Then again the Pharisees also asked him how he had received his sight. He said unto them, "He put clay upon my eyes, and I washed, and do see." Therefore said

some of the Pharisees, "This man is not of God, because he does not keep 5
the sabbath day." Others said, "How can a man that is a sinner do such miracles?" And there was a division among them. They said unto the blind man
again, "What do you say of him, that he has opened your eyes?" He said,
"He is a prophet."

But the Jews did not believe concerning him, that he had been blind, 6
and received his sight, until they called the parents of him that had received
his sight. And they asked them, saying, "Is this your son, who you say was
born blind? how then does he now see?"

His parents answered them and said, "We know that this is our son, 7
and that he was born blind: but by what means he now sees, we know not;
or who has opened his eyes, we know not: he is of age; ask him: he shall
speak for himself." These words spoke his parents, because they feared the
Jews: for the Jews had agreed already, that if any man did confess that he
was Christ, he should be put out of the synagogue. Therefore his parents
said, "He is of age; ask him."

Then again called they the man that was blind, and said unto him, 8
"Give God the praise: we know that this man is a sinner." He answered and
said, "Whether he be a sinner or not, I know not: one thing I know, that,
whereas I was blind, now I see."

Then they said to him again, "What did he to you? how opened he 9
your eyes?" He answered them, "I have told you already, and you did not
hear: why would you hear it again? will you also be his disciples?"

Then they insulted him, and said, "You are his disciple; but we are 10
Moses' disciples. We know that God spoke unto Moses: as for this fellow,
we know not from where he is."

The man answered and said unto them, "Why herein is a marvelous 11
thing, that you know not from where he is, and yet he has opened my eyes.
Now we know that God hears not sinners: but if any man be a worshiper of
God, and does his will, him he hears. Since the world began it was not heard
that any man opened the eyes of one that was born blind. If this man were
not of God, he could do nothing."

They answered and said unto him, "You were altogether born in sins, 12
and do you teach us?" And they cast him out.

Spiritual Blindness
John 9:35-41

Jesus heard that they had cast him out; and when he had found him, 13
he said unto him, "Do you believe on the Son of God?" He answered and
said, "Who is he, Lord, that I might believe on him?" And Jesus said unto
him, "You have both seen him, and it is he that talks with you." And he said,
"Lord, I believe." And he worshiped him. And Jesus said, "For judgment I
am come into this world, that they which see not might see; and that they
which see might be made blind."

14   And some of the Pharisees which were with him heard these words, and said unto him, "Are we blind also?" Jesus said unto them, "If you were blind, you should have no sin: but now you say, 'We see;' therefore your sin remains."

"I Am the Good Shepherd"
John 10:1-21

15   "Truly, truly, I say unto you, He that enters not by the door into the sheepfold, but climbs up some other way, the same is a thief and a robber. But he that enters in by the door is the shepherd of the sheep. To him the doorkeeper opens; and the sheep hear his voice: and he calls his own sheep by name, and leads them out. And when he puts forth his own sheep, he goes before them, and the sheep follow him: for they know his voice. And a stranger will they not follow, but will flee from him: for they do not know the voice of strangers." This illustration Jesus spoke unto them: but they did not understand what things they were which he spoke unto them.

16   Then said Jesus unto them again, "Truly, truly, I say unto you, I am the door of the sheep. All that ever came before me are thieves and robbers: but the sheep did not hear them. I am the door: by me if any man enters in, he shall be saved, and shall go in and out, and find pasture. The thief does not come, except to steal, and to kill, and to destroy: I am come that they might have life, and that they might have it more abundantly.

> "I AM COME THAT THEY MIGHT HAVE LIFE, AND THAT THEY MIGHT HAVE IT MORE ABUNDANTLY."

17   "I am the good shepherd: the good shepherd gives his life for the sheep. But he that is a hireling, and not the shepherd, whose own the sheep are not, sees the wolf coming, and leaves the sheep, and flees: and the wolf catches them, and scatters the sheep. The hireling flees, because he is a hireling, and cares not for the sheep.

18   "I am the good shepherd, and know my sheep, and am known of mine. As the Father knows me, even so I know the Father: and I lay down my life for the sheep. And other sheep I have, which are not of this fold: them also I must bring, and they shall hear my voice; and there shall be one flock, and one shepherd. Therefore does my Father love me, because I lay down my life, that I might take it again. No man takes it from me, but I lay it down of myself. I have power to lay it down, and I have power to take it again. This commandment have I received of my Father."

19   There was a division therefore again among the Jews for these sayings. And many of them said, "He has a demon, and is gone mad; why do you hear him?" Others said, "These are not the words of him that has a demon. Can a demon open the eyes of the blind?"

CHAPTER 28

JESUS' MINISTRY MULTIPLIES

Seventy Sent Forth to Minister
Luke 10:1-12

After these things the Lord appointed seventy others also, and sent 1 them two and two before his face into every city and place, where he himself would come. Therefore he said unto them, "The harvest truly is great, but the laborers are few: pray therefore the Lord of the harvest, that he would send forth laborers into his harvest. Go your ways: behold, I send you forth as lambs among wolves. Carry neither purse, nor bag, nor shoes: and greet no man on the road.

"And into whatsoever house you enter, first say, 'Peace be to this 2 house.' And if the son of peace be there, your peace shall rest upon it: if not, it shall turn to you again. And in the same house remain, eating and drinking such things as they give: for the laborer is worthy of his wages. Go not from house to house.

"And into whatsoever city you enter, and they receive you, eat such 3 things as are set before you: and heal the sick that are therein, and say unto them, 'The kingdom of God is come near unto you.'

"But into whatsoever city you enter, and they do not receive you, go 4 your ways out into the streets of the same, and say, 'Even the very dust of your city, which cleaves on us, we do wipe off against you: nevertheless be sure of this, that the kingdom of God is come near unto you.' But I say unto you, that it shall be more tolerable in that day for Sodom, than for that city."

Jesus Laments for Four Cities
Matthew 11:20-24; Luke 10:13-16

Then he began to denounce the cities wherein most of his mighty 5 works were done, because they had not repented: "Woe unto you, Chorazin! woe unto you, Bethsaida! for if the mighty works, which were done in you, had been done in Tyre and Sidon, they would have repented long ago, sitting

5 in sackcloth and ashes. But I say unto you, It shall be more tolerable for Tyre and Sidon at the day of judgment, than for you.

6   "And you, Capernaum, which are exalted unto heaven, shall be brought down to Hades: for if the mighty works, which have been done in you, had been done in Sodom, it would have remained until this day. But I say unto you, That it shall be more tolerable for the land of Sodom in the day of judgment, than for you.

7   "He that hears you hears me; and he that rejects you rejects me; and he that rejects me rejects him that sent me."

Seventy Return and Are Given Authority
Luke 10:17-20

8   And the seventy returned again with joy, saying, "Lord, even the demons are subject unto us through your name." And he said unto them,

> "REJOICE, BECAUSE YOUR NAMES ARE WRITTEN IN HEAVEN."

"I saw Satan fall as lightning from heaven. Behold, I give unto you authority to trample on serpents and scorpions, and over all the power of the enemy: and nothing shall by any means hurt you. Nevertheless in this rejoice not, that the spirits are subject unto you; but rather rejoice, because your names are written in heaven."

Jesus Rejoices in Spirit and Prayer
Matthew 11:25-30; Luke 10:21-24

9   In that hour Jesus rejoiced in spirit, and said, "I thank you, O Father, Lord of heaven and earth, that you have hidden these things from the wise and prudent, and have revealed them unto babies: even so, Father; for so it seemed good in your sight. All things are delivered to me of my Father: and no man knows who the Son is, but the Father; and who the Father is, but the Son, and he to whom the Son chooses to reveal him.

10   "Come unto me, all you that labor and are heavy laden, and I will give

> "COME UNTO ME, ALL YOU THAT LABOR AND ARE HEAVY LADEN, AND I WILL GIVE YOU REST."

you rest. Take my yoke upon you, and learn of me; for I am meek and lowly in heart: and you shall find rest unto your souls. For my yoke is easy, and my burden is light."

11   And he turned himself unto his disciples, and said privately, "Blessed are the eyes which see the things that you see: for I tell you, that many prophets and kings have desired to see those things which you see, and have not seen them; and to hear those things which you hear, and have not heard them."

Parable of the Good Samaritan
Luke 10:25-37

12   And, behold, a certain lawyer stood up, and tempted him, saying, "Teacher, what shall I do to inherit eternal life?" He said unto him, "What

is written in the law? how do you read?" And he answering said, "*You shall* 12
love the Lord your God with all your heart, and with all your soul, and with
all your strength, and with all your mind; and your neighbor as yourself."
And he said unto him, "You have answered rightly: this do, and you shall
live."

But he, willing to justify himself, said unto Jesus, "And who is my 13
neighbor?" And Jesus answering said, "A certain man went down from
Jerusalem to Jericho, and fell among thieves, which stripped him of his
clothing, and wounded him, and departed, leaving him half dead.

"And by chance there came down a certain priest that way: and when 14
he saw him, he passed by on the other side. And likewise a Levite, when he
was at the place, came and looked on him, and passed by on the other side.

"But a certain Samaritan, as he journeyed, came where he was: and 15
when he saw him, he had compassion on him, and went to him, and bound
up his wounds, pouring in oil and wine, and set him on his own animal, and
brought him to an inn, and took care of him. And the next day when he
departed, he took out two silver coins, and gave them to the host, and said
unto him, 'Take care of him; and whatsoever you spend more, when I come
again, I will repay you.'

"Which now of these three, do you think, was neighbor unto him that 16
fell among the thieves?" And he said, "He that showed mercy on him." Then
said Jesus unto him, "Go, and do likewise."

Jesus Visits Martha and Mary
Luke 10:38-42

Now it came to pass, as they went, that he entered into a certain vil- 17
lage: and a certain woman named Martha received him into her house. And
she had a sister called Mary, which also sat at Jesus' feet, and heard his
word. But Martha was distracted about much serving, and came to him, and
said, "Lord, do you not care that my sister has left me to serve alone? tell
her therefore that she help me." And Jesus answered and said unto her,
"Martha, Martha, you are anxious and troubled about many things: but one
thing is needful: and Mary has chosen that good part, which shall not be
taken away from her."

CHAPTER 29

WORDS OF TRUTH TO THE PHARISEES

Prayer (repeated)
Luke 11:1-4

1   And it came to pass, that, as he was praying in a certain place, when he ceased, one of his disciples said unto him, "Lord, teach us to pray, as John also taught his disciples." And he said unto them, "When you pray, say, Our Father which are in heaven, Hallowed be your name. Your kingdom come. Your will be done, as in heaven, so on earth. Give us day by day our daily bread. And forgive us our sins; for we also forgive everyone that is indebted to us. And lead us not into temptation; but deliver us from evil."

Parable of the Persistent Friend
Luke 11:5-13

2   And he said unto them, "Which of you shall have a friend, and shall go unto him at midnight, and say unto him, 'Friend, lend me three loaves; for a friend of mine in his journey is come to me, and I have nothing to set before him'? And he from within shall answer and say, 'Do not trouble me: the door is now shut, and my children are with me in bed; I cannot rise and give you.' I say unto you, Though he will not rise and give him, because he is his friend, yet because of his persistence he will rise and give him as many as he needs.

3   "And I say unto you, Ask, and it shall be given you; seek, and you shall find; knock, and it shall be opened unto you. For everyone that asks receives; and he that seeks finds; and to him that knocks it shall be opened.

4   "If a son shall ask for bread of any of you that is a father, will he give him a stone? or if he asks for a fish, will he for a fish give him a serpent? Or if he shall ask for an egg, will he offer him a scorpion? If you then, being evil, know how to give good gifts unto your children: how much more shall your heavenly Father give the Holy Spirit to them that ask him?"

Jesus Is Not Beelzebub (repeated)
Luke 11:14-23

5   And he was casting out a demon, and it was mute. And it came to pass, when the demon was gone out, the mute spoke; and the people wondered.

But some of them said, "He casts out demons through Beelzebub the prince 5 of the demons." And others, tempting him, sought of him a sign from heaven.

But he, knowing their thoughts, said unto them, "Every kingdom 6 divided against itself is brought to desolation; and a house divided against a house falls. If Satan also be divided against himself, how shall his kingdom stand? because you say that I cast out demons through Beelzebub.

"And if I by Beelzebub cast out demons, by whom do your sons cast 7 them out? therefore shall they be your judges. But if I with the finger of God cast out demons, no doubt the kingdom of God is come upon you.

"When a strong man armed keeps his palace, his goods are in peace: but 8 when a stronger than he shall come upon him, and overcome him, he takes from him all his armor wherein he trusted, and divides his belongings. He that is not with me is against me: and he that gathers not with me scatters."

Unclean Spirits (repeated)
Luke 11:24-26

"When the unclean spirit is gone out of a man, it walks through dry 9 places, seeking rest; and finding none, it says, 'I will return unto my house from which I came out.' And when it comes, it finds it swept and put in order. Then it goes, and takes to itself seven other spirits more wicked than itself; and they enter in, and dwell there: and the last state of that man is worse than the first."

"Blessed Are They That Hear"
Luke 11:27-28

And it came to pass, as he spoke these things, a certain woman of the 10 company lifted up her voice, and said unto him, "Blessed is the womb that bore you, and the breasts which you have nursed." But he said, "Yes rather, blessed are they that hear the word of God, and keep it."

Seeking a Sign (repeated)
Luke 11:29-32

And when the people were gathered thickly together, he began to say, 11 "This is an evil generation: they seek a sign; and there shall no sign be given it, but the sign of Jonah the prophet. For as Jonah was a sign unto the Ninevites, so shall also the Son of man be to this generation.

"The queen of the south shall rise up in the judgment with the men of 12 this generation, and condemn them: for she came from the utmost parts of the earth to hear the wisdom of Solomon; and, behold, a greater than Solomon is here."

"The men of Nineveh shall rise up in the judgment with this genera- 13 tion, and shall condemn it: for they repented at the preaching of Jonah; and, behold, a greater than Jonah is here."

Light of the World (repeated)
Luke 11:33

"No man, when he has lit a lamp, puts it in a secret place, neither under 14 a tub, but on a lampstand, that they which come in may see the light."

Light of the Body (repeated)
Luke 11:34-36

15   "The light of the body is the eye: therefore when your eye is single, your whole body also is full of light; but when your eye is evil, your body also is full of darkness. Take heed therefore that the light which is in you be not darkness. If your whole body therefore be full of light, having no part dark, the whole shall be full of light, as when the bright shining of a lamp does give you light."

Woe! Pharisees and Lawyers
Luke 11:37-54

16   And as he spoke, a certain Pharisee asked him to dine with him: and he went in, and sat down to eat. And when the Pharisee saw it, he marveled that he had not first washed before dinner. And the Lord said unto him, "Now do you Pharisees make clean the outside of the cup and the platter; but your inward part is full of greediness and wickedness. You fools, did not he that made that which is outside make that which is inside also? But rather give charitable deeds of such things as you have; and, behold, all things are clean unto you.

17   "But woe unto you, Pharisees! for you tithe mint and rue and all manner of herbs, and pass over judgment and the love of God: these ought you to have done, and not to leave the others undone.

18   "Woe unto you, Pharisees! for you love the uppermost seats in the synagogues, and greetings in the marketplaces.

19   "Woe unto you, scribes and Pharisees, hypocrites! for you are as graves which are not seen, and the men that walk over them are not aware of them."

20   Then answered one of the lawyers, and said unto him, "Teacher, thus saying you reproach us also." And he said, "Woe unto you also, you lawyers! for you load men with burdens grievous to be borne, and you yourselves do not touch the burdens with one of your fingers.

21   "Woe unto you! for you build the tombs of the prophets, and your fathers killed them. Truly you bear witness that you approve the deeds of your fathers: for they indeed killed them, and you build their tombs. Therefore also said the wisdom of God, I will send them prophets and apostles, and some of them they shall slay and persecute: that the blood of all the prophets, which was shed from the foundation of the world, may be required of this generation; from the blood of Abel unto the blood of Zacharias, which perished between the altar and the temple: yes I say unto you, It shall be required of this generation.

22   "Woe unto you, lawyers! for you have taken away the key of knowledge: you did not enter in yourselves, and them that were entering in you hindered."

23   And as he said these things unto them, the scribes and the Pharisees began to urge him strongly, and to provoke him to speak of many things: laying wait for him, and seeking to catch something out of his mouth, that they might accuse him.

CHAPTER 30

THE KEYS OF THE KINGDOM

Beware of Hypocrisy
Luke 12:1-3

In the meantime, when there were gathered together an innumerable 1 multitude of people, insomuch that they trampled one upon another, he began to say unto his disciples first of all, "Beware of the leaven of the Pharisees, which is hypocrisy. For there is nothing covered, that shall not be revealed; neither hidden, that shall not be known. Therefore whatsoever you have spoken in darkness shall be heard in the light; and that which you have spoken in the ear in inner rooms shall be proclaimed upon the housetops."

Whom Shall You Fear Most?
Luke 12:4-7

"And I say unto you my friends, Be not afraid of them that kill the 2 body, and after that have no more that they can do. But I will forewarn you whom you shall fear: Fear him, which after he has killed has power to cast into hell; yes, I say unto you, Fear him. Are not five sparrows sold for two copper coins, and not one of them is forgotten before God? But even the very hairs of your head are all numbered. Fear not therefore: you are of more value than many sparrows."

Confess Christ Before Men
Luke 12:8-9

"Also I say unto you, Whosoever shall confess me before men, him 3 shall the Son of man also confess before the angels of God: but he that denies me before men shall be denied before the angels of God."

The One Unforgiven Sin (repeated)
Luke 12:10-12

"And whosoever shall speak a word against the Son of man, it shall be 4 forgiven him: but unto him that blasphemes against the Holy Ghost it shall

4 not be forgiven. And when they bring you unto the synagogues, and unto magistrates, and authorities, worry not how or what thing you shall answer, or what you shall say: for the Holy Ghost shall teach you in the same hour what you ought to say."

Parable of the Rich Fool
Luke 12:13-21

5 And one of the company said unto him, "Teacher, speak to my brother, that he divide the inheritance with me." And he said unto him, "Man, who made me a judge or a divider over you?" And he said unto them, "Take heed, and beware of covetousness: for a man's life consists not in the abundance of the things which he possesses."

6 And he spoke a parable unto them, saying, "The ground of a certain rich man brought forth plentifully: and he thought within himself, saying, 'What shall I do, because I have no room where to store my fruits?' And he said, 'This will I do: I will pull down my barns, and build greater; and there will I store all my fruits and my goods. And I will say to my soul, "Soul, you have many goods laid up for many years; take your ease, eat, drink, and be merry." ' But God said unto him, 'You fool, this night your soul shall be required of you: then whose shall those things be, which you have provided?' So is he that lays up treasure for himself, and is not rich toward God."

> "BEWARE OF COVETOUSNESS: FOR A MAN'S LIFE CONSISTS NOT IN THE ABUNDANCE OF THE THINGS WHICH HE POSSESSES."

Consider This (repeated)
Luke 12:22-34

7 And he said unto his disciples, "Therefore I say unto you, Be not anxious for your life, what you shall eat; neither for the body, what you shall put on. The life is more than food, and the body is more than clothing. Consider the ravens: for they neither sow nor reap; which neither have storehouse nor barn; and God feeds them: how much more are you better than the birds? And which of you with worrying can add to his stature one cubit?

> "LIFE IS MORE THAN FOOD, AND THE BODY IS MORE THAN CLOTHING."

8 "If you then be not able to do that thing which is least, why be anxious for the rest? Consider the lilies how they grow: they toil not, they spin not; and yet I say unto you, that Solomon in all his glory was not arrayed like one of these. If then God so clothe the grass, which is today in the field, and tomorrow is cast into the oven; how much more will he clothe you, O you of little faith?

9 "And seek not what you shall eat, or what you shall drink, neither be of doubtful mind. For all these things do the nations of the world seek after:

and your Father knows that you have need of these things. But rather seek 9 the kingdom of God; and all these things shall be added unto you.

"Fear not, little flock; for it is your Father's good pleasure to give you 10 the kingdom. Sell that you have, and give charitable deeds; provide yourselves bags which grow not old, a treasure in the heavens that fails not, where no thief approaches, neither moth corrupts. For where your treasure is, there will your heart be also."

> "WHERE YOUR TREASURE IS, THERE WILL YOUR HEART BE ALSO."

Be as Watchful Servants
Luke 12:35-40

"Let your loins be girded about, and your lamps burning; and you 11 yourselves like men that wait for their master, when he will return from the wedding; that when he comes and knocks, they may open unto him immediately. Blessed are those servants, whom the master when he comes shall find watching: truly I say unto you, that he shall dress himself, and make them to sit down to eat, and will come forth and serve them.

"And if he shall come in the second watch, or come in the third watch, 12 and find them so, blessed are those servants. And this know, that if the owner of the house had known what hour the thief would come, he would have watched, and not have allowed his house to be broken into. Be therefore ready also: for the Son of man comes at an hour when you think not."

Faithful and Wise Steward
Luke 12:41-48

Then Peter said unto him, "Lord, do you speak this parable unto us, or 13 even to all?" And the Lord said, "Who then is that faithful and wise steward, whom his master shall make ruler over his household, to give them their portion of food in due season? Blessed is that servant, whom his master when he comes shall find so doing. Of a truth I say unto you, that he will make him ruler over all that he has.

"But and if that servant says in his heart, 'My master delays his com- 14 ing'; and shall begin to beat the men servants and women servants, and to eat and drink, and to be drunk; the master of that servant will come in a day when he does not look for him, and at an hour when he is not aware, and will cut him in pieces, and will appoint him his portion with the unbelievers.

"And that servant, which knew his master's will, and prepared not 15 himself, neither did according to his will, shall be beaten with many stripes. But he that knew not, and did commit things worthy of stripes, shall be beaten with few stripes. For unto whomsoever much is given, of him shall be much required: and to whom men have committed much, of him they will ask the more."

> "UNTO WHOMSOEVER MUCH IS GIVEN, OF HIM SHALL BE MUCH REQUIRED."

"I Have a Baptism"
Luke 12:49-53

16   "I am come to send fire on the earth; and how I wish, that it be already kindled? But I have a baptism to be baptized with; and how I am distressed till it be accomplished!

17   "Do you suppose that I am come to give peace on earth? I tell you, No; but rather division: for from henceforth there shall be five in one house divided, three against two, and two against three. The father shall be divided against the son, and the son against the father; the mother against the daughter, and the daughter against the mother; the mother-in-law against her daughter-in-law, and the daughter-in-law against her mother-in-law."

"Discern This Time"
Luke 12:54-56

18   And he said also to the people, "When you see a cloud rise out of the west, straightway you say,' 'There comes a shower'; and so it is. And when you see the south wind blow, you say, 'There will be heat'; and it comes to pass. You hypocrites, you can discern the face of the sky and of the earth; but how is it that you do not discern this time?"

Reconciliation (repeated)
Luke 12:57-59

19   "Yes, and why even of yourselves do you not judge what is right? When you go with your adversary to the magistrate, as you are on the way, give diligence that you may be delivered from him; lest he drag you to the judge, and the judge deliver you to the officer, and the officer cast you into prison. I tell you, you shall not depart from there, till you have paid the very last small copper coin."

CHAPTER 31

⁜Jesus Answers His Adversaries⁜

Repent or Perish
Luke 13:1-5

There were present at that season some that told him of the Galileans, 1
whose blood Pilate had mingled with their sacrifices. And Jesus answering
said unto them, "Do you suppose that these Galileans were sinners above all
the Galileans, because they suffered such things? I tell you, No: but, except
you repent, you shall all likewise perish.

"Or those eighteen, upon whom the tower in Siloam fell, and killed them, 2
do you think that they were sinners above all men that dwelt in Jerusalem?
I tell you, No: but, except you repent, you shall all likewise perish."

Parable of the Barren Fig Tree
Luke 13:6-9

He spoke also this parable; "A certain man had a fig tree planted in his 3
vineyard; and he came and sought fruit thereon, and found none. Then he
said unto the dresser of his vineyard, 'Behold, these three years I come seeking fruit on this fig tree, and find none: cut it down; why does it use up the
ground?' And he answering said unto him, 'Master, let it alone this year
also, till I shall dig about it, and fertilize it: and if it bears fruit, well: and if
not, then after that you shall cut it down.' "

Healing on the Sabbath
Luke 13:10-17

And he was teaching in one of the synagogues on the sabbath. And, 4
behold, there was a woman which had a spirit of infirmity eighteen years,
and was bowed together, and could in no way lift up herself. And when Jesus
saw her, he called her to him, and said unto her, "Woman, you are loosed
from your infirmity." And he laid his hands on her: and immediately she was
made straight, and glorified God.

5   And the ruler of the synagogue answered with indignation, because Jesus had healed on the sabbath day, and said unto the people, "There are six days in which men ought to work: in them therefore come and be healed, and not on the sabbath day." The Lord then answered him, and said, "You hypocrite, does not each one of you on the sabbath loose his ox or his donkey from the stall, and lead it away to watering? And ought not this woman, being a daughter of Abraham, whom Satan has bound, lo, these eighteen years, be loosed from this bond on the sabbath day?"

6   And when he had said these things, all his adversaries were ashamed: and all the people rejoiced for all the glorious things that were done by him.

Parable of Mustard Seed (repeated)
Luke 13:18-19

7   Then he said, "Unto what is the kingdom of God like? and to what shall I compare it? It is like a grain of mustard seed, which a man took, and cast into his garden; and it grew, and became a great tree; and the birds of the air lodged in the branches of it."

Parable of the Leaven (repeated)
Luke 13:20-21

8   And again he said, "To what shall I liken the kingdom of God? It is like leaven, which a woman took and hid in three measures of meal, till the whole was leavened."

CHAPTER 32

·+· FOURTH MINISTRY AT JERUSALEM ·+·

"The Father Is in Me, and I in Him."
John 10:22-38

And it was at Jerusalem the feast of the dedication, and it was winter. 1
And Jesus walked in the temple in Solomon's porch. Then came the Jews
round about him, and said unto him, "How long do you make us to doubt?
If you be the Christ, tell us plainly." Jesus answered them, "I told you, and
you believed not: the works that I do in my Father's name, they bear witness
of me. But you do not believe, because you are not of my sheep, as I said
unto you. My sheep hear my voice, and I know them, and they follow me:
and I give unto them eternal life; and they shall never perish, neither shall
any man pluck them out of my hand. My Father, which gave them to me, is
greater than all; and no man is able to pluck them out of my Father's hand.
I and my Father are one."

Then the Jews took up stones again to stone him. Jesus answered 2
them, "Many good works have I shown you from my Father; for which of
those works do you stone me?" The Jews answered him, saying, "For a good
work we do not stone you; but for blasphemy; and because you, being a
man, make yourself God."

Jesus answered them, "Is it not written in your law, 'I said, "You are 3
gods" '? If he called them gods, unto whom the word of God came, and the
scripture cannot be broken; you say of him, whom the Father has sanctified,
and sent into the world, 'You blaspheme'; because I said, 'I am the Son of
God'? If I do not the works of my Father, do not believe me. But if I do,
though you do not believe me, believe the works: that you may know, and
believe, that the Father is in me, and I in him."

Return to Place of John's Baptism
John 10:39-42

Therefore they sought again to take him: but he escaped out of their 4
hand, and went away again beyond Jordan into the place where John at first
baptized; and there he stayed. And many came unto him, and said, "John did
no miracle: but all things that John spoke of this man were true." And many
believed on him there.

PART 8

SERVING AND SERVITUDE

Jesus showed no preference of persons. Understanding that the rich can be poor in spirit, and the poor can be rich in spirit, He taught humility and deference as the true signets of grace. He instructed those who would follow Him to exchange the love of material things for the love of God, knowing that which we serve will become our master. He gave the promise that those who love God will one day be lifted up above those who love the world. In that day, the first shall be last and the last shall be first.

"THEY SHALL COME FROM THE EAST, AND FROM THE WEST, AND FROM THE NORTH, AND FROM THE SOUTH, AND SHALL SIT DOWN IN THE KINGDOM OF GOD. AND, BEHOLD, THERE ARE LAST WHICH SHALL BE FIRST, AND THERE ARE FIRST WHICH SHALL BE LAST." (LUKE 13:29-30)

CHAPTER 33

THE COST OF SERVING

The Gateway to the Kingdom
Luke 13:22-30

And he went through the cities and villages, teaching, and journeying 1 toward Jerusalem. Then said one unto him, "Lord, are there few that be saved?" And he said unto them, "Strive to enter in at the strait gate: for many, I say unto you, will seek to enter in, and shall not be able.

"When once the master of the house is risen up, and has shut the door, 2 and you begin to stand outside, and to knock at the door, saying, 'Lord, Lord, open unto us'; and he shall answer and say unto you, 'I know not from where you are': then shall you begin to say, 'We have eaten and drunk in your presence, and you have taught in our streets.' But he shall say, 'I tell you, I know not from where you are; depart from me, all you workers of iniquity.'

"There shall be weeping and gnashing of teeth, when you shall see 3 Abraham, and Isaac, and Jacob, and all the prophets, in the kingdom of God, and you yourselves thrust out. And they shall come from the east, and from the west, and from the north, and from the south, and shall sit down in the kingdom of God. And, behold, there are last which shall be first, and there are first which shall be last."

Jesus Laments for Jerusalem
Luke 13:31-35

The same day there came certain of the Pharisees, saying unto him, 4 "Get out, and depart from here: for Herod will kill you." And he said unto them, "Go, and tell that fox, 'Behold, I cast out demons, and I do cures today and tomorrow, and the third day I shall be perfected.' Nevertheless I must walk today, and tomorrow, and the day following: for it cannot be that a prophet perish outside of Jerusalem.

"O Jerusalem, Jerusalem, which kill the prophets, and stone them that 5 are sent unto you; how often would I have gathered your children together,

5   as a hen does gather her brood under her wings, and you would not! Behold, your house is left unto you desolate: and truly I say unto you, You shall not see me, until the time comes when you shall say, *Blessed is he that comes in the name of the Lord.*"

Man Healed on the Sabbath Day
Luke 14:1-6

6   And it came to pass, as he went into the house of one of the chief Pharisees to eat bread on the sabbath day, that they watched him. And, behold, there was a certain man before him which had the dropsy. And Jesus answering spoke unto the lawyers and Pharisees, saying, "Is it lawful to heal on the sabbath day?" And they held their peace. And he took him, and healed him, and let him go; and answered them, saying, "Which of you shall have a donkey or an ox fallen into a pit, and will not straightway pull it out on the sabbath day?" And they could not answer him again to these things.

Parable of the Wedding Guest
Luke 14:7-11

7   And he put forth a parable to those which were invited, when he noticed how they chose out the chief places; saying unto them, "When you are invited of any man to a wedding, do not sit down in the highest place; lest a more prominent man than you be invited of him; and he that invited you and him come and say to you, 'Give this man your place'; and you begin with shame to take the lowest place.

8   "But when you are invited, go and sit down in the lowest place; that when he that invited you comes, he may say unto you, 'Friend, go up higher': then shall you have honor in the presence of them that sit at the table with you. For whosoever exalts himself shall be humbled; and he that

> "HE THAT HUMBLES HIMSELF SHALL BE EXALTED."

humbles himself shall be exalted."

Parable of the Great Repayment
Luke 14:12-14

9   Then he said also to him that invited him, "When you make a dinner or a supper, call not your friends, nor your brethren, neither your relatives, nor your rich neighbors; lest they also invite you in return, and a repayment be made you. But when you make a feast, call the poor, the maimed, the lame, the blind: and you shall be blessed; for they cannot repay you: for you shall be repaid at the resurrection of the just."

Parable of the Great Supper
Luke 14:15-24

10   And when one of them that sat at the table with him heard these things, he said unto him, "Blessed is he that shall eat bread in the kingdom of God." Then said he unto him, "A certain man made a great supper, and

invited many: and sent his servant at supper time to say to them that were 10 invited, 'Come; for all things are now ready.'

"And they all with one purpose began to make excuses. The first said 11 unto him, 'I have bought a piece of ground, and I must of necessity go and see it: I ask you have me excused.' And another said, 'I have bought five yoke of oxen, and I go to test them: I ask you have me excused.' And another said, 'I have married a wife, and therefore I cannot come.'

"So that servant came, and showed his master these things. Then the 12 master of the house being angry said to his servant, 'Go out quickly into the streets and lanes of the city, and bring in here the poor, and the maimed, and the lame, and the blind.' And the servant said, 'Master, it is done as you have commanded, and yet there is room.' And the master said unto the servant, 'Go out into the highways and country roads, and compel them to come in, that my house may be filled. For I say unto you, That none of those men which were invited shall taste of my supper.' "

Counting the Cost to Follow
Luke 14:25-33

And there went great multitudes with him: and he turned, and said 13 unto them, "If any man comes to me, and does not hate his father, and mother, and wife, and children, and brethren, and sisters, yes, and his own life also, he cannot be my dis-

> "WHOSOEVER DOES NOT BEAR HIS CROSS, AND COME AFTER ME, CANNOT BE MY DISCIPLE."

ciple. And whosoever does not bear his cross, and come after me, cannot be my disciple.

"For which of you, intending to build a tower, sits not down first, and 14 counts the cost, whether he has sufficient to finish it? Lest perhaps, after he has laid the foundation, and is not able to finish it, all that behold it begin to mock him, saying, 'This man began to build, and was not able to finish.'

"Or what king, going to make war against another king, sits not down 15 first, and consults whether he be able with ten thousand to meet him that comes against him with twenty thousand? Or else, while the other is yet a great way off, he sends a delegation, and desires conditions of peace. So likewise, whosoever he be of you that forsakes not all that he has, he cannot be my disciple."

Salt of the Earth (repeated)
Luke 14:34-35

"Salt is good: but if the salt has lost its savor, with what shall it be sea- 16 soned? It is neither fit for the land, nor even for the waste pile; but men cast it out. He that has ears to hear, let him hear."

CHAPTER 34

THE RESPONSIBILITIES OF SERVING

Parable of the Lost Sheep (repeated)
Luke 15:1-7

1   Then drew near unto him all the tax collectors and sinners to hear him. And the Pharisees and scribes murmured, saying, "This man receives sinners, and eats with them."

2   And he spoke this parable unto them, saying, "What man of you, having a hundred sheep, if he loses one of them, does not leave the ninety and nine in the wilderness, and go after that which is lost, until he finds it? And when he has found it, he lays it on his shoulders, rejoicing. And when he comes home, he calls together his friends and neighbors, saying unto them, 'Rejoice with me; for I have found my sheep which was lost.' I say unto you, that likewise joy shall be in heaven over one sinner that repents, more than over ninety and nine just persons, which need no repentance."

Parable of the Lost Coin
Luke 15:8-10

3   "Or what woman having ten pieces of silver, if she loses one piece, does not light a lamp, and sweep the house, and seek diligently till she finds it? And when she has found it, she calls her friends and her neighbors together, saying, 'Rejoice with me; for I have found the piece which I had lost.' Likewise, I say unto you, there is joy in the presence of the angels of God over one sinner that repents."

Parable of the Prodigal Son
Luke 15:11-32

4   And he said, "A certain man had two sons: and the younger of them said to his father, 'Father, give me the portion of goods that falls to me.' And he divided unto them his livelihood. And not many days afterward the younger son gathered all together, and took his journey into a far country,

and there wasted his possessions with reckless living. And when he had 4
spent all, there arose a mighty famine in that land; and he began to be in
need. And he went and joined himself to a citizen of that country; and he
sent him into his fields to feed swine. And he would gladly have filled his
belly with the husks that the swine did eat: and no man gave unto him.

"And when he came to himself, he said, 'How many hired servants of 5
my father's have bread enough and to spare, and I perish with hunger! I will
arise and go to my father, and will say unto him, "Father, I have sinned
against heaven, and before you, and am no more worthy to be called your
son: make me as one of your hired servants." ' And he arose, and came to
his father. But when he was yet a great way off, his father saw him, and had
compassion, and ran, and fell on his neck, and kissed him. And the son said
unto him, 'Father, I have sinned against heaven, and in your sight, and am
no more worthy to be called your son.'

"But the father said to his servants, 'Bring forth the best robe, and put 6
it on him; and put a ring on his hand, and shoes on his feet: and bring here the
fatted calf, and kill it; and let us eat, and be merry: for this my son was dead,
and is alive again; he was lost, and is found.' And they began to be merry.

"Now his older son was in the field: and as he came and drew near to 7
the house, he heard music and dancing. And he called one of the servants,
and asked what these things meant. And he said unto him, 'Your brother is
come; and your father has killed the fatted calf, because he has received him
safe and sound.'

"And he was angry, and would not go in: therefore his father came out, 8
and pleaded with him. And he answering said to his father, 'Lo, these many
years do I serve you, neither trans-
gressed I at any time your commandment: and yet you never gave me a
young goat, that I might make merry
with my friends: but as soon as this

> SON, YOU ARE EVER WITH ME,
> AND ALL THAT I HAVE IS
> YOURS.

your son was come, which has devoured your livelihood with harlots, you
have killed for him the fatted calf.' And he said unto him, 'Son, you are ever
with me, and all that I have is yours. It was fitting that we should make
merry, and be glad: for this your brother was dead, and is alive again; and
was lost, and is found.' "

Parable of the Shrewd Steward
Luke 16:1-13

And he said also unto his disciples, "There was a certain rich man, 9
which had a steward; and the same was accused unto him that he had
wasted his goods. And he called him, and said unto him, 'How is it that
I hear this of you? give an account of your stewardship; for you may be
no longer steward.' Then the steward said within himself, 'What shall I
do? for my master takes away from me the stewardship: I cannot dig; to
beg I am ashamed. I am resolved what to do, that, when I am put out of
the stewardship, they may receive me into their houses.'

10 "So he called every one of his master's debtors unto him, and said unto the first, 'How much do you owe unto my master?' And he said, 'A hundred measures of oil.' And he said unto him, 'Take your bill, and sit down quickly, and write fifty.' Then he said to another, 'And how much do you owe?' And he said, 'A hundred measures of wheat.' And he said unto him, 'Take your bill, and write eighty.'

11 "And the master commended the unjust steward, because he had done shrewdly: for the children of this world are in their generation more shrewd than the children of light. And I say unto you, Make to yourselves friends of the money of unrighteousness; that, when you fail, they may receive you into everlasting dwellings. He that is faithful in that which is least is faithful also in much: and he that is unjust in the least is unjust also in much.

12 "If therefore you have not been faithful in the unrighteous money, who will commit to your trust the true riches? And if you have not been faithful in that which is another man's, who shall give you that which is your own? No servant can serve two masters: for either he will hate the one, and love the other; or else he will hold to the one, and despise the other. You cannot serve God and money."

The Law and the Prophets
Luke 16:14-17

13 And the Pharisees also, who were covetous, heard all these things: and they scoffed at him. And he said unto them, "You are they which justify yourselves before men; but God knows your hearts: for that which is highly esteemed among men is abomination in the sight of God.

14 "The law and the prophets were until John: since that time the kingdom of God is preached, and every man presses into it. And it is easier for heaven and earth to pass, than one little stroke of the law to fail."

Divorce (repeated)
Luke 16:18

15 "Whosoever puts away his wife, and marries another, commits adultery: and whosoever marries her that is put away from her husband commits adultery."

Rich Man and Beggar Lazarus
Luke 16:19-31

16 "There was a certain rich man, which was clothed in purple and fine linen, and feasted sumptuously every day: and there was a certain beggar named Lazarus, which was laid at his gate, full of sores, and desiring to be fed with the crumbs which fell from the rich man's table: moreover the dogs came and licked his sores.

17 "And it came to pass, that the beggar died, and was carried by the angels into Abraham's bosom: the rich man also died, and was buried; and in Hades he lifted up his eyes, being in torments, and saw Abraham afar off, and Lazarus in his bosom. And he cried and said, 'Father Abraham, have

mercy on me, and send Lazarus, that he may dip the tip of his finger in 17
water, and cool my tongue; for I am tormented in this flame.'

"But Abraham said, 'Son, remember that you in your lifetime
received your good things, and likewise Lazarus evil things: but now he is 18
comforted, and you are tormented. And besides all this, between us and
you there is a great gulf fixed: so that they which would pass from here to
you cannot; neither can they pass to us, that would come from there.'

"Then he said, 'I beg you therefore, father, that you would send him to
my father's house: for I have five brethren; that he may testify unto them, 19
lest they also come into this place of torment.' Abraham said unto him,
'They have Moses and the prophets; let them hear them.' And he said, 'No,
father Abraham: but if one went unto them from the dead, they will repent.'

"And he said unto him, 'If they hear not Moses and the prophets, neither will they be persuaded, though one rose from the dead.'"   20

The Reward for Causing Sin
Luke 17:1-2

Then he said unto the disciples, "It is impossible that no causes to sin
will come: but woe unto him, through whom they come! It would be better 21
for him that a millstone were hung around his neck, and he cast into the sea,
than that he should cause one of these little ones to sin."

Forgiving Those Who Repent of Sin
Luke 17:3-4

"Take heed to yourselves: If your brother trespasses against you, 22
rebuke him; and if he repents, forgive him. And if he trespasses against you
seven times in a day, and seven times in a day turns again to you, saying, 'I
repent'; you shall forgive him."

The Power of Faith
Luke 17:5-6

And the apostles said unto the Lord, "Increase our faith." And the Lord 23
said, "If you had faith as a grain of mustard seed, you might say unto this
mulberry tree, 'Be plucked up by the root, and be planted in the sea'; and it
should obey you."

Duties of a Servant
Luke 17:7-10

"But which of you, having a servant plowing or feeding sheep, will say 24
unto him at once, when he is come from the field, 'Go and sit down to eat'?
And will not rather say unto him, 'Make ready with what I may dine, and
dress yourself, and serve me, till I have eaten and drunk; and afterward you
shall eat and drink'? Does he thank that servant because he did the things
that were commanded him? I think not. So likewise you, when you shall
have done all those things which are commanded you, say, 'We are unprofitable servants: we have done that which was our duty to do.'"

CHAPTER 35

Lazarus Raised From the Dead

"Lazarus Is Dead"
John 11:1-16

1   Now a certain man was sick, named Lazarus, of Bethany, the town of Mary and her sister Martha. (It was that Mary which anointed the Lord with ointment, and wiped his feet with her hair, whose brother Lazarus was sick.) Therefore his sisters sent unto him, saying, "Lord, behold, he whom you love is sick." When Jesus heard that, he said, "This sickness is not unto death, but for the glory of God, that the Son of God might be glorified thereby." Now Jesus loved Martha, and her sister, and Lazarus.

2   When he had heard therefore that he was sick, he stayed two days still in the same place where he was. Then after that he said to his disciples, "Let us go into Judea again." His disciples say unto him, "Rabbi, the Jews of late sought to stone you; and do you go there again?" Jesus answered, "Are there not twelve hours in the day? If any man walks in the day, he does not stumble, because he sees the light of this world. But if a man walks in the night, he stumbles, because there is no light in him."

3   These things said he: and after that he said unto them, "Our friend Lazarus sleeps; but I go, that I may awake him out of sleep." Then said his disciples, "Lord, if he sleeps, he shall get well." Howbeit Jesus spoke of his death: but they thought that he had spoken of taking of rest in sleep.

4   Then Jesus said unto them plainly, "Lazarus is dead. And I am glad for your sakes that I was not there, to the intent you may believe; nevertheless let us go unto him." Then said Thomas, which is called Didymus, unto his fellow disciples, "Let us also go, that we may die with him."

"I Am the Resurrection"
John 11:17-27

5   Then when Jesus came, he found that he had lain in the grave four days already. Now Bethany was near unto Jerusalem, about two miles away:

and many of the Jews came to Martha and Mary, to comfort them concern- 5
ing their brother. Then Martha, as soon as she heard that Jesus was coming,
went and met him: but Mary sat still in the house. Then Martha said unto
Jesus, "Lord, if you had been here, my brother would not have died. But I
know, that even now, whatsoever you will ask of God, God will give you."

Jesus said unto her, "Your brother shall rise again." Martha said 6
unto him, "I know that he shall rise again in the resurrection at the last
day." Jesus said unto her, "I am the
resurrection, and the life: he that
believes in me, though he were dead,
yet shall he live: and whosoever lives
and believes in me shall never die.
Do you believe this?" She said unto

> "I AM THE RESURRECTION, AND
> THE LIFE: HE THAT BELIEVES IN
> ME, THOUGH HE WERE DEAD,
> YET SHALL HE LIVE."

him, "Yes, Lord: I believe that you are the Christ, the Son of God, which
should come into the world."

Jesus Weeps
John 11:28-37

And when she had so said, she went her way, and called Mary her sis- 7
ter secretly, saying, "The Teacher is come, and calls for you." As soon as she
heard that, she arose quickly, and came unto him. Now Jesus was not yet
come into the town, but was in that place where Martha met him. The Jews
then which were with her in the house, and comforted her, when they saw
Mary, that she rose up hastily and went out, followed her, saying, "She goes
unto the grave to weep there."

Then when Mary was come where Jesus was, and saw him, she fell 8
down at his feet, saying unto him, "Lord, if you had been here, my brother
would not have died." When Jesus therefore saw her weeping, and the Jews
also weeping which came with her, he groaned in the spirit, and was troubled, and said, "Where have you laid him?" They said unto him, "Lord,
come and see." Jesus wept. Then said the Jews, "Behold how he loved him!"
And some of them said, "Could not this man, which opened the eyes of the
blind, have caused that even this man should not have died?"

Restoring Life to Lazarus
John 11:38-46

Jesus therefore again groaning in himself came to the grave. It was a 9
cave, and a stone lay upon it. Jesus said, "Take away the stone." Martha, the
sister of him that was dead, said unto him, "Lord, by this time he stinks: for
he has been dead four days." Jesus said unto her, "Said I not unto you, that,
if you would believe, you should see the glory of God?"

Then they took away the stone from the place where the dead was laid. 10
And Jesus lifted up his eyes, and said, "Father, I thank you that you have
heard me. And I knew that you hear me always: but because of the people
which stand by I said it, that they may believe that you have sent me." And

10 when he thus had spoken, he cried with a loud voice, "Lazarus, come forth." And he that was dead came forth, bound hand and foot with graveclothes: and his face was bound about with a cloth. Jesus said unto them, "Loose him, and let him go."

11 Then many of the Jews which came to Mary, and had seen the things which Jesus did, believed on him. But some of them went their ways to the Pharisees, and told them what things Jesus had done.

Priests Plot to Kill Jesus
John 11:47-54

12 Then gathered the chief priests and the Pharisees a council, and said, "What do we? for this man does many miracles. If we let him alone like this, all men will believe on him: and the Romans shall come and take away both our place and nation."

13 And one of them, named Caiaphas, being the high priest that same year, said unto them, "You know nothing at all, nor consider that it is expedient for us, that one man should die for the people, and that the whole nation not perish." And this spoke he not of himself: but being high priest that year, he prophesied that Jesus should die for that nation; and not for that nation only, but that also he should gather together in one the children of God that were scattered abroad. Then from that day forth they plotted together to put him to death.

14 Jesus therefore walked no more openly among the Jews; but went from there unto a country near to the wilderness, into a city called Ephraim, and there continued with his disciples.

PART 9

FINAL JOURNEY

Jesus began His last journey to Jerusalem knowing that betrayal and death awaited Him. Still He continued, teaching through healings and parables that the kingdom of heaven is not attained through intellect, riches, and pride—but rather that gratitude, childlike humility, and virtue embody the spiritual essence and power of Christ. Those who possess such qualities are assured that the kingdom of heaven is not a distant hope, but a very present reality here and now.

> THEN HE TOOK UNTO HIM THE TWELVE, AND
> SAID UNTO THEM, "BEHOLD, WE GO UP TO
> JERUSALEM, AND ALL THINGS THAT ARE WRITTEN
> BY THE PROPHETS CONCERNING THE SON OF
> MAN SHALL BE ACCOMPLISHED." (LUKE 18:31)

CHAPTER 36

LIVING THE KINGDOM LIFE

Jesus Cleanses Ten Lepers
Luke 17:11-19

1   And it came to pass, as he went to Jerusalem, that he passed through the midst of Samaria and Galilee. And as he entered into a certain village, there met him ten men that were lepers, which stood afar off: and they lifted up their voices, and said, "Jesus, Master, have mercy on us." And when he saw them, he said unto them, "Go show yourselves unto the priests." And it came to pass, that, as they went, they were cleansed.

2   And one of them, when he saw that he was healed, turned back, and with a loud voice glorified God, and fell down on his face at his feet, giving him thanks: and he was a Samaritan. And Jesus answering said, "Were there not ten cleansed? but where are the nine? There are not found that returned to give glory to God, except this foreigner." And he said unto him, "Arise, go your way: your faith has made you whole."

About the Coming of the Kingdom
Luke 17:20-37

3   And when he was asked of the Pharisees, when the kingdom of God should come, he answered them and said, "The kingdom of God comes not with observation: neither shall they say, 'Lo here!' or, 'lo there!' for, behold, the kingdom of God is within you."

4   And he said unto the disciples, "The days will come, when you shall desire to see one of the days of the Son of man, and you shall not see it. And they shall say to you, 'See here'; or, 'see there': go not after them, nor follow them. For as the lightning, that flashes out of the one part under heaven, shines unto the other part under heaven; so shall also the Son of man be in his day. But first he must suffer many things, and be rejected of this generation.

5   "And as it was in the days of Noah, so shall it be also in the days of the Son of man. They did eat, they drank, they married wives, they were

given in marriage, until the day that Noah entered into the ark, and the flood 5
came, and destroyed them all. Likewise also as it was in the days of Lot;
they did eat, they drank, they bought, they sold, they planted, they built; but
the same day that Lot went out of Sodom it rained fire and brimstone from
heaven, and destroyed them all.

"Even thus shall it be in the day when the Son of man is revealed. In 6
that day, he which shall be upon the housetop, and his stuff in the house, let
him not come down to take it away: and he that is in the field, let him likewise not return back. Remember Lot's wife. Whosoever shall seek to save
his life shall lose it; and whosoever shall lose his life shall preserve it.

"I tell you, in that night there shall be two men in one bed; the one 7
shall be taken, and the other shall be left. Two women shall be grinding
together; the one shall be taken, and the other left. Two men shall be in the
field; the one shall be taken, and the other left."

And they answered and said unto him, "Where, Lord?" And he said 8
unto them, "Wheresoever the body is, there will the eagles be gathered
together."

Parable of the Persistent Widow
Luke 18:1-8

And he spoke a parable unto them to this end, that men ought always 9
to pray, and not to lose heart; saying, "There was in a city a judge, which
feared not God, neither respected man:
and there was a widow in that city; and

> MEN OUGHT ALWAYS TO PRAY,
> AND NOT TO LOSE HEART.

she came unto him, saying, 'Avenge
me of my adversary.' And he would
not for a while: but afterward he said within himself, 'Though I fear not
God, nor respect man; yet because this widow troubles me, I will avenge
her, lest by her continual coming she wearies me.' "

And the Lord said, "Hear what the unjust judge says. And shall not 10
God avenge his own elect, which cry day and night unto him, though he
delays long with them? I tell you that he will avenge them speedily. Nevertheless when the Son of man comes, shall he find faith on the earth?"

Parable of the Self-Righteous Pharisee
Luke 18:9-14

And he spoke this parable unto certain which trusted in themselves 11
that they were righteous, and despised others: "Two men went up into the
temple to pray; the one a Pharisee, and the other a tax collector.

"The Pharisee stood and prayed thus with himself, 'God, I thank you, 12
that I am not as other men are, extortioners, unjust, adulterers, or even as
this tax collector. I fast twice in the week, I give tithes of all that I possess.'

"And the tax collector, standing afar off, would not lift up so much as 13
his eyes unto heaven, but struck down upon his breast, saying, 'God be merciful to me a sinner.' I tell you, this man went down to his house justified

13 rather than the other: for everyone that exalts himself shall be humbled; and he that humbles himself shall be exalted."

About Marriage and Divorce
Matthew 19:1-9; Mark 10:1-12

14 And it came to pass, that when Jesus had finished these sayings, he departed from Galilee, and came into the region of Judea beyond Jordan; and great multitudes followed him; and he healed them there: and, as he was accustomed, he taught them again.

15 And the Pharisees also came unto him, tempting him, and saying unto him, "Is it lawful for a man to put away his wife for every cause?" And he answered and said unto them, "What did Moses command you?" And they said, "Moses gave permission to *write a bill of divorcement, and to put her away.*" And Jesus answered and said unto them, "For the hardness of your heart he wrote you this precept."

16 And he answered and said unto them, "Have you not read, that God which made them at the beginning of the creation *made them male and female,* and said, '*For this cause shall a man leave father and mother, and shall cleave to his wife: and they two shall be one flesh*'? Therefore they are no more two, but one flesh. What therefore God has joined together, let not man put asunder."

> "WHAT THEREFORE GOD HAS JOINED TOGETHER, LET NOT MAN PUT ASUNDER."

17 They said unto him, "Why did Moses then give permission to *give a writing of divorcement, and to put her away?*" He said unto them, "Moses because of the hardness of your hearts permitted you to put away your wives: but from the beginning it was not so. And I say unto you, Whosoever shall put away his wife, except it be for fornication, and shall marry another, commits adultery: and whoever marries her which is put away does commit adultery."

18 And in the house his disciples asked him again of the same matter. And he said unto them, "Whosoever shall put away his wife, and marry another, commits adultery against her. And if a woman shall put away her husband, and be married to another, she commits adultery."

About Celibacy
Matthew 19:10-12

19 His disciples said unto him, "If the case of the man be so with his wife, it is not good to marry." But he said unto them, "All men cannot receive this saying, except they to whom it is given. For there are some eunuchs, which were so born from their mother's womb: and there are some eunuchs, which were made eunuchs of men: and there be eunuchs, which have made themselves eunuchs for the kingdom of heaven's sake. He that is able to receive it, let him receive it."

CHAPTER 37

Gaining Eternal Life

Blessing Little Children
Matthew 19:13-15; Mark 10:13-16; Luke 18:15-17

Then were there brought unto him little children, that he should put his 1
hands on them, and pray: and they brought unto him also infants, that he
would touch them: but when his disciples saw it, they rebuked those that
brought them. But when Jesus saw it, he was much displeased, and said unto
them, "Allow the little children to come unto me, and do not forbid them:
for of such is the kingdom of God." Jesus called them unto him, and said,
"Truly I say unto you, Whosoever shall not receive the kingdom of God as
a little child shall in no way enter therein." And he took them up in his arms,
put his hands upon them, and blessed them, and departed from there.

The Rich Ruler and Eternal Life
Matthew 19:16-22; Mark 10:17-22; Luke 18:18-23

And when he was gone forth into the road, behold, there came a cer- 2
tain ruler running, and kneeled to him, and asked him, saying, "Good
Teacher, what good thing shall I do, that I may inherit eternal life?" And
Jesus said unto him, "Why do you call me good? there is none good but one,
that is, God: but if you would enter into life, keep the commandments."

He said unto him, "Which?" Jesus said, "You know the command- 3
ments, '*You shall do no murder, You shall not commit adultery, You shall not
steal, You shall not bear false witness, Defraud not, Honor your father and
your mother: and, You shall love your neighbor as yourself.*'"

The young man answered and said unto him, "Teacher, all these have 4
I observed from my youth: what lack I yet?" Then Jesus beholding him
loved him, and said unto him, "If you would be perfect, one thing you lack:
go your way, sell whatsoever you have, and give to the poor, and you shall
have treasure in heaven: and come, take up the cross, and follow me."

5   But when the young man heard this, he was very sorrowful: for he was very rich. And he was sad at that saying, and went away grieved: for he had great possessions.

All Things Are Possible With God
Matthew 19:23-30; Mark 10:23-31; Luke 18:24-30

6   And when Jesus saw that he was very sorrowful, he looked round about, and said unto his disciples, "How hard shall they that have riches find it to enter into the kingdom of God!" And the disciples were astonished at his words. But Jesus answered again, and said unto them, "Children, how hard it is for them that trust in riches to enter into the kingdom of God! It is easier for a camel to go through the eye of a needle, than for a rich man to enter into the kingdom of God."

7   When his disciples heard it, they were astonished out of measure, saying among themselves, "Who then can be saved?" And Jesus looking upon them said, "With men it is impossible, but not with God: for the things which are impossible with men are possible with God. For with God all things are possible."

> "THE THINGS WHICH ARE IMPOSSIBLE WITH MEN ARE POSSIBLE WITH GOD."

8   Then Peter answered and said unto him, "Lo, we have left all, and have followed you; what shall we have therefore?" And Jesus said unto them, "Truly I say unto you, That you which have followed me, in the regeneration when the Son of man shall sit in the throne of his glory, you also shall sit upon twelve thrones, judging the twelve tribes of Israel.

9   And Jesus answered and said unto them, "Truly I say unto you, everyone that has left house, or brethren, or sisters, or father, or mother, or wife, or children, or lands, for the kingdom of God's sake, for my name's sake, and the gospel's, shall receive many times more in this present time a hundredfold, houses, and brethren, and sisters, and mothers, and children, and lands, with persecutions; and in the world to come, shall inherit life everlasting.

10   "But many that are first shall be last; and the last shall be first."

Parable of the Laborers
Matthew 20:1-16

11   "For the kingdom of heaven is like a man that is a landowner, which went out early in the morning to hire laborers into his vineyard. And when he had agreed with the laborers for a silver coin a day, he sent them into his vineyard.

12   "And he went out about the third hour, and saw others standing idle in the marketplace, and said unto them; 'Go also into the vineyard, and whatsoever is right I will give you.' And they went their way. Again he went out about the sixth and ninth hour, and did likewise.

"And about the eleventh hour he went out, and found others standing 13 idle, and said unto them, 'Why do you stand here all the day idle?' They said unto him, 'Because no man has hired us.' He said unto them, 'Go also into the vineyard; and whatsoever is right, that shall you receive.'

"So when evening was come, the owner of the vineyard said unto 14 his steward, 'Call the laborers, and give them their wages, beginning from the last unto the first.' And when they came that were hired about the eleventh hour, they received every man a silver coin. But when the first came, they supposed that they should have received more; and they likewise received every man a silver coin.

"And when they had received it, they murmured against the owner of 15 the land, saying, 'These last have labored but one hour, and you have made them equal unto us, which have borne the burden and heat of the day.' But he answered one of them, and said, 'Friend, I do you no wrong: did not you agree with me for a silver coin?'

" 'Take what is yours, and go your way: I will give unto this last, even 16 as unto you. Is it not lawful for me to do what I will with my own? Is your eye evil, because I am good?' So the last shall be first, and the first last: for many be called, but few chosen."

CHAPTER 38

Gaining Spiritual Life

Jesus Again Predicts His Death
Matthew 20:17-19; Mark 10:32-34; Luke 18:31-34

1   Then he took unto him the twelve, and said unto them, "Behold, we go up to Jerusalem, and all things that are written by the prophets concerning the Son of man shall be accomplished."

2   And they were on the road going up to Jerusalem; and Jesus went before them: and they were amazed; and as they followed, they were afraid. And he took again the twelve disciples apart on the road, and began to tell them what things should happen unto him, saying, "Behold, we go up to Jerusalem; and the Son of man shall be betrayed unto the chief priests, and unto the scribes; and they shall condemn him to death, and shall deliver him to the Gentiles: and they shall mock him, and shall scourge him, and shall spit upon him, and shall put him to death: and the third day he shall rise again."

3   And they understood none of these things: and this saying was hidden from them, neither knew they the things which were spoken.

Greatness in Serving
Matthew 20:20-28; Mark 10:35-45

4   Then came to him the mother of Zebedee's children with her sons, worshiping him, and desiring a certain thing of him. And he said unto her, "What will you?" She said unto him, "Grant that these my two sons may sit, the one on your right hand, and the other on the left, in your kingdom." And James and John, the sons of Zebedee, came unto him, saying, "Teacher, we would that you should do for us whatsoever we shall desire." And he said unto them, "What would you that I should do for you?" They said unto him, "Grant unto us that we may sit, one on your right hand, and the other on your left hand, in your glory."

5   But Jesus answered and said, "You know not what you ask. Are you able to drink of the cup that I shall drink of, and to be baptized with the baptism

that I am baptized with?" And they said unto him, "We are able." And Jesus 5 said unto them, "You shall drink indeed of my cup, and be baptized with the baptism that I am baptized with: but to sit on my right hand, and on my left hand, is not mine to give, but it shall be given to them for whom it is prepared of my Father."

And when the ten heard it, they were moved with indignation against 6 the two brethren, James and John. But Jesus called them unto him, and said, "You know that they which are accounted to rule over the Gentiles exercise dominance over them, and they that are great exercise authority upon them.

"But it shall not be so among you: but whosoever will be great among you, let him be your minister; and whosoever will be chief among you, let him be your servant: and 7

> "EVEN THE SON OF MAN CAME NOT TO BE MINISTERED UNTO, BUT TO MINISTER."

whosoever of you will be the first, shall be servant of all. For even the Son of man came not to be ministered unto, but to minister, and to give his life a ransom for many."

Healing the Blind at Jericho
Matthew 20:29-34; Mark 10:46-52; Luke 18:35-43

And it came to pass, that as he was come near unto Jericho, a certain 8 blind man, blind Bartimaeus, the son of Timaeus, sat by the wayside begging: and hearing the multitude pass by, he asked what it meant. And they told him, that Jesus of Nazareth passes by. And when he heard that it was Jesus of Nazareth, he began to cry out, and say, "Jesus, Son of David, have mercy on me." And they which went before warned him, that he should hold his peace: but he cried so much the more, "Son of David, have mercy on me."

And Jesus stood still, and commanded him to be called. And they 9 called the blind man, saying unto him, "Be of good cheer, rise; he calls you." And he, casting away his garment, rose, and came to Jesus. And Jesus answered and said unto him, "What will you that I should do unto you?" The blind man said unto him, "Rabboni, that I might receive my sight." And Jesus said unto him, "Receive your sight: go your way; your faith has made you whole." And immediately he received his sight, and followed Jesus on the road, glorifying God: and all the people, when they saw it, gave praise unto God.

And as they departed from Jericho, a great multitude followed him. 10 And, behold, two blind men sitting by the wayside, when they heard that Jesus passed by, cried out, saying, "Have mercy on us, O Lord, Son of David." And the multitude warned them, because they should hold their peace: but they cried the more, saying, "Have mercy on us, O Lord, Son of David." And Jesus stood still, and called them, and said, "What will you that I shall do unto you?" They said unto him, "Lord, that our eyes may be opened." So Jesus had compassion on them, and touched their eyes: and immediately their eyes received sight, and they followed him.

A Tax Collector Finds Salvation
Luke 19:1-10

11   And Jesus entered and passed through Jericho. And, behold, there was a man named Zacchaeus, which was the chief among the tax collectors, and he was rich. And he sought to see Jesus who he was; and could not for the crowd, because he was little of stature. And he ran ahead, and climbed up into a sycamore tree to see him: for he was to pass that way.

12   And when Jesus came to the place, he looked up, and saw him, and said unto him, "Zacchaeus, make haste, and come down; for today I must stay at your house." And he made haste, and came down, and received him joyfully. And when they saw it, they all murmured, saying, "That he was gone to be guest with a man that is a sinner."

13   And Zacchaeus stood, and said unto the Lord; "Behold, Lord, the half of my goods I give to the poor; and if I have taken anything from

> "THE SON OF MAN IS COME TO SEEK AND TO SAVE THAT WHICH WAS LOST."

any man by false accusation, I restore him fourfold." And Jesus said unto him, "This day is salvation come to this house, forasmuch as he also is a son of Abraham. For the Son of man is come to seek and to save that which was lost."

Parable of Good Stewardship
Luke 19:11-28

14   And as they heard these things, he added and spoke a parable, because he was near to Jerusalem, and because they thought that the kingdom of God should immediately appear. He said therefore, "A certain nobleman went into a far country to receive for himself a kingdom, and to return. And he called his ten servants, and delivered them ten gold coins, and said unto them, 'Conduct business till I come.' But his citizens hated him, and sent a message after him, saying, 'We will not have this man to reign over us.'

15   "And it came to pass, that when he was returned, having received the kingdom, then he commanded these servants to be called unto him, to whom he had given the money, that he might know how much every man had gained by trading. Then came the first, saying, 'Master, your gold coin has gained ten gold coins.' And he said unto him, 'Well, good servant: because you have been faithful in a very little, you have authority over ten cities.'

16   "And the second came, saying, 'Master, your gold coin has gained five gold coins.' And he said likewise to him, 'Be you also over five cities.'

17   "And another came, saying, 'Master, behold, here is your gold coin, which I have kept laid up in a cloth: for I feared you, because you are a stern man: you take up that you did not lay down, and reap that you did not sow.' And he said unto him, 'Out of your own mouth will I judge you, you wicked servant. You knew that I was a stern man, taking up that I did not lay down, and reaping that I did not sow: why then did you not give my money into the bank, that at my coming I might have collected my own with interest?'

"And he said unto them that stood by, 'Take from him the gold coin, 18
and give it to him that has ten gold coins.' (And they said unto him, 'Master, he has ten gold coins.') 'For I say unto you, That unto everyone which has shall be given; and from him that has not, even that he has shall be taken away from him. But those my enemies, which would not that I should reign over them, bring here, and slay them before me.' "

And when he had thus spoken, he went ahead, ascending up to 19
Jerusalem.

Priests Plot to Kill Jesus
John 11:55-57

And the Jews' passover was near at hand: and many went out of the 20
country up to Jerusalem before the passover, to purify themselves. Then they searched for Jesus, and spoke among themselves, as they stood in the temple, "What do you think, that he will not come to the feast?" Now both the chief priests and the Pharisees had given a commandment, that, if any man knew where he were, he should show it, that they might take him.

Priests Plot to Kill Lazarus
John 12:1, 9-11

Then Jesus six days before the passover came to Bethany, where 21
Lazarus was which had been dead, whom he raised from the dead.

Many people of the Jews therefore knew that he was there: and they 22
came not for Jesus' sake only, but that they might see Lazarus also, whom he had raised from the dead. But the chief priests consulted that they might put Lazarus also to death; because by reason of him many of the Jews went away, and believed on Jesus.

PART 10

LAST SUPPER

Jesus' life had fulfilled the prophecies recorded in the Old Testament, and He had often described the precise manner of His death. His actions proved that He was most assuredly the Christ. During His final journey to Jerusalem, He instructed those who followed Him, and all that would follow thereafter, to be vigilant in their adherence to the Word, even unto the end of days, for in this way only could they hope to enter into the kingdom of heaven. In the twilight of a glorious mission with shadows fast falling around, Jesus broke bread with His disciples and washed their feet, knowing He would soon be betrayed into the hands of sinners for thirty pieces of silver.

"IN MY FATHER'S HOUSE ARE MANY MANSIONS: IF
IT WERE NOT SO, I WOULD HAVE TOLD YOU. I GO
TO PREPARE A PLACE FOR YOU." (JOHN 14:2)

CHAPTER 39

THE FINAL ENTRY

Triumphal Entry of Jesus
Matthew 21:1-9; Mark 11:1-10; Luke 19:29-40; John 12:12-19

On the next day many people that were come to the feast, when they 1
heard that Jesus was coming to Jerusalem, took branches of palm trees, and
went forth to meet him, and cried, "Hosanna: *Blessed is the King of Israel
that comes in the name of the Lord.*"

And it came to pass, when they came near to Jerusalem, unto Beth- 2
phage and Bethany, at the mount called the mount of Olives, he sent forth
two of his disciples, saying unto them, "Go your way into the village opposite you: and as soon as you be entered into it, you shall find a donkey tied,
and a colt with it, whereon yet never man sat: loose them, and bring them
unto me. And if any man says unto you, 'Why do you this?' you shall say,
'The Lord has need of them'; and straightway he will send them here."

All this was done, that it might be fulfilled which was spoken by the 3
prophet, saying, "*Tell the daughter of Zion, Behold, your King comes unto
you, meek, and sitting upon a donkey, and a colt the foal of a donkey.*" And
the disciples that were sent went their way, and did as Jesus commanded
them, and found the colt tied by the door outside in a place where two roads
met, even as he had said unto them. And as they were loosing the colt, the
owners thereof said unto them, "Why do you loose the colt?" And they said
unto them, "The Lord has need of it," even as Jesus had commanded: and
they let them go. And they brought the donkey, and the colt to Jesus, and
put on them their clothes, and they set Jesus thereon.

And as he went, a very great multitude spread their clothes on the 4
road; and others cut down branches from the trees, and spread them on the
road. And the multitudes that went before, and that followed, cried, saying,
"Hosanna to the Son of David: *Blessed is he that comes in the name of the
Lord*; Hosanna in the highest. Blessed be the kingdom of our father David,
that comes in the name of the Lord: Hosanna in the highest."

5 And when he was come near, even now at the descent of the mount of Olives, the whole multitude of the disciples began to rejoice and praise God with a loud voice for all the mighty works that they had seen; saying, "Blessed be the King that comes in the name of the Lord: peace in heaven, and glory in the highest."

6 And some of the Pharisees from among the multitude said unto him, "Teacher, rebuke your disciples." And he answered and said unto them, "I tell you that, if these should hold their peace, the stones would immediately cry out."

7 These things his disciples did not understand at the first: but when Jesus was glorified, then they remembered that these things were written of him, and that they had done these things unto him.

8 The people therefore that were with him when he called Lazarus out of his grave, and raised him from the dead, bore record. For this cause the people also met him, because they heard that he had done this miracle.

9 The Pharisees therefore said among themselves, "Do you perceive how you prevail nothing? behold, the world is gone after him."

Jesus Laments Jerusalem's Fate
Luke 19:41-44

10 And when he was come near, he beheld the city, and wept over it, saying, "If you had known, even you, at least in this your day, the things which belong unto your peace! but now they are hidden from your eyes. For the days shall come upon you, that your enemies shall cast a trench around you, and circle you round, and close you in on every side, and shall lay you even with the ground, and your children within you; and they shall not leave in you one stone upon another; because you knew not the time of your visitation."

Jesus Enters Jerusalem
Matthew 21:10-11; Mark 11:11

11 And when Jesus entered into Jerusalem, all the city was moved, saying, "Who is this?" And the multitude said, "This is Jesus the prophet of Nazareth of Galilee." And Jesus entered into the temple: and when he had looked round about upon all things, and now the evening hour was come, he went out unto Bethany with the twelve.

Jesus Condemns Barren Fig Tree
Matthew 21:18-19; Mark 11:12-14

12 Now in the morning as he returned into the city, when they were come from Bethany, he was hungry: and seeing a fig tree afar off having leaves, he came to it, if perhaps he might find anything thereon: and when he came to it, he found nothing but leaves; for the time of figs was not yet. And Jesus said unto it, "Let no fruit grow on you henceforth for ever." And at once the fig tree withered away. And Jesus answered and said unto it, "No man shall eat fruit of you hereafter for ever." And his disciples heard it.

Jesus Again Clears the Temple
Matthew 21:12-17; Mark 11:15-19; Luke 19:45-48

And they came to Jerusalem: and Jesus went into the temple of God, 13 and cast out all them that sold and bought in the temple, and overturned the tables of the money changers, and the seats of them that sold doves; and would not allow that any man should carry any vessel through the temple. And he taught, saying unto them, "Is it not written, *'My house shall be called of all nations the house of prayer'*? but you have made it *'a den of thieves.'*"

And the blind and the lame came to him in the temple; and he healed 14 them. And when the chief priests and scribes saw the wonderful things that he did, and the children crying in the temple, and saying, "Hosanna to the Son of David"; they were very displeased, and said unto him, "Do you hear what these say?" And Jesus said unto them, "Yes; have you never read, *'Out of the mouth of babies and nursing infants you have perfected praise'*?" And the scribes and chief priests heard it, and sought how they might destroy him: for they feared him, because all the people were astonished at his doctrine.

And he taught daily in the temple. But the chief priests and the scribes 15 and the leaders of the people sought to destroy him, and could not find what they might do: for all the people were very attentive to hear him.

And when evening was come, he left them, and went out of the city 16 into Bethany; and he lodged there.

CHAPTER 40

THE FINAL LESSONS

Lesson From Withered Fig Tree
Matthew 21:20-22; Mark 11:20-24

1   And in the morning, as they passed by, they saw the fig tree dried up from the roots, and when the disciples saw it, they marveled, saying, "How soon is the fig tree withered away!" And Peter calling to remembrance said unto him, "Rabbi, behold, the fig tree which you cursed is withered away."

2   And Jesus answering said unto them, "Have faith in God. For truly I say unto you, If you have faith, you shall not only do this which is done to the fig tree, but also if you shall say unto this mountain, 'Be removed, and be cast into the sea'; and shall not doubt in his heart, but shall believe that those things which he says shall come to pass; he shall have whatsoever he says. Therefore I say unto you, Whatsoever things you desire, when you pray, believe that you receive them, and you shall have them."

"When You Stand Praying, Forgive"
Mark 11:25-26

3   "And when you stand praying, forgive, if you have anything against any: that your Father also which is in heaven may forgive you your trespasses. But if you do not forgive, neither will your Father which is in heaven forgive your trespasses."

Authority of Jesus Questioned
Matthew 21:23-27; Mark 11:27-33; Luke 20:1-8

4   And they came again to Jerusalem: and it came to pass, that on one of those days, as he taught the people in the temple, and preached the gospel, the chief priests and the scribes came upon him with the elders, as he was walking in the temple: and spoke unto him, saying, "Tell us, by what authority do you these things? and who gave you this authority to do these things?"

And Jesus answered and said unto them, "I also will ask of you one 5
question, which if you answer me, I will tell you by what authority I do
these things. The baptism of John, from where was it? from heaven, or of
men?" And they reasoned with themselves, saying, "If we shall say, 'From
heaven'; he will say unto us, 'Why then did you not believe him?' But if we
shall say, 'Of men'; we fear the people; all the people will stone us: for all
hold John as a prophet."

And they answered and said unto Jesus, "We cannot tell from where it 6
was." And Jesus answering said unto them, "Neither do I tell you by what
authority I do these things."

Parable of the Two Sons
Matthew 21:28-32

And he began to speak unto them by parables. "But what do you 7
think? A certain man had two sons; and he came to the first, and said, 'Son,
go work today in my vineyard.' He answered and said, 'I will not': but
afterward he repented, and went. And he came to the second, and said likewise. And he answered and said, 'I go, sir': and did not go.

"Which of these two did the will of his father?" They said unto him, 8
"The first." Jesus said unto them, "Truly I say unto you, That the tax collectors and the harlots go into the kingdom of God before you. For John
came unto you in the way of righteousness, and you did not believe him: but
the tax collectors and the harlots believed him: and you, when you had seen
it, did not repent afterward, that you might believe him.

Parable of the Vinedressers
Matthew 21:33-46; Mark 12:1-12; Luke 20:9-19

"Hear another parable: There was a certain landowner, which *planted* 9
a vineyard, and set a hedge around it, and dug a place for the winepress,
and built a tower, and rented it out to vinedressers, and went into a far country for a long time. And at the season when the time of the fruit drew near,
he sent a servant to the vinedressers, that they should give him of the fruit
of the vineyard. And they caught him, and beat him, and sent him away
empty.

"And again he sent unto them another servant: and they beat him also, 10
and at him they cast stones, and wounded him in the head, and sent him
away empty. And again he sent a third: and him they killed, and many others; beating some, and killing some.

"Then said the owner of the vineyard, 'What shall I do? I will send my 11
beloved son: it may be they will respect him when they see him.' Having yet
therefore one son, his beloved, he sent him also last unto them, saying,
'They will respect my son.' But when the vinedressers saw him, they reasoned among themselves, saying, 'This is the heir: come, let us kill him,
that the inheritance may be ours.'

12   "So they caught him, and cast him out of the vineyard, and killed him. When the owner therefore of the vineyard comes, what will he do unto these vinedressers?" They said unto him, "He will miserably destroy those wicked men, and will rent out his vineyard unto other vinedressers, which shall render him the fruits in their seasons."

13   "What shall therefore the owner of the vineyard do? he will come and destroy the vinedressers, and will give the vineyard unto others." And when they heard it, they said, "God forbid."

14   And Jesus beheld them, and said, "What is this then that is written, did you never read in the scriptures, '*The stone which the builders rejected, the same is become the head of the cornerstone: this is the Lord's doing, and it is marvelous in our eyes'*?

15   "Therefore say I unto you, The kingdom of God shall be taken from you, and given to a nation bringing forth the fruits thereof. And whosoever shall fall on this stone shall be broken: but on whomsoever it shall fall, it will grind him to powder."

16   And when the chief priests and Pharisees had heard his parables, they perceived that he spoke of them. And they and the scribes the same hour sought to lay hands on him; and they feared the people, because they took him for a prophet: and they left him, and went their way.

CHAPTER 41

WISE ANSWERS TO SLY QUESTIONS

Parable of the Wedding Feast
Matthew 22:1-14

And Jesus answered and spoke unto them again by parables, and said, 1
"The kingdom of heaven is like a certain king, which made a marriage for
his son, and sent forth his servants to call them that were invited to the wedding: and they would not come. Again, he sent forth other servants, saying,
'Tell them which are invited, "Behold, I have prepared my dinner: my oxen
and my fatlings are killed, and all things are ready: come unto the marriage." '

"But they made light of it, and went their ways, one to his farm, another 2
to his business: and the remaining ones took his servants, and treated them
spitefully, and killed them. But when the king heard thereof, he was angry:
and he sent forth his armies, and destroyed those murderers, and burned up
their city.

"Then he said to his servants, 'The wedding is ready, but they which 3
were invited were not worthy. Go therefore into the highways, and as many
as you shall find, invite to the marriage.' So those servants went out into the
highways, and gathered together all as many as they found, both bad and
good: and the wedding was filled with guests.

"And when the king came in to see the guests, he saw there a man 4
which did not have on a wedding garment: and he said unto him, 'Friend,
how came you in here not having a wedding garment?' And he was speechless. Then the king said to the servants, 'Bind him hand and foot, and take
him away, and cast him into outer darkness; there shall be weeping and
gnashing of teeth.' For many are called, but few are chosen."

Paying Taxes to Caesar
Matthew 22:15-22; Mark 12:13-17; Luke 20:20-26

Then the Pharisees went, and plotted how they might entangle him in 5
his talk. And they watched him, and sent forth spies, which should pretend

5 themselves just men, that they might catch him in his words, that so they might deliver him unto the power and authority of the governor. And they sent out unto him their disciples with the Herodians, saying, "Teacher, we know that you are true, and teach the way of God in truth, neither do you favor any man: for you do not regard the person of men. Tell us therefore, What do you think? Is it lawful to give tribute unto Caesar, or not?

6 "Shall we give, or shall we not give?" But Jesus perceived their wickedness, knowing their hypocrisy, said unto them, "Why do you tempt me, you hypocrites? Show me the tribute money. Bring me a silver coin, that I may see it." And they brought unto him a silver coin. "Whose image and superscription has it?" They answered and said, "Caesar's." And Jesus answering said unto them, "Render to Caesar the things that are Caesar's, and to God the things that are God's." And they could not take hold of his words before the people: and they marveled at his answer, and held their peace, and left him, and went their way.

> "RENDER TO CAESAR THE THINGS THAT ARE CAESAR'S, AND TO GOD THE THINGS THAT ARE GOD'S."

No Marriage in the Resurrection
Matthew 22:23-33; Mark 12:18-27; Luke 20:27-40

7 The same day came to him certain of the Sadducees, which deny that there is any resurrection; and they asked him, saying, "Teacher, Moses wrote unto us, '*If any man's brother dies, having a wife, and he dies without children, that his brother should marry his wife, and raise up seed unto his brother.*'

8 "Now there were with us seven brethren: and the first took a wife, and died without children, left his wife unto his brother. And the second took her as wife, and he died childless. And the third took her; and in like manner the seven also: and they left no children, and died. And last of all the woman died also.

9 "Therefore in the resurrection, when they shall rise, whose wife shall she be of them? for the seven had her as wife." Jesus answered and said unto them, "You do err, not knowing the scriptures, nor the power of God. For in the resurrection they neither marry, nor are given in marriage, but are as the angels of God in heaven. The children of this world marry, and are given in marriage: but they which shall be accounted worthy to obtain that world, and the resurrection from the dead, neither marry, nor are given in marriage: neither can they die anymore: but are as the angels which are in heaven; and are the children of God, being the children of the resurrection.

10 "But as concerning the resurrection of the dead, have you not read in the book of Moses, how in the bush God spoke unto him, saying, '*I am the God of Abraham, and the God of Isaac, and the God of Jacob*'? He is not the God of the dead, but the God of the living: for all live unto him: you therefore do greatly err." And when the multitude heard this, they were astonished at his doctrine.

Then certain of the scribes answering said, "Teacher, you have well 11 said." And after that they dared not ask him any question at all.

First and Greatest Commandment
Matthew 22:34-40; Mark 12:28-34

But when the Pharisees had heard that he had put the Sadducees to 12 silence, they were gathered together. Then one of them, which was a scribe, came, and having heard them reasoning together, and perceiving that he had answered them well, asked him a question, tempting him, and saying, "Teacher, which is the great commandment in the law? which is the first commandment of all?" And Jesus answered him, "The first of all the commandments is, '*Hear, O Israel; The Lord our God is one Lord: and You shall love the Lord your God with all your heart, and with all your soul, and with all your mind, and with all your strength.*' This is the first and great commandment.

"And the second is like it, namely this, '*You shall love your neighbor 13 as yourself.*' There is no other commandment greater than these. On these two commandments hang all the law and the prophets."

And the scribe said unto him, "Well, Teacher, you have said the truth: 14 *for there is one God*; and *there is no other but he*: and to *love him with all the heart, and with all the understanding, and with all the soul, and with all the strength*, and to *love his neighbor as himself*, is more than all the whole of burnt offerings and sacrifices."

And when Jesus saw that he answered wisely, he said unto him, "You 15 are not far from the kingdom of God." And no man after that dared ask him any question.

Whose Son Is Christ?
Matthew 22:41-46; Mark 12:35-37; Luke 20:41-44

While the Pharisees were gathered together, Jesus asked them, saying, 16 "What do you think of Christ? whose son is he?" They said unto him, "The Son of David." He said unto them, "How then does David in spirit call him 'Lord'?" And Jesus answered and said unto them, while he taught in the temple, "How said the scribes that Christ is the Son of David? for David himself said by the Holy Ghost in the book of Psalms, '*The Lord said unto my Lord, "Sit on my right hand, till I make your enemies your footstool."* '

"If David himself therefore calls him 'Lord,' how is he then his son?" 17 And no man was able to answer him a word, neither dared any man from that day forth ask him any more questions. And the common people heard him gladly.

CHAPTER 42

Blunt Words to the Hypocrites

Beware of Scribes and Pharisees
Matthew 23:1-12; Mark 12:38-40; Luke 20:45-47

1   Then in the audience of all the people he said unto his disciples in his doctrine, "Beware of the scribes, which love to go in long robes, and love greetings in the marketplaces, and the chief seats in the synagogues, and the uppermost rooms at feasts; which devour widows' houses, and for a show make long prayers: the same shall receive greater condemnation."

2   Then Jesus spoke to the multitude, and to his disciples, saying, "The scribes and the Pharisees sit in Moses' seat: all therefore whatsoever they tell you observe, that observe and do; but do not according to their works: for they say, and do not. For they bind heavy burdens grievous to be borne, and lay them on men's shoulders; but they themselves will not move them with one of their fingers. But all their works they do to be seen of men: they make broad their phylacteries (scripture boxes), and enlarge the borders of their garments, and love the uppermost rooms at feasts, and the chief seats in the synagogues, and greetings in the marketplaces, and to be called of men, 'Rabbi, Rabbi.'

3   "But be not called 'Rabbi': for one is your Teacher, even Christ; and all you are brethren. And call no man your father upon the earth: for one is your Father, which is in heaven. Neither be called teachers: for one is your Teacher, even Christ. But he that is greatest among you shall be your servant. And whosoever shall exalt himself shall be humbled; and he that shall humble himself shall be exalted."

Scribes and Pharisees: Hypocrites
Matthew 23:13-36

4   "But woe unto you, scribes and Pharisees, hypocrites! for you shut up the kingdom of heaven against men: for you neither go in yourselves, neither allow them that are entering to go in.

"Woe unto you, scribes and Pharisees, hypocrites! for you devour wid- 5 ows' houses, and for a pretense make long prayers: therefore you shall receive the greater condemnation.

"Woe unto you, scribes and Pharisees, hypocrites! for you journey sea 6 and land to make one convert, and when he is made, you make him twofold more the child of hell than yourselves.

"Woe unto you, you blind guides, which say, 'Whosoever shall swear 7 by the temple, it is nothing; but whosoever shall swear by the gold of the temple, he is a debtor!' You fools and blind: for which is greater, the gold, or the temple that sanctifies the gold? And, 'Whosoever shall swear by the altar, it is nothing; but whosoever swears by the gift that is upon it, he is bound.' You fools and blind: for which is greater, the gift, or the altar that sanctifies the gift? Whoever therefore shall swear by the altar, swears by it, and by all things thereon. And whoever shall swear by the temple, swears by it, and by him that dwells therein. And he that shall swear by heaven, swears by the throne of God, and by him that sits thereon.

"Woe unto you, scribes and Pharisees, hypocrites! for you pay tithe of 8 mint and anise and cummin, and have omitted the weightier matters of the law, judgment, mercy, and faith: these ought you to have done, and not to leave the others undone. You blind guides, which strain out a gnat, and swallow a camel.

"Woe unto you, scribes and Pharisees, hypocrites! for you make clean 9 the outside of the cup and of the platter, but inside they are full of extortion and excess. You blind Pharisee, cleanse first that which is inside the cup and platter, that the outside of them may be clean also.

"Woe unto you, scribes and Pharisees, hypocrites! for you are like 10 whitewashed tombs, which indeed appear beautiful outwardly, but are inside full of dead men's bones, and of all uncleanness. Even so you also outwardly appear righteous unto men, but inside you are full of hypocrisy and iniquity.

"Woe unto you, scribes and Pharisees, hypocrites! because you build 11 the tombs of the prophets, and decorate the monuments of the righteous, and say, 'If we had been in the days of our fathers, we would not have been partakers with them in the blood of the prophets.' Therefore you be witnesses unto yourselves, that you are the children of them which killed the prophets. Fill up then the measure of your fathers. You serpents, you generation of vipers, how can you escape the condemnation of hell?

"Therefore, behold, I send unto you prophets, and wise men, and 12 scribes: and some of them you shall kill and crucify; and some of them shall you scourge in your synagogues, and persecute them from city to city: that upon you may come all the righteous blood shed upon the earth, from the blood of righteous Abel unto the blood of Zacharias son of Barachiah, whom you slew between the temple and the altar.

"Truly I say unto you, All these things shall come upon this generation." 13

Jesus Again Laments for Jerusalem
Matthew 23:37-39

14   "O Jerusalem, Jerusalem, you that kill the prophets, and stone them which are sent unto you, how often would I have gathered your children together, even as a hen gathers her chickens under her wings, and you would not! Behold, your house is left unto you desolate. For I say unto you, You shall not see me henceforth, till you shall say, 'Blessed is he that comes in the name of the Lord.'"

The Poor Widow's Two-Coin Offering
Mark 12:41-44; Luke 21:1-4

15   And Jesus sat opposite the treasury, and beheld how the people cast money into the treasury: and many that were rich cast in much. And there came a certain poor widow, and she threw in two small copper coins, which make a copper coin.

16   And he called unto him his disciples, and said unto them, "Truly I say unto you, That this poor widow has cast more in, than all they which have cast into the treasury: for all these have of their abundance cast in unto the offerings of God: but she of her poverty has cast in all the livelihood that she had, even all her livelihood."

Jesus Invites All Men to Serve Him
John 12:20-26

17   And there were certain Greeks among them that came up to worship at the feast: the same came therefore to Philip, which was of Bethsaida of Galilee, and desired him, saying, "Sir, we would see Jesus." Philip came and told Andrew: and in turn Andrew and Philip told Jesus.

18   And Jesus answered them, saying, "The hour is come, that the Son of man should be glorified. Truly, truly, I say unto you, Except a grain of wheat falls into the ground and dies, it remains alone: but if it dies, it brings forth much fruit. He that loves his life shall lose it; and he that hates his life in this world shall keep it unto life eternal.

> "HE THAT LOVES HIS LIFE SHALL LOSE IT."

19   "If any man serves me, let him follow me; and where I am, there shall also my servant be: if any man serves me, him will my Father honor."

"Now Is the Judgment of This World"
John 12:27-36

20   "Now is my soul troubled; and what shall I say? 'Father, save me from this hour': but for this cause came I unto this hour. Father, glorify your name." Then came there a voice from heaven, saying, "I have both glorified it, and will glorify it again."

21   The people therefore, that stood by, and heard it, said that it thundered: others said, "An angel spoke to him." Jesus answered and said, "This voice

came not because of me, but for your sakes. Now is the judgment of this 21
world: now shall the prince of this world be cast out. And I, if I be lifted up
from the earth, will draw all men unto me." This he said, signifying what
death he should die.

The people answered him, "We have heard out of the law that Christ 22
remains for ever: and how do you say, 'The Son of man must be lifted up'?
who is this Son of man?" Then Jesus said unto them, "Yet a little while is
the light with you. Walk while you have the light, lest darkness come upon
you: for he that walks in darkness does not know where he goes. While you
have light, believe in the light, that you may be the children of light." These
things spoke Jesus, and departed, and did hide himself from them.

As a Light Into the World
John 12:37-50

But though he had done so many miracles before them, yet they had 23
not believed on him: that the saying of Isaiah the prophet might be fulfilled,
which he spoke, *"Lord, who has believed our report? and to whom has the
arm of the Lord been revealed?"* Therefore they could not believe, because
Isaiah said again, *"He has blinded their eyes, and hardened their hearts;
that they should not see with their eyes, nor understand with their hearts,
and be converted, and I should heal them."*

These things said Isaiah, when he saw his glory, and spoke of him. 24
Nevertheless among the chief rulers also many believed on him; but
because of the Pharisees they did not confess him, lest they should be put
out of the synagogue: for they loved the praise of men more than the praise
of God.

Jesus cried and said, "He that believes on me, believes not on me, but 25
on him that sent me. And he that sees
me sees him that sent me. I am come
a light into the world, that whosoever
believes on me should not abide in
darkness. And if any man hears my
words, and does not believe, I do not
judge him: for I came not to judge the world, but to save the world.

> "I AM COME A LIGHT INTO THE
> WORLD, THAT WHOSOEVER
> BELIEVES ON ME SHOULD NOT
> ABIDE IN DARKNESS."

"He that rejects me, and receives not my words, has one that judges 26
him: the word that I have spoken, the same shall judge him in the last day.
For I have not spoken of myself; but the Father which sent me, he gave me
a commandment, what I should say, and what I should speak. And I know
that his commandment is life everlasting: whatsoever I speak therefore,
even as the Father said unto me, so I speak."

CHAPTER 43

THE END TIMES

Signs: The End of the Age
Matthew 24:1-14; Mark 13:1-13; Luke 21:5-19

1   And as he went out of the temple, one of his disciples said unto him, "Teacher, see what manner of stones and what buildings are here!" And Jesus answering said unto him, "Do you see these great buildings? there shall not be left one stone upon another, that shall not be thrown down." And Jesus went out, and departed from the temple: and his disciples came to him to show him the buildings of the temple. And as some spoke of the temple, how it was adorned with beautiful stones and gifts, he said unto them, "Do you not see all these things? truly I say unto you, As for these things which you behold, the days will come, in which there shall not be left one stone upon another, that shall not be thrown down."

2   And as he sat upon the Mount of Olives opposite the temple, Peter and James and John and Andrew asked him privately, "Tell us, when shall these things be? and what shall be the sign when all these things shall come to pass?" And they asked him, saying, "Teacher, but what shall be the sign of your coming, and of the end of the world?"

3   And Jesus answering them began to say, "Take heed that no man deceives you. For many shall come in my name, saying, 'I am Christ'; and shall deceive many. And 'the time draws near': go not therefore after them. And you shall hear of wars and rumors of wars: see that you be not troubled: for all these things must first come to pass; but the end is not yet, is not immediately.

4   "For nation shall rise against nation, and kingdom against kingdom: and there shall be great earthquakes in various places, and there shall be famines, and pestilences; and fearful sights and great signs shall there be from heaven. All these are the beginning of sorrows.

"But before all these, take heed to yourselves: for they shall lay their 5
hands on you, and persecute you, and shall kill you: delivering you up to
councils and into prisons. And in the synagogues you shall be beaten: and
you shall be brought before rulers and kings for my sake, for a testimony
against them. And the gospel must first be published among all nations.
And you shall be hated of all nations for my name's sake. And it shall turn
to you for a testimony.

"But when they shall lead you, and deliver you up, settle it in your 6
hearts, worry not beforehand what you
shall speak, neither premeditate what
you shall answer: for I will give you a
mouth and wisdom, which all your
adversaries shall not be able to contra-
dict nor resist: but whatsoever shall be given you in that hour, that speak:
for it is not you that speak, but the Holy Ghost.

> "I WILL GIVE YOU A MOUTH AND WISDOM."

"And then shall many fall away, and shall betray one another, and shall 7
hate one another. And many false
prophets shall rise, and shall deceive
many. And because iniquity shall
abound, the love of many shall grow
cold. And you shall be betrayed both
by parents, and brethren, and relatives,
and friends; and some of you shall
they cause to be put to death. Now the brother shall betray the brother to
death, and the father the son; and children shall rise up against their parents,
and shall cause them to be put to death.

> "THIS GOSPEL OF THE KING-DOM SHALL BE PREACHED IN ALL THE WORLD FOR A WIT-NESS UNTO ALL NATIONS."

"And you shall be hated of all men for my name's sake: but he that 8
shall endure unto the end, the same shall be saved. But there shall not a hair
of your head perish. In your patience you possess your souls. And this
gospel of the kingdom shall be preached in all the world for a witness unto
all nations; and then shall the end come."

Signs: The Great Tribulation
Matthew 24:15-28; Mark 13:14-23; Luke 21:20-24

"And when you shall see Jerusalem surrounded with armies, then 9
know that the desolation thereof is near. When you therefore shall see the
'abomination of desolation,' spoken of by Daniel the prophet, stand in the
holy place, standing where it ought not, (let him that reads understand).
Then let them that be in Judea flee to the mountains; and let them which are
in the midst of the city depart out; and let not them that are in the country
enter thereinto. And let him that is on the housetop not go down into the
house, neither enter therein, to take anything out of his house: neither let
him which is in the field return back to take his clothes. For these be the
days of vengeance, that all things which are written may be fulfilled.

"And woe unto them that are with child, and to them that nurse 10
babies, in those days! for there shall be great distress in the land, and
wrath upon this people. And pray that your flight be not in the winter,

10   neither on the sabbath day: for in those days shall be affliction, then shall be great tribulation, such as was not since the beginning of the world to this time, no, nor ever shall be.

11   "And they shall fall by the edge of the sword, and shall be led away captive into all nations: and Jerusalem shall be trampled down of the Gentiles, until the times of the Gentiles be fulfilled.

12   "And except that the Lord had shortened those days, no flesh should be saved: but for the elect's sake, whom he has chosen, he has shortened the days.

13   "Then if any man shall say to you, 'Lo, here is Christ'; or, 'lo, he is there'; do not believe him: for there shall arise false Christs, and false prophets, and shall show great signs and wonders; insomuch that, if it were possible, they shall deceive the very elect. But take heed: behold, I have foretold you all things.

> "BEHOLD, I HAVE FORETOLD YOU ALL THINGS."

14   "Therefore if they shall say unto you, 'Behold, he is in the desert'; go not forth: 'behold, he is in the inner rooms'; do not believe it. For as the lightning comes out of the east, and shines even unto the west; so shall also the coming of the Son of man be. For wheresoever the carcass is, there will the eagles be gathered together."

Signs: Second Coming of the Son
Matthew 24:29-31; Mark 13:24-27; Luke 21:25-28

15   "But in those days, immediately after that tribulation, the sun shall be darkened, and the moon shall not give its light, and the stars shall fall from heaven, and the powers of the heavens shall be shaken. And there shall be signs in the sun, and in the moon, and in the stars; and upon the earth distress of nations, with perplexity; the sea and the waves roaring; men's hearts failing them for fear, and for awaiting those things which are coming on the earth: for the powers of heaven shall be shaken. And then shall appear the sign of the Son of man in heaven: and then shall all the tribes of the earth mourn, and they shall see *the Son of man coming in the clouds of heaven* with power and great glory.

16   "And he shall send his angels with a great sound of a trumpet, and they shall gather together his elect from the four winds, from one end of heaven to the other, from the uttermost part of the earth to the uttermost part of heaven. And when these things begin to come to pass, then look up, and lift up your heads; for your redemption draws near."

Signs: Parable of the Fig Tree
Matthew 24:32-35; Mark 13:28-31; Luke 21:29-33

17   And he spoke to them a parable; "Behold the fig tree, and all the trees. Now learn a parable of the fig tree; When its branch is yet tender, and puts forth leaves, you see and know of your own selves that summer is now near at hand. So likewise you, when you shall see all these things come to pass, know that the kingdom of God is near, even at the doors.

"Truly I say unto you, This generation shall not pass away, till all 18 these things be fulfilled. Heaven and earth shall pass away, but my words shall not pass away."

Signs: No One Knows the Hour
Matthew 24:36-44; Mark 13:32-37; Luke 21:34-36

"But of that day and that hour knows no man, no, not the angels which 19 are in heaven, neither the Son, but the Father only. But as the days of Noah were, so shall also the coming of the Son of man be. For as in the days that were before the flood they were eating and drinking, marrying and giving in marriage, until the day that Noah entered into the ark, and knew not until the flood came, and took them all away; so shall also the coming of the Son of man be. Take heed, watch and pray: for you know not when the time is.

> "OF THAT DAY AND THAT HOUR KNOWS NO MAN, NO, NOT THE ANGELS WHICH ARE IN HEAVEN, NEITHER THE SON, BUT THE FATHER ONLY."

"And take heed to yourselves, lest at any time your hearts be weighted 20 down with carousing, and drunkenness, and cares of this life, and so that day come upon you suddenly. For as a snare shall it come on all them that dwell on the face of the whole earth. Then shall two be in the field; the one shall be taken, and the other left. Two women shall be grinding at the mill; the one shall be taken, and the other left.

"Watch therefore: for you know not what hour your Lord does come. 21 But know this, that if the owner of the house had known in what watch the thief would come, he would have watched, and would not have allowed his house to be broken into. Therefore be also ready: for in such an hour as you think not the Son of man comes.

"Watch therefore, and pray always, that you may be accounted worthy 22 to escape all these things that shall come to pass, and to stand before the Son of man.

"For the Son of man is as a man taking a far journey, who left his 23 house, and gave authority to his servants, and to every man his work, and commanded the doorkeeper to watch. Watch therefore: for you know not when the master of the house comes, at evening, or at midnight, or at the cockcrowing, or in the morning: lest coming suddenly he find you sleeping. And what I say unto you I say unto all, Watch."

Signs: Faithful and Wise Servant
Matthew 24:45-51

"Who then is a faithful and wise servant, whom his master has made 24 ruler over his household, to give them food in due season? Blessed is that servant, whom his master when he comes shall find so doing. Truly I say unto you, That he shall make him ruler over all his goods.

"But and if that evil servant shall say in his heart, 'My master delays 25 his coming'; and shall begin to strike his fellow servants, and to eat and drink with the drunkards; the master of that servant shall come in a day

25 when he does not look for him, and in an hour that he is not aware of, and shall cut him to pieces, and appoint him his portion with the hypocrites: there shall be weeping and gnashing of teeth."

Signs: Parable of the Ten Virgins
Matthew 25:1-13

26 "Then shall the kingdom of heaven be likened unto ten virgins, which took their lamps, and went forth to meet the bridegroom. And five of them were wise, and five were foolish. They that were foolish took their lamps, and took no oil with them: but the wise took oil in their vessels with their lamps. While the bridegroom tarried, they all slumbered and slept.

27 "And at midnight there was a cry made, 'Behold, the bridegroom comes; go out to meet him.' Then all those virgins arose, and trimmed their lamps. And the foolish said unto the wise, 'Give us of your oil; for our lamps are gone out.' But the wise answered, saying, 'Not so; lest there be not enough for us and you: but go rather to them that sell, and buy for yourselves.'

28 "And while they went to buy, the bridegroom came; and they that were ready went in with him to the marriage: and the door was shut.

29 "Afterward came also the other virgins, saying, 'Lord, Lord, open to us.' But he answered and said, 'Truly I say unto you, I do not know you.'

30 "Watch therefore, for you know neither the day nor the hour wherein the Son of man comes."

Signs: Parable of the Talents
Matthew 25:14-30

31 "For the kingdom of heaven is as a man traveling into a far country, who called his own servants, and delivered unto them his goods. And unto one he gave five talents, to another two, and to another one; to every man according to his particular ability; and straightway took his journey. Then he that had received the five talents went and traded with the same, and made them another five talents. And likewise he that had received two, he also gained another two. But he that had received one went and dug in the earth, and hid his master's money.

32 "After a long time the master of those servants came, and reckoned with them. And so he that had received five talents came and brought another five talents, saying, 'Master, you delivered unto me five talents: behold, I have gained besides them five talents more.' His master said unto him, 'Well done, good and faithful servant: you have been faithful over a few things, I will make you ruler over many things: enter into the joy of your master.'

33 "He also that had received two talents came and said, 'Master, you delivered unto me two talents: behold, I have gained two other talents besides them.' His master said unto him, 'Well done, good and faithful servant; you have been faithful over a few things, I will make you ruler over many things: enter into the joy of your master.'

34 "Then he which had received the one talent came and said, 'Master, I knew you that you are a hard man, reaping where you have not sown, and gathering where you have not scattered: and I was afraid, and went and hid

your talent in the earth: lo, there you have that is yours.' His master 34 answered and said unto him, 'You wicked and lazy servant, you knew that I reap where I have not sowed, and gather where I have not scattered: you ought therefore to have put my money to the exchangers, and then at my coming I should have received my own with interest.

"Take therefore the talent from him, and give it unto him which has 35 ten talents. For unto everyone that has shall be given, and he shall have abundance: but from him that has not shall be taken away even that which he has. And cast the unprofitable servant into outer darkness: there shall be weeping and gnashing of teeth."

Signs: The Final Judgment
Matthew 25:31-46; Luke 21:37-38

"When the Son of man shall come in his glory, and all the holy angels 36 with him, then shall he sit upon the throne of his glory: and before him shall be gathered all nations: and he shall separate them one from another, as a shepherd divides his sheep from the goats: and he shall set the sheep on his right hand, but the goats on the left.

"Then shall the King say unto them on his right hand, 'Come, you 37 blessed of my Father, inherit the kingdom prepared for you from the foundation of the world: for I was hungry, and you gave me food: I was thirsty, and you gave me drink: I was a stranger, and you took me in: naked, and you clothed me: I was sick, and you visited me: I was in prison, and you came unto me.'

"Then shall the righteous answer him, saying, 'Lord, when did we see 38 you hungry, and fed you? or thirsty, and gave you drink? When did we see you a stranger, and took you in? or naked, and clothed you? Or when did we see you sick, or in prison, and came unto you?' And the King shall answer and say unto them, 'Truly I say unto you, Inasmuch as you have done it unto one of the least of these my brethren, you have done it unto me.'

> "INASMUCH AS YOU HAVE DONE IT UNTO ONE OF THE LEAST OF THESE MY BRETHREN, YOU HAVE DONE IT UNTO ME."

"Then shall he say also unto them on the left hand, 'Depart from me, 39 you cursed, into everlasting fire, prepared for the devil and his angels: for I was hungry, and you gave me no food: I was thirsty, and you gave me no drink: I was a stranger, and you did not take me in: naked, and you did not clothe me: sick, and in prison, and you did not visit me.'

"Then shall they also answer him, saying, 'Lord, when did we see you 40 hungry, or thirsty, or a stranger, or naked, or sick, or in prison, and did not minister unto you?' Then shall he answer them, saying, 'Truly I say unto you, Inasmuch as you did it not to one of the least of these, you did it not to me.' And these shall go away into everlasting punishment: but the righteous into life eternal."

And in the daytime he was teaching in the temple; and at night he went 41 out, and stayed in the mount that is called the Mount of Olives. And all the people came early in the morning to him in the temple, to hear him.

CHAPTER 44

THE EVIL PLOT AWAITS

Priests Plot to Kill Jesus
Matthew 26:1-5; Mark 14:1-2; Luke 22:1-2

1   And it came to pass, when Jesus had finished all these sayings, he said unto his disciples, "You know that after two days is the feast of the passover, and the Son of man is betrayed to be crucified."

2   After two days was the feast of the passover, and of unleavened bread, which is called the Passover. And the chief priests and scribes sought how they might take him by deceit, and put him to death. Then assembled together the chief priests and the scribes, and the elders of the people, unto the palace of the high priest, who was called Caiaphas, and plotted that they might take Jesus by deceit, and kill him. But they said, "Not on the feast day, lest there be an uproar of the people"; for they feared the people.

Jesus Anointed at Bethany
Matthew 26:6-13; Mark 14:3-9; John 12:2-8

3   Now when Jesus was in Bethany, in the house of Simon the leper, they made him a supper; and Martha served: but Lazarus was one of them that sat at the table with him. There came unto him a woman having an alabaster jar of very precious ointment, and she broke open the jar, and poured it on his head, as he sat at the table. Then Mary took a pound of ointment of spikenard, very costly, and anointed the feet of Jesus, and wiped his feet with her hair: and the house was filled with the fragrance of the ointment.

4   But when his disciples saw it, there were some that had indignation within themselves, and said, "Why was this waste of the ointment made? To what purpose is this waste?" Then said one of his disciples, Judas Iscariot, Simon's son, which should betray him, "Why was not this ointment sold for three hundred silver coins, and given to the poor?" This he said, not that he cared for the poor; but because he was a thief, and had the bag, and took what was put therein. And they murmured against her. When Jesus

understood it, he said unto them, "Why trouble the woman? for she has 4 wrought a good work upon me."

Then Jesus said, "Let her alone: for the day of my burial has she kept 5 this. For in that she has poured this ointment on my body, she did it for my burial. For you have the poor with you always, and whensoever you will you may do them good: but me you have not always. She has done what she could: she is come beforehand to anoint my body to the burial.

> "SHE HAS DONE WHAT SHE COULD."

"Truly I say unto you, Wheresoever this gospel shall be preached 6 throughout the whole world, this also that she has done shall be spoken of for a memorial of her."

Judas Agrees to Betray Jesus
Matthew 26:14-16; Mark 14:10-11; Luke 22:3-6

Then entered Satan into Judas surnamed Iscariot, being of the number 7 of the twelve. And he went his way, and went unto the chief priests, and communed with the chief priests and captains, how he might betray him unto them. And said unto them, "What will you give me, and I will deliver him unto you?" And when they heard it, they were glad, and promised to give him money. And they bargained

> AND THEY BARGAINED WITH HIM FOR THIRTY PIECES OF SILVER.

with him for thirty pieces of silver. And he promised, and from that time, he sought opportunity to betray him unto them in the absence of the multitude.

CHAPTER 45

THE LAST SUPPER

Passover: Preparation
Matthew 26:17-19; Mark 14:12-16; Luke 22:7-13

1   Then came the day of unleavened bread, when the passover must be killed. Now the first day of the feast of unleavened bread the disciples came to Jesus, saying unto him, "Where will you that we go and prepare that you may eat the passover?"

2   And he said, "Go into the city to such a man, and say unto him, 'The Teacher says, "My time is at hand; I will keep the passover at your house with my disciples."'" And he sent Peter and John, saying, "Go and prepare us the passover, that we may eat." And they said unto him, "Where?" And he said unto them, "Behold, when you are entered into the city, there shall a man meet you, bearing a pitcher of water; follow him into the house where he enters in. And you shall say unto the owner of the house, 'The Teacher says unto you, "Where is the guest room, where I shall eat the passover with my disciples?"' And he will show you a large upper room furnished and prepared: there make ready for us."

3   And his disciples did as Jesus had appointed them, and came into the city, and found as he had said unto them: and they made ready the passover.

Passover: Observance Begins
Matthew 26:20; Mark 14:17; Luke 22:14-18; John 13:1-4

4   Now before the feast of the passover, when Jesus knew that his hour was come that he should depart out of this world unto the Father, having loved his own which were in the world, he loved them unto the end.

5   And in the evening he came with the twelve. And when the hour was come, he sat down, and the twelve apostles with him. And he said unto them, "With desire I have desired to eat this passover with you before I suffer: for I say unto you, I will not eat thereof anymore, until it be fulfilled in the kingdom of God."

And he took the cup, and gave thanks, and said, "Take this, and divide 6 it among yourselves: for I say unto you, I will not drink of the fruit of the vine, until the kingdom of God shall come."

And supper being ended, the devil having now put into the heart of 7 Judas Iscariot, Simon's son, to betray him; Jesus knowing that the Father had given all things into his hands, and that he was come from God, and went to God; he rose from supper, and laid aside his garments; and took a towel, and girded himself.

Passover: Washing Disciples' Feet
John 13:5-17

After that he poured water into a basin, and began to wash the disci- 8 ples' feet, and to wipe them with the towel with which he was girded. Then he came to Simon Peter: and Peter said unto him, "Lord, do you wash my feet?" Jesus answered and said unto him, "What I do you know not now; but you shall know hereafter."

Peter said unto him, "You shall never wash my feet." Jesus answered 9 him, "If I do not wash you, you have no part with me." Simon Peter said unto him, "Lord, not my feet only, but also my hands and my head." Jesus said to him, "He that is bathed needs not except to wash his feet, but is clean every bit: and you are clean, but not all." For he knew who should betray him; therefore he said, "You are not all clean."

So after he had washed their feet, and had taken his garments, and 10 was seated again, he said unto them, "Do you know what I have done to you? You call me Teacher and Lord: and you say well; for so I am. If I then, your Lord and Teacher, have washed your feet; you also ought to wash one another's feet. For I have given you an example, that you should do as I have done to you.

> "I HAVE GIVEN YOU AN EXAM-
> PLE, THAT YOU SHOULD DO AS
> I HAVE DONE TO YOU."

"Truly, truly, I say unto you, The servant is not greater than his mas- 11 ter; neither he that is sent greater than he that sent him. If you know these things, happy are you if you do them.

Passover: Prediction of Betrayal
John 13:18-20

"I speak not of you all: I know whom I have chosen: but that the scrip- 12 ture may be fulfilled, '*He that eats bread with me has lifted up his heel against me.*' Now I tell you before it comes, that, when it is come to pass, you may believe that I am he. Truly, truly, I say unto you, He that receives whomsoever I send receives me; and he that receives me receives him that sent me."

> "HE THAT RECEIVES WHOMSO-
> EVER I SEND RECEIVES ME;
> AND HE THAT RECEIVES ME
> RECEIVES HIM THAT SENT ME."

Passover: Betrayer Revealed
Matthew 26:21-25; Mark 14:18-21; Luke 22:21-23; John 13:21-30

13   When Jesus had said these things, and as they sat and did eat, he was troubled in spirit, and testified, and said, "Truly, truly, I say unto you, One of you which eats with me shall betray me." Then the disciples looked one on another, doubting of whom he spoke. And they began to be exceedingly sorrowful, and to say unto him one by one, "Is it I?" and another said, "Is it I?" And he answered and said unto them, "It is one of the twelve," and said, "He that dips his hand with me in the dish, the same shall betray me. But, behold, the hand of him that betrays me is with me on the table.

> "ONE OF YOU WHICH EATS WITH ME SHALL BETRAY ME."

14   "And truly the Son of man goes, as it was determined, as it is written of him: but woe unto that man by whom he is betrayed! it had been good for that man if he had never been born." Then Judas, which betrayed him, answered and said, "Rabbi, is it I?" He said unto him, "You have said."

15   And they began to inquire among themselves, which of them it was that should do this thing. Now there was leaning on Jesus' bosom one of his disciples, whom Jesus loved. Simon Peter therefore beckoned to him, that he should ask who it should be of whom he spoke. He then lying on Jesus' breast said unto him, "Lord, who is it?"

16   Jesus answered, "He it is, to whom I shall give a piece of bread, when I have dipped it." And when he had dipped the piece of bread, he gave it to Judas Iscariot, the son of Simon. And after the piece of bread Satan entered into him. Then said Jesus unto him, "That you do, do quickly."

17   Now no man at the table knew for what intent he spoke this unto him. For some of them thought, because Judas had the bag, that Jesus had said unto him, "Buy those things that we have need of for the feast"; or, that he should give something to the poor.

18   He then having received the piece of bread went immediately out: and it was night.

Passover: Greatest Is He Who Serves
Luke 22:24-30

19   And there was also a dispute among them, which of them should be considered the greatest. And he said unto them, "The kings of the Gentiles exercise dominance over them; and they that exercise authority upon them are called benefactors.

20   "But you shall not be so: but he that is greatest among you, let him be as the younger; and he that is leader, as he that does serve. For which is greater, he that sits at the table, or he that serves? is not he that sits at the table ? but I am among you as he that serves.

21   "You are they which have continued with me in my temptations. And I appoint unto you a kingdom, as my Father has appointed unto me; that you

may eat and drink at my table in my kingdom, and sit on thrones judging 21 the twelve tribes of Israel."

Passover: The Last Supper
Matthew 26:26-29; Mark 14:22-25; Luke 22:19-20

And as they were eating, Jesus took bread, and blessed it, and broke it, 22 and gave it to the disciples, and said, "Take, eat: this is my body which is given for you: this do in remembrance of me."

Likewise also the cup after sup- 23 per, saying, "This cup is the new testament in my blood, which is shed for you." And he took the cup, and when he had given thanks, he gave it to them, saying, "Drink it all of you; for

> "THIS IS MY BLOOD OF THE NEW TESTAMENT, WHICH IS SHED FOR MANY FOR THE REMISSION OF SINS."

this is my blood of the new testament, which is shed for many for the remission of sins." And they all drank of it.

"Truly I say unto you, I will drink no more of the fruit of the vine, until 24 that day when I drink it new with you in my Father's kingdom."

CHAPTER 46

WHAT MUST BE WILL BE

Passover: The New Commandment
John 13:31-35

1   Therefore, when he was gone out, Jesus said, "Now is the Son of man glorified, and God is glorified in him. If God be glorified in him, God shall also glorify him in himself, and shall straightway glorify him. Little children, yet a little while I am with you. You shall seek me: and as I said unto the Jews, Where I go, you cannot come; so now I say to you.

2   "A new commandment I give unto you, That you love one another; as I have loved you, that you also love one another. By this shall all men know that you are my disciples, if you have love one to another."

Passover: Prediction of Denials
Matthew 26:31-35; Mark 14:27-31; Luke 22:31-34; John 13:36-38

3   Simon Peter said unto him, "Lord, where do you go?" Jesus answered him, "Where I go, you cannot follow me now; but you shall follow me afterward."

4   And the Lord said, "Simon, Simon, behold, Satan has desired to have you, that he may sift you as wheat: but I have prayed for you, that your faith not fail: and when you are converted, strengthen your brethren."

5   Then Jesus said unto them, "All you shall fall away because of me this night: for it is written, '*I will strike the shepherd, and the sheep of the flock shall be scattered abroad.*' But after I am risen again, I will go before you into Galilee."

6   Peter answered and said unto him, "Though all men shall fall away because of you, yet will I never fall away." And Jesus said unto him, "Truly I say unto you, That this day, even in this night, before the cock crows twice, you shall deny me three times." Peter said unto him, "Lord, why cannot I follow you now? I will lay down my life for your sake. Lord, I am ready to

go with you, both into prison, and to death." Jesus answered him, "Will you 6
lay down your life for my sake? Truly, truly, I say unto you, Peter, the cock
shall not crow this day, before that you shall three times deny that you
know me."

But Peter spoke the more emphatically, "Though I should die with 7
you, yet will I not deny you in any way." Likewise also said all the disciples.

Passover: What Is Written Must Be
Luke 22:35-38

And he said unto them, "When I sent you without purse, and bag, and 8
shoes, did you lack anything?" And they said, "Nothing." Then he said unto
them, "But now, he that has a purse, let him take it, and likewise his bag:
and he that has no sword, let him sell his garment, and buy one.

"For I say unto you, that this that is written must yet be accomplished 9
in me, '*And he was numbered among the transgressors*': for the things concerning me have an end." And they said, "Lord, behold, here are two swords."
And he said unto them, "That is enough."

CHAPTER 47

·⊶·————— THE PRECIOUS PROMISES —————·⊷·

Passover: In My Father's House
John 14:1-14

1   "Let not your heart be troubled: you believe in God, believe also in me. In my Father's house are many mansions: if it were not so, I would have told you. I go to prepare a place for you. And if I go and prepare a place for you, I will come again, and receive you unto myself; that where I am, there you may be also. And where I go you know, and the way you know."

2   Thomas said unto him, "Lord, we know not where you go; and how can we know the way?" Jesus said unto him, "I am the way, the truth, and the life: no man comes unto the Father, but by me. If you had known me, you should have known my Father also: and from henceforth you know him, and have seen him."

3   Philip said unto him, "Lord, show us the Father, and it suffices us." Jesus said unto him, "Have I been so long time with you, and yet have you not known me, Philip? he that has seen me has seen the Father; and how do you say then, 'Show us the Father'? Do you not believe that I am in the Father, and the Father in me? the words that I speak unto you I speak not of myself: but the Father that dwells in me, he does the works. Believe me that I am in the Father, and the Father in me: or else believe me for the very works' sake.

4   "Truly, truly, I say unto you, He that believes on me, the works that I do shall he do also; and greater works than these shall he do; because I go unto my Father. And whatsoever you shall ask in my name, that will I do, that the Father may be glorified in the Son. If you shall ask anything in my name, I will do it."

Passover: Promise of a Comforter
John 14:15-24

5   "If you love me, keep my commandments. And I will ask the Father, and he shall give you another Comforter, that he may be with you for ever;

even the Spirit of truth; whom the world cannot receive, because it sees him 5
not, neither knows him: but you know
him; for he dwells with you, and shall
be in you. I will not leave you com-
fortless: I will come to you.

> "I WILL NOT LEAVE YOU COM-
> FORTLESS."

"Yet a little while, and the world sees me no more; but you see me: 6
because I live, you shall live also. At that day you shall know that I am in
my Father, and you in me, and I in you. He that has my commandments, and
keeps them, he it is that loves me: and he that loves me shall be loved of my
Father, and I will love him, and will manifest myself to him."

Judas said unto him, not Iscariot, "Lord, how is it that you will mani- 7
fest yourself unto us, and not unto the world?" Jesus answered and said unto
him, "If a man loves me, he will keep my words: and my Father will love
him, and we will come unto him, and make our home with him. He that
does not love me does not keep my sayings: and the word which you hear
is not mine, but the Father's which sent me."

Passover: "Peace I Leave With You"
Matthew 26:30; Mark 14:26; John 14:25-31

"These things have I spoken unto you, being yet present with you. But 8
the Comforter, which is the Holy Ghost, whom the Father will send in my
name, he shall teach you all things, and bring all things to your remembrance, whatsoever I have said unto you.

"Peace I leave with you, my peace I give unto you: not as the world 9
gives, give I unto you. Let not your heart be troubled, neither let it be afraid.
You have heard how I said unto you, 'I go away, and come again unto you.'
If you loved me, you would rejoice, because I said, 'I go unto the Father':
for my Father is greater than I.

"And now I have told you before it comes to pass, that, when it is come 10
to pass, you might believe. Hereafter I will not talk much with you: for the
prince of this world comes, and has nothing in me. But that the world may
know that I love the Father; and as the Father gave me commandment, even
so I do. Arise, let us go from here."

And when they had sung a hymn, they went out into the Mount of Olives. 11

CHAPTER 48

THE ETERNAL CONNECTION

"Abide in Me, and I in You"
John 15:1-10

1   "I am the true vine, and my Father is the vinedresser. Every branch in me that bears no fruit he takes away: and every branch that bears fruit, he prunes it, that it may bring forth more fruit. Now you are clean through the word which I have spoken unto you.

2   "Abide in me, and I in you. As the branch cannot bear fruit of itself, except it remains in the vine; no more can you, except you abide in me. I am the vine, you are the branches: He that abides in me, and I in him, the same brings forth much fruit: for without me you can do nothing. If a man does not abide in me, he is cast forth as a branch, and is withered; and men gather them, and cast them into the fire, and they are burned.

3   "If you abide in me, and my words abide in you, you shall ask what you will, and it shall be done unto you. Herein is my Father glorified, that you bear much fruit; so shall you be my disciples. As the Father has loved me, so have I loved you: continue in my love. If you keep my commandments, you shall abide in my love; even as I have kept my Father's commandments, and abide in his love."

"Love One Another"
John 15:11-17

4   "These things have I spoken unto you, that my joy might remain in you, and that your joy might be full. This is my commandment, That you love one another, as I have loved you.

5   "Greater love has no man than this, that a man lay down his life for his friends. You are my friends, if you do whatsoever I command you. Henceforth I do not call you servants; for the servant does not know what his master does: but I have called you friends; for all things that I

have heard of my Father I have made known unto you. You have not cho- 5
sen me, but I have chosen you, and
ordained you, that you should go and
bring forth fruit, and that your fruit
should remain: so that whatsoever
you shall ask of the Father in my

> "GREATER LOVE HAS NO MAN THAN THIS, THAT A MAN LAY DOWN HIS LIFE FOR HIS FRIENDS."

name, he may give it you. These things I command you, that you love
one another."

"You Also Shall Bear Witness"
John 15:18-27
6

"If the world hates you, you know that it hated me before it hated you.
If you were of the world, the world would love its own: but because you are
not of the world, but I have chosen you out of the world, therefore the world
hates you. Remember the word that I said unto you, 'The servant is not
greater than his master.' If they have persecuted me, they will also persecute
you; if they have kept my saying, they will keep yours also. But all these
things will they do unto you for my name's sake, because they know not him
that sent me.
7

"If I had not come and spoken unto them, they would have no sin: but
now they have no excuse for their sin. He that hates me hates my Father
also. If I had not done among them the works which no other man did, they
would have no sin: but now they have both seen and hated both me and my
Father. But this comes to pass, that the word might be fulfilled that is written in their law, '*They hated me without a cause.*'
8

"But when the Comforter is come, whom I will send unto you from
the Father, even the Spirit of truth, which proceeds from the Father, he shall
testify of me: and you also shall bear witness, because you have been with
me from the beginning."

CHAPTER 49

THE PROMISE TO RETURN

"These Things Have I Told You"
John 16:1-4

1   "These things have I spoken unto you, that you should not fall away. They shall put you out of the synagogues: yes, the time comes, that whosoever kills you will think that he does God service. And these things will they do unto you, because they have not known the Father, nor me.

2   "But these things have I told you, that when the time shall come, you may remember that I told you of them. And these things I have not said unto you at the beginning, because I was with you."

The Spirit of Truth Will Come
John 16:5-15

3   "But now I go my way to him that sent me; and none of you asks me, 'Where do you go?' But because I have said these things unto you, sorrow has filled your hearts. Nevertheless I tell you the truth; It is expedient for you that I go away: for if I do not go away, the Comforter will not come unto you; but if I depart, I will send him unto you. And when he is come, he will expose the world of sin, and of righteousness, and of judgment: of sin, because they do not believe on me; of righteousness, because I go to my Father, and you see me no more; of judgment, because the prince of this world is judged.

4   "I have yet many things to say unto you, but you cannot bear them now. Howbeit when he, the Spirit of truth, is come, he will guide you into all truth: for he shall not speak of himself; but whatsoever he shall hear, that shall he speak: and he will show you things to come. He shall glorify me: for he shall receive of mine, and shall show it unto you. All things that the Father has are mine: therefore said I, that he shall take of mine, and shall show it unto you."

Your Sorrow Will Become Joy
John 16:16-33

"A little while, and you shall not see me: and again, a little while, and 5
you shall see me, because I go to the Father." Then said some of his disciples among themselves, "What is this that he says unto us, 'A little while, and you shall not see me: and again, a little while, and you shall see me': and, 'Because I go to the Father'? They said therefore, "What is this that he says, 'A little while'? we cannot know what he says." Now Jesus knew that they were desirous to ask him, and said unto them, "Do you inquire among yourselves of that I said, 'A little while, and you shall not see me: and again, a little while, and you shall see me'?

"Truly, truly, I say unto you, That you shall weep and lament, but the 6
world shall rejoice: and you shall be sorrowful, but your sorrow shall be turned into joy. A woman when she is in labor has sorrow, because her hour is come: but as soon as she is delivered of the child, she remembers no more the anguish, for joy that a child is born into the world. And you now therefore have sorrow: but I will see you again, and your heart shall rejoice, and your joy no man takes from you. And in that day you shall ask me nothing. Truly, truly, I say unto you, Whatsoever you shall ask the Father in my name, he will give you. Until now have you asked nothing in my name: ask, and you shall receive, that your joy may be full.

"These things have I spoken unto you in figures of speech: but the 7
time comes, when I shall no more speak unto you in figures of speech, but I shall show you plainly of the Father. At that day you shall ask in my name: and I say not unto you, that I will ask the Father for you: for the Father himself loves you, because you have loved me, and have believed that I came out from God. I came forth from the Father, and am come into the world: again, I leave the world, and go to the Father."

His disciples said unto him, "Lo, now you speak plainly, and speak no 8
figure of speech. Now are we sure that you know all things, and need not that any man should ask you: by this we believe that you came forth from God." Jesus answered them, "Do you now believe?

"Behold, the hour comes, yes, is 9
now come, that you shall be scattered, every man to his own, and shall leave me alone: and yet I am not alone, because the Father is with me. These things I have spoken unto you, that in me you might have peace. In the world you shall have tribulation: but be of good cheer; I have overcome the world."

> "IN THE WORLD YOU SHALL HAVE TRIBULATION: BUT BE OF GOOD CHEER; I HAVE OVERCOME THE WORLD."

CHAPTER 50

THE INTERCESSORY PRAYER

Jesus Prays for Himself
John 17:1-5

1   These words spoke Jesus, and lifted up his eyes to heaven, and said, "Father, the hour is come; glorify your Son, that your Son also may glorify you: as you have given him authority over all flesh, that he should give eternal life to as many as you have given him. And this is life eternal, that they might know you the only true God, and Jesus Christ, whom you have sent.

2   "I have glorified you on the earth: I have finished the work which you gave me to do. And now, O Father, glorify me with your own self with the glory which I had with you before the world was."

Jesus Prays for All Disciples
John 17:6-19

3   "I have manifested your name unto the men which you gave me out of the world: yours they were, and you gave them to me; and they have kept your word. Now they have known that all things whatsoever you have given me are of you. For I have given unto them the words which you gave me; and they have received them, and have known surely that I came out from you, and they have believed that you did send me.

4   "I pray for them: I pray not for the world, but for them which you have given me; for they are yours. And all mine are yours, and yours are mine; and I am glorified in them. And now I am no more in the world, but these are in the world, and I come to you. Holy Father, keep through your own name those whom you have given me, that they may be one, as we are. While I was with them in the world, I kept them in your name: those that you gave me I have kept, and none of them is lost, but the son of perdition; that the scripture might be fulfilled.

"And now I come to you; and these things I speak in the world, that 5 they might have my joy fulfilled in themselves. I have given them your word; and the world has hated them, because they are not of the world, even as I am not of the world.

"I pray not that you should take them out of the world, but that you 6 should keep them from the evil. They are not of the world, even as I am not of the world. Sanctify them through your truth: your word is truth. As you have sent me into the world, even so have I also sent them into the world. And for their sakes I sanctify myself, that they also might be sanctified through the truth."

Jesus Prays for All Believers
John 17:20-26

"Neither pray I for these alone, but for them also which shall believe 7 on me through their word; that they all may be one; as you, Father, are in me, and I in you, that they also may be one in us: that the world may believe that you have sent me. And the glory which you gave me I have given them; that they may be one, even as we are one: I in them, and you in me, that they may be made perfect in one; and that the world may know that you have sent me, and have loved them, as you have loved me.

"Father, I desire that they also, whom you have given me, be with me 8 where I am; that they may behold my glory, which you have given me: for you loved me before the foundation of the world.

"O righteous Father, the world has not known you: but I have known 9 you, and these have known that you have sent me. And I have declared unto them your name, and will declare it: that the love with which you have loved me may be in them, and I in them."

PART 11

BETRAYAL, TRIAL, AND DEATH

In anticipation of His final hour, Jesus withdrew to the Mount of Olives to pray. In speechless agony He pleaded with His Father to spare Him from this trial. Yet He knew that there was a cross to be borne before He could make the supreme demonstration of God's power over evil, of joy over sorrow, of life over death. Embracing His divine mission with renewed faith, He asserted His oneness with the Father in the face of His adversaries. For this He was about to suffer violence and offer up the final vestige of His mortal soul. This final act of faith proved the all-encompassing power of God's love for all mankind and for all time.

THERE APPEARED AN ANGEL UNTO HIM FROM HEAVEN, STRENGTHENING HIM. AND BEING IN AGONY HE PRAYED MORE EARNESTLY.

(LUKE 22:43-44)

CHAPTER 51

THE TRIAL BEFORE DAWN

Gethsemane: Jesus Prays in Agony
Matthew 26:36-46; Mark 14:32-42; Luke 22:39-46; John 18:1

When Jesus had spoken these words, he came out, and went forth over 1 the brook Cedron, where was a garden, as he was accustomed, to the Mount of Olives; and his disciples also followed him. And they came to a place which was named Gethsemane, into which he entered, and his disciples. And when he was at the place, he said unto them, "Pray that you enter not into temptation." And he said to his disciples, "Sit here, while I go and pray yonder." And he took with him Peter and the two sons of Zebedee, James and John, and began to be sorrowful and very heavy.

Then said he unto them, "My soul is exceedingly sorrowful, even unto 2 death: tarry here, and watch with me." And he went forward about a stone's cast, and kneeled down, and fell on his face, and prayed that, if it were possible, the hour might pass from him. And he said, "Abba, Father, all things are possible unto you; take away this cup from me: nevertheless not my will, but yours, be done."

And he came unto the disciples, and found them asleep, and said unto 3 Peter, "Simon, do you sleep? What, could you not watch with me one hour? Watch and pray, that you enter not into temptation: the spirit indeed is willing, but the flesh is weak."

He went away again the second time, and prayed, saying, "O my 4 Father, if this cup may not pass away from me, unless I drink it, your will be done." And there appeared an angel unto him from heaven, strengthening him. And being in agony he prayed more earnestly: and his sweat was as it were great drops of blood falling down to the ground.

And when he rose up from prayer, and was come to his disciples, he 5 found them asleep again, sleeping for sorrow, for their eyes were heavy. And said unto them, "Why do you sleep? rise and pray, lest you enter into temptation." And neither knew they what to answer him.

6   And he left them, and went away again, and prayed the third time, saying the same words. And he came to his disciples the third time, and said unto them, "Sleep on now, and take your rest: it is enough, the hour is come; behold, the Son of man is betrayed into the hands of sinners. Rise up, let us go; lo, he that betrays me is at hand."

Judas Betrays Jesus
Matthew 26:47-56; Mark 14:43-52; Luke 22:47-53; John 18:2-11

7   And immediately, while he yet spoke, lo, Judas, one of the twelve, came, and with him a great multitude with swords and staves, from the chief priests and the scribes and the elders of the people. And Judas also, which betrayed him, knew the place: for Jesus often met there with his disciples. Judas then, having received a band of men and officers from the chief priests and Pharisees, came there with lanterns and torches and weapons.

8   Jesus therefore, knowing all things that should come upon him, went forth, and said unto them, "Whom do you seek?" They answered him, "Jesus of Nazareth." Jesus said unto them, "I am he." And Judas also, which betrayed him, stood with them. As soon then as he had said unto them, "I am he," they went backward, and fell to the ground.

9   Then he asked them again, "Whom do you seek?" And they said, "Jesus of Nazareth." Jesus answered, "I have told you that I am he: if therefore you seek me, let these go their way": that the saying might be fulfilled, which he spoke, "Of them which you gave me have I lost none."

10   And while he yet spoke, he that was called Judas, one of the twelve, went before them, and drew near unto Jesus to kiss him. Now he that betrayed him had given them a sign, saying, "Whomsoever I shall kiss, that same is he; take him, and lead him away under guard." But Jesus said unto him, "Judas, do you betray the Son of man with a kiss?" And forthwith he came to Jesus, and said, "Hail, Rabbi"; and kissed him. And Jesus said unto him, "Friend, for what purpose are you come?" Then they came, and laid hands on Jesus, and took him.

11   When they which were about him saw what would follow, they said unto him, "Lord, shall we strike with the sword?" Then Simon Peter having a sword drew it, and struck the high priest's servant, and cut off his right ear. The servant's name was Malchus.

12   Then Jesus said unto Peter, "Resist no more." And he touched his ear, and healed him. "Put up your sword into the sheath: for all they that take the sword shall perish with the sword.

> "THEY THAT TAKE THE SWORD SHALL PERISH WITH THE SWORD."

Do you think that I cannot now appeal to my Father, and he shall at once give me more than twelve legions of angels? But how then shall the scriptures be fulfilled, that thus it must be? The cup which my Father has given me, shall I not drink it?"

Then Jesus said unto the chief priests, and captains of the temple, and 13 the elders, which were come to him, "Are you come out, as against a thief, with swords and staves to take me? When I sat daily with you teaching in the temple, you stretched forth no hands against me: but this is your hour, and the power of darkness. But all this was done, that the scriptures of the prophets might be fulfilled." Then all the disciples forsook him, and fled.

And there followed him a certain young man, having a linen cloth cast 14 about his naked body; and the young men laid hold on him: and he left the linen cloth, and fled from them naked.

Jesus Is Seized and Taken Away
Matthew 26:57-58; Mark 14:53-54; Luke 22:54-55; John 18:12-16

Then the band and the captain and officers of the Jews took Jesus, and 15 bound him, and led him away to Annas first; for he was father-in-law to Caiaphas, which was the high priest that same year. Now Caiaphas was he, which gave advice to the Jews, that it was expedient that one man should die for the people.

And they that had laid hold on Jesus led him away to Caiaphas the 16 high priest, and brought him into the high priest's house, where the chief priests and the scribes and the elders were assembled. And Simon Peter followed Jesus afar off unto the high priest's palace, and so did another disciple: that disciple was known unto the high priest, and went in with Jesus into the palace of the high priest. But Peter stood at the door outside. Then went out that other disciple, which was known unto the high priest, and spoke unto her that kept the door, and brought in Peter. And when they had kindled a fire in the midst of the hall, and were seated together, Peter sat down among the servants, and warmed himself at the fire, to see the end.

Council: Questioned and Struck
John 18:19-24

The high priest then asked Jesus of his disciples, and of his doctrine. 17 Jesus answered him, "I spoke openly to the world; I ever taught in the synagogues, and in the temple, where the Jews always meet; and in secret have I said nothing. Why do you ask me? ask them which heard me, what I have said unto them: behold, they know what I said."

And when he had thus spoken, one of the officers which stood by 18 struck Jesus with the palm of his hand, saying, "Do you answer the high priest so?" Jesus answered him, "If I have spoken evil, bear witness of the evil: but if well, why do you strike me?" Now Annas had sent him bound unto Caiaphas the high priest.

Council: The False Witnesses
Matthew 26:59-62; Mark 14:55-60

Now the chief priests, and elders, and all the council, sought for wit- 19 ness against Jesus to put him to death; but found none. For many bore false

19 witness against him, but their witness had not agreed together. At the last came two false witnesses, and said, "This fellow said, 'I am able to destroy the temple of God, and to build it in three days.'" And saying, "We heard him say, 'I will destroy this temple that is made with hands, and within three days I will build another made without hands.'" But neither so did their witness agree together.

20   And the high priest stood up in the midst, and asked Jesus, saying, "Do you answer nothing? what is it which these witness against you?"

Council: Questioned and Beaten
Matthew 26:63-68; Mark 14:61-65; Luke 22:63-65

21   But Jesus held his peace, and answered nothing. And the high priest answered and said unto him, "I charge you by the living God, that you tell us whether you be the Christ, the Son of God." Jesus said unto him, "You have said: nevertheless I say unto you, Hereafter shall you see *the Son of man sitting on the right hand of power, and coming in the clouds of heaven.*" Again the high priest asked him, and said unto him, "Are you the Christ, the Son of the Blessed?" And Jesus said, "I am."

22   Then the high priest tore his clothes, saying, "He has spoken blasphemy; what further need have we of witnesses? behold, now you have heard his blasphemy. What do you think?" They answered and said, "He is guilty of death." And they all condemned him to be guilty of death.

23   And the men that held Jesus mocked him, and struck him. And some began to spit in his face, and the servants did strike him with the palms of their hands. And when they had blindfolded him, they struck him on the face, and asked him, saying, "Prophesy unto us, you Christ, Who is it that struck you?" And many other things blasphemously spoke they against him.

Council: Outside Peter Denies Jesus
Matthew 26:69-75; Mark 14:66-72; Luke 22:56-62; John 18:17-18, 25-27

24   Now Peter sat outside in the palace. And the servants and officers stood there, who had made a fire of coals; for it was cold: and they warmed themselves: and Peter stood with them, and warmed himself. And there came one of the servant girls of the high priest that kept the door. And when she saw Peter warming himself, she closely looked upon him, and said, "Are not you also one of this man's disciples? You also were with Jesus of Galilee." But he denied him before them all, saying, "I know not, neither do I understand what you say." And he went out into the porch; and the cock crowed.

25   And when he was gone out into the porch, after a little while, another girl saw him, and said unto them that were there, "This fellow was also with Jesus of Nazareth." They said therefore unto him, "Are not you also one of his disciples?" And again he denied with an oath, "I do not know the man."

26   And about the space of one hour later, one of the servants of the high priest, being his relative whose ear Peter cut off, said, "Did not I see you in

the garden with him? Surely you also are one of them: for you are a 26 Galilean; for your speech betrays you." But he began to curse and to swear, saying, "Man, I know not what you say. I know not this man of whom you speak." And immediately, while he yet spoke, the cock crowed the second time. And the Lord turned, and looked upon Peter. And Peter called to mind the word that Jesus said unto him, "Before the cock crows twice, you shall deny me three times." And when he thought thereon, Peter went out, and wept bitterly.

Council: Condemned to Pilate
Matthew 27:1-2; Mark 15:1; Luke 22:66-71; 23:1

When the morning was come, all the chief priests and elders of the 27 people and the scribes plotted against Jesus to put him to death: and led him into their council, saying, "Are you the Christ? tell us." And he said unto them, "If I tell you, you will not believe: and if I also ask you, you will not answer me, nor let me go. Hereafter shall *the Son of man sit on the right hand of the power of God.*" Then said they all, "Are you then the Son of God?" And he said unto them, "You say that I am." And they said, "What need we any further witness? for we ourselves have heard of his own mouth." And the whole multitude of them arose, and when they had bound Jesus, they led him away, and delivered him to Pontius Pilate the governor.

Judas Hangs Himself
Matthew 27:3-10

Then Judas, which had betrayed him, when he saw that he was con- 28 demned, repented himself, and brought back the thirty pieces of silver to the chief priests and elders, saying, "I have sinned in that I have betrayed the innocent blood." And they said, "What is that to us? you see to that." And he cast down the pieces of silver in the temple, and departed, and went and hanged himself.

And the chief priests took the silver pieces, and said, "It is not lawful 29 to put them into the treasury, because it is the price of blood." And they con- ferred, and bought with them the potter's field, to bury foreigners in. There- fore that field was called, The Field of Blood, unto this day. Then was fulfilled that which was spoken by Jeremiah the prophet, saying, "*And they took the thirty pieces of silver, the price of him that was valued, whom they of the children of Israel did value; and gave them for the potter's field, as the Lord appointed me.*"

CHAPTER 52

THE ROMAN TRIAL

Before Pilate: Accusations
Luke 23:2; John 18:28-32

1   Then they led Jesus from Caiaphas unto the hall of judgment: and it was early; and they themselves went not into the judgment hall, lest they should be defiled; but that they might eat the passover. Pilate then went out unto them, and said, "What accusation do you bring against this man?"

2   They answered and said unto him, "If he were not an evildoer, we would not have delivered him up unto you." Then said Pilate unto them, "Take him, and judge him according to your law." The Jews therefore said unto him, "It is not lawful for us to put any man to death": that the saying of Jesus might be fulfilled, which he spoke, signifying what death he should die.

3   And they began to accuse him, saying, "We found this fellow perverting the nation, and forbidding to give tribute to Caesar, saying that he himself is Christ a King."

Before Pilate: King of the Jews?
Matthew 27:11-14; Mark 15:2-5; Luke 23:3-7; John 18:33-38

4   And Jesus stood before the governor: and the governor asked him, saying, "Are you the King of the Jews?" And Jesus said unto him, "You say it." And the chief priests and elders accused him of many things: but he answered nothing. And Pilate asked him again, saying, "Do you answer nothing? behold how many things they witness against you." But Jesus answered him to never a word; insomuch that the governor marveled greatly.

5   Then Pilate entered into the judgment hall again, and called Jesus, and said unto him, "Are you the King of the Jews?" Jesus answered him, "Do you say this thing of yourself, or did others tell you it of me?" Pilate answered, "Am I a Jew? Your own nation and the chief priests have delivered you unto me: what have you done?"

Jesus answered, "My kingdom is not of this world: if my kingdom 6 were of this world, then would my servants fight, that I should not be delivered to the Jews: but now is my kingdom not from here."

Pilate therefore said unto him, "Are you a king then?" Jesus answered, 7 "You say that I am a king. To this end was I born, and for this cause came I into the world, that I should bear witness unto the truth. Everyone that is of the truth hears my voice." Pilate said unto him, "What is truth?" And when he had said this, he went out again

> "TO THIS END WAS I BORN, AND FOR THIS CAUSE CAME I INTO THE WORLD, THAT I SHOULD BEAR WITNESS UNTO THE TRUTH."

unto the Jews, and said to the chief priests and to the people, "I find no fault in this man at all."

And they were the more fierce, saying, "He stirs up the people, teach- 8 ing throughout all Judea, beginning from Galilee to this place."

When Pilate heard of Galilee, he asked whether the man were a 9 Galilean. And as soon as he knew that he belonged unto Herod's jurisdiction, he sent him to Herod, who himself also was at Jerusalem at that time.

Before Pilate: Sent to Herod
Luke 23:8-12

And when Herod saw Jesus, he was exceedingly glad: for he was 10 desirous to see him of a long time, because he had heard many things of him; and he hoped to have seen some miracle done by him. Then he questioned with him in many words; but he answered him nothing. And the chief priests and scribes stood and strongly accused him.

And Herod with his men of war rejected him, and mocked him, and 11 arrayed him in a gorgeous robe, and sent him again to Pilate.

And the same day Pilate and Herod were made friends together: for 12 before they were at hostility between themselves.

Before Pilate: Whom to Release?
Matthew 27:15-16; Mark 15:6-7; Luke 23:13-17

And Pilate, when he had called together the chief priests and the rulers 13 and the people, said unto them, "You have brought this man unto me, as one that perverts the people: and, behold, I, having examined him before you, have found no fault in this man concerning those things whereof you accuse him: no, nor Herod: for I sent you to him; and, lo, nothing deserving of death is done by him. I will therefore chastise him, and release him."

Now at that feast the governor was accustomed to release unto the 14 people one prisoner, whomsoever they desired. And there was then a notorious prisoner, named Barabbas, which lay bound with them that had made insurrection with him, who had committed murder in the insurrection.

Before Pilate: "Crucify Him!"
Matthew 27:17-23; Mark 15:8-14; Luke 23:18-23; John 18:39-40

15   And the multitude crying aloud began to desire him to do as he had ever done unto them. Therefore when they were gathered together, Pilate answered them, saying, "Whom will you that I release unto you? Barabbas, or Jesus which is called Christ? For you have a custom, that I should release unto you one at the passover: will you therefore that I release unto you the King of the Jews?" For he knew that the chief priests had delivered him for envy.

16   When he was seated on the judgment seat, his wife sent unto him, saying, "Have nothing to do with that just man: for I have suffered many things this day in a dream because of him."

17   But the chief priests and elders persuaded the multitude that he should rather release Barabbas unto them, and destroy Jesus. The governor answered and said unto them, "Which of the two will you that I release unto you?" They said, "Barabbas." And they all cried out at once, saying, "Away with this man, and release unto us Barabbas": (who for a certain insurrection made in the city, and for murder, was cast into prison). Then they all cried again, saying, "Not this man, but Barabbas." Now Barabbas was a robber.

18   And Pilate answered and said again unto them, "What will you then that I shall do with Jesus which is called Christ, whom you call the King of the Jews?" They all said unto him, "Let him be crucified." And they cried out again, "Crucify him."

19   Then Pilate said unto them, "Why, what evil has he done?" And they cried out the more, saying, "Let him be crucified." Pilate therefore, willing to release Jesus, spoke again to them. But they cried, saying, "Crucify him, crucify him."

20   Then Pilate the governor said unto them the third time, "Why, what evil has he done? I have found no cause of death in him: I will therefore chastise him, and let him go." And they were insistent with loud voices, requiring that he might be crucified. And the voices of them and of the chief priests prevailed.

Before Pilate: Jesus Is to Die
Matthew 27:24-26; Mark 15:15; Luke 23:24-25; John 19:1

21   When Pilate saw that he could prevail nothing, but that rather a tumult was made, he took water, and washed his hands before the multitude, saying, "I am innocent of the blood of this just person: you see to it." Then answered all the people, and said, "His blood be on us, and on our children."

22   And Pilate gave sentence that it should be as they required. And he released unto them him that for insurrection and murder was cast into prison, whom they had desired; but he delivered Jesus to their will. And so Pilate, willing to satisfy the people, released Barabbas unto them, and when he had scourged Jesus, he delivered Jesus to be crucified.

Before Pilate: Crown of Thorns
Matthew 27:27-30; Mark 15:16-19; John 19:2-3

Then the soldiers of the governor led Jesus away into the common 23 hall, called Praetorium; and gathered unto him the whole band of soldiers. And they stripped him, and they clothed him with a purple robe. And when they had twisted a crown of thorns, they put it upon his head, and a reed in his right hand: and they bowed the knee before him, and mocked him, and said, "Hail, King of the Jews!" and they struck him with their hands. And they spit upon him, and took the reed, and struck him on the head.

Before Pilate: Final Decision
John 19:4-16

Pilate therefore went forth again, and said unto them, "Behold, I bring 24 him forth to you, that you may know that I find no fault in him." Then came Jesus forth, wearing the crown of thorns, and the purple robe. And Pilate said unto them, "Behold the man!"

When the chief priests therefore and officers saw him, they cried out, 25 saying, "Crucify him, crucify him." Pilate said unto them, "Take him, and crucify him: for I find no fault in him." The Jews answered him, "We have a law, and by our law he ought to die, because he made himself the Son of God."

When Pilate therefore heard that saying, he was the more afraid; and 26 went again into the judgment hall, and said unto Jesus, "From where are you?" But Jesus gave him no answer. Then said Pilate unto him, "Do you not speak unto me? know you not that I have power to crucify you, and have power to release you?"

Jesus answered, "You could have no power at all against me, except it 27 were given you from above: therefore he that delivered me unto you has the greater sin." And from then on Pilate sought to release him: but the Jews cried out, saying, "If you let this man go, you are not Caesar's friend: whosoever makes himself a king speaks against Caesar."

When Pilate therefore heard that saying, he brought Jesus forth, and 28 sat down in the judgment seat in a place that is called the Pavement, but in the Hebrew, Gabbatha. And it was the preparation of the passover, and about the sixth hour: and he said unto the Jews, "Behold your King!"

But they cried out, "Away with him, away with him, crucify him." 29 Pilate said unto them, "Shall I crucify your King?" The chief priests answered, "We have no king but Caesar." Then he delivered him therefore unto them to be crucified. And they took Jesus, and led him away.

Before Pilate: Jesus Is Mocked
Matthew 27:31; Mark 15:20

And when they had mocked him, they took off the purple robe from 30 him, and put his own clothes on him, and led him out to crucify him.

CHAPTER 53

THE DARKEST DAY

The Son of God Is Crucified
Matthew 27:32-44; Mark 15:21-32; Luke 23:26-43; John 19:17-24

1   And as they came out, they found a man of Cyrene, Simon by name, coming out of the country, the father of Alexander and Rufus: him they compelled to bear his cross. And as they led him away, on him they laid the cross, that he might bear it after Jesus.

2   And there followed him a great company of people, and of women, which also bewailed and lamented him. But Jesus turning unto them said, "Daughters of Jerusalem, weep not for me, but weep for yourselves, and for your children. For, behold, the days are coming, in which they shall say, 'Blessed are the barren, and the wombs that never bore, and the breasts which never nursed babies.' Then shall they beg ?in *to say to the mountains, "Fall on us"; and to the hills, "Cover us."* ' For if they do these things in a green tree, what shall be done in the dry?"

3   And there were also two others, criminals, led with him to be put to death.

4   And they bring him bearing his cross unto a place called Golgotha in the Hebrew, that is to say, a place of a skull, which is called Calvary: where they crucified him, and the two criminals, one on the right hand, and the other on the left, and Jesus in the middle. And they gave him to drink wine, sour wine mingled with myrrh, gall: and when he had tasted thereof, he would not drink. Then Jesus said, "Father, forgive them; for they know not what they do."

5   And it was the third hour, and they crucified him. Then the soldiers, when they had crucified Jesus, took his garments, and made four parts, and parted his garments, to every soldier a part; and also his coat: now the coat was without seam, woven from the top throughout. They said therefore among themselves, "Let us not tear it, but cast lots for it, whose it shall be": that the scripture might be fulfilled, which says, "*They parted my garments*

among them, and for my clothing they did cast lots." These things therefore 5 the soldiers did.

And sitting down they watched him there. And Pilate wrote a title, and 6 put it on the cross. And the writing was, JESUS OF NAZARETH THE KING OF THE JEWS. This title then read many of the Jews: for the place where Jesus was crucified was near to the city: and it was written in Hebrew, and Greek, and Latin. Then said the chief priests of the Jews to Pilate, "Write not, 'The King of the Jews'; but that 'he said, "I am King of the Jews." ' " Pilate answered, "What I have written I have written."

Then there were two thieves crucified with him, one on the right hand, 7 and another on the left. And the scripture was fulfilled, which says, *"And he was numbered with the transgressors."* And they that passed by hurled insults on him, wagging their heads, and saying, "Ah, you that destroy the temple, and build it in three days, save yourself, and come down from the cross. If you be the Son of God, come down from the cross."

And the people stood beholding. And the rulers also with them scoffed 8 at him, saying, "He saved others; let him save himself, if he be Christ, the chosen of God." And the soldiers also mocked him, coming to him, and offering him sour wine, and saying, "If you be the king of the Jews, save yourself."

Likewise also the chief priests mocking him, with the scribes and eld- 9 ers, said among themselves, "He saved others; himself he cannot save. If he be the King of Israel, let him now come down from the cross, that we may see, and we will believe him. He trusted in God; let him deliver him now, if he will have him: for he said, 'I am the Son of God.' " The thieves also, which were crucified with him, hurled insults on him.

And one of the criminals which were hanged hurled insults on him, 10 saying, "If you be Christ, save yourself and us." But the other answering rebuked him, saying, "Do you not fear God, seeing you are in the same condemnation? And we indeed justly; for we receive the due reward of our deeds: but this man has done nothing wrong." And he said unto Jesus, "Lord, remember me when you come into your kingdom." And Jesus said unto him, "Truly I say unto you, Today shall you be with me in paradise."

Jesus Provides for His Mother
John 19:25-27

Now there stood by the cross of Jesus his mother, and his mother's sis- 11 ter, Mary the wife of Clopas, and Mary Magdalene. When Jesus therefore saw his mother, and the disciple standing by, whom he loved, he said unto his mother, "Woman, behold your son!" Then he said to the disciple, "Behold your mother!" And from that hour that disciple took her unto his own home.

Jesus Dies on the Cross
Matthew 27:45-56; Mark 15:33-41; Luke 23:44-49; John 19:28-37

And it was about the sixth hour, and from the sixth hour there was 12 darkness over the whole land until the ninth hour.

13   And at about the ninth hour Jesus cried with a loud voice, saying, "Eloi, Eloi, lama sabachthani?" which is, being interpreted, *"My God, my*

> "MY GOD, MY GOD, WHY HAVE YOU FORSAKEN ME?"

God, why have you forsaken me?" Some of them that stood there, when they heard that, said, "Behold, he calls for Elijah."

14   After this, Jesus knowing that all things were now accomplished, that the scripture might be fulfilled, said, "I thirst." Now there was set a vessel full of sour wine: and straightway one of them ran, and took a sponge, and filled it with sour wine, and put it on a hyssop reed, and put it to his mouth, and gave him to drink, saying "Let alone; let us see whether Elijah will come to take him down."

15   The rest said, "Let him be, let us see whether Elijah will come to save him."

16   When Jesus therefore had received the sour wine, he said, "It is fin-

> "IT IS FINISHED"..."FATHER, INTO YOUR HANDS I COMMEND MY SPIRIT."

ished": and when Jesus had cried again with a loud voice, he said, *"Father, into your hands I commend my spirit"*: and having said thus, he bowed his head, and gave up the ghost.

17   And the sun was darkened, and, behold, the veil of the temple was torn in two, in the middle, from the top to the bottom; and the earth did quake, and the rocks split; and the graves were opened; and many bodies of the saints which slept arose, and came out of the graves after his resurrection, and went into the holy city, and appeared unto many.

18   Now when the centurion, and they that were with him, watching Jesus, saw the earthquake, and those things that were done, they feared greatly. And when the centurion, which stood opposite him, saw that he so cried out, and gave up the ghost, he glorified God, saying, "Certainly this was a righteous man. Truly this man was the Son of God."

19   And all the people that came together to that sight, beholding the things which were done, struck down their breasts, and returned. And all his acquaintances, and the women that followed him from Galilee, stood afar off, beholding these things: among whom was Mary Magdalene, and Mary the mother of James the less and of Joses, and Salome, the mother of Zebedee's children; (who also, when he was in Galilee, followed him, and ministered unto him); and many other women which came up with him unto Jerusalem.

20   The Jews therefore, because it was the preparation, that the bodies should not remain upon the cross on the sabbath day, (for that sabbath day was a high day), besought Pilate that their legs might be broken, and that they might be taken away. Then came the soldiers, and broke the legs of the first, and of the other which was crucified with him. But when they came to Jesus, and saw that he was dead already, they did not break his legs: but one of the soldiers with a spear pierced his side, and at once came there out blood and water.

And he that saw it bore witness, and his witness is true: and he knows 21 that he says true, that you might believe. For these things were done, that the scripture should be fulfilled, *"A bone of him shall not be broken."* And again another scripture says, *"They shall look on him whom they pierced."*

Burial of Jesus
Matthew 27:57-61; Mark 15:42-47; Luke 23:50-56; John 19:38-42

And after this when the evening was come, because it was the prepa- 22 ration, that is, the day before the sabbath, behold, there was a rich man of Arimathea, a city of the Jews, named Joseph, a prominent council member, a good man, and just: (the same had not consented to the purpose and deed of them); who also himself waited for the kingdom of God. And being a disciple of Jesus, but secretly for fear of the Jews, came, and went in boldly unto Pilate, and asked for the body of Jesus. And Pilate marveled that he were already dead: and calling unto him the centurion, he asked him whether he had been already dead. And when he knew it of the centurion, Pilate gave him permission. Then Pilate commanded the body to be delivered to Joseph. He came therefore, and took the body of Jesus.

Now in the place where he was crucified there was a garden; and in 23 the garden a new tomb, wherein was never man yet laid. And he bought fine linen, and when Joseph had taken the body down, he wrapped it in a clean linen cloth: and laid it in his own new tomb, which he had hewn out in the rock. And there came also Nicodemus, which at the first came to Jesus by night, and brought a mixture of myrrh and aloes, about a hundred pounds in weight. Then they took the body of Jesus, and wound it in linen clothes with the spices, as the manner of the Jews is to bury. There they laid Jesus; for the tomb was near at hand: and rolled a great stone unto the door of the tomb, and departed.

And that day was the preparation, and the sabbath drew on. And there 24 was Mary Magdalene, and the other Mary the mother of Joses, sitting opposite the tomb, and beheld where he was laid. And the women also, which came with him from Galilee, followed after, and beheld the tomb, and how his body was laid. And they returned, and prepared spices and ointments; and rested the sabbath day according to the commandment.

Pilate Places a Watch at the Tomb
Matthew 27:62-66

Now the next day, that followed the day of the preparation, the chief 25 priests and Pharisees came together unto Pilate, saying, "Sir, we remember that that deceiver said, while he was yet alive, 'After three days I will rise again.' Command therefore that the tomb be made sure until the third day, lest his disciples come by night, and steal him away, and say unto the people, 'He is risen from the dead': so the last error shall be worse than the first."

Pilate said unto them, "You have a guard: go your way, make it as 26 secure as you can." So they went, and made the tomb secure, sealing the stone, and setting a guard.

PART 12

RESURRECTION AND ASCENSION

Just three days past the pain, humiliation, and sorrow of His death on the cross, Jesus rose from the dead in radiant glory, victorious over the grave. He rolled away the stone of doubt from the hearts of all mankind and wiped the tears of sorrow from their eyes. With one divine act He vanquished evil and overcame the last enemy, called death. Then He revealed Himself—as He does today—to all prepared to accept the infinite possibilities of God.

> FOR, BEHOLD, THERE WAS A GREAT EARTHQUAKE:
> FOR THE ANGEL OF THE LORD DESCENDED FROM
> HEAVEN, AND CAME AND ROLLED BACK THE
> STONE FROM THE DOOR. (MATTHEW 28:2)

CHAPTER 54

THE BRIGHTEST DAWN

Jesus Is Raised From the Dead
Matthew 28:1-8; Mark 16:1-8; Luke 24:1-7; John 20:1-2

1 Now when the sabbath was past, upon the first day of the week when it was yet dark, Mary Magdalene, and the other Mary the mother of James, and Salome, had bought sweet spices, that they might come and anoint him. And very early in the morning as it began to dawn at the rising of the sun, they came unto the tomb, bringing the spices which they had prepared, and certain others with them. And they said among themselves, "Who shall roll us away the stone from the door of the tomb?" And when they looked, they saw that the stone was rolled away: for it was very great.

2 For, behold, there was a great earthquake: for the angel of the Lord descended from heaven, and came and rolled back the stone from the door, and sat upon it. His countenance was like lightning, and his clothing white as snow: and for fear of him the guards did shake, and became as dead men.

3 And the angel answered and said unto the women, "Fear not: for I know that you seek Jesus, which was crucified. He is not here: for he is risen, as he said. Come, see the place where the Lord lay. And go quickly, and tell his disciples that he is risen from the dead; and, behold, he goes before you into Galilee; there shall you see him: lo, I have told you."

4 And they entered into the tomb, and did not find the body of the Lord Jesus. And they saw a young man sitting on the right side, clothed in a long white robe; and they were alarmed. And he said unto them, "Be not alarmed: You seek Jesus of Nazareth, which was crucified: he is risen; he is not here: behold the place where they laid him."

5 And it came to pass, as the women were much perplexed about this, behold, two men stood by them in shining clothes: and as the women were afraid, and bowed down their faces to the earth, they said unto them, "Why do you seek the living among the dead? He is not here, but is risen:

5 remember how he spoke unto you when he was yet in Galilee, saying, 'The Son of man must be delivered into the hands of sinful men, and be crucified, and the third day rise again.'

6   "But go your way, tell his disciples and Peter that he goes before you into Galilee: there shall you see him, as he said unto you." And they went out quickly, and fled from the tomb; for they trembled and were amazed: neither said they anything to any man; for they were afraid.

7   Then Mary Magdalene ran, and came to Simon Peter, and to the other disciple, whom Jesus loved, and said unto them, "They have taken away the Lord out of the tomb, and we know not where they have laid him."

8   And they departed from the tomb with fear and great joy; and did run to bring his disciples word.

John and Peter See Empty Tomb
Luke 24:12; John 20:3-10

9   Peter therefore went forth, and that other disciple, and came to the tomb. So they ran both together: and the other disciple did outrun Peter, and came first to the tomb. And he stooping down, and looking in, saw the linen clothes lying; yet he went not in.

10   Then came Simon Peter following him unto the tomb; and stooping down, he beheld the linen clothes laid by themselves, and went into the tomb, and saw the linen clothes lie, and the cloth, that was about his head, not lying with the linen clothes, but wrapped together in a place by itself, wondering in himself at that which was come to pass.

11   Then went in also that other disciple, which came first to the tomb, and he saw, and believed. For as yet they knew not the scripture, that he must rise again from the dead. Then the disciples went away again unto their own homes.

Jesus Appears to Mary Magdalene
Mark 16:9-11; John 20:11-18

12   But Mary stood outside at the tomb weeping: and as she wept, she stooped down, and looked into the tomb, and saw two angels in white sitting, the one at the head, and the other at the feet, where the body of Jesus had lain. And they said unto her, "Woman, why do you weep?" She said unto them, "Because they have taken away my Lord, and I do not know where they have laid him."

13   And when she had thus said, she turned herself around, and saw Jesus standing, and knew not that it was Jesus. Now when Jesus was risen early the first day of the week, he appeared first to Mary Magdalene, out of whom he had cast seven demons.

14   Jesus said unto her, "Woman, why do you weep? whom do you seek?" She, supposing him to be the gardener, said unto him, "Sir, if you have

carried him from here, tell me where you have laid him, and I will take him 14
away."

Jesus said unto her, "Mary." She turned herself, and said unto him, 15
"Rabboni"; which is to say, Teacher. Jesus said unto her, "Do not touch me;
for I am not yet ascended to my Father: but go to my brethren, and say unto
them, 'I ascend unto my Father, and your Father; and to my God, and your
God.'"

Mary Magdalene came and told the disciples that had been with him, 16
as they mourned and wept, that she had seen the Lord, and that he had spoken these things unto her. And they, when they had heard that he was alive,
and had been seen of her, did not believe her.

Jesus Appears to the Women
Matthew 28:9-10

And as they (the women) went to tell his disciples, behold, Jesus met 17
them, saying, "All hail." And they came and held him by the feet, and worshiped him. Then said Jesus unto them, "Be not afraid: go tell my brethren
that they go into Galilee, and there shall they see me."

Women Give Witness to Resurrection
Luke 24:8-11

And they remembered his words, and told all these things unto the 18
eleven, and to all the rest. It was Mary Magdalene, and Joanna, and Mary
the mother of James, and other women that were with them, which told
these things unto the apostles. And their words seemed to them as idle tales,
and they did not believe them.

Report of the Watch Made False
Matthew 28:11-15

Now when they were going, behold, some of the guard came into the 19
city, and showed unto the chief priests all the things that were done. And
when they were assembled with the elders, and had conferred, they gave a
large sum of money unto the soldiers, saying, "You say, 'His disciples came
by night, and stole him away while we slept.' And if this comes to the governor's ears, we will persuade him, and secure you." So they took the
money, and did as they were instructed: and this saying is commonly
reported among the Jews until this day.

Jesus Appears to Two on the Road
Mark 16:12-13; Luke 24:13-35

After that he appeared in another form unto two of them, as they 20
walked, and went into the country. And, behold, two of them went that same
day to a village called Emmaus, which was from Jerusalem about seven
miles. And they talked together of all these things which had happened.

And it came to pass, that, while they talked together and reasoned, Jesus 21
himself drew near, and went with them. But their eyes were constrained that

21 they should not know him. And he said unto them, "What manner of communications are these that you have one to another, as you walk, and are sad?"

22 And the one of them, whose name was Cleopas, answering said unto him, "Are you only a visitor in Jerusalem, and have not known the things which are come to pass there in these days?" And he said unto them, "What things?" And they said unto him, "Concerning Jesus of Nazareth, which was a prophet mighty in deed and word before God and all the people: and how the chief priests and our rulers delivered him to be condemned to death, and have crucified him. But we trusted that it had been he which should have redeemed Israel: and besides all this, today is the third day since these things were done.

23 "Yes, and certain women also of our company made us astonished, which were early at the tomb; and when they did not find his body, they came, saying, that they had also seen a vision of angels, which said that he was alive.

24 "And certain of them which were with us went to the tomb, and found it even so as the women had said: but him they did not see." Then he said unto them, "O fools, and slow of heart to believe all that the prophets have spoken: ought not Christ to have suffered these things, and to enter into his glory?" And beginning at Moses and all the prophets, he explained unto them in all the scriptures the things concerning himself.

25 And they drew near unto the village, where they went: and he made as though he would have gone farther. But they stopped him, saying, "Stay with us: for it is toward evening, and the day is far spent." And he went in to tarry with them.

26 And it came to pass, as he sat at the table with them, he took bread, and blessed it, and broke, and gave to them. And their eyes were opened, and they knew him; and he vanished out of their sight. And they said one to another, "Did not our heart burn within us, while he talked with us on the road, and while he opened to us the scriptures?"

27 And they rose up the same hour, and returned to Jerusalem, and found the eleven gathered together, and them that were with them, saying, "The Lord is risen indeed, and has appeared to Simon." And they told what things were done on the road, and how he was known of them in breaking of bread: neither did they believe them.

Jesus Appears to Disciples
Mark 16:14; Luke 24:36-43; John 20:19-25

28 Then the same day at evening, being the first day of the week, when the doors were shut where the disciples were assembled for fear of the Jews, he appeared unto the eleven as they sat at the table, and rebuked them with their unbelief and hardness of heart, because they had not believed them which had seen him after he was risen. And as they thus spoke, Jesus himself stood in the midst of them, and said unto them, "Peace be unto you."

But they were terrified and frightened, and supposed that they had 29 seen a spirit. And he said unto them, "Why are you troubled? and why do thoughts arise in your hearts? Behold my hands and my feet, that it is I myself: handle me, and see; for a spirit has not flesh and bones, as you see me have."

And when he had thus spoken, he showed them his hands and his feet 30 and his side. And while they yet had not believed for joy, and wondered, he said unto them, "Have you here any food?" And they gave him a piece of a broiled fish, and of a honeycomb. And he took it, and did eat before them. Then were the disciples glad, when they saw the Lord.

Then Jesus said to them again, "Peace be unto you: as my Father has 31 sent me, even so I send you." And when he had said this, he breathed on them, and said unto them, "Receive the Holy Ghost: those whose sins you forgive, they are forgiven unto them; and those whose sins you retain, they are retained."

> "RECEIVE THE HOLY GHOST."

But Thomas, one of the twelve, called Didymus, was not with them 32 when Jesus came. The other disciples therefore said unto him, "We have seen the Lord." But he said unto them, "Unless I shall see in his hands the print of the nails, and put my finger into the print of the nails, and thrust my hand into his side, I will not believe."

CHAPTER 55

THE GREAT COMMISSION

Jesus Appears to Thomas
John 20:26-29

1   And after eight days again his disciples were inside, and Thomas with them: then Jesus came, the doors being shut, and stood in the midst, and said, "Peace be unto you." Then he said to Thomas, "Reach here your finger, and behold my hands; and reach here your hand, and thrust it into my side: and be not faithless, but believing."

2   And Thomas answered and said unto him, "My Lord and my God." Jesus said unto him, "Thomas, because you have seen me, you have believed: blessed are they that have not seen, and yet have believed."

Jesus Appears at the Sea of Galilee
John 21:1-14

3   After these things Jesus showed himself again to the disciples at the sea of Galilee; and in this way he showed himself. There were together Simon Peter, and Thomas called Didymus, and Nathanael of Cana in Galilee, and the sons of Zebedee, and two others of his disciples. Simon Peter said unto them, "I go fishing." They said unto him, "We also go with you." They went forth, and entered into a ship immediately; and that night they caught nothing. But when the morning was now come, Jesus stood on the shore: but the disciples did not know that it was Jesus.

4   Then Jesus said unto them, "Children, have you any fish?" They answered him, "No." And he said unto them, "Cast the net on the right side of the ship, and you shall find." They cast therefore, and now they were not able to draw it for the multitude of fishes.

5   Therefore that disciple whom Jesus loved said unto Peter, "It is the Lord." Now when Simon Peter heard that it was the Lord, he wrapped his fisher's coat unto him, (for he was naked), and did cast himself into the sea.

And the other disciples came in a little ship; (for they were not far from 5 land, but as it were three hundred feet), dragging the net with fishes.

As soon then as they were come to land, they saw a fire of coals there, 6 and fish laid thereon, and bread. Jesus said unto them, "Bring of the fish which you have now caught." Simon Peter went up, and drew the net to land full of great fishes, a hundred and fifty and three: and although there were so many, yet the net was not broken.

Jesus said unto them, "Come and have breakfast." And none of the 7 disciples dared ask him, "Who are you?" knowing that it was the Lord. Jesus then came, and took bread, and gave them, and fish likewise. This is now the third time that Jesus showed himself to his disciples, after that he was risen from the dead.

Jesus Counsels Peter
John 21:15-24

So when they had finished breakfast, Jesus said to Simon Peter, 8 "Simon, son of Jonah, do you totally love me more than these?" He said unto him, "Yes, Lord; you know that I love you." He said unto him, "Feed my lambs." He said to him again the second time, "Simon, son of Jonah, do you totally love me?" He said unto him, "Yes, Lord; you know that I love you." He said unto him, "Tend my sheep." He said unto him the third time, "Simon, son of Jonah, do you love me?" Peter was grieved because he said unto him the third time, "Do you love me?" And he said unto him, "Lord, you know all things; you know that I love you." Jesus said unto him, "Feed my sheep.

"Truly, truly, I say unto you, When you were young, you dressed your- 9 self, and walked where you would: but when you shall be old, you shall stretch forth your hands, and another shall dress you, and carry you where you would not." This he spoke, signifying by what death he should glorify God. And when he had spoken this, he said unto him, "Follow me."

Then Peter, turning about, saw the disciple whom Jesus loved follow- 10 ing; which also leaned on his breast at supper, and said, "Lord, which is he that betrays you?" Peter seeing him said to Jesus, "Lord, and what shall this man do?" Jesus said unto him, "If I will that he tarry till I come, what is that to you? You follow me."

Then went this saying abroad among the brethren, that that disciple 11 should not die: yet Jesus did not say unto him, "He shall not die"; but, "If I will that he tarry till I come, what is that to you?" This is the disciple which testifies of these things, and wrote these things: and we know that his testimony is true.

Jesus Appears to Give Commission
Matthew 28:16-20; Mark 16:15-18

Then the eleven disciples went away into Galilee, into a mountain 12 where Jesus had appointed them. And when they saw him, they worshiped him: but some doubted.

13   And Jesus came and spoke unto them, saying, "All authority is given unto me in heaven and on earth. Go therefore, and teach all nations, baptizing them in the name of the Father, and of the Son, and of the Holy Ghost: teaching them to observe all things whatsoever I have commanded you: and, lo, I am with you always, even unto the end of the world."

14   And he said unto them, "Go into all the world, and preach the gospel to every creature. He that believes and is baptized shall be saved; but he that believes not shall be condemned. And these signs shall follow them that believe: In my name shall they cast out demons; they shall speak with new tongues; they shall take up serpents; and if they drink any deadly thing, it shall not hurt them; they shall lay hands on the sick, and they shall recover."

Await the Promise of the Father
Luke 24:44-49

15   And he said unto them, "These are the words which I spoke unto you, while I was yet with you, that all things must be fulfilled, which were written in the law of Moses, and in the prophets, and in the psalms, concerning me. Then he opened their minds, that they might understand the scriptures, and said unto them, Thus it is written, and thus it behooved Christ to suffer, and to rise from the dead the third day: and that repentance and remission of sins should be preached in his name among all nations, beginning at Jerusalem. And you are witnesses of these things.

16   "And, behold, I send the promise of my Father upon you: but tarry in the city of Jerusalem, until you be endued with power from on high."

Jesus Ascends to Heaven
Mark 16:19; Luke 24:50-51

17   And he led them out as far as to Bethany, and he lifted up his hands, and blessed them. And it came to pass, while he blessed them, he was parted from them, and carried up into heaven, and sat on the right hand of God.

Disciples Obey Jesus' Commission
Mark 16:20; Luke 24:52-53

18   And they worshiped him, and returned to Jerusalem with great joy: and were continually in the temple, praising and blessing God.

19   And they went forth, and preached everywhere, the Lord working with them, and confirming the word with signs following.

Written That You Might Believe
John 20:30-31; 21:25

20   And many other signs truly did Jesus in the presence of his disciples, which are not written in this book: but these are written, that you might believe that Jesus is the Christ, the Son of God; and that believing you might have life through his name.

21   And there are also many other things which Jesus did, which, if they should be written every one, I suppose that even the world itself could not contain the books that should be written. Amen.

CHAPTER 56

GENEALOGY OF JESUS

The Two Genealogies of Jesus
Matthew 1:1-17; Luke 3:23-38

The book of the genealogy of Jesus Christ, the son of David, the son 1
of Abraham. Abraham begot Isaac; and Isaac begot Jacob; and Jacob begot
Judah and his brethren; and Judah begot Perez and Zerah by Tamar; and
Perez begot Hezron; and Hezron begot Ram; and Ram begot Amminadab;
and Amminadab begot Nahshon; and Nahshon begot Salmon; and Salmon
begot Boaz of Rahab; and Boaz begot Obed by Ruth; and Obed begot Jesse;
and Jesse begot David the king; and David the king begot Solomon by her
who had been the wife of Uriah; and Solomon begot Rehoboam; and
Rehoboam begot Abijah; and Abijah begot Asa; and Asa begot Jehoshaphat;
and Jehoshaphat begot Joram; and Joram begot Uzziah; and Uzziah begot
Jotham; and Jotham begot Ahaz; and Ahaz begot Hezekiah; and Hezekiah
begot Manasseh; and Manasseh begot Amon; and Amon begot Josias; and
Josias begot Jeconiah and his brethren, about the time they were carried
away to Babylon: and after they were brought to Babylon, Jeconiah begot
Shealtiel; and Shealtiel begot Zerubbabel; and Zerubbabel begot Abiud;
and Abiud begot Eliakim; and Eliakim begot Azor; and Azor begot Zadok;
and Zadok begot Achim; and Achim begot Eliud; and Eliud begot Eleazar;
and Eleazar begot Matthan; and Matthan begot Jacob; and Jacob begot
Joseph the husband of Mary, of whom was born Jesus, who is called Christ.

So all the generations from Abraham to David are fourteen genera- 2
tions; and from David until the carrying away into Babylon are fourteen
generations; and from the carrying away into Babylon unto Christ are fourteen generations.

And Jesus himself began to be about thirty years of age, being (as was 3
supposed) the son of Joseph, which was the son of Heli, which was the son
of Matthat, which was the son of Levi, which was the son of Melchi, which

3 was the son of Janna, which was the son of Joseph, which was the son of Mattathiah, which was the son of Amos, which was the son of Nahum, which was the son of Esli, which was the son of Naggai, which was the son of Maath, which was the son of Mattathiah, which was the son of Semei, which was the son of Joseph, which was the son of Judah, which was the son of Joannas, which was the son of Rhesa, which was the son of Zerubbabel, which was the son of Shealtiel, which was the son of Neri, which was the son of Melchi, which was the son of Addi, which was the son of Cosam, which was the son of Elmodam, which was the son of Er, which was the son of Jose, which was the son of Eliezer, which was the son of Jorim, which was the son of Matthat, which was the son of Levi, which was the son of Simeon, which was the son of Judah, which was the son of Joseph, which was the son of Jonan, which was the son of Eliakim, which was the son of Melea, which was the son of Menan, which was the son of Mattathah, which was the son of Nathan, which was the son of David, which was the son of Jesse, which was the son of Obed, which was the son of Boaz, which was the son of Salmon, which was the son of Nahshon, which was the son of Amminadab, which was the son of Ram, which was the son of Hezron, which was the son of Perez, which was the son of Judah, which was the son of Jacob, which was the son of Isaac, which was the son of Abraham, which was the son of Terah, which was the son of Nahor, which was the son of Serug, which was the son of Reu, which was the son of Peleg, which was the son of Eber, which was the son of Shelah, which was the son of Cainan, which was the son of Arphaxad, which was the son of Shem, which was the son of Noah, which was the son of Lamech, which was the son of Methuselah, which was the son of Enoch, which was the son of Jared, which was the son of Mahalalel, which was the son of Cainan, which was the son of Enos, which was the son of Seth, which was the son of Adam, which was the son of God.

This greatest of all stories is much more than a collection of many stories. It demonstrates the science of being by which to live. It opens the way to an understanding of God as the one true being—overlying, underlying, and encompassing all true being. Jesus taught no mere theory or doctrine of worship. It was the divine Principle of all real being that enabled Him to perform miracles—miracles that are as natural now as they were then to all who are willing to follow in His footsteps.

The Journey of the Apostles

PART 13

EMERGENCE OF THE APOSTLES

The mission of Jesus was exemplified not only through His own works, but also through the acts of the Apostles who continued His work after His death. His resurrection was their resurrection, enabling them to demonstrate with full assurance the same healing power of God's love that Jesus had proved. His reappearance unchanged after death proved to them the eternal nature of man's unbroken relationship with God. His ascension before their eyes confirmed the boundless power and presence of God's love and sealed forever the highest hope of life everlasting in the hearts of all men. In renewed faith, they took up His cross and went forward with boldness. From the first assembly of faithful disciples, the word of God spread across the country to thousands, bridging religious boundaries. Frightful persecutions followed and many fled from Jerusalem beyond the reach of the Jewish leaders.

"YOU SHALL RECEIVE POWER, AFTER THE HOLY GHOST IS COME UPON YOU: AND YOU SHALL WITNESS UNTO ME BOTH IN JERUSALEM...AND UNTO THE UTTERMOST PART OF THE EARTH."

(ACTS 1:8)

CHAPTER 57

THE COMING OF THE HOLY GHOST

The Promise
Acts 1:1-5

The former writing have I made of all that Jesus began both to do and teach, until the day in which he was taken up, after that he through the Holy Ghost had given commandments unto the apostles whom he had chosen: to whom also he showed himself alive after his suffering by many infallible proofs, being seen of them forty days, and speaking of the things pertaining to the kingdom of God. 1

And, being assembled together with them, commanded them that they should not depart from Jerusalem, but wait for the promise of the Father, which, he said, "you have heard of me. For John truly baptized with water; but you shall be baptized with the Holy Ghost not many days from now." 2

Jesus' Ascension Into Heaven
Acts 1:6-11

When they therefore were come together, they asked of him, saying, "Lord, will you at this time restore again the kingdom to Israel?" And he said unto them, "It is not for you to know the times or the seasons, which the Father has put in his own authority. But you shall receive power, after the Holy Ghost is come upon you: and you shall be witnesses unto me both in Jerusalem, and in all Judea, and in Samaria, and unto the uttermost part of the earth." 3

And when he had spoken these things, while they beheld, he was taken up; and a cloud received him out of their sight. 4

And while they looked steadfastly toward heaven as he went up, behold, two men stood by them in white apparel; which also said, "You men of Galilee, why do you stand gazing up into heaven? this same Jesus, which is taken up from you into heaven, shall so come in like manner as you have seen him go into heaven." 5

One Accord in the Upper Room
Acts 1:12-14

6   Then they returned unto Jerusalem from the mount called Olivet, which is from Jerusalem a sabbath day's journey.

7   And when they were come in, they went up into an upper room, where remained both Peter, and James, and John, and Andrew, Philip, and Thomas, Bartholomew, and Matthew, James the son of Alphaeus, and Simon Zelotes, and Judas the brother of James.

8   These all continued with one accord in prayer and supplication, with the women, and Mary the mother of Jesus, and with his brethren.

Election of a New Apostle
Acts 1:15-26

9   And in those days Peter stood up in the midst of the disciples, and said, (the number of names together were about a hundred and twenty), "Men and brethren, this scripture must of necessity have been fulfilled, which the Holy Ghost by the mouth of David spoke before concerning Judas, which was guide to them that took Jesus. For he was numbered with us, and had obtained part of this ministry."

10   (Now this man purchased a field with the reward of iniquity; and falling headlong, he burst asunder in the middle, and all his bowels gushed out. And it was known unto all the dwellers at Jerusalem; insomuch as that field is called in their own tongue, Aceldama, that is to say, The Field of Blood.) "For it is written in the book of Psalms, '*Let his habitation be desolate, and let no man dwell therein*': and '*his overseer position let another take.*'

11   "Therefore of these men which have companied with us all the time that the Lord Jesus went in and out among us, beginning from the baptism of John, unto that same day that he was taken up from us, must one be ordained to be a witness with us of his resurrection."

12   And they appointed two, Joseph called Barsabas, who was surnamed Justus, and Matthias. And they prayed, and said, "You, Lord, which know the hearts of all men, show which of these two you have chosen, that he may take part of this ministry and apostleship, from which Judas by transgression fell, that he might go to his own place." And they gave forth their lots; and the lot fell upon Matthias; and he was numbered with the eleven apostles.

Arrival of the Holy Ghost
Acts 2:1-13

13   And when the day of Pentecost was fully come, they were all with one accord in one place. And suddenly there came a sound from heaven as of a rushing mighty wind, and it filled all the house where they were sitting. And there appeared unto them divided tongues like as of fire, and it sat upon each of them. And they were all filled

> "SUDDENLY THERE CAME A SOUND FROM HEAVEN AS OF A RUSHING MIGHTY WIND."

with the Holy Ghost, and began to speak with other tongues, as the Spirit gave them utterance.

And there were dwelling at Jerusalem Jews, devout men, out of every 14
nation under heaven. Now when this was heard, the multitude came together,
and were confounded, because that every man heard them speak in his own
language. And they were all amazed and marveled, saying one to another,
"Behold, are not all these which speak Galileans? And how hear we every
man in our own tongue, wherein we were born? Parthians, and Medes, and
Elamites, and the dwellers in Mesopotamia, and in Judea, and Cappadocia,
in Pontus, and Asia, Phrygia, and Pamphylia, in Egypt, and in the parts of
Libya about Cyrene, and visitors of Rome, Jews and converts to Judaism,
Cretans and Arabians, we do hear them speak in our tongues the wonderful
works of God."

And they were all amazed, and were in doubt, saying one to another, "What 15
does this mean?" Others mocking said, "These men are full of new wine."

Peter's Address to the Crowd
Acts 2:14-36

But Peter, standing up with the eleven, lifted up his voice, and said 16
unto them, "You men of Judea, and all you that dwell at Jerusalem, be this
known unto you, and hearken to my words: for these are not drunk, as you
suppose, seeing it is but the third hour of the day.

"But this is that which was spoken by the prophet Joel: '*And it shall* 17
come to pass in the last days, says God, I will pour out of my Spirit upon all
flesh: and your sons and your daughters shall prophesy, and your young men
shall see visions, and your old men shall dream dreams: and on my servants
and on my handmaidens I will pour out in those days of my Spirit; and they
shall prophesy: and I will show wonders in heaven above, and signs in the
earth beneath; blood, and fire, and vapor of smoke: the sun shall be turned
into darkness, and the moon into blood, before that great and terrible day of
the Lord comes: and it shall come to pass, that whosoever shall call on the
name of the Lord shall be saved.'

"You men of Israel, hear these words; Jesus of Nazareth, a man 18
approved of God among you by miracles and wonders and signs, which God
did by him in the midst of you, as you yourselves also know: him, being
delivered by the predetermined purpose and foreknowledge of God, you
have taken, and by wicked hands have crucified and slain: whom God has
raised up, having loosed the pains of death: because it was not possible that
he should be held of it.

"For David speaks concerning him, '*I foresaw the Lord always before* 19
my face, for he is on my right hand, that I should not be moved: therefore
did my heart rejoice, and my tongue was glad; moreover also my flesh shall
rest in hope: because you will not leave my soul in Hades, neither will you
allow your Holy One to see corruption. You have made known to me the
ways of life; you shall make me full of joy with your countenance.'

20   "Men and brethren, let me freely speak unto you of the patriarch David, that he is both dead and buried, and his tomb is with us unto this day. Therefore being a prophet, and knowing that God had *sworn with an oath to him, that of the fruit of his loins, according to the flesh, he would raise up Christ to sit on his throne*; he seeing this before spoke of the resurrection of Christ, that *his soul was not left in Hades, neither his flesh did see corruption.*

21   "This Jesus has God raised up, of which we all are witnesses. Therefore being by the right hand of God exalted, and having received of the Father the promise of the Holy Ghost, he has poured forth this, which you now see and hear. For David is not ascended into the heavens: but he says himself, '*The Lord said unto my Lord, "Sit you on my right hand, until I make your foes your footstool."*'

> "JESUS HAS GOD RAISED UP, OF WHICH WE ALL ARE WITNESSES."

22   "Therefore let all the house of Israel know assuredly, that God has made that same Jesus, whom you have crucified, both Lord and Christ."

Response of the Crowd
Acts 2:37-42

23   Now when they heard this, they were stung in their heart, and said unto Peter and to the rest of the apostles, "Men and brethren, what shall we do?" Then Peter said unto them, "Repent, and be baptized every one of you in the name of Jesus Christ for the remission of sins, and you shall receive the gift of the Holy Ghost. For the promise is unto you, and to your children, and to all that are afar off, even as many as the Lord our God shall call."

24   And with many other words did he testify and exhort, saying, "Save yourselves from this corrupt generation." Then they that gladly received his word were baptized: and the same day there were added unto them about three thousand souls.

25   And they continued steadfastly in the apostles' doctrine and fellowship, and in breaking of bread, and in prayers.

Life Among the Believers
Acts 2:43-47

26   And fear came upon every soul: and many wonders and signs were done by the apostles. And all that believed were together, and had all things common; and sold their possessions and goods, and parted them to all men, as every man had need.

27   And they, continuing daily with one accord in the temple, and breaking bread from house to house, did eat their food with gladness and singleness of heart, praising God, and having favor with all the people. And the Lord added to the church daily such as should be saved.

> "AND THE LORD ADDED TO THE CHURCH DAILY."

CHAPTER 58

PREACHING AND PERSECUTION

Healing a Lame Man
Acts 3:1-10

Now Peter and John went up together into the temple at the hour of 1
prayer, being the ninth hour. And a certain man lame from his mother's
womb was carried, whom they laid daily at the gate of the temple which is
called Beautiful, to ask donations of them that entered into the temple; who
seeing Peter and John about to go into the temple asked a donation. And
Peter, fastening his eyes upon him with John, said, "Look on us." And he
gave heed unto them, expecting to receive something of them.

Then Peter said, "Silver and gold have I none; but such as I have give 2
I you: In the name of Jesus Christ of Nazareth rise up and walk." And he
took him by the right hand, and lifted him up: and immediately his feet and
ankle bones received strength. And he leaping up stood, and walked, and
entered with them into the temple, walking, and leaping, and praising God.

And all the people saw him walking and praising God: and they knew 3
that it was he which sat for donations at the Beautiful gate of the temple:
and they were filled with wonder and amazement at that which had happened unto him.

Peter Speaks in Solomon's Porch
Acts 3:11-26

And as the lame man which was healed held Peter and John, all the 4
people ran together unto them in the porch that is called Solomon's, greatly
wondering. And when Peter saw it, he answered unto the people, "You men
of Israel, why do you marvel at this? or why do you look so earnestly on us,
as though by our own power or holiness we had made this man to walk?

"*The God of Abraham, and of Isaac, and of Jacob, the God of our* 5
fathers, has glorified his Son Jesus; whom you delivered up, and denied

5   him in the presence of Pilate, when he was determined to let him go. But you denied the Holy One and the Just, and desired a murderer to be granted unto you; and killed the Prince of life, whom God has raised from the dead; of which we are witnesses. And his name through faith in his name has made this man strong, whom you see and know: yes, the faith which is by him has given him this perfect soundness in the presence of you all.

6   "And now, brethren, I know that through ignorance you did it, as did also your rulers. But those things, which God before had showed by the mouth of all his prophets, that Christ should suffer, he has so fulfilled.

> "REPENT YOU THEREFORE, AND BE CONVERTED, THAT YOUR SINS MAY BE BLOTTED OUT."

Repent you therefore, and be converted, that your sins may be blotted out, when the times of refreshing shall come from the presence of the Lord; and he shall send Jesus Christ, which before was preached unto you: whom the heaven must receive until the times of restoration of all things, which God has spoken by the mouth of all his holy prophets since the world began.

7   "For Moses truly said unto the fathers, '*A prophet shall the Lord your God raise up unto you of your brethren, like unto me; him shall you hear in all things whatsoever he shall say unto you. And it shall come to pass, that every soul, which will not hear that prophet, shall be destroyed from among the people.*'

8   "Yes, and all the prophets from Samuel and those that follow afterward, as many as have spoken, have likewise foretold of these days. You are the children of the prophets, and of the covenant which God made with our fathers, saying unto Abraham, '*And in your seed shall all the families of the earth be blessed.*' Unto you first God, having raised up his Son Jesus, sent him to bless you, in turning away every one of you from his iniquities."

Peter and John Before the Council
Acts 4:1-12

9   And as they spoke unto the people, the priests, and the captain of the temple, and the Sadducees, came upon them, being grieved that they taught the people, and preached through Jesus the resurrection from the dead. And they laid hands on them, and put them in custody unto the next day: for it was now evening. Howbeit many of them which heard the word believed; and the number of the men was about five thousand.

10   And it came to pass the next day, that their rulers, and elders, and scribes, and Annas the high priest, and Caiaphas, and John, and Alexander, and as many as were of the family of the high priest, were gathered together at Jerusalem. And when they had set them in the midst, they asked, "By what power, or by what name, have you done this?"

11   Then Peter, filled with the Holy Ghost, said unto them, "You rulers of the people, and elders of Israel, If we this day be examined of the good deed done to the crippled man, by what means he is made whole; be it known unto you all, and to all the people of Israel, that by the name of Jesus Christ

of Nazareth, whom you crucified, whom God raised from the dead, even by 11
him does this man stand here before you whole.

"This is *the stone which was rejected of you builders, which is become* 12
the head of the cornerstone. Neither is there salvation in any other: for there is
no other name under heaven given among men, whereby we must be saved."

Apostles Are Threatened
Acts 4:13-22

Now when they saw the boldness of Peter and John, and perceived that 13
they were uneducated and untrained men, they marveled; and they took
knowledge of them, that they had been with Jesus. And beholding the man
which was healed standing with them, they could say nothing against it.

But when they had commanded them to go aside out of the council, 14
they conferred among themselves, saying, "What shall we do to these men?
for that indeed a notable miracle has been done by them is evident to all
them that dwell in Jerusalem; and we cannot deny it. But that it spreads no
further among the people, let us strictly threaten them, that they speak
henceforth to no man in this name."

And they called them, and commanded them not to speak at all nor 15
teach in the name of Jesus. But Peter and John answered and said unto them,
"Whether it be right in the sight of God to hearken unto you more than unto
God, you judge. For we cannot but speak the things which we have seen and
heard."

So when they had further threatened them, they let them go, finding 16
nothing how they might punish them, because of the people: for all men
glorified God for that which was done. For the man was above forty years
old, on whom this miracle of healing was shown.

Believers Pray for Boldness
Acts 4:23-31

And being let go, they went to their own company, and reported all 17
that the chief priests and elders had said unto them. And when they heard
that, they lifted up their voice to God
with one accord, and said, "Lord, you
are God, which have made heaven, and
earth, and the sea, and all that is in
them: who by the mouth of your servant David have said, *'Why did the*

> "LORD, YOU ARE GOD, WHICH
> HAVE MADE HEAVEN, AND
> EARTH, AND THE SEA, AND ALL
> THAT IS IN THEM."

heathen rage, and the people imagine vain things? The kings of the earth
stood up, and the rulers were gathered together against the Lord, and
against his Christ.'

"For of a truth against your holy child Jesus, whom you have 18
anointed, both Herod (Antipas), and Pontius Pilate, with the Gentiles,
and the people of Israel, were gathered together, to do whatsoever your
hand and your purpose determined before to be done.

19   "And now, Lord, behold their threats: and grant unto your servants, that with all boldness they may speak your word, by stretching forth your hand to heal; and that signs and wonders may be done by the name of your holy child Jesus."

20   And when they had prayed, the place was shaken where they were assembled together; and they were all filled with the Holy Ghost, and they spoke the word of God with boldness.

Believers Share in All Things
Acts 4:32-37

21   And the multitude of them that believed were of one heart and of one soul: neither said any of them that any of the things which he possessed was his own; but they had all things common. And with great power gave the apostles witness of the resurrection of the Lord Jesus: and great grace was upon them all. Neither was there any among them that lacked: for as many as were possessors of lands or houses sold them, and brought the prices of the things that were sold, and laid them down at the apostles' feet: and distribution was made unto every man according as he had need.

> "WITH GREAT POWER GAVE THE APOSTLES WITNESS OF THE RESURRECTION OF THE LORD JESUS: AND GREAT GRACE WAS UPON THEM ALL."

22   And Joses, who by the apostles was surnamed Barnabas, (which is, being interpreted, The son of consolation), a Levite, and of the country of Cyprus, having land, sold it, and brought the money, and laid it at the apostles' feet.

CHAPTER 59

DECEIVERS AND DECISIONS

Lying to Man and to God
Acts 5:1-11

But a certain man named Ananias, with Sapphira his wife, sold a pos- 1
session, and kept back part of the price, his wife also being a party to it, and
brought a certain part, and laid it at the apostles' feet.

But Peter said, "Ananias, why has Satan filled your heart to lie to the 2
Holy Ghost, and to keep back part of the price of the land? While it
remained, was it not your own? and after it was sold, was it not in your own
control? why have you conceived this thing in your heart? you have not lied
unto men, but unto God."

And Ananias hearing these words fell down, and gave up the ghost: 3
and great fear came on all them that heard these things. And the young men
arose, wrapped him up, and carried him out, and buried him.

And it was about the space of three hours afterward, when his wife, 4
not knowing what was done, came in. And Peter answered unto her, "Tell
me whether you sold the land for so much?" And she said, "Yes, for so
much." Then Peter said unto her, "How is it that you have agreed together
to tempt the Spirit of the Lord? behold, the feet of them which have buried
your husband are at the door, and shall carry you out."

Then she fell down straightway at his feet, and yielded up the ghost: 5
and the young men came in, and found her dead, and, carrying her forth,
buried her by her husband. And great fear came upon all the church, and
upon as many as heard these things.

Many Signs and Wonders
Acts 5:12-16

And by the hands of the apostles were many signs and wonders 6
worked among the people; (and they were all with one accord in Solomon's
porch. And of the rest dared no man join himself to them: but the people

6 magnified them. And believers were the more added to the Lord, multitudes both of men and women). Insomuch that they brought forth the sick into the streets, and laid them on beds and couches, that at the least the shadow of Peter passing by might overshadow some of them. There came also a multitude out of the cities round about unto Jerusalem, bringing sick folks, and them which were tormented with unclean spirits: and they were healed every one.

Apostles Put in Prison
Acts 5:17-26

7 Then the high priest rose up, and all they that were with him, (which is the sect of the Sadducees), and were filled with indignation, and laid their hands on the apostles, and put them in the common prison. But the angel of the Lord by night opened the prison doors, and brought them forth, and said, "Go, stand and speak in the temple to the people all the words of this life."

> THE ANGEL OF THE LORD BY NIGHT OPENED THE PRISON DOORS.

8 And when they heard that, they entered into the temple early in the morning, and taught. But the high priest came, and they that were with him, and called the council together, and all the elders of the children of Israel, and sent to the prison to have them brought. But when the officers came, and found them not in the prison, they returned, and told, saying, "The prison truly we found shut with all security, and the guards standing outside before the doors: but when we had opened, we found no man inside."

9 Now when the high priest and the captain of the temple and the chief priests heard these things, they wondered of them to what this would grow.

10 Then came one and told them, saying, "Behold, the men whom you put in prison are standing in the temple, and teaching the people." Then went the captain with the officers, and brought them without violence: for they feared the people, lest they should have been stoned.

Apostles Before the Council
Acts 5:27-42

11 And when they had brought them, they set them before the council: and the high priest asked them, saying, "Did not we strictly command you that you should not teach in this name? and, behold, you have filled Jerusalem with your doctrine, and intend to bring this man's blood upon us."

12 Then Peter and the other apostles answered and said, "We ought to obey God rather than men. The God of our fathers raised up Jesus, whom you slew and hanged on a tree. Him has God exalted with his right hand to be a Prince and a Savior, to give repentance to Israel, and forgiveness of sins. And we are his witnesses of these things; and so is also the Holy Ghost, whom God has given to them that obey him."

13 When they heard that, they were cut to the heart, and plotted to slay them. Then there stood up one in the council, a Pharisee, named Gamaliel,

a teacher of the law, held in respect among all the people, and commanded 13
to put the apostles forth a little space; and said unto them, "You men of
Israel, take heed to yourselves what you intend to do as concerning these
men. For before these days rose up Theudas, boasting himself to be somebody; to whom a number of men, about four hundred, joined themselves:
who was slain; and all, as many as obeyed him, were scattered, and brought
to nothing. After this man Judas of Galilee rose up in the days of the taxing,
and drew away many people after him: he also perished; and all, even as
many as obeyed him, were dispersed.

"And now I say unto you, Refrain from these men, and let them alone: 14
for if this purpose or this work be of men, it will come to nothing: but if it
be of God, you cannot overthrow it; lest perhaps you be found even to fight
against God." And to him they agreed: and when they had called the apostles, and beaten them, they commanded that they should not speak in the
name of Jesus, and let them go.

And they departed from the presence of the council, rejoicing that they 15
were counted worthy to suffer shame for his name. And daily in the temple,
and in every house, they ceased not to teach and preach Jesus Christ.

Seven Disciples Chosen to Serve
Acts 6:1-7

And in those days, when the number of the disciples was multiplied, 16
there arose a murmuring of the Grecians against the Hebrews, because their
widows were neglected in the daily distribution. Then the twelve called the
multitude of the disciples unto them,
and said, "It is not reasonable that we
should leave the word of God, and
serve tables. Therefore, brethren, pick
out among you seven men of honest
report, full of the Holy Ghost and wis-

> "WE WILL GIVE OURSELVES CONTINUALLY TO PRAYER, AND TO THE MINISTRY OF THE WORD."

dom, whom we may appoint over this business. But we will give ourselves
continually to prayer, and to the ministry of the word."

And the saying pleased the whole multitude: and they chose Stephen, 17
a man full of faith and of the Holy Ghost, and Philip, and Prochorus, and
Nicanor, and Timon, and Parmenas, and Nicolas a convert to Judaism of
Antioch: whom they set before the apostles: and when they had prayed, they
laid their hands on them.

And the word of God increased; and the number of the disciples mul- 18
tiplied in Jerusalem greatly; and a great company of the priests were obedient to the faith.

CHAPTER 60

MARTYRDOM OF A DISCIPLE

Stephen Before the Council
Acts 6:8-15

1   And Stephen, full of faith and power, did great wonders and miracles among the people. Then there arose certain of the synagogue, which is called the synagogue of the Libertines, and Cyrenians, and Alexandrians, and of them of Cilicia and of Asia, disputing with Stephen. And they were not able to resist the wisdom and the spirit by which he spoke.

2   Then they secretly induced men, which said, "We have heard him speak blasphemous words against Moses, and against God." And they stirred up the people, and the elders, and the scribes, and came upon him, and caught him, and brought him to the council, and set up false witnesses, which said, "This man ceases not to speak blasphemous words against this holy place, and the law: for we have heard him say, that this Jesus of Nazareth shall destroy this place, and shall change the customs which Moses delivered us."

3   And all that sat in the council, looking steadfastly on him, saw his face as it had been the face of an angel.

Stephen's Defense: History of Founders
Acts 7:1-8

4   Then said the high priest, "Are these things so?"

5   And he said, "Men, brethren, and fathers, hearken: The God of glory appeared unto our father Abraham, when he was in Mesopotamia, before he dwelt in Haran, and said unto him, '*Get you out of your country, and from your relatives, and come into the land which I shall show you.*'

6   "Then he came out of the land of the Chaldeans, and dwelt in Haran: and from there, when his father was dead, he moved him into this land, in which you now dwell. And he gave him no inheritance in it, no, not so much

as to set his foot on: yet *he promised that he would give it to him for a pos-* 6
session, and to his seed after him, when as yet he had no child. And God
spoke in this way, *That his seed should dwell in a foreign land; and that they
should bring them into bondage, and treat them evil four hundred years.
'And the nation to whom they shall be in bondage will I judge,' said God:
'and after that shall they come forth, and serve me in this place.'*

"And he gave him the covenant of circumcision: and so Abraham 7
begot Isaac, and circumcised him the eighth day; and Isaac begot Jacob; and
Jacob begot the twelve patriarchs."

Stephen's Defense: History of Patriarchs
Acts 7:9-19

"And the patriarchs, moved with envy, sold Joseph into Egypt: but 8
God was with him, and delivered him out of all his afflictions, and gave him
favor and wisdom in the sight of Pharaoh king of Egypt; and he made him
governor over Egypt and all his house.

"Now there came a famine over all the land of Egypt and Canaan, and 9
great affliction: and our fathers found no sustenance. But when Jacob heard
that there was grain in Egypt, he sent out our fathers first. And at the second time Joseph was made known to his brethren; and Joseph's family was
made known unto Pharaoh. Then Joseph sent, and called his father Jacob to
him, and all his family, sixty and fifteen souls. So Jacob went down into
Egypt, and died, he, and our fathers, and were carried over into Shechem,
and laid in the tomb that Abraham bought for a sum of money of the sons
of Hamor the father of Shechem.

"But when the time of the promise drew near, which God had sworn 10
to Abraham, the people grew and multiplied in Egypt, till *another king
arose, which knew not Joseph.* The same dealt treacherously with our race,
and evil treated our fathers, so that they cast out their young children, to the
end they might not live."

Stephen's Defense: History of Moses
Acts 7:20-43

"In which time Moses was born, and was exceedingly beautiful, and 11
nourished up in his father's house three months: and when he was cast out,
Pharaoh's daughter took him up, and nourished him for her own son. And
Moses was learned in all the wisdom of the Egyptians, and was mighty in
words and in deeds.

"And when he was fully forty years old, it came into his heart to visit 12
his brethren the children of Israel. And seeing one of them suffer wrong, he
defended him, and avenged him that was oppressed, and struck down the
Egyptian: for he supposed his brethren would have understood that God by
his hand would deliver them: but they understood not.

"And the next day he showed himself unto them as they quarreled, and 13
would have set them at one again, saying, 'Sirs, you are brethren; why do

13   you wrong one to another?' But he that did his neighbor wrong thrust him
away, saying, '*Who made you a ruler and a judge over us? Will you kill me,
as you did the Egyptian yesterday?*' Then Moses fled at this saying, and was
a stranger in the land of Midian, where he begot two sons.

14   "And when forty years were expired, *there appeared to him in the
wilderness of mount Sinai an angel of the Lord in a flame of fire in a bush.*
When Moses saw it, he wondered at the sight: and as he drew near to behold
it, the voice of the Lord came unto him, saying, '*I am the God of your
fathers, the God of Abraham, and the God of Isaac, and the God of Jacob.*'
Then Moses trembled, and dared not behold.

15   " '*Then said the Lord to him, "Put off your shoes from your feet: for
the place where you stand is holy ground. I have seen, I have seen the affliction of my people which are in Egypt, and I have heard their groaning, and
am come down to deliver them. And now come, I will send you into Egypt."* '

16   "This Moses whom they refused, saying, '*Who made you a ruler and
a judge?*' the same did God send to be a ruler and a deliverer by the hand
of the angel which appeared to him in the bush. He brought them out, after
he had showed wonders and signs in the land of Egypt, and in the Red sea,
and in the wilderness forty years.

17   "This is that Moses, which said unto the children of Israel, '*A prophet
shall the Lord your God raise up unto you of your brethren, like unto me;
him shall you hear.*' This is he, that was in the church in the wilderness with
the angel which spoke to him in the mount Sinai, and with our fathers: who
received the living oracles to give unto us: to whom our fathers would not
obey, but thrust him from them, and in their hearts turned back again into
Egypt, saying unto Aaron, '*Make us gods to go before us: for as for this
Moses, which brought us out of the land of Egypt, we do not know what is
become of him.*'

18   "And they made a calf in those days, and offered sacrifices unto the
idol, and rejoiced in the works of their own hands. Then God turned, and
gave them up to worship the host of heaven; as it is written in the book of
the prophets, '*O you house of Israel, have you offered to me slain beasts and
sacrifices by the space of forty years in the wilderness? Yes, you took up the
tabernacle of Moloch, and the star of your god Remphan, figures which you
made to worship them: and I will carry you away beyond Babylon.*' "

Stephen's Defense: History of Worship
Acts 7:44-53

19   "Our fathers had the tabernacle of witness in the wilderness, as he had
appointed, speaking unto Moses, that he should make it according to the
fashion that he had seen. Which also our fathers that came afterward
brought in with Joshua into the possession of the Gentiles, whom God drove
out before the face of our fathers, unto the days of David; who found favor

before God, and desired to find a tabernacle for the God of Jacob. But 19
Solomon built him a house.

"Howbeit the most High dwells not in temples made with hands; as 20
says the prophet, *'Heaven is my throne, and earth is my footstool: what
house will you build me? says the Lord: or what is the place of my rest? has
not my hand made all these things?'*

"You stiff-necked and uncircumcised in heart and ears, you do always 21
resist the Holy Ghost: as your fathers did, so do you. Which of the prophets
have not your fathers persecuted? and they have slain them which showed
before of the coming of the Just One; of whom you have been now the
betrayers and murderers: who have received the law by the disposition of
angels, and have not kept it."

Stephen Stoned to Death
Acts 7:54-60

When they heard these things, they were cut to the heart, and they 22
gnashed on him with their teeth. But
he, being full of the Holy Ghost,
looked up steadfastly into heaven, and
saw the glory of God, and Jesus standing on the right hand of God, and said,
"Behold, I see the heavens opened, and
the Son of man standing on the right hand of God."

> "BEHOLD, I SEE THE HEAVENS
> OPENED, AND THE SON OF
> MAN STANDING ON THE
> RIGHT HAND OF GOD."

Then they cried out with a loud voice, and stopped their ears, and ran 23
upon him with one accord, and cast him out of the city, and stoned him: and
the witnesses laid down their clothes at a young man's feet, whose name
was Saul.

And they stoned Stephen, he calling upon God, and saying, "Lord 24
Jesus, receive my spirit." And he kneeled down, and cried with a loud voice,
"Lord, lay not this sin against them." And when he had said this, he fell asleep.

Saul Persecutes Congregations
Acts 8:1-3

And Saul was consenting unto his death. And at that time there was a 25
great persecution against the church which was at Jerusalem; and they were
all scattered abroad throughout the regions of Judea and Samaria, except the
apostles. And devout men carried Stephen to his burial, and made great
lamentation over him. As for Saul, he made havoc of the church, entering into
every house, and dragging off men and women committing them to prison.

PART 14

CONVERSION OF BELIEVERS

When those who fled Jerusalem continued preaching the gospel, Jewish leaders appointed a man called Saul to persecute the followers of Jesus' teachings wherever he found them. This was a time of uncertainty, testing the faith of all believers in God and His Christ. But as Saul set about his task, the Holy Ghost came upon him in a profound transformation of the persecutor. Having his eyes opened by the revelation of Christ in a blinding vision of light, Saul now sees clearly that one Spirit governs all people. He is instructed by God to take the gospel into the world—to the scattered Jews, the Grecian Jews, and the Gentiles—and to turn the people away from their idols to serve the one and only true God. Converted in faith to the works of God, Saul obeys his new calling. Then came a period of peace and preaching as conversion of those faithful to God began.

THEN THE CHURCHES HAD PEACE THROUGHOUT ALL JUDEA AND GALILEE AND SAMARIA, AND WERE BUILT UP; AND WALKING IN THE FEAR OF THE LORD, AND IN THE COMFORT OF THE HOLY GHOST, WERE MULTIPLIED.   (ACTS 9:31)

CHAPTER 61

CONVERSION OF AN ETHIOPIAN
Philip Preaches in Samaria
Acts 8:4-25

Therefore they that were scattered abroad went everywhere preaching the word. ¹

Then Philip went down to the city of Samaria, and preached Christ ² unto them. And the people with one accord gave heed unto those things which Philip spoke, hearing and seeing the miracles which he did. For unclean spirits, crying with loud voice, came out of many that were possessed with them: and many taken with paralysis, and that were lame, were healed. And there was great joy in that city.

But there was a certain man, called Simon, which previously in the ³ same city used sorcery, and amazed the people of Samaria, claiming that he himself was some great one: to whom they all gave heed, from the least to the greatest, saying, "This man is the great power of God." And to him they had regard, because for a long time he had amazed them with sorceries.

But when they believed Philip preaching the things concerning the ⁴ kingdom of God, and the name of Jesus Christ, they were baptized, both men and women. Then Simon himself believed also: and when he was baptized, he continued with Philip, and wondered, beholding the miracles and signs which were done.

Now when the apostles which were at Jerusalem heard that Samaria ⁵ had received the word of God, they sent unto them Peter and John: who, when they were come down, prayed for them, that they might receive the Holy Ghost: (for as yet it was fallen upon none of them: only they were baptized in the name of the Lord Jesus). Then they laid their hands on them, and they received the Holy Ghost.

6   And when Simon saw that through laying on of the apostles' hands the Holy Ghost was given, he offered them money, saying, "Give me also this power, that on whomsoever I lay hands, he may receive the Holy Ghost."

7   But Peter said unto him, "Your money perish with you, because you have thought that the gift of God may be purchased with money. You have neither part nor lot in this matter: for your heart is not right in the sight of God. Repent therefore of this your wickedness, and pray God, if perhaps the thought of your heart may be forgiven you. For I perceive that you are in the gall of bitterness, and in the bond of iniquity."

8   Then Simon answered, and said, "Pray you to the Lord for me, that none of these things which you have spoken come upon me."

9   And they, when they had testified and preached the word of the Lord, returned to Jerusalem, and preached the gospel in many villages of the Samaritans.

Philip and the Ethiopian Eunuch
Acts 8:26-40

10   And the angel of the Lord spoke unto Philip, saying, "Arise, and go toward the south unto the road that goes down from Jerusalem unto Gaza, which is desert." And he arose and went: and, behold, a man of Ethiopia, a eunuch of great authority under Candace queen of the Ethiopians, who had the charge of all her treasury, and had come to Jerusalem to worship, was returning, and sitting in his chariot read Isaiah the prophet.

11   Then the Spirit said unto Philip, "Go near, and join yourself to this chariot." And Philip ran there to him, and heard him read the prophet Isaiah, and said, "Do you understand what you read?" And he said, "How can I, except some man should guide me?" And he desired Philip that he would come up and sit with him.

12   The place of the scripture which he read was this, "*He was led as a sheep to the slaughter; and like a lamb dumb before his shearer, so opened he not his mouth: in his humiliation his judgment was taken away: and who shall declare his generation? for his life is taken from the earth.*"

13   And the eunuch answered Philip, and said, "I ask you, of whom speaks the prophet this? of himself, or of some other man?" Then Philip opened his mouth, and began at the same scripture, and preached unto him Jesus.

14   And as they went on their way, they came unto a certain water: and the eunuch said, "See, here is water; what does hinder me to be baptized?" And Philip said, "If you believe with all your heart, you may." And he answered and said, "I believe that Jesus Christ is the Son of God." And he commanded the chariot to stand still: and they went down both into the water, both Philip and the eunuch; and he baptized him. And when they were come up out of the water, the Spirit of the Lord caught away Philip, that the eunuch saw him no more: and he went on his way rejoicing.

15   But Philip was found at Azotus: and passing through he preached in all the cities, till he came to Caesarea.

CHAPTER 62

CONVERSION OF THE FORMER ENEMY

The Conversion of Saul
Acts 9:1-19

And Saul, yet breathing out threats and slaughter against the disciples 1
of the Lord, went unto the high priest, and desired of him letters to Damascus to the synagogues, that if he found any of this way, whether they were men or women, he might bring them bound unto Jerusalem. And as he journeyed, he came near Damascus: and suddenly there shined round about him a light from heaven: and he fell to the earth, and heard a voice saying unto him, "Saul, Saul, why do you persecute me?" And he said, "Who are you, Lord?" And the Lord said, "I am Jesus whom you persecute: it is hard for you to kick against the prods." And he trembling and astonished said, "Lord, what will you have me to do?" And the Lord said unto him, "Arise, and go into the city, and it shall be told you what you must do."

And the men which journeyed with him stood speechless, hearing a 2
voice, but seeing no man. And Saul arose from the earth; and when his eyes were opened, he saw no man: but they led him by the hand, and brought him into Damascus. And he was three days without sight, and neither did eat nor drink.

And there was a certain disciple at Damascus, named Ananias; and to 3
him said the Lord in a vision, "Ananias." And he said, "Behold, I am here, Lord." And the Lord said unto him, "Arise, and go into the street which is called Straight, and inquire in the house of Judas for one called Saul, of Tarsus: for, behold, he prays, and has seen in a vision a man named Ananias coming in, and putting his hand on him, that he might receive his sight."

Then Ananias answered, "Lord, I have heard by many of this man, how 4
much evil he has done to your saints at Jerusalem: and here he has authority from the chief priests to bind all that call on your name." But the Lord said unto him, "Go your way: for he is a chosen vessel unto me, to bear my

4   name before the Gentiles, and kings, and the children of Israel: for I will show him what great things he must suffer for my name's sake."

5   And Ananias went his way, and entered into the house; and putting his hands on him said, "Brother Saul, the Lord, even Jesus, that appeared unto you on the road as you came, has sent me, that you might receive your sight, and be filled with the Holy Ghost." And immediately there fell from his eyes as it had been scales: and he received sight at once, and arose, and was baptized. And when he had received food, he was strengthened. Then was Saul certain days with the disciples which were at Damascus.

Saul Proclaims Jesus
Acts 9:20-30

6   And straightway he preached Christ in the synagogues, that he is the Son of God. But all that heard him were amazed, and said; "Is not this he that destroyed them which called on this name in Jerusalem, and came here for that intent, that he might bring them bound unto the chief priests?" But Saul increased the more in strength, and confounded the Jews which dwelt at Damascus, proving that this is the very Christ.

7   And after many days were fulfilled, the Jews plotted to kill him: but their laying in ambush was known of Saul. And they watched the gates day and night to kill him. Then the disciples took him by night, and let him down by the wall in a basket.

8   And when Saul was come to Jerusalem, he attempted to join himself to the disciples: but they were all afraid of him, and believed not that he was a disciple. But Barnabas took him, and brought him to the apostles, and declared unto them how he had seen the Lord on the road, and that he had spoken to him, and how he had preached boldly at Damascus in the name of Jesus.

9   And he was with them coming in and going out at Jerusalem. And he spoke boldly in the name of the Lord Jesus, and disputed against the Grecians: but they went about to slay him. Which when the brethren knew, they brought him down to Caesarea, and sent him forth to Tarsus.

CHAPTER 63

CONVERSION OF WILLING GENTILES

Peter Heals Aeneas
Acts 9:31-35

Then the churches had peace throughout all Judea and Galilee and 1 Samaria, and were built up; and walking in the fear of the Lord, and in the comfort of the Holy Ghost, were multiplied.

And it came to pass, as Peter passed throughout all areas, he came 2 down also to the saints which dwelt at Lydda. And there he found a certain man named Aeneas, which had kept his bed eight years, and was sick of the paralysis. And Peter said unto him, "Aeneas, Jesus Christ makes you whole: arise, and make your bed." And he arose immediately. And all that dwelt at Lydda and Sharon saw him, and turned to the Lord.

Peter Raises Tabitha
Acts 9:36-43

Now there was at Joppa a certain disciple named Tabitha, which by 3 interpretation is called Dorcas: this woman was full of good works and charitable deeds which she did. And it came to pass in those days, that she was sick, and died: whom when they had washed, they laid her in an upper room. And Inasmuch as Lydda was near to Joppa, and the disciples had heard that Peter was there, they sent unto him two men, desiring him that he would not delay to come to them.

Then Peter arose and went with them. When he was come, they 4 brought him into the upper room: and all the widows stood by him weeping, and showing the coats and garments which Dorcas made, while she was with them. But Peter put them all out, and kneeled down, and prayed; and turning to the body said, "Tabitha, arise." And she opened her eyes: and when she saw Peter, she sat up. And he gave her his hand, and lifted her up, and when he had called the saints and widows, presented her alive. And it was known throughout all Joppa; and many believed in the Lord.

5 And it came to pass, that he tarried many days in Joppa with one Simon a tanner.

Cornelius Receives a Vision
Acts 10:1-8

6 There was a certain man in Caesarea called Cornelius, a centurion of the army called the Italian Regiment, a devout man, and one that feared God with all his household, which gave many donations to the people, and prayed to God always. He saw in a vision clearly about the ninth hour of the day an angel of God coming in to him, and saying unto him, "Cornelius."

7 And when he looked on him, he was afraid, and said, "What is it, Lord?" And he said unto him, "Your prayers and your donations are come up for a memorial before God. And now send men to Joppa, and call for one Simon, whose surname is Peter: he lodges with one Simon a tanner, whose house is by the seaside: he shall tell you what you ought to do."

> "YOUR PRAYERS AND YOUR DONATIONS ARE COME UP FOR A MEMORIAL BEFORE GOD."

8 And when the angel which spoke unto Cornelius was departed, he called two of his household servants, and a devout soldier of them that waited on him continually; and when he had declared all these things unto them, he sent them to Joppa.

Peter Receives a Corresponding Vision
Acts 10:9-23

9 The next day, as they went on their journey, and drew near unto the city, Peter went up upon the housetop to pray about the sixth hour: and he became very hungry, and would have eaten: but while they made ready, he fell into a trance, and saw heaven opened, and a certain vessel descending unto him, as it had been a great sheet bound at the four corners, and let down to the earth: wherein were all manner of four-footed animals of the earth, and wild beasts, and creeping things, and birds of the air.

10 And there came a voice to him, "Rise, Peter; kill, and eat." But Peter said, "Not so, Lord; for I have never eaten anything that is impure or unclean." And the voice spoke unto him again the second time, "What God has cleansed, that do not you call impure." This was done three times: and the vessel was received up again into heaven.

11 Now while Peter doubted within himself what this vision which he had seen should mean, behold, the men which were sent from Cornelius had made inquiry for Simon's house, and stood before the gate, and called, and asked whether Simon, which was surnamed Peter, were lodged there.

12 While Peter thought on the vision, the Spirit said unto him, "Behold, three men seek you. Arise therefore, and get you down, and go with them, doubting nothing: for I have sent them."

13 Then Peter went down to the men which were sent unto him from Cornelius; and said, "Behold, I am he whom you seek: what is the reason for

which you are come?" And they said, "Cornelius the centurion, a just man, 13
and one that fears God, and of good reputation among all the nation of the
Jews, was warned from God by a holy angel to send for you into his house,
and to hear words of you." Then he called them in, and lodged them. And
the next day Peter went away with them, and certain brethren from Joppa
accompanied him.

Peter Meets With the Gentile Cornelius
Acts 10:24-33

And the next day they entered into Caesarea. And Cornelius waited for 14
them, and had called together his relatives and close friends. And as Peter
was coming in, Cornelius met him, and fell down at his feet, and worshiped
him. But Peter took him up, saying, "Stand up; I myself also am a man."

And as he talked with him, he went in, and found many that were 15
come together. And he said unto them, "You know how that it is an unlawful thing for a man that is a Jew to keep company, or come unto one of
another nation; but God has shown me that I should not call any man common or unclean. Therefore I came unto you without objection, as soon as I
was sent for: I ask therefore for what purpose you have sent for me?"

And Cornelius said, "Four days ago I was fasting until this hour; and 16
at the ninth hour I prayed in my house, and, behold, a man stood before me
in bright clothing, and said, 'Cornelius, your prayer is heard, and your donations are had in remembrance in the sight of God. Send therefore to Joppa,
and call here Simon, whose surname is Peter; he is lodged in the house of
one Simon a tanner by the seaside: who, when he comes, shall speak unto
you.' Immediately therefore I sent to you; and you have done well that you
are come. Now therefore are we all here present before God, to hear all
things that are commanded you of God."

Peter Brings Jesus' Message to Cornelius
Acts 10:34-43

Then Peter opened his mouth, and said, "Of a truth I perceive that God 17
has no partiality of persons: but in every nation he that fears him, and works
righteousness, is accepted with him.
The word which God sent unto the
children of Israel, preaching peace by
Jesus Christ: (he is Lord of all): that
word, I say, you know, which was published throughout all Judea, and began
from Galilee, after the baptism which
John preached; how God anointed
Jesus of Nazareth with the Holy Ghost

> "I PERCEIVE THAT GOD HAS
> NO PARTIALITY OF PERSONS:
> BUT IN EVERY NATION HE
> THAT FEARS HIM, AND WORKS
> RIGHTEOUSNESS, IS ACCEPTED
> WITH HIM."

and with power: who went about doing good, and healing all that were
oppressed of the devil; for God was with him.

"And we are witnesses of all things which he did both in the land of 18
the Jews, and in Jerusalem; whom they slew and hanged on a tree: him God
raised up the third day, and showed him openly; not to all the people, but

18 unto witnesses chosen before of God, even to us, who did eat and drink with him after he rose from the dead.

19 "And he commanded us to preach unto the people, and to testify that it is he which was ordained of God to be the Judge of the quick and the dead. To him give all the prophets witness, that through his name whosoever believes in him shall receive remission of sins."

Peter Converts Cornelius and Family
Acts 10:44-48

20 While Peter yet spoke these words, the Holy Ghost fell on all them which heard the word. And they of the circumcision which believed were astonished, as many as came with Peter, because on the Gentiles also was poured out the gift of the Holy Ghost. For they heard them speak with tongues, and magnify God. Then answered Peter, "Can any man forbid water, that these should not be baptized, which have received the Holy Ghost as well as we?"

> THE HOLY GHOST FELL ON ALL THEM WHICH HEARD THE WORD.

21 And he commanded them to be baptized in the name of the Lord. Then they asked him to tarry certain days.

CHAPTER 64

REPORT OF GENTILES' CONVERSION

Peter's Report to Jerusalem Assembly
Acts 11:1-18

And the apostles and brethren that were in Judea heard that the Gentiles had also received the word of God. And when Peter was come up to Jerusalem, they that were of the circumcision contended with him, saying, "You went in to men uncircumcised, and did eat with them." 1

But Peter explained the matter from the beginning, and explained it in order unto them, saying, "I was in the city of Joppa praying: and in a trance I saw a vision, a certain vessel descend, as it had been a great sheet, let down from heaven by four corners; and it came even to me: upon which when I had fastened my eyes, I considered, and saw four-footed animals of the earth, and wild beasts, and creeping things, and birds of the air. 2

"And I heard a voice saying unto me, 'Arise, Peter; kill and eat.' But I said, 'Not so, Lord: for nothing impure or unclean has at any time entered into my mouth.' But the voice answered me again from heaven, 'What God has cleansed, that do not you call impure.' And this was done three times: and all were drawn up again into heaven. 3

"And, behold, immediately there were three men already come unto the house where I was, sent from Caesarea unto me. And the Spirit told me to go with them, doubting nothing. Moreover these six brethren accompanied me, and we entered into the man's house. And he showed us how he had seen an angel in his house, which stood and said unto him, 'Send men to Joppa, and call for Simon, whose surname is Peter; who shall tell you words, whereby you and all your household shall be saved.' 4

"And as I began to speak, the Holy Ghost fell on them, as on us at the beginning. Then I remembered the word of the Lord, how he said, 'John indeed baptized with water; but you shall be baptized with the Holy Ghost.' 5

5 Inasmuch then as God gave them the like gift as he did unto us, who believed on the Lord Jesus Christ; what was I, that I could withstand God?"

6 When they heard these things, they held their peace, and glorified God, saying, "Then has God also to the Gentiles granted repentance unto life."

Antioch Disciples Called Christians
Acts 11:19-30

7 Now they which were scattered abroad upon the persecution that arose about Stephen traveled as far as Phoenicia, and Cyprus, and Antioch, preaching the word to none but unto the Jews only. And some of them were men of Cyprus and Cyrene, which, when they were come to Antioch, spoke unto the Grecians, preaching the Lord Jesus. And the hand of the Lord was with them: and a great number believed, and turned unto the Lord.

8 Then news of these things came unto the ears of the church which was

> MANY PEOPLE WERE ADDED UNTO THE LORD.

in Jerusalem: and they sent forth Barnabas, that he should go as far as Antioch. who, when he came, and had seen the grace of God, was glad, and encouraged them all, that with purpose of heart they would cleave unto the Lord. For he was a good man, and full of the Holy Ghost and of faith: and many people were added unto the Lord.

9 Then Barnabas departed to Tarsus, to seek Saul: and when he had found him, he brought him unto Antioch. And it came to pass, that a whole year they assembled themselves with the church, and taught many people. And the disciples were called Christians first in Antioch.

10 And in these days came prophets from Jerusalem unto Antioch. And there stood up one of them named Agabus, and signified by the Spirit that there should be great famine throughout all the world: which came to pass in the days of Claudius Caesar.

11 Then the disciples, every man according to his ability, determined to send relief unto the brethren which dwelt in Judea: which also they did, and sent it to the elders by the hands of Barnabas and Saul.

PART 15

LETTER FROM JAMES

It was fifteen years after the death of Jesus that His brother James, now leader of the Jerusalem church, wrote to the Jewish faithful, reminding them about subjects they had previously been taught. His letter is a mixture of familiar Hebrew proverbs, well-known Greek wisdom of daily life, and gospel beliefs in life everlasting. It illustrates a convergence of Jewish, Grecian, and Christian meanings in a blending of faith for living a life filled with good works for God. This earliest letter serves as a pause in the order of events and is key to understanding the letters written by others that follow.

BLESSED IS THE MAN THAT ENDURES TEMPTA-
TION: FOR WHEN HE IS APPROVED, HE SHALL
RECEIVE THE CROWN OF LIFE, WHICH THE LORD
HAS PROMISED TO THEM THAT LOVE HIM.

(JAMES 1:12)

CHAPTER 65

LIVING WITHIN GOD'S COMMANDMENTS

Greeting From James
James 1:1

1   James, a servant of God and of the Lord Jesus Christ, to the twelve
tribes which are scattered abroad, greeting.

Faith and Wisdom
James 1:2-8

2   My brethren, count it all joy when you fall into various temptations;
knowing this, that the testing of your faith works perseverance. But let perseverance have its perfect work, that you may be perfect and complete, lacking nothing.

3   If any of you lacks wisdom, let him ask of God, that gives to all men
liberally, and does not find fault; and it shall be given him. But let him ask
in faith, nothing wavering. For he that wavers is like a wave of the sea driv-
en with the wind and tossed. For let not that man think that he shall receive
anything of the Lord. A double-minded man is unstable in all his ways.

Rich and Poor
James 1:9-11

4   Let the brother of low degree rejoice in that he is exalted: but the rich,
in that he is made low: because as the flower of the grass he shall pass away.
For the sun is no sooner risen with a burning heat, but it withers the grass,
and the flower thereof falls, and the grace of the fashion of it perishes: so
also shall the rich man fade away in his ways.

Crown of Life
James 1:12-18

5   Blessed is the man that endures temptation: for when he is tried, he
shall receive the crown of life, which the Lord has promised to them that

love him. Let no man say when he is tempted, "I am tempted of God": for 5
God cannot be tempted with evil, neither tempts he any man: but every man
is tempted, when he is drawn away of his own lust, and enticed. Then when
lust has conceived, it brings forth sin: and sin, when it is finished, brings
forth death.

Do not be deceived, my beloved brethren. Every good gift and every per- 6
fect gift is from above, and comes down
from the Father of lights, with whom is
no variation, neither shadow of turning.
Of his own will he brought us forth with
the word of truth, that we should be a
kind of first fruits of his creatures.

> EVERY GOOD GIFT AND EVERY
> PERFECT GIFT IS FROM ABOVE,
> AND COMES DOWN FROM THE
> FATHER OF LIGHTS.

Doers of the Word
James 1:19-27

Therefore, my beloved brethren, let every man be swift to hear, slow 7
to speak, slow to anger: for the anger of man does not work the righteousness of God. Therefore lay aside all filthiness and overflow of wickedness,
and receive with meekness the implanted word, which is able to save your
souls.

But be you doers of the word, and not hearers only, deceiving your 8
own selves. For if anyone be a hearer of the word, and not a doer, he is like
unto a man beholding his natural face
in a mirror: for he beholds himself,
and goes his way, and straightway for-
gets what manner of man he was. But
whoever looks into the perfect law of

> "BE YOU DOERS OF THE WORD,
> AND NOT HEARERS ONLY,
> DECEIVING YOUR OWN SELVES."

liberty, and continues therein, he being not a forgetful hearer, but a doer of
the work, this man shall be blessed in his deed.

If any man among you seems to be religious, and bridles not his 9
tongue, but deceives his own heart, this man's religion is useless. Pure religion and undefiled before God and the Father is this, To visit the fatherless
and widows in their distress, and to keep himself unstained from the world.

Royal Law of Scripture
James 2:1-13

My brethren, have not the faith in our Lord Jesus Christ, the Lord of 10
glory, with partiality of persons. For if there comes unto your assembly a
man with a gold ring, in fine apparel, and there comes in also a poor man
in filthy clothing; and you have partiality to him that wears the fine clothing, and say unto him, "You sit here in a good place"; and say to the poor,
"You stand there," or "sit here under my footstool": are you not then partial
in yourselves, and are become judges with evil thoughts?

Hearken, my beloved brethren, Has not God chosen the poor of this 11
world rich in faith, and heirs of the kingdom which he has promised to them

11 that love him? But you have dishonored the poor. Do not rich men oppress you, and draw you before the judgment seats? Do not they blaspheme that noble name by which you are called?

12 If you fulfill the royal law according to the scripture, "*You shall love your neighbor as yourself*," you do well: but if you have partiality to persons, you commit sin, and are convicted of the law as transgressors. For whosoever shall keep the whole law, and yet fails in one point, he is guilty of all. For he that said, "*Do not commit adultery*," said also, "*Do not kill*." Now if you commit no adultery, yet if you kill, you are become a transgressor of the law.

13 So speak, and so do, as they that shall be judged by the law of liberty. For he shall have judgment without mercy, that has shown no mercy; and mercy triumphs over judgment.

Faith and Works
James 2:14-26

14 What does it profit, my brethren, though a man says he has faith, and does not have works? can that faith save him? If a brother or sister be naked, and destitute of daily food, and one of you says unto them, "Depart in peace, be warmed and filled"; however you do not give them those things which are needful to the body; what does it profit? Even so faith, if it has not works, is dead, being alone.

15 Yes, a man may say, "You have faith, and I have works": show me your faith without your works, and I will show you my faith by my works. You believe that there is one God; you do well: the demons also believe, and tremble. But will you know, O foolish man, that faith without works is dead?

> SHOW ME YOUR FAITH WITHOUT YOUR WORKS, AND I WILL SHOW YOU MY FAITH BY MY WORKS.

16 Was not Abraham our father justified by works, when he had offered Isaac his son upon the altar? Do you see how faith worked with his works, and by works was faith made perfect? And the scripture was fulfilled which says, "*Abraham believed God, and it was counted unto him for righteousness*": and he was called the Friend of God.

17 You see then how that by works a man is justified, and not by faith only. Likewise also was not Rahab the harlot justified by works, when she had received the messengers, and had sent them out another way? For as the body without the spirit is dead, so faith without works is dead also.

> AS THE BODY WITHOUT THE SPIRIT IS DEAD, SO FAITH WITHOUT WORKS IS DEAD ALSO.

CHAPTER 66

LIVING ACCORDING TO CHRIST'S PROMISES
Taming the Tongue
James 3:1-12

My brethren, let not many be teachers, knowing that we shall receive 1 the greater condemnation. For in many things we all falter. If any man does not falter in word, the same is a perfect man, and able also to bridle the whole body.

Behold, we put bits in the horses' mouths, that they may obey us; and 2 we turn about their whole body. Behold also the ships, which though they be so great, and are driven of fierce winds, yet are they turned about with a very small rudder, wherever the pilot chooses.

Even so the tongue is a little member, and boasts great things. Behold, 3 how great a matter a little fire kindles! And the tongue is a fire, a world of iniquity: so is the tongue among our members, that it defiles the whole body, and sets on fire the course of nature; and it is set on fire of hell. For every kind of beasts, and of birds, and of serpents, and of things in the sea, is tamed, and has been tamed of mankind. But the tongue can no man tame; it is an unruly evil, full of deadly poison.

Therewith we bless God, even the Father; and therewith we curse men, 4 which are made after the likeness of God. Out of the same mouth proceeds blessing and cursing. My brethren, these things ought not to be so.

Does a fountain send forth at the same opening sweet water and bit- 5 ter? Can the fig tree, my brethren, bear olive berries? either a grapevine, figs? so can no fountain both yield salt water and fresh.

True Wisdom
James 3:13-18

Who is a wise man and endued with understanding among you? let 6 him show out of a good manner of life his works with meekness of wisdom.

6 But if you have bitter envying and contention in your hearts, boast not, and lie not against the truth. This wisdom descends not from above, but is earthly, sensual, devilish. For where envying and contention is, there is confusion and every evil work.

7 But the wisdom that is from above is first pure, then peaceable, gentle, and easy to be submissive, full of mercy and good fruits, without partiality, and without hypocrisy. And the fruit of righteousness is sown in peace of them that make peace.

One Lawgiver
James 4:1-17

8 From where come wars and quarrels among you? come they not from here, even of your passions that war in your own selves? You desire, and have not: you kill, and desire to have, and cannot obtain: you quarrel and war, yet you have not, because you ask not. You ask, and receive not, because you ask wrongly, that you may consume it upon your passions.

> THE WISDOM THAT IS FROM ABOVE IS FIRST PURE, THEN PEACEABLE.

9 You adulterers and adulteresses, do you not know that the friendship of the world is hostility with God? whosoever therefore will be a friend of the world is the enemy of God. Do you think that the scripture says in vain, "The spirit that dwells in us lusts to jealousy"? But he gives more grace. Therefore he says, "God resists the proud, but gives grace unto the humble."

10 Submit yourselves therefore to God. Resist the devil, and he will flee from you. Draw near to God, and he will draw near to you. Cleanse your hands, you sinners; and purify your hearts, you double-minded. Be sorrowful, and mourn, and weep: let your laughter be turned to mourning, and your joy to gloom. Humble yourselves in the sight of the Lord, and he shall lift you up.

> RESIST THE DEVIL, AND HE WILL FLEE FROM YOU.

11 Do not speak evil one of another, brethren. He that speaks evil of his brother, and judges his brother, speaks evil of the law, and judges the law: but if you judge the law, you are not a doer of the law, but a judge. There is one lawgiver, who is able to save and to destroy: who are you that judge another?

12 Listen now, you that say, "Today or tomorrow we will go into such a city, and continue there a year, and buy and sell, and get gain": whereas you know not what shall be tomorrow. For what is your life? It is even a vapor, that appears for a little time, and then vanishes away.

13 For you ought to say, "If the Lord is willing, we shall live, and do this, or that." But now you boast in your boastings: all such boasting is evil. Therefore to him that knows to do good, and does not do it, to him it is sin.

Patience
James 5:1-12

Listen now, you rich men, weep and howl for your miseries that shall 14 come upon you. Your riches are corrupted, and your garments are moth-eaten. Your gold and silver is corroded; and the corrosion of them shall be a witness against you, and shall eat your flesh as if it were fire. You have heaped treasure together for the last days.

Behold, the wages of the laborers who have reaped down your fields, 15 which is of you kept back by fraud, cries: and the cries of them which have reaped are entered into the ears of the Lord of hosts. You have lived in luxury on the earth, and been self-indulgent; you have fattened your hearts, as in a day of slaughter. You have condemned and killed the just; and he does not resist you.

Be patient therefore, brethren, unto the coming of the Lord. Behold, 16 the farmer waits for the precious fruit of the earth, and has long patience for it, until he receives the early and latter rain. Be you also patient; establish your hearts: for the coming of the Lord draws near. Do not grumble one against another, brethren, lest you be condemned: behold, the judge stands before the door.

Take, my brethren, the prophets, who have spoken in the name of the 17 Lord, for an example of suffering affliction, and of patience. Behold, we count them blessed which endure. You have heard of the patience of Job, and have seen the end from the Lord; that the Lord is very compassionate, and of tender mercy.

> THE LORD IS VERY COMPASSIONATE, AND OF TENDER MERCY.

But above all things, my brethren, swear not, neither by heaven, nei- 18 ther by the earth, neither by any other oath: but let your "yes" be "yes"; and your "no", "no"; lest you fall into condemnation.

Prayer of Faith
James 5:13-18

Is anyone among you suffering? let him pray. Is anyone cheerful? let 19 him sing psalms. Is anyone sick among you? let him call for the elders of the church; and let them pray over him, anointing him with oil in the name of the Lord: and the prayer of faith shall save the sick, and the Lord shall raise him up; and if he has committed sins, they shall be forgiven him. Confess your faults one to another, and pray one for another, that you may be healed. The effective fervent prayer of a righteous man avails much.

> THE PRAYER OF FAITH SHALL SAVE THE SICK.

Elijah was a man subject to like natures as we are, and he prayed 20 earnestly that it might not rain: and it did not rain on the earth in the space of three years and six months. And he prayed again, and the heaven gave rain, and the earth brought forth its fruit.

Saving a Soul
James 5:19-20

21   Brethren, if any of you do wander from the truth, and one converts
him; let him know, that he which converts the sinner from the error of his
way shall save a soul from death, and shall cover a multitude of sins.

CHAPTER 67

MARTYRDOM OF AN APOSTLE

Herod (Agrippa I) Executes James
Acts 12:1-5

Now about that time Herod (Agrippa I) the king stretched forth his 1 hands to harm certain of the church. And he killed James the brother of John with the sword.

And because he saw it pleased the Jews, he proceeded further to seize 2 Peter also. (Then were the days of unleavened bread.) And when he had apprehended him, he put him in prison, and delivered him to four squads of soldiers to keep him; intending after passover to bring him forth to the people.

Peter therefore was kept in prison: but prayer was made without ceas- 3 ing of the church unto God for him.

Peter's Deliverance From Prison
Acts 12:6-17

And when Herod would have brought him forth, the same night Peter 4 was sleeping between two soldiers, bound with two chains: and the guards before the door kept the prison. And, behold, the angel of the Lord came upon him, and a light shined in the prison: and he struck Peter on the side, and raised him up, saying, "Arise up quickly." And his chains fell off from his hands. And the angel said unto him, "Dress yourself, and bind on your sandals." And he did so. And he said unto him, "Cast your garment about you, and follow me."

And he went out, and followed him; and knew not that it was true 5 which was done by the angel; but thought he saw a vision. When they were past the first and the second guard posts, they came unto the iron gate that leads unto the city; which opened to them of its own accord: and they went out, and passed on through one street; and immediately the angel departed from him. And when Peter was come to himself, he said, "Now I know of a

5 certainty, that the Lord has sent his angel, and has delivered me out of the hand of Herod, and from all the expectation of the people of the Jews."

6 And when he had considered the thing, he came to the house of Mary the mother of John, whose surname was Mark; where many were gathered together praying. And as Peter knocked at the door of the gate, a girl came to answer, named Rhoda. And when she knew Peter's voice, she opened not the gate for gladness, but ran in, and told how Peter stood before the gate. And they said unto her, "You are mad." But she constantly affirmed that it was even so. Then they said, "It is his angel."

7 But Peter continued knocking: and when they had opened the door, and saw him, they were astonished. But he, beckoning unto them with the hand to hold their peace, declared unto them how the Lord had brought him out of the prison. And he said, "Go show these things to James (brother of Jesus), and to the brethren." And he departed, and went into another place.

Herod Puts Guards to Death
Acts 12:18-19

8 Now as soon as it was day, there was no small stir among the soldiers, what was become of Peter. And when Herod had sought for him, and not found him, he examined the guards, and commanded that they should be put to death. And he went down from Judea to Caesarea, and there stayed.

Death of Herod (Agrippa I)
Acts 12:20-25

9 And Herod was highly displeased with them of Tyre and Sidon: but they came with one accord to him, and, having made Blastus the king's chamberlain their friend, desired peace; because their country was nourished by the king's country. And upon a set day Herod, arrayed in royal apparel, sat upon his throne, and made an oration unto them. And the people gave a shout, saying, "It is the voice of a god, and not of a man." And immediately the angel of the Lord struck him, because he gave not God the glory: and he was eaten of worms, and gave up the ghost.

10 But the word of God grew and multiplied. And Barnabas and Saul returned from Jerusalem, when they had fulfilled their ministry, and took with them John, whose surname was Mark.

PART 16

FIRST MISSIONARY JOURNEY

In recognition of Saul's conversion of faith and renewed spirit, God changed his name from Saul to Paul. Selected by God and sent from Palestine to carry God's message, Paul and Barnabas, now faithful to the calling, took the gospel message to other towns and cities. But when the unbelievers saw the people turn their hearts to the word of God, they stirred the people up with false accusations and divided them among themselves, so that they turned against the disciples and persecuted them, stoning Paul nearly to death.

Amid outcries from the people that this new faith would destroy their old traditional beliefs, Paul and Barnabas sought advice from the Council of Jerusalem about the matter. With letters of confirmation from the elders, they returned to the people, assuring them that God made no distinction among people of different faiths because of their rituals, but that, setting aside the religious rules that would divide them, all would be made pure in one faith by turning their hearts to God. With this they succeeded in bringing the people together in one accord.

THE HOLY GHOST SAID, "SEPARATE TO ME BARNABAS AND SAUL FOR THE WORK TO WHICH I HAVE CALLED THEM." (ACTS 13:2)

CHAPTER 68

FOUNDING NEW CONGREGATIONS

First Journey Begins
Acts 13:1-3

1   Now there were in the church that was at Antioch certain prophets and teachers; as Barnabas, and Simeon that was called Niger, and Lucius of Cyrene, and Manaen, which had been brought up with Herod (Antipas) the tetrarch (ruler), and Saul. As they ministered to the Lord, and fasted, the Holy Ghost said, "Separate to me Barnabas and Saul for the work to which I have called them." And when they had fasted and prayed, and laid their hands on them, they sent them away.

Saul Is Now Called Paul
Acts 13:4-12

2   So they, being sent forth by the Holy Ghost, departed unto Seleucia; and from there they sailed to Cyprus. And when they were at Salamis, they preached the word of God in the synagogues of the Jews: and they had also John (Mark) as their helper.

3   And when they had gone through the island unto Paphos, they found a certain sorcerer, a false prophet, a Jew, whose name was Bar-Jesus: which was with the proconsul of the country, Sergius Paulus, a prudent man; who called for Barnabas and Saul, and desired to hear the word of God. But Elymas the sorcerer (for so is his name by interpretation) withstood them, seeking to turn away the proconsul from the faith.

4   Then Saul, (who also is called Paul), filled with the Holy Ghost, set his eyes on him, and said, "O full of all deceit and all trickery, you child of the devil, you enemy of all righteousness, will you not cease to pervert the right ways of the Lord? And now, behold, the hand of the Lord is upon you, and you shall be blind, not seeing the sun for a season." And immediately there fell on him a mist and a darkness; and he went about seeking some to

lead him by the hand. Then the proconsul, when he saw what was done, 4
believed, being astonished at the doctrine of the Lord.

Mark Returns Home
Acts 13:13-15

Now when Paul and his company sailed from Paphos, they came to 5
Perga in Pamphylia: and John departing from them returned to Jerusalem.
But when they departed from Perga, they came to Antioch in Pisidia, and
went into the synagogue on the sabbath day, and sat down. And after the
reading of the law and the prophets, the rulers of the synagogue sent unto
them, saying, "You men and brethren, if you have any word of exhortation
for the people, say on."

Paul's Sermon
Acts 13:16-41

Then Paul stood up, and beckoning with his hand said, "Men of 6
Israel, and you that fear God, give audience. The God of this people of
Israel chose our fathers, and exalted the people when they dwelt as foreigners in the land of Egypt, and with a high arm brought he them out of
it. And about the time of forty years he tolerated their ways in the wilderness. And when he had destroyed seven nations in the land of Canaan, he
divided their land to them by lot.

"And after that he gave unto them judges about the space of four hun- 7
dred and fifty years, until Samuel the prophet. And afterward they desired
a king: and God gave unto them Saul the son of Kish, a man of the tribe of
Benjamin, by the space of forty years. And when he had removed him, he
raised up unto them David to be their king; to whom also he gave testimony, and said, '*I have found David* the son of Jesse, *a man after my own
heart*, which shall fulfill all my will.'

"Of this man's seed has God according to his promise raised unto 8
Israel a Savior, Jesus: when John (the Baptist) had first preached before his
coming the baptism of repentance to all the people of Israel. And as John
fulfilled his course, he said, 'Whom do you think that I am? I am not he.
But, behold, there comes one after me, whose shoes of his feet I am not worthy to loose.'

"Men and brethren, children of the stock of Abraham, and whosoever 9
among you fears God, to you is the word of this salvation sent. For they that
dwell at Jerusalem, and their rulers,
because they knew him not, nor the
voices of the prophets which are read
every sabbath day, they have fulfilled
them in condemning him. And though
they found no cause of death in him,

> "WHOSOEVER AMONG YOU
> FEARS GOD, TO YOU IS THE
> WORD OF THIS SALVATION
> SENT."

yet desired they Pilate that he should be slain. And when they had fulfilled
all that was written of him, they took him down from the cross, and laid him
in a tomb. But God raised him from the dead: and he was seen many days

9 of them which came up with him from Galilee to Jerusalem, who are his witnesses unto the people.

10   "And we declare unto you glad tidings, how that the promise which was made unto the fathers, God has fulfilled the same unto us their children, in that he has raised up Jesus again; as it is also written in the second psalm, '*You are my Son, this day have I begotten you.*' And as concerning that he raised him up from the dead, now no more to return to corruption, he said in this way, '*I will give you the sure mercies of David.*' Therefore he says also in another psalm, '*You shall not allow your Holy One to see corruption.*' For David, after he had served his own generation by the will of God, fell on sleep, and was laid unto his fathers, and saw corruption: but he, whom God raised again, saw no corruption.

11   "Be it known unto you therefore, men and brethren, that through this man is preached unto you the forgiveness of sins: and by him all that believe are justified from all things, from which you could not be justified by the law of Moses. Beware therefore, lest that come upon you, which is spoken of in the prophets; '*Behold, you despisers, and wonder, and perish: for I work a work in your days, a work which you shall in no way believe, though a man declares it unto you.*'"

> "BY HIM ALL THAT BELIEVE ARE JUSTIFIED FROM ALL THINGS."

Paul's Decision
Acts 13:42-52

12   And when the Jews were gone out of the synagogue, the Gentiles asked that these words might be preached to them the next sabbath. Now when the congregation was broken up, many of the Jews and religious converts to Judaism followed Paul and Barnabas: who, speaking to them, persuaded them to continue in the grace of God.

13   And the next sabbath day came almost the whole city together to hear the word of God. But when the Jews saw the multitudes, they were filled with envy, and spoke against those things which were spoken by Paul, contradicting and insulting. Then Paul and Barnabas became bold, and said, "It was necessary that the word of God should first have been spoken to you: but seeing you put it from you, and judge yourselves unworthy of everlasting life, lo, we turn to the Gentiles. For so has the Lord commanded us, saying, 'I have set you to be a light of the Gentiles, that you should be for salvation unto the ends of the earth.'"

14   And when the Gentiles heard this, they were glad, and glorified the word of the Lord: and as many as were ordained to eternal life believed. And the word of the Lord was published throughout all the region. But the Jews stirred up the devout and prominent women, and the chief men of the city, and raised persecution against Paul and Barnabas, and expelled them out of their region. But they shook off the dust of their feet against them, and came unto Iconium. And the disciples were filled with joy, and with the Holy Ghost.

CHAPTER 69

Confirming the New Disciples

Under Assault
Acts 14:1-7

And it came to pass in Iconium, that they went both together into the 1
synagogue of the Jews, and so spoke, that a great multitude both of the Jews
and also of the Greeks believed. But the unbelieving Jews stirred up the
Gentiles, and made their minds poisoned against the brethren. Therefore
they remained a long time speaking boldly in the Lord, which gave testimony unto the word of his grace, and granted signs and wonders to be done
by their hands.

But the multitude of the city was divided: and part held with the Jews, 2
and part with the apostles. And when there was an assault made both of the
Gentiles, and also of the Jews with their rulers, to use them despitefully, and
to stone them, they were aware of it, and fled unto Lystra and Derbe, cities
of Lycaonia, and unto the region that lies round about: and there they
preached the gospel.

Accused as Gods and Stoned
Acts 14:8-20

And there sat a certain man at Lystra, crippled in his feet, being a crip- 3
ple from his mother's womb, who never had walked: the same heard Paul
speak: who steadfastly beholding him, and perceiving that he had faith to
be healed, Said with a loud voice, "Stand upright on your feet." And he
leaped and walked.

And when the people saw what Paul had done, they lifted up their 4
voices, saying in the language of Lycaonia, "The gods are come down to us
in the likeness of men." And they called Barnabas, Jupiter; and Paul, Mer-
curius, because he was the chief speaker. Then the priest of Jupiter, which
was before their city, brought oxen and garlands unto the gates, and would
have done sacrifice with the people.

5   Which when the apostles, Barnabas and Paul, heard of, they tore their clothes, and ran in among the people, crying out, and saying, "Sirs, why do you these things? We also are men of like natures with you, and preach unto you that you should turn from these foolish things unto the living God, which made heaven, and earth, and the sea, and all things that are therein: who in times past allowed all nations to walk in their own ways. Nevertheless he has not left himself without witness, in that he did good, and gave us rain from heaven, and fruitful seasons, filling our hearts with food and gladness." And with these sayings scarcely restrained they the people, that they had not done sacrifice unto them.

> "TURN FROM THESE FOOLISH THINGS UNTO THE LIVING GOD, WHICH MADE HEAVEN, AND EARTH, AND THE SEA, AND ALL THINGS THAT ARE THEREIN."

6   And there came there certain Jews from Antioch and Iconium, who persuaded the people, and, having stoned Paul, dragged him out of the city, supposing he had been dead. Howbeit, as the disciples stood round about him, he rose up, and came into the city: and the next day he departed with Barnabas to Derbe.

Appointed Elders Confirmed
Acts 14:21-23

7   And when they had preached the gospel to that city, and had taught many, they returned again to Lystra, and to Iconium, and Antioch, confirming the souls of the disciples, and encouraging them to continue in the faith, and that "we must through much tribulation enter into the kingdom of God." And when they had appointed of them elders in every church, and had prayed with fasting, they commended them to the Lord, on whom they believed.

First Journey Ends
Acts 14:24-28

8   And after they had passed throughout Pisidia, they came to Pamphylia. And when they had preached the word in Perga, they went down into Attalia: and from there sailed to Antioch, from where they had been commended to the grace of God for the work which they fulfilled.

9   And when they were come, and had gathered the church together, they explained all that God had done with them, and how he had opened the door of faith unto the Gentiles. And there they stayed a long time with the disciples.

CHAPTER 70

JERUSALEM COUNCIL DECISION
Debate and Decision
Acts 15:1-21

And certain men which came down from Judea taught the brethren, 1 and said, "Except you be circumcised after the manner of Moses, you cannot be saved."

When therefore Paul and Barnabas had no small dissension and dis- 2 pute with them, they determined that Paul and Barnabas, and certain others of them, should go up to Jerusalem unto the apostles and elders about this question. And being brought on their way by the church, they passed through Phoenicia and Samaria, declaring the conversion of the Gentiles: and they caused great joy unto all the brethren.

And when they were come to Jerusalem, they were received of the 3 church, and of the apostles and elders, and they declared all things that God had done with them. But there rose up certain of the sect of the Pharisees which believed, saying, "That it was needful to circumcise them, and to command them to keep the law of Moses."

And the apostles and elders came together to consider of this matter. 4 And when there had been much disputing, Peter rose up, and said unto them, "Men and brethren, you know how that a good while ago God made choice among us, that the Gentiles by my mouth should hear the word of the gospel, and believe. And God, which knows the hearts, bore them witness, giving them the Holy Ghost, even as he did unto us; and put no distinction between us and them, purifying their hearts by faith.

"Now therefore why tempt you God, to put a yoke upon the neck of 5 the disciples, which neither our fathers nor we were able to bear? But we believe that through the grace of the Lord Jesus Christ we shall be saved, even as they."

6   Then all the multitude kept silent, and gave audience to Barnabas and Paul, declaring what miracles and wonders God had wrought among the Gentiles by them.

7   And after they had held their peace, James answered, saying, "Men and brethren, hearken unto me: Simon has declared how God at the first did visit the Gentiles, to take out of them a people for his name. And to this agree the words of the prophets; as it is written, 'After this I will return, and will build again the tabernacle of David, which is fallen down; and I will build again the ruins thereof, and I will set it up: that the residue of men might seek after the Lord, and all the Gentiles, upon whom my name is called, says the Lord, who does all these things.' Known unto God are all his works from the beginning of the world.

8   "Therefore my judgement is, that we do not trouble them, which from among the Gentiles are turned to God: but that we write unto them, that they abstain from pollutions of idols, and from fornication, and from things slaughtered, and from blood. For Moses of old time has in every city them that preach him, being read in the synagogues every sabbath day."

Agreement Letter to Gentiles
Acts 15:22-35

9   Then it pleased the apostles and elders, with the whole church, to send chosen men of their own company to Antioch with Paul and Barnabas; namely, Judas surnamed Barsabas, and Silas, chief men among the brethren. And they wrote letters by them after this manner: The apostles and elders and brethren send greeting unto the brethren which are of the Gentiles in Antioch and Syria and Cilicia.

10   Inasmuch as we have heard, that certain ones which went out from us have troubled you with words, unsettling your souls, saying, "You must be circumcised, and keep the law": to whom we gave no such instruction: it seemed good unto us, being assembled with one accord, to send chosen men unto you with our beloved Barnabas and Paul, men that have hazarded their lives for the name of our Lord Jesus Christ.

11   We have sent therefore Judas and Silas, who shall also tell you the same things by mouth. For it seemed good to the Holy Ghost, and to us, to lay upon you no greater burden than these necessary things; that you abstain from foods offered to idols, and from blood, and from things slaughtered, and from fornication: from which if you keep yourselves, you shall do well. Fare you well.

12   So when they were dismissed, they came to Antioch: and when they had gathered the multitude together, they delivered the letter: which when they had read, they rejoiced for the consolation.

13   And Judas and Silas, being prophets also themselves, encouraged the brethren with many words, and confirmed them. And after they had remained there a time, they were let go in peace from the brethren unto the apostles. However it pleased Silas to stay on there. Paul also and Barnabas continued in Antioch, teaching and preaching the word of the Lord, with many others also.

PART 17

SECOND MISSIONARY JOURNEY

And so, following the same course they had traveled in their earlier journey, Paul and Barnabas, traveling separately and joined by other disciples, revisited the same cities, delivering the letters written by the Jerusalem elders that rescinded the Jewish rituals for joining the Christian faith. They preached to Jews, Greeks, and Gentiles, and all who would believe, persuading many to join the faith. Paul received visions to guide him in his way. Though suffering many persecutions and even imprisonment, the Apostles are protected at every turn and delivered from their enemies by the hand of God.

> As they went through the cities, they delivered them the decrees to keep, that were decided by the apostles and elders which were at Jerusalem. And so were the churches established in the faith, and increased in number daily. (Acts 16:4-5)

CHAPTER 71

Establishing Churches Among Gentiles

Second Journey Begins
Acts 15:36-41

1   And some days later Paul said unto Barnabas, "Let us go again and visit our brethren in every city where we have preached the word of the Lord, and see how they do." And Barnabas determined to take with them John, whose surname was Mark.

2   But Paul thought not good to take him with them, who departed from them from Pamphylia, and went not with them to the work. And the contention was so sharp between them, that they departed separately one from the other: and so Barnabas took Mark, and sailed unto Cyprus; and Paul chose Silas, and departed, being commended by the brethren unto the grace of God. And he went through Syria and Cilicia, confirming the churches.

Timothy Joins Journey
Acts 16:1-5

3   Then he came to Derbe and Lystra: and, behold, a certain disciple was there, named Timothy, the son of a certain woman, which was a Jewess, and believed; but his father was a Greek: which was well reported of by the brethren that were at Lystra and Iconium. Him would Paul have to go forth with him; and took and circumcised him because of the Jews which were in those areas: for they all knew that his father was a Greek.

4   And as they went through the cities, they delivered them the decrees to keep, that were decided by the apostles and elders which were at Jerusalem. And so were the churches established in the faith, and increased in number daily.

Paul Receives a Vision to Go to Europe
Acts 16:6-10

5   Now when they had gone throughout Phrygia and the region of Galatia, and were forbidden of the Holy Ghost to preach the word in Asia, after

they were come to Mysia, they attempted to go into Bithynia: but the Spir- 5
it did not allow them. And they passing by Mysia came down to Troas.

And a vision appeared to Paul in the night; There stood a man of 6
Macedonia, and pleaded with him, saying, "Come over into Macedonia, and
help us." And after he had seen the vision, immediately we endeavored to
go into Macedonia, assuredly concluding that the Lord had called us to
preach the gospel unto them.

Baptism of Lydia at Philippi
Acts 16:11-15

Therefore sailing from Troas, we came with a straight course to 7
Samothrace, and the next day to Neapolis; and from there to Philippi, which
is the chief city of that part of Macedonia, and a colony: and we were in that
city staying certain days.

And on the sabbath we went out of the city by a riverside, where prayer 8
was by custom to be made; and we sat down, and spoke unto the women
which gathered there.

And a certain woman named Lydia, a seller of purple, of the city of 9
Thyatira, which worshiped God, heard
us: whose heart the Lord opened, that | "IF YOU HAVE JUDGED ME TO
she attended unto the things which | BE FAITHFUL TO THE LORD,
were spoken of Paul. And when she | COME INTO MY HOUSE, AND
was baptized, and her household, she | STAY."
asked us, saying, "If you have judged
me to be faithful to the Lord, come into my house, and stay there." And she
persuaded us.

Cast Into Prison
Acts 16:16-24

And it came to pass, as we went to prayer, a certain servant girl pos- 10
sessed with a spirit of divination met us, which brought her masters much
gain by soothsaying: the same followed Paul and us, and cried, saying,
"These men are the servants of the most high God, which show unto us the
way of salvation." And this she did many days. But Paul, being troubled,
turned and said to the spirit, "I command you in the name of Jesus Christ to
come out of her." And it came out the same hour.

And when her masters saw that the hope of their gains was gone, they 11
caught Paul and Silas, and dragged them into the marketplace unto the
rulers, and brought them to the magistrates, saying, "These men, being
Jews, do exceedingly trouble our city, and teach customs, which are not
lawful for us to receive, neither to observe, being Romans."

And the multitude rose up together against them: and the magistrates 12
tore off their clothes, and commanded to beat them. And when they had laid
many stripes upon them, they cast them into prison, charging the jailer to
keep them securely: who, having received such a charge, thrust them into
the inner prison, and made their feet secure in the stocks.

Earthquake Opens Prison Doors
Acts 16:25-34

13   And at midnight Paul and Silas prayed, and sang praises unto God: and the prisoners heard them. And suddenly there was a great earthquake, so that the foundations of the prison were shaken: and immediately all the doors were opened, and everyone's chains were loosed. And the jailer of the prison awaking out of his sleep, and seeing the prison doors open, he drew out his sword, and would have killed himself, supposing that the prisoners had escaped. But Paul cried with a loud voice, saying, "Do yourself no harm: for we are all here."

> SUDDENLY THERE WAS A GREAT EARTHQUAKE, SO THAT THE FOUNDATIONS OF THE PRISON WERE SHAKEN: AND IMMEDIATELY ALL THE DOORS WERE OPENED.

14   Then he called for a light, and sprang in, and came trembling, and fell down before Paul and Silas, and brought them out, and said, "Sirs, what must I do to be saved?" And they said, "Believe on the Lord Jesus Christ, and you shall be saved, and your household." And they spoke unto him the word of the Lord, and to all that were in his household.

> "WHAT MUST I DO TO BE SAVED?"

15   And he took them the same hour of the night, and washed their stripes; and was baptized, he and all his, straightway. And when he had brought them into his house, he set food before them, and rejoiced, believing in God with all his household.

Release From Prison
Acts 16:35-40

16   And when it was day, the magistrates sent the officers, saying, "Let those men go." And the jailer of the prison told this saying to Paul, "The magistrates have sent to let you go: now therefore depart, and go in peace." But Paul said unto them, "They have beaten us openly uncondemned, being Romans, and have cast us into prison; and now do they thrust us out secretly? no indeed; but let them come themselves and bring us out."

17   And the officers told these words unto the magistrates: and they feared, when they heard that they were Romans. And they came and apologized to them, and brought them out, and desired them to depart out of the city.

18   And they went out of the prison, and entered into the house of Lydia: and when they had seen the brethren, they encouraged them, and departed.

CHAPTER 72

⚜ CONTINUING WITH THE GENTILE DISCIPLES ⚜

Troubles Continue at Thessalonica
Acts 17:1-9

Now when they had passed through Amphipolis and Apollonia, they 1
came to Thessalonica, where was a synagogue of the Jews: and Paul, as his
manner was, went in unto them, and three sabbath days reasoned with them
out of the scriptures, explaining and proving, that Christ must of necessity
have suffered, and risen again from the dead; and that "this Jesus, whom I
preach unto you, is Christ." And some of them believed, and joined with
Paul and Silas; and of the devout Greeks a great multitude, and of the
prominent women not a few.

But the Jews which believed not, moved with envy, took unto them- 2
selves certain wicked fellows of the rabble sort, and gathered a crowd, and
set all the city on an uproar, and assaulted the house of Jason, and sought to
bring them out to the people. And when they had not found them, they
dragged Jason and certain brethren unto the rulers of the city, crying,
"These that have turned the world upside down are come here also; whom
Jason has received: and these all do contrary to the decrees of Caesar, saying that there is another king, one Jesus."

And they troubled the people and the rulers of the city, when they 3
heard these things. And when they had taken security from Jason, and from
the others, they let them go.

Stirred Up People and Departure
Acts 17:10-15

And the brethren immediately sent away Paul and Silas by night unto 4
Berea: who coming there went into the synagogue of the Jews. These were
more open-minded than those in Thessalonica, in that they received the
word with all readiness of mind, and searched the scriptures daily, whether

4 those things were so. Therefore many of them believed; also of prominent women which were Greeks, and of men, not a few.

5   But when the Jews of Thessalonica had knowledge that the word of God was preached of Paul at Berea, they came there also, and stirred up the people. And then immediately the brethren sent away Paul to go as it were to the sea: but Silas and Timothy stayed on there. And they that conducted Paul brought him unto Athens: and receiving a command unto Silas and Timothy to come to him with all speed, they departed.

Paul and Philosophers at Athens
Acts 17:16-21

6   Now while Paul waited for them at Athens, his spirit was stirred in him, when he saw the city wholly given to idolatry. Therefore he reasoned in the synagogue with the Jews, and with the devout persons, and in the marketplace daily with them that met with him.

7   Then certain philosophers of the Epicureans, and of the Stoics, encountered him. And some said, "What will this babbler say?" some others, "He seems to be a proclaimer of strange gods": because he preached unto them Jesus, and the resurrection. And they took him, and brought him unto Areopagus, saying, "May we know what this new doctrine, of which you speak, is? For you bring certain strange things to our ears: we would know therefore what these things

> "MAY WE KNOW WHAT THIS NEW DOCTRINE, OF WHICH YOU SPEAK, IS?"

mean." (For all the Athenians and foreigners which were there spent their time in nothing else, but either to tell, or to hear some new thing.)

Paul's Gospel Speech
Acts 17:22-34

8   Then Paul stood in the midst of Mars' hill, and said, "You men of Athens, I perceive that in all things you are very religious. For as I passed by, and beheld your devotions, I found an altar with this inscription, TO THE UNKNOWN GOD. Whom therefore you ignorantly worship, him I declare unto you.

9   "God that made the world and all things therein, seeing that he is Lord of heaven and earth, dwells not in temples made with hands; neither is worshiped with men's hands, as though he needed anything, seeing he gives to all life, and breath, and all things. And has made of one blood all nations of men to dwell on all the face of the

> "HE GIVES TO ALL LIFE, AND BREATH, AND ALL THINGS' ...FOR IN HIM WE LIVE, AND MOVE, AND HAVE OUR BEING."

earth, and has determined beforehand the times appointed, and the boundaries of their habitation; that they should seek the Lord, if perhaps they might feel after him, and find him, though he be not far from every one of us: for in him we live, and move, and have our

being; as certain also of your own poets have said, 'For we are also his off- 9
spring.'

"Inasmuch then as we are the offspring of God, we ought not to think 10
that the Godhead is like unto gold, or silver, or stone, graven by art and
man's device. And the times of this
ignorance God overlooked; but now | "HE HAS APPOINTED A DAY, IN
commands all men everywhere to | WHICH HE WILL JUDGE THE
repent: because he has appointed a | WORLD IN RIGHTEOUSNESS."
day, in which he will judge the world
in righteousness by that man whom he has ordained; of which he has given
assurance unto all men, in that he has raised him from the dead."

And when they heard of the resurrection of the dead, some mocked: 11
and others said, "We will hear you again of this matter." So Paul departed
from among them. Howbeit certain men joined unto him, and believed:
among which was Dionysius the Areopagite, and a woman named Damaris,
and others with them.

Paul's Announcement at Corinth
Acts 18:1-6

After these things Paul departed from Athens, and came to Corinth; 12
and found a certain Jew named Aquila, born in Pontus, recently come from
Italy, with his wife Priscilla; (because Claudius had commanded all Jews
to depart from Rome): and came unto them. And because he was of the
same craft, he stayed with them, and worked: for by their occupation they
were tentmakers. And he reasoned in the synagogue every sabbath, and
persuaded the Jews and the Greeks.

And when Silas and Timothy were come from Macedonia, Paul was 13
occupied in the spirit, and testified to the Jews that Jesus was Christ. And
when they opposed themselves, and became insulting, he shook his clothing, and said unto them, "Your blood be upon your own heads; I am clean:
from now on I will go unto the Gentiles."

Paul Receives a Vision to Speak
Acts 18:7-11

And he departed from there, and entered into a certain man's house, 14
named Justus, one that worshiped God, whose house joined walls with the
synagogue. And Crispus, the chief ruler of the synagogue, believed on the
Lord with all his household; and many of the Corinthians hearing believed,
and were baptized.

Then the Lord spoke to Paul in the night by a vision, "Be not afraid, 15
but speak, and hold not your peace: for I am with you, and no man shall set
on you to hurt you: for I have many people in this city." And he continued
there a year and six months, teaching the word of God among them.

PART 18

First Letter to Thessalonians

*In one of the most beautiful and comforting of the letters, Paul deliv-
ers words of praise and promise to those who have remained faithful
to the word of God. Praying that they might continue in good works
and abound in love for one another, Paul gives them assurance of their
delivery at the second coming of Christ, when the dead will be caught
up together with the living in the everlasting circle of God's love.*

THE LORD HIMSELF SHALL DESCEND FROM
HEAVEN WITH A SHOUT, WITH THE VOICE OF THE
ARCHANGEL, AND WITH THE TRUMPET OF GOD:
AND THE DEAD IN CHRIST SHALL RISE FIRST:
THEN WE WHICH ARE ALIVE AND REMAIN SHALL
BE CAUGHT UP TOGETHER WITH THEM IN THE
CLOUDS, TO MEET THE LORD IN THE AIR: AND SO
SHALL WE EVER BE WITH THE LORD.

(1 THESSALONIANS 4:16-17)

CHAPTER 73

PROGRESS AMID PERSECUTIONS

Greeting to Thessalonians
1 Thessalonians 1:1

Paul, and Silas, and Timothy, unto the church of the Thessalonians 1
which is in God the Father and in the Lord Jesus Christ: Grace be unto you,
and peace, from God our Father, and the Lord Jesus Christ.

Giving Thanks
1 Thessalonians 1:2-10

We give thanks to God always for you all, making mention of you in 2
our prayers; remembering without ceasing your work of faith, and labor of
love, and patience of hope in our Lord Jesus Christ, in the sight of God and
our Father; knowing, brethren beloved, your election of God.

For our gospel came not unto you in word only, but also in power, and 3
in the Holy Ghost, and in much assurance; as you know what manner of
men we were among you for your sake. And you became imitators of us,
and of the Lord, having received the word in much affliction, with joy of the
Holy Ghost: so that you were examples to all that believe in Macedonia and
Achaia. For from you rang forth the word of the Lord not only in Macedonia and Achaia, but also in every place your faith toward God is spread
abroad; so that we need not to speak anything.

For they themselves show of us what manner of entering in we had 4
unto you, and how you turned to God from idols to serve the living and true
God; and to wait for his Son from heaven, whom he raised from the dead,
even Jesus, which delivered us from the wrath to come.

Paul's Gospel Work
1 Thessalonians 2:1-16

5   For yourselves, brethren, know our coming unto you, that it was not in vain: but even after we had suffered before, and were spitefully treated, as you know, at Philippi, we were bold in our God to speak unto you the gospel of God with much opposition.

6   For our exhortation was not of error, nor of uncleanness, nor in deceit: but as we were approved of God to be put in trust with the gospel, even so we speak; not as pleasing men, but God, which tests our hearts.

7   For neither at any time used we flattering words, as you know, nor a cloak of covetousness; God is witness: nor of men sought we glory, neither of you, nor of others, when we might have been burdensome, as the apostles of Christ.

8   But we were gentle among you, even as a nurse cherishes her children: so being affectionately desirous of you, we were ready to have imparted unto you, not the gospel of God only, but also our own selves, because you were dear unto us. For you remember, brethren, our labor and toil: for laboring night and day, because we would not be a burden unto any of you, we preached unto you the gospel of God.

9   You are witnesses, and God also, how holy and justly and blamelessly we behaved ourselves among you that believe: as you know how we

> WALK WORTHY OF GOD, WHO HAS CALLED YOU UNTO HIS KINGDOM.

exhorted and comforted and charged every one of you, as a father does his children, that you would walk worthy of God, who has called you unto his kingdom and glory.

10   For this cause also we thank God without ceasing, because, when you received the word of God which you heard of us, you received it not as the word of men, but as it is in truth, the word of God, which effectively works also in you that believe. For you, brethren, became imitators of the churches of God which in Judea are in Christ Jesus: for you also have suffered like things of your own countrymen, even as they have of the Jews: who both killed the Lord Jesus, and their own prophets, and have persecuted us; and they please not God, and are contrary to all men: forbidding us to speak to the Gentiles that they might be saved, to fill up their sins always: for the wrath is come upon them to the uttermost.

Wish to Visit Again
1 Thessalonians 2:17-20

11   But we, brethren, being taken from you for a short time in presence, not in heart, endeavored the more eagerly to see your face with great desire. Therefore we would have come unto you, even I Paul, once and again; but Satan hindered us. For what is our hope, or joy, or crown of rejoicing? Are not even you in the presence of our Lord Jesus Christ at his coming? For you are our glory and joy.

Report of Your Progress
1 Thessalonians 3:1-13

Therefore when we could no longer endure, we thought it good to be 12 left at Athens alone; and sent Timothy, our brother, and minister of God, and our fellow laborer in the gospel of Christ, to strengthen you, and to encourage you concerning your faith: that no man should be unsettled by these afflictions: for you yourselves know that we are appointed thereto.

For in fact, when we were with you, we told you before that we should 13 suffer tribulation; even as it came to pass, and you know. For this reason, when I could no longer endure, I sent to know your faith, lest by some means the tempter have tempted you, and our labor be in vain.

But now when Timothy came from you unto us, and brought us good 14 news of your faith and love, and that you have good remembrance of us always, desiring greatly to see us, as we also to see you: therefore, brethren,

> NOW WE LIVE, IF YOU STAND FAST IN THE LORD.

we were comforted over you in all our affliction and distress by your faith: For now we live, if you stand fast in the Lord.

For what thanks can we render to God again for you, for all the joy 15 with which we joy for your sakes before our God; night and day praying earnestly that we might see your face, and might supply that which is lacking in your faith?

Now God himself and our Father, and our Lord Jesus Christ, direct our 16 way unto you. And the Lord make you to increase and abound in love one toward another, and toward all men, even as we do toward you: to the end he may establish your hearts blameless in holiness before God, even our Father, at the coming of our Lord Jesus Christ with all his saints.

> INCREASE AND ABOUND IN LOVE ONE TOWARD ANOTHER, AND TOWARD ALL MEN.

CHAPTER 74

⚬ MAJESTIC MANNER OF THE SECOND COMING ⚬

Living to Please God
1 Thessalonians 4:1-12

1   Furthermore then we ask you, brethren, and urge you by the Lord Jesus, that as you have received of us how you ought to walk and to please God, so you would abound more and more. For you know what instructions we gave you by the Lord Jesus.

2   For this is the will of God, even your sanctification, that you should abstain from fornication: that every one of you should know how to possess his body in sanctification and honor; not in the lust of evil desire, even as the Gentiles which know not God: that no man go beyond and wrong his brother in any matter: because the Lord is the avenger of all such, as we also have forewarned you and testified. For God has not called us unto uncleanness, but unto holiness. He therefore that rejects, rejects not man, but God, who has also given unto us his Holy Spirit.

3   But as concerning brotherly love you need not that I write unto you: for you yourselves are taught of God to love one another. And indeed you do it toward all the brethren which are in all Macedonia: but we urge you, brethren, that you increase more and more; and that you strive to be quiet, and to do your own business, and to work with your own hands, as we instructed you; that you may walk decently toward them that are outside, and that you may have lack of nothing.

Those That Sleep Shall Rise
1 Thessalonians 4:13-18

4   But I would not have you to be ignorant, brethren, concerning them which are asleep, that you do not sorrow, even as others which have no hope. For if we believe that Jesus died and rose again, even so them also which sleep in Jesus will God bring with him. For this we say unto you by

the word of the Lord, that we which are alive and remain unto the coming 4
of the Lord shall not precede them
which are asleep. For the Lord himself
shall descend from heaven with a
shout, with the voice of the archangel,
and with the trumpet of God: and the
dead in Christ shall rise first: then we
which are alive and remain shall be

> IF WE BELIEVE THAT JESUS DIED AND ROSE AGAIN, EVEN SO THEM ALSO WHICH SLEEP IN JESUS WILL GOD BRING WITH HIM.

caught up together with them in the clouds, to meet the Lord in the air: and
so shall we ever be with the Lord.

Therefore comfort one another with these words.   5

Being Ready for the Coming
1 Thessalonians 5:1-11

But of the times and the seasons, brethren, you have no need that I 6
write unto you. For you yourselves
know perfectly that the day of the
Lord so comes as a thief in the night.
For when they shall say, "Peace and
security"; then sudden destruction

> THE DAY OF THE LORD SO COMES AS A THIEF IN THE NIGHT.

comes upon them, as labor pains upon a woman with child; and they shall
not escape.

But you, brethren, are not in darkness, that that day should overtake 7
you as a thief. You are all the children of light, and the children of the day:
we are not of the night, nor of darkness. Therefore let us not sleep, as do
others; but let us watch and be sober. For they that sleep sleep in the night;
and they that be drunk are drunk in the night.

But let us, who are of the day, be sober, putting on the breastplate 8
of faith and love; and for a helmet,
the hope of salvation. For God has
not appointed us to wrath, but to
obtain salvation by our Lord Jesus
Christ, who died for us, that,
whether we wake or sleep, we

> BE SOBER, PUTTING ON THE BREASTPLATE OF FAITH AND LOVE; AND FOR A HELMET, THE HOPE OF SALVATION.

should live together with him. Therefore comfort yourselves together,
and build up one another, even as also you do.

Faithful Instructions
1 Thessalonians 5:12-25

And we appeal to you, brethren, to know them which labor among 9
you, and are over you in the Lord, and admonish you; and to esteem them
very highly in love for their work's sake. And be at peace among yourselves.

Now we urge you, brethren, warn them that are idle, encourage the 10
fainthearted, support the weak, be patient toward all men. See that none render evil for evil unto any man; but ever follow that which is good, both
among yourselves, and to all men.

11 Rejoice evermore. Pray without ceasing. In everything give thanks: for this is the will of God in Christ Jesus concerning you. Do not quench the Spirit. Do not despise prophesy-ings. Test all things; hold fast that which is good. Abstain from all appearance of evil.

> ABSTAIN FROM ALL APPEAR-ANCE OF EVIL.

12 And the very God of peace sanctify you wholly; and I pray God your whole spirit and soul and body be preserved blameless unto the coming of our Lord Jesus Christ. Faithful is he that calls you, who also will do it.

13 Brethren, pray for us.

Conclusion
1 Thessalonians 5:26-28

14 Greet all the brethren with a holy kiss. I charge you by the Lord that this letter be read unto all the holy brethren.

15 The grace of our Lord Jesus Christ be with you. Amen.

PART 19

SECOND LETTER TO THESSALONIANS

With words of profound encouragement and praise, Paul exhorts the people of the church of Thessalonians to remain strong in their faith until the coming of the Lord Jesus Christ and not to abide with those who despise the Truth. The unbelievers will be consumed at the brightness of His coming; but God will give everlasting consolation to those who love Him and will establish them in every good work.

284

> THE LORD IS FAITHFUL, WHO SHALL ESTABLISH
> YOU, AND KEEP YOU FROM EVIL. AND WE HAVE
> CONFIDENCE IN THE LORD CONCERNING YOU,
> THAT YOU BOTH DO AND WILL DO THE THINGS
> WHICH WE INSTRUCT YOU.
>
> (2 THESSALONIANS 3:3-4)

CHAPTER 75

PRELUDE TO THE SECOND COMING

Greeting to Thessalonians
2 Thessalonians 1:1-2

1   Paul, and Silas, and Timothy, unto the church of the Thessalonians in
God our Father and the Lord Jesus Christ: Grace unto you, and peace, from
God our Father and the Lord Jesus Christ.

Giving Thanks
2 Thessalonians 1:3-12

2   We are bound to thank God always for you, brethren, as it is fitting,
because that your faith grows exceedingly, and the love of every one of you
all toward each other abounds; so that we ourselves boast in you in the
churches of God for your patience and faith in all your persecutions and
tribulations that you endure: which is a manifest proof of the righteous
judgment of God, that you may be counted worthy of the kingdom of God,
for which you also suffer: seeing it is a righteous thing with God to repay
tribulation to them that trouble you; and to you who are troubled rest with
us, when the Lord Jesus shall be revealed from heaven with his mighty
angels, in flaming fire taking vengeance on them that know not God, and
that do not obey the gospel of our Lord Jesus Christ.

3   They shall be punished with everlasting destruction from the presence
of the Lord, and from the glory of his power; when he shall come to be glorified in his saints, and to be admired in all them that believe (because our
testimony among you was believed) in that day.

4   Therefore also we pray always for you, that our God would count you
worthy of this calling, and fulfill all the good pleasure of his goodness, and
the work of faith with power: that the name of our Lord Jesus Christ may
be glorified in you, and you in him, according to the grace of our God and
the Lord Jesus Christ.

Mystery of Iniquity
2 Thessalonians 2:1-12

Now we beg you, brethren, by the coming of our Lord Jesus Christ, 5 and by our gathering together unto him, that you be not soon shaken in mind, or be troubled, neither by spirit, nor by word, nor by letter as from us, as though the day of the Lord is at hand. Let no man deceive you by any means: for that day shall not come, except there comes a falling away first, and that man of sin be revealed, the son of perdition; who opposes and exalts himself above all that is called God, or that is worshiped; so that he as God sits in the temple of God, showing himself that he is God.

> LET NO MAN DECEIVE YOU BY ANY MEANS: FOR THAT DAY SHALL NOT COME, EXCEPT THERE COMES A FALLING AWAY FIRST.

Do you not remember, that, when I was yet with you, I told you these 6 things? And now you know what is withheld that he might be revealed in his time. For the mystery of iniquity does already work: only he who now restrains will restrain, until he be taken out of the way.

And then shall that Wicked be revealed, whom the Lord shall con- 7 sume with the spirit of his mouth, and shall destroy with the brightness of his coming: even him, whose coming is according to the working of Satan with all power and signs and false wonders, and with all deceptiveness of unrighteousness in them that perish; because they had not received the love of the truth, that they might be saved. And for this cause God shall send them strong delusion, that they should believe a lie: that they all might be condemned who had not believed the truth, but had pleasure in unrighteousness.

Standing for Salvation
2 Thessalonians 2:13-17

But we are bound to give thanks always to God for you, brethren 8 beloved of the Lord, because God has from the beginning chosen you to salvation through sanctification of the Spirit and belief of the truth: to which he called you by our gospel, to the obtaining of the glory of our Lord Jesus Christ. Therefore, brethren, stand fast, and hold the traditions which you have been taught, whether by word, or our letter.

> STAND FAST, AND HOLD THE TRADITIONS WHICH YOU HAVE BEEN TAUGHT.

Now our Lord Jesus Christ himself, and God, even our Father, which 9 has loved us, and has given us everlasting consolation and good hope through grace, comfort your hearts, and establish you in every good word and work.

CHAPTER 76

Preparation for the Second Coming

Faithfulness of the Lord
2 Thessalonians 3:1-5

1   Finally, brethren, pray for us, that the word of the Lord may have free course, and be glorified, even as it is with you: and that we may be delivered from unreasonable and wicked men: for not all men have faith.

2   But the Lord is faithful, who shall establish you, and keep you from evil. And we have confidence in the Lord concerning you, that you both do and will do the things which we instruct you. And the Lord direct your hearts into the love of God, and into the patient waiting for Christ.

Providing for Your Own
2 Thessalonians 3:6-15

3   Now we instruct you, brethren, in the name of our Lord Jesus Christ, that you withdraw yourselves from every brother that walks disorderly, and not after the tradition which he received of us. For yourselves know how you ought to imitate us: for we behaved not ourselves disorderly among you; neither did we eat any man's bread for nothing; but worked with labor and toil night and day, that we might not be a burden to any of you: not because we have not authority, but to make ourselves an example unto you to imitate us. For even when we were with you, this we instructed you, that if any would not work, neither should he eat.

4   For we hear that there are some which walk among you disorderly, working not at all, but are busybodies. Now them that are such we instruct and call on by our Lord Jesus Christ, that with quietness they work, and eat their own bread. But you, brethren, be not weary in well doing.

5   And if any man does not obey our word by this letter, note that man, and have no company with him, that he may be ashamed. Yet count him not as an enemy, but admonish him as a brother.

Conclusion
2 Thessalonians 3:16-18

Now the Lord of peace himself give you peace always by all means. 6
The Lord be with you all.

The greeting of Paul with my own hand, which is the mark in every 7
letter: this is how I write.

The grace of our Lord Jesus Christ be with you all. Amen.   8

CHAPTER 77

⸎ Mission's Success and Support ⸎

Important Roman Ruling at Corinth
Acts 18:12-17

1   And when Gallio was the proconsul of Achaia, the Jews made insurrection with one accord against Paul, and brought him to the judgment seat, saying, "This fellow persuades men to worship God contrary to the law."

2   And when Paul was now about to open his mouth, Gallio said unto the Jews, "If it were a matter of wrongdoing or wicked crime, O you Jews, reason would that I should bear with you. But if it be a question of words and names, and of your law, you see to it; for I will be no judge of such matters."

3   And he drove them from the judgment seat. Then all the Greeks took Sosthenes, the chief ruler of the synagogue, and beat him before the judgment seat. And Gallio cared for none of those things.

Second Journey Ends
Acts 18:18-21

4   And Paul after this tarried there yet a good while, and then took his leave of the brethren, and sailed from there into Syria, and with him Priscilla and Aquila; having sheared his head in Cenchrea: for he had a vow. And he came to Ephesus, and left them there: but he himself entered into the synagogue, and reasoned with the Jews.

5   When they desired him to tarry a longer time with them, he did not consent; but told them farewell, saying, "I must by all means keep this feast that comes in Jerusalem: but I will return again unto you, if God wills." And he sailed from Ephesus.

PART 20

THIRD MISSIONARY JOURNEY

*As Paul and the Apostles continue their missionary journey through-
out the Roman province of Asia, ministering to those who accept
Jesus' teachings and who struggle to practice the Christian faith,
their cause is beset by many adversaries. Itinerant Jews, exorcists,
magicians, and those who craft idols fear that the growing belief in
this new unseen God will deprive them of their livelihood and try vig-
orously to upset their cause. This is a time of both trouble and triumph for the young church and its leaders.*

THIS CONTINUED BY THE SPACE OF TWO YEARS;
SO THAT ALL THEY WHICH DWELT IN ASIA HEARD
THE WORD OF THE LORD JESUS, BOTH JEWS AND
GREEKS. (ACTS 19:10)

CHAPTER 78

SPREADING THE GOSPEL FROM EPHESUS

Third Journey Begins
Acts 18:22-23

1   And when he had landed at Caesarea, and gone up, and greeted the church, he went down to Antioch. And after he had spent some time there, he departed, and went over all the region of Galatia and Phrygia in order, strengthening all the disciples.

Apollos Joins the Mission at Ephesus
Acts 18:24-28

2   And a certain Jew named Apollos, born at Alexandria, an eloquent man, and mighty in the scriptures, came to Ephesus. This man was instructed in the way of the Lord; and being fervent in the spirit, he spoke and taught diligently the things of the Lord, knowing only the baptism of John. And he began to speak boldly in the synagogue: whom when Aquila and Priscilla had heard, they took him unto them, and explained unto him the way of God more accurately.

3   And when he was disposed to cross into Achaia, the brethren wrote, urging the disciples to receive him: who, when he was come, helped them greatly which had believed through grace: for he mightily refuted the Jews, and that publicly, showing by the scriptures that Jesus was Christ.

Paul's Mixed Success
Acts 19:1-10

4   And it came to pass, that, while Apollos was at Corinth, Paul having passed through the upper regions came to Ephesus: and finding certain disciples, he said unto them, "Have you received the Holy Ghost since you believed?" And they said unto him, "We have not so much as heard whether there be any Holy Ghost."

5   And he said unto them, "Unto what then were you baptized?" And they said, "Unto John's baptism." Then said Paul, "John indeed baptized

with the baptism of repentance, saying unto the people, that they should 5 believe on him which should come after him, that is, on Christ Jesus." When they heard this, they were baptized in the name of the Lord Jesus. And when Paul had laid his hands upon them, the Holy Ghost came on them; and they spoke with tongues, and prophesied. And all the men were about twelve.

> WHEN PAUL HAD LAID HIS HANDS UPON THEM, THE HOLY GHOST CAME ON THEM.

And he went into the synagogue, and spoke boldly for the space of 6 three months, reasoning and persuading the things concerning the kingdom of God. But when several were hardened, and believed not, but spoke evil of that way before the multitude, he departed from them, and withdrew the disciples, reasoning daily in the school of one Tyrannus. And this continued by the space of two years; so that all they which dwelt in Asia heard the word of the Lord Jesus, both Jews and Greeks.

Seven Sons of Sceva
Acts 19:11-20

And God wrought special miracles by the hands of Paul: so that from 7 his body were brought unto the sick handkerchiefs or aprons, and the diseases departed from them, and the evil spirits went out of them.

Then certain of the itinerant Jews, exorcists, took upon themselves to 8 pronounce over those which had evil spirits the name of the Lord Jesus, saying, "We command you by Jesus whom Paul preaches." And there were seven sons of one Sceva, a Jew, and chief of the priests, which did so.

And the evil spirit answered and said, "Jesus I know, and Paul I know; 9 but who are you?" And the man in whom the evil spirit was leaped on them, and overpowered them, and prevailed against them, so that they fled out of that house naked and wounded.

And this was known to all the Jews and Greeks also dwelling at Eph- 10 esus; and fear fell on them all, and the name of the Lord Jesus was magnified. And many that believed came, and confessed, and showed their deeds.

> THE NAME OF THE LORD JESUS WAS MAGNIFIED.

Many of them also which practiced magic brought their books together, 11 and burned them before all men: and they counted the price of them, and found it fifty thousand pieces of silver. So mightily grew the word of God and prevailed.

Uproar Over Shrines of Diana
Acts 19:21-41

After these things were ended, Paul purposed in the spirit, when he 12 had passed through Macedonia and Achaia, to go to Jerusalem, saying, "After I have been there, I must also see Rome." So he sent into Macedonia two of them that ministered unto him, Timothy and Erastus; but he himself stayed in Asia for a season.

13   And the same time there arose no small stir about that way. For a certain man named Demetrius, a silversmith, which made silver shrines for Diana, brought no small gain unto the craftsmen; whom he called together with the workmen of like occupation, and said, "Sirs, you know that by this craft we have our wealth.

14   "Moreover you see and hear, that not alone at Ephesus, but almost throughout all Asia, this Paul has persuaded and turned away many people, saying that they be no gods, which are made with hands. So that not only this our craft is in danger to be discredited; but also that the temple of the great goddess Diana should be despised, and her magnificence should be destroyed, whom all Asia and the world worship."

15   And when they heard these sayings, they were full of anger, and cried out, saying, "Great is Diana of the Ephesians." And the whole city was filled with confusion: and having caught Gaius and Aristarchus, men of Macedonia, Paul's companions in travel, they rushed with one accord into the theater.

16   And when Paul would have entered in unto the people, the disciples did not permit him. And certain of the officials of Asia, which were his friends, sent unto him, begging him that he would not venture himself into the theater. Some therefore cried one thing, and some another: for the assembly was confused; and the majority knew not why they were come together.

17   And they drew Alexander out of the multitude, the Jews putting him forward. And Alexander beckoned with the hand, and would have made his defense unto the people. But when they knew that he was a Jew, all with one voice about the space of two hours cried out, "Great is Diana of the Ephesians."

18   And when the town clerk had quieted the people, he said, "You men of Ephesus, what man is there that knows not how the city of the Ephesians is a worshiper of the great goddess Diana, and of the image which fell down from Jupiter? Seeing then that these things cannot be spoken against, you ought to be quiet, and to do nothing rashly.

19   "For you have brought here these men, which are neither robbers of churches, nor blasphemers of your goddess. Therefore if Demetrius, and the craftsmen which are with him, have a matter against any man, the law is open, and there are proconsuls: let them bring charges against one another. But if you inquire any thing concerning other matters, it shall be determined in a lawful assembly.

20   "For we are in danger to be called in question for this day's uproar, there being no cause whereby we may give an account of this commotion." And when he had thus spoken, he dismissed the assembly.

PART 21

FIRST LETTER TO CORINTHIANS

In his first letter to the Corinthians, Paul offers guidance to the people in patience, love, and meekness. He instructs them to abstain from boasting and excessive ways and to do all things in deference to one another. In patient and thoughtful ministry he admonishes them to part from those of wicked ways, yet also should they not condemn them, for we are all given different gifts by the same Spirit. Therefore, we should not judge another's beliefs, for this judgment belongs only to God. Rather let all things be done through love, that those who are faithful to His word until His coming may partake also in the final resurrection. It is here that Paul delivers what some believe to be the most compelling description of love ever written.

HOW THAT CHRIST DIED FOR OUR SINS
ACCORDING TO THE SCRIPTURES; AND THAT HE
WAS BURIED, AND THAT HE ROSE AGAIN THE
THIRD DAY ACCORDING TO THE SCRIPTURES:
AND THAT HE WAS SEEN OF CEPHAS, THEN OF
THE TWELVE. AFTER THAT, HE WAS SEEN BY MORE
THAN FIVE HUNDRED BRETHREN....AFTER THAT,
HE WAS SEEN OF JAMES; THEN OF ALL THE APOS-
TLES. AND LAST OF ALL HE WAS SEEN OF ME ALSO.
(1 CORINTHIANS 15:3-8)

CHAPTER 79

CONDITIONS AND CORRECTIONS AT CORINTH

Greeting to Corinthians
1 Corinthians 1:1-3

1   Paul, called to be an apostle of Jesus Christ through the will of God, and Sosthenes our brother, unto the church of God which is at Corinth, to them that are sanctified in Christ Jesus, called to be saints, with all that in every place call upon the name of Jesus Christ our Lord, both theirs and ours: Grace be unto you, and peace, from God our Father, and from the Lord Jesus Christ.

Giving Thanks
1 Corinthians 1:4-9

2   I thank my God always on your behalf, for the grace of God which is given you by Jesus Christ; that in every way you are enriched by him, in all utterance, and in all knowledge; even as the testimony of Christ was confirmed in you: so that you come lacking in no gift; waiting for the coming of our Lord Jesus Christ: who shall also confirm you unto the end, that you may be blameless in the day of our Lord Jesus Christ. God is faithful, by whom you were called unto the fellowship of his Son Jesus Christ our Lord.

Divisions in the Church
1 Corinthians 1:10-17

3   Now I appeal to you, brethren, by the name of our Lord Jesus Christ, that you all speak the same thing, and that there be no divisions among you; but that you be perfectly joined together in the same mind and in the same judgment. For it has been declared unto me of you, my brethren, by them which are of the household of Chloe, that there are contentions among you.

Now this I say, that every one of you says, "I am of Paul"; and "I of 4
Apollos"; and "I of Cephas"; and "I of Christ." Is Christ divided? was Paul
crucified for you? or were you baptized in the name of Paul? I thank God
that I baptized none of you, but Cris-
pus and Gaius; lest any should say that
I had baptized in my own name. And
I baptized also the household of
Stephanas: besides, I do not know

> CHRIST SENT ME NOT TO BAP-
> TIZE, BUT TO PREACH THE
> GOSPEL.

whether I baptized any other. For Christ sent me not to baptize, but to
preach the gospel: not with wisdom of words, lest the cross of Christ should
be made of no effect.

God's Power and Wisdom
1 Corinthians 1:18-31

For the message of the cross is to them that perish foolishness; but 5
unto us which are saved it is the power of God. For it is written, *"I will
destroy the wisdom of the wise, and will bring to nothing the understanding
of the prudent."*

Where is the wise? where is the scribe? where is the disputer of this 6
world? has not God made foolish the wisdom of this world? For after that
in the wisdom of God the world by wisdom knew not God, it pleased God
by the foolishness of preaching to save them that believe. For the Jews
require a sign, and the Greeks seek after wisdom: but we preach Christ crucified, unto the Jews a stumbling block, and unto the Greeks foolishness;
but unto them which are called, both Jews and Greeks, Christ the power of
God, and the wisdom of God. Because the foolishness of God is wiser than
men; and the weakness of God is stronger than men.

For you see your calling, brethren, how that not many wise men accord- 7
ing to the flesh, not many mighty, not many noble, are called: but God has
chosen the foolish things of the world
to shame the wise; and God has chosen
the weak things of the world to shame
the things which are mighty; and lowly
things of the world, and things which

> GOD HAS CHOSEN THE FOOL-
> ISH THINGS OF THE WORLD
> TO CONFOUND THE WISE.

are despised, has God chosen, yes, and things which are not, to bring to
nothing things that are: that no flesh should boast in his presence.

But of him are you in Christ Jesus, who of God is made unto us wis- 8
dom, and righteousness, and sanctification, and redemption: that, according
as it is written, "He that boasts, let him boast in the Lord."

Faith and Power
1 Corinthians 2:1-5

And I, brethren, when I came to you, came not with excellence of 9
speech or of wisdom, declaring unto you the testimony of God. For I
determined not to know anything among you, except Jesus Christ, and him

9 crucified. And I was with you in weakness, and in fear, and in much trembling. And my speech and my preaching was not with enticing words of man's wisdom, but in demonstration of the Spirit and of power: that your faith should not stand in the wisdom of men, but in the power of God.

God's Hidden Things
1 Corinthians 2:6-16

10   Howbeit we speak wisdom among them that are mature: yet not the wisdom of this world, nor of the rulers of this world, that come to nothing: but we speak the wisdom of God in a mystery, even the hidden wisdom, which God ordained before the world unto our glory: which none of the rulers of this world knew: for had they known it, they would not have crucified the Lord of glory. But as it is written, *"Eye has not seen, nor ear heard, neither have entered into the heart of man, the things which God has prepared for them that love him."*

11   But God has revealed them unto us by his Spirit: for the Spirit searches all things, yes, the deep things of God. For what man knows the things of a man, except the spirit of man which is in him? even so the things of God knows no man, but the Spirit of God. Now we have received, not the spirit of the world, but the spirit which is of God; that we might know the things that are freely given to us of God.

> THE SPIRIT SEARCHES ALL THINGS, YES, THE DEEP THINGS OF GOD.

Which things also we speak, not in the words which man's wisdom teaches, but which the Holy Ghost teaches; comparing spiritual things with spiritual.

12   But the natural man receives not the things of the Spirit of God: for they are foolishness unto him: neither can he know them, because they are spiritually discerned. But he that is spiritual judges all things, yet he himself is judged of no man. For *"who has known the mind of the Lord, that he may instruct him?"* But we have the mind of Christ.

CHAPTER 80

SERVICE AND CONDUCT

Effect of Divisions
1 Corinthians 3:1-23

And I, brethren, could not speak unto you as unto spiritual, but as unto 1
carnal, even as unto infants in Christ. I have fed you with milk, and not with
food: for previously you were not able to bear it, neither yet now are you
able. For you are yet carnal: for whereas there is among you envy, and strife,
and divisions, are you not carnal, and walk as men? For while one says, "I
am of Paul"; and another, "I am of Apollos"; are you not carnal?

Who then is Paul, and who is Apollos, but ministers by whom you 2
believed, even as the Lord gave to every man? I have planted, Apollos
watered; but God gave the increase. So then neither is he that plants anything, neither he that waters; but God that gives the increase.

Now he that plants and he that waters are one: and every man shall 3
receive his own reward according to his own labor. For we are laborers
together with God: you are God's garden, you are God's building.

According to the grace of God which is given unto me, as a wise mas- 4
ter builder, I have laid the foundation, and another builds thereon. But let
every man take heed how he builds thereupon. For another foundation can
no man lay than that which is laid, which is Jesus Christ.

Now if any man builds upon this foundation gold, silver, precious 5
stones, wood, hay, stubble; every man's work shall be made manifest: for the
day shall declare it, because it shall be revealed by fire; and the fire shall
test every man's work of what sort it is. If any man's work survives which
he has built thereupon, he shall receive a reward. If any man's work shall be
burned, he shall suffer loss: but he himself shall be saved; yet so as by fire.

Do you not know that you are the temple of God, and that the Spirit of 6
God dwells in you? If any man defiles the temple of God, him shall God
destroy; for the temple of God is holy, which temple you are.

7 Let no man deceive himself. If any man among you seems to be wise in this world, let him become a fool, that he may be wise. For the wisdom of this world is foolishness with God.

> THE WISDOM OF THIS WORLD IS FOOLISHNESS WITH GOD.

For it is written, "*He takes the wise in their own craftiness.*" And again, "*The Lord knows the thoughts of the wise, that they are vain.*"

8 Therefore let no man boast in men. For all things are yours; whether Paul, or Apollos, or Cephas, or the world, or life, or death, or things present, or things to come; all are yours; and you are Christ's; and Christ is God's.

Ministry and Secret Things
1 Corinthians 4:1-13

9 Let a man so think of us, as of the ministers of Christ, and stewards of the mysteries of God. Moreover it is required in stewards, that a man be found faithful.

> IT IS REQUIRED IN STEWARDS, THAT A MAN BE FOUND FAITHFUL.

But with me it is a very small thing that I should be judged of you, or of man's judgment: yes, I judge not my own self. For I know nothing against myself; yet am I not hereby justified: but he that judges me is the Lord.

10 Therefore judge nothing before the time, until the Lord comes, who both will bring to light the hidden things of darkness, and will make manifest the purposes of the hearts: and then shall every man have praise from God.

11 And these things, brethren, I have as an example transferred to myself and to Apollos for your sakes; that you might learn in us not to think of men above that which is written, that no one of you be puffed up for one against another. For who makes you to differ from another? and what have you that you did not receive? now if you did receive it, why do you boast, as if you had not received it?

12 Now you are full, now you are rich, you have reigned as kings without us: and I would to God you did reign, that we also might reign with you. For I think that God has set forth us the apostles last, as it were appointed to death: for we are made a spectacle unto the world, and to angels, and to men. We are fools for Christ's sake, but you are wise in Christ; we are weak, but you are strong; you are honorable, but we are dishonored.

13 Even unto this present hour we both hunger, and thirst, and are naked, and are beaten, and have no certain dwelling place; and labor, working with our own hands: being insulted, we bless; being persecuted, we endure it. Being defamed, we answer kindly: we are made as the filth of the world, and are the scum of all things unto this day.

Assurances
1 Corinthians 4:14-21

14 I do not write these things to shame you, but as my beloved children I warn you. For though you have ten thousand instructors in Christ, yet you

have not many fathers: for in Christ Jesus I have begotten you through the 14 gospel. Therefore I urge you, be imitators of me. For this cause have I sent unto you Timothy, who is my beloved son, and faithful in the Lord, who shall bring you into remembrance of my ways which be in Christ, as I teach everywhere in every church.

Now some are puffed up, as though I would not come to you. But I 15 will come to you shortly, if the Lord wills, and will know, not the words of them which are puffed up, but the power. For the kingdom of God is not in word, but in power. What will you? shall I come unto you with a rod, or in love, and in the spirit of meekness?

> THE KINGDOM OF GOD IS NOT IN WORD, BUT IN POWER.

CHAPTER 81

Scandals and Solutions

Sexual Immorality
1 Corinthians 5:1-13

1   It is reported commonly that there is sexual immorality among you, and such sexual immorality as is not so much as named among the Gentiles, that one should have his father's wife. And you are puffed up, and have not rather mourned, that he that has done this deed might be taken away from among you.

2   For I indeed, as absent in body, but present in spirit, have judged already, as though I were present, concerning him that has so done this deed. In the name of our Lord Jesus Christ, when you are gathered together, and my spirit, with the power of our Lord Jesus Christ, to deliver such a one unto Satan for the destruction of the flesh, that the spirit may be saved in the day of the Lord Jesus.

3   Your boasting is not good. Know you not that a little leaven leavens the whole lump? Purge out therefore the old leaven, that you may be a new lump, since you are unleavened. For even Christ our passover is sacrificed for us: therefore let us keep the feast, not with old leaven, neither with the leaven of malice and wickedness; but with the unleavened bread of sincerity and truth.

4   I wrote unto you in a letter not to company with fornicators: yet not altogether with the fornicators of this world, or with the covetous, or extortioners, or with idolaters; for then you must of necessity go out of the world. But now I have written unto you not to keep company, if any man that is called a brother be a fornicator, or covetous, or an idolater, or a slanderer, or a drunkard, or an extortioner; no not to eat with such a one.

5   For what have I to do to judge them also that are outside? do not you judge them that are inside? But them that are outside God judges. Therefore *"put away from among yourselves that wicked person."*

Lawsuits Among Members
1 Corinthians 6:1-11

Dare any of you, having a matter against another, go to law before the 6 unjust, and not before the saints? Do you not know that the saints shall judge the world? and if the world shall be judged by you, are you unworthy to judge the smallest matters? Do you not know that we shall judge angels? how much more things that pertain to this life?

If then you have judgments of things pertaining to this life, set them 7 to judge who are least esteemed in the church. I speak to your shame. Is it so, that there is not a wise man among you? no, not one that shall be able to judge between his brethren? But brother goes to law against brother, and that before the unbelievers.

Now therefore there is utterly a fault among you, because you go to 8 law one against another. Why do you not rather accept wrong? why do you not rather permit yourselves to be defrauded? No, you do wrong, and defraud, and that your brethren.

Do you not know that the unrighteous shall not inherit the kingdom of 9 God? Be not deceived: neither fornicators, nor idolaters, nor adulterers, nor effeminate, nor abusers of themselves with mankind, nor thieves, nor covetous, nor drunkards, nor slanderers, nor extortioners, shall inherit the kingdom of God. And such were some of you: but you are washed, but you are sanctified, but you are justified in the name of the Lord Jesus, and by the Spirit of our God.

Sexual Morality
1 Corinthians 6:12-20

All things are lawful unto me, but all things are not expedient: all 10 things are lawful for me, but I will not be brought under the power of any. Foods for the belly, and the belly for foods: but God shall destroy both it and them. Now the body is not for fornication, but for the Lord; and the Lord for the body.

And God has both raised up the Lord, and will also raise up us by his 11 own power. Do you not know that your bodies are the members of Christ? shall I then take the members of Christ, and make them the members of a harlot? God forbid.

What? do you not know that he which is joined to a harlot is one body? 12 for "two," says he, "shall be one flesh." But he that is joined unto the Lord is one spirit.

Flee fornication. Every sin that a man does is outside the body; but he 13 that commits fornication sins against his own body.

What? do you not know that your body is the temple of the Holy Ghost 14 which is in you, which you have of God, and you are not your own? For you are bought with a price: therefore glorify God in your body, and in your spirit, which are God's.

CHAPTER 82

Guidance in Relationships

Marriage
1 Corinthians 7:1-16

1   Now concerning the things of which you wrote unto me: It is good for a man not to touch a woman. Nevertheless, to avoid fornication, let every man have his own wife, and let every woman have her own husband.

2   Let the husband render unto the wife due benevolence: and likewise also the wife unto the husband. The wife has not full right of her own body, but the husband: and likewise also the husband has not full right of his own body, but the wife. Do not deprive one another, except it be with consent for a time, that you may give yourselves to fasting and prayer; and come together again, that Satan does not tempt you for your lack of self-control.

3   But I speak this by permission, and not of commandment. For I wish that all men were even as I myself. But every man has his own gift of God, one after this manner, and another after that.

4   I say therefore to the unmarried and widows, It is good for them if they remain even as I. But if they cannot contain, let them marry: for it is better to marry than to burn.

5   And unto the married I command, yet not I, but the Lord, Let not the wife depart from her husband: but and if she departs, let her remain unmarried, or be reconciled to her husband: and let not the husband put away his wife.

6   But to the rest I speak, not the Lord: If any brother has a wife that does not believe, and she be pleased to dwell with him, let him not put her away. And the woman which has a husband that does not believe, and if he be pleased to dwell with her, let her not leave him. For the unbelieving husband is sanctified by the wife, and the unbelieving wife is sanctified by the husband: else were your children unclean; but now they are holy.

But if the unbelieving departs, let him depart. A brother or a sister is 7
not under bondage in such cases: but God has called us to peace. For what
do you know, O wife, whether you shall save your husband? or how do you
know, O man, whether you shall save your wife?

Calling
1 Corinthians 7:17-24

But as God has distributed to every man, as the Lord has called every 8
one, so let him walk. And so I ordain in all churches. Is any man called
being circumcised? let him not become uncircumcised. Is anyone called in
uncircumcision? let him not be circumcised. Circumcision is nothing, and
uncircumcision is nothing, but the keeping of the commandments of God.
Let every man remain in the same calling wherein he was called.

Are you called being a servant? do not worry for it: but if you may be 9
made free, use it rather. For he that is
called in the Lord, being a servant, is | LET EVERY MAN ABIDE IN THE
the Lord's freedman: likewise also he | SAME CALLING WHEREIN HE WAS
that is called, being free, is Christ's | CALLED.
servant. You are bought with a price;
do not be the servants of men. Brethren, let every man, wherein he is called,
therein remain with God.

Wives and Virgins
1 Corinthians 7:25-40

Now concerning virgins I have no commandment of the Lord: yet I 10
give my judgment, as one that has obtained mercy of the Lord to be faithful. I suppose therefore that this is good for the present distress, I say, that
it is good for a man so to be. Are you bound unto a wife? seek not to be
loosed. Are you loosed from a wife? seek not a wife. But and if you marry,
you have not sinned; and if a virgin marries, she has not sinned. Nevertheless such shall have trouble in the flesh: but I spare you.

But this I say, brethren, the time is short: it remains, that both they that 11
have wives be as though they had
none; and they that weep, as though | THE FASHION OF THIS WORLD
they wept not; and they that rejoice, as | PASSES AWAY.
though they rejoiced not; and they that
buy, as though they possessed not; and they that use this world, as not abus-
ing it: for the fashion of this world passes away.

But I would have you without anxieties. He that is unmarried cares 12
for the things that belong to the Lord, how he may please the Lord: but he
that is married cares for the things that are of the world, how he may please
his wife.

There is difference also between a wife and a virgin. The unmarried 13
woman cares for the things of the Lord, that she may be holy both in body
and in spirit: but she that is married cares for the things of the world, how

13 she may please her husband. And this I speak for your own profit; not that
I may put a restraint upon you, but for that which is proper, and that you
may attend upon the Lord without distraction.

14   But if any man thinks that he behaves himself improperly toward his
virgin, if she is past the flower of her age, and needs so require, let him do
what he will, he sins not: let them marry. Nevertheless he that stands steadfast in his heart, having no necessity, but has power over his own will, and
has so decreed in his heart that he will keep his virgin, does well. So then
he that gives her in marriage does well; but he that gives her not in marriage
does better.

15   The wife is bound by the law as long as her husband lives; but if her
husband be dead, she is at liberty to be married to whom she will; only in
the Lord. But she is happier if she so remains, according to my judgment:
and I think also that I have the Spirit of God.

CHAPTER 83

GUIDANCE IN LIBERTY

Offerings to Idols
1 Corinthians 8:1-13

Now as concerning things offered unto idols, we know that we all have 1 knowledge. Knowledge puffs up, but love builds up. And if any man thinks that he knows anything, he knows nothing yet as he ought to know. But if any man loves God, the same is known of him.

As concerning therefore the eating of those things that are offered in 2 sacrifice unto idols, we know that an idol is nothing in the world, and that there is no other God but one. For though there be that are called gods, whether in heaven or on earth, (as there be many gods, and many lords), but to us there is but one God, the Father, of whom are all things, and we in him; and one Lord Jesus Christ, by whom are all things, and we by him.

Howbeit there is not in every man that knowledge: for some with con- 3 sciousness of the idol unto this hour eat it as a thing offered unto an idol; and their conscience being weak is defiled. But food commends us not to God: for neither, if we eat, are we the better; neither, if we eat not, are we the worse.

But take heed lest by any means this liberty of yours become a stum- 4 bling block to them that are weak. For if any man sees you which have knowledge sit eating in the idol's temple, shall not the conscience of him which is weak be emboldened to eat those things which are offered to idols; and through your knowledge shall the weak brother perish, for whom Christ died?

But when you sin so against the brethren, and wound their weak 5 conscience, you sin against Christ. Therefore, if food makes my brother fall away, I will eat no flesh while the world stands, lest I make my brother fall away.

Conduct of Apostles
1 Corinthians 9:1-27

6　　　Am I not an apostle? am I not free? have I not seen Jesus Christ our Lord? are not you my work in the Lord? If I be not an apostle unto others, yet doubtless I am to you: for the seal of my apostleship are you in the Lord.

7　　　My answer to them that do examine me is this, Have we not the right to eat and to drink? Have we not the right to lead about a sister, a wife, as well as other apostles, and as the brethren of the Lord, and Cephas? Or I only and Barnabas, have we not the right to refrain from working? Who goes to war any time at his own expense? who plants a vineyard, and eats not of the fruit thereof? or who feeds a flock, and eats not of the milk of the flock?

8　　　Say I these things as a man? or says not the law the same also? For it is written in the law of Moses, *"You shall not muzzle the mouth of the ox that treads out the grain."* Does God take care for oxen? Or says he it altogether for our sakes? For our sakes, no doubt, this is written: that he that plows should plow in hope; and that he that threshes in hope should be partaker of his hope.

9　　　If we have sown unto you spiritual things, is it a great thing if we shall reap your material things? If others be partakers of this right over you, are not we the more? Nevertheless we have not used this right; but endure all things, lest we should hinder the gospel of Christ.

10　　　Do you not know that they which minister about holy things live of the things of the temple? and they which wait at the altar are partakers with the altar? Even so has the Lord ordained that they which preach the gospel should live of the gospel.

> THEY WHICH PREACH THE GOSPEL SHOULD LIVE OF THE GOSPEL.

11　　　But I have used none of these things: neither have I written these things, that it should be so done unto me: for it would be better for me to die, than that any man should make my boasting void. For though I preach the gospel, I have nothing to boast of: for necessity is laid upon me; yes, woe is unto me, if I do not preach the gospel! For if I do this thing willingly, I have a reward: but if against my will, a stewardship of the gospel is committed unto me. What is my reward then? Just that, when I preach the gospel, I may present the gospel of Christ without expense, that I abuse not my authority in the gospel.

12　　　For though I be free from all men, yet have I made myself servant unto all, that I might gain the more. And unto the Jews I became as a Jew, that I might gain the Jews; to them that are under the law, as under the law, that I might gain them that are under the

> I AM MADE ALL THINGS TO ALL MEN, THAT I MIGHT BY ALL MEANS SAVE SOME.

law; to them that are without law, as without law, (being not without law to

God, but under the law to Christ), that I might gain them that are without 12
law. To the weak I became as weak, that I might gain the weak: I am made
all things to all men, that I might by all means save some. And this I do for
the gospel's sake, that I might be partaker thereof with you.

Do you not know that they which run in a race all run, but one receives 13
the prize? So run, that you may obtain. And every man that strives for the
mastery is temperate in all things. Now they do it to obtain a corruptible
crown; but we an incorruptible.

I therefore so run, not as uncertainly; so I fight, not as one that beats the 14
air: but I keep control of my body, and bring it into subjection: lest that by
any means, when I have preached to others, I myself should be disqualified.

Temptation of Evil
1 Corinthians 10:1-22

Moreover, brethren, I would not that you should be ignorant, how that 15
all our fathers were under the cloud, and all passed through the sea; and
were all baptized unto Moses in the cloud and in the sea; and did all eat the
same spiritual food; and did all drink the same spiritual drink: for they
drank of that spiritual Rock that followed them: and that Rock was Christ.
But with many of them God was not well pleased: for they were overthrown
in the wilderness.

Now these things were our examples, to the intent we should not lust 16
after evil things, as they also lusted. Neither be you idolaters, as were some
of them; as it is written, "*The people sat down to eat and drink, and rose up
to play.*" Neither let us commit sexual immorality, as some of them committed, and fell in one day three and twenty thousand. Neither let us tempt
Christ, as some of them also tempted, and were destroyed of serpents. Neither grumble you, as some of them also grumbled, and were destroyed of
the destroyer.

Now all these things happened unto them for examples: and they are 17
written for our admonition, upon
whom the ends of the world are come.
Therefore let him that thinks he stands
take heed lest he fall. There has no
temptation overtaken you except such
as is common to man: but God is faithful, who will not allow you to be
tempted above that you are able; but

> GOD IS FAITHFUL, WHO WILL
> NOT ALLOW YOU TO BE
> TEMPTED ABOVE THAT YOU
> ARE ABLE; BUT WILL WITH THE
> TEMPTATION ALSO MAKE A
> WAY TO ESCAPE.

will with the temptation also make a way to escape, that you may be able to
bear it.

Therefore, my dearly beloved, flee from idolatry. I speak as to wise 18
men; judge you what I say. The cup of blessing which we bless, is it not the
communion of the blood of Christ? The bread which we break, is it not the
communion of the body of Christ? For we being many are one bread, and
one body: for we are all partakers of that one bread.

19   Behold Israel after the flesh: are not they which eat of the sacrifices partakers of the altar? What do I say then? that the idol is anything, or that which is offered in sacrifice to idols is anything? But I say, that the things which the Gentiles sacrifice, they sacrifice to demons, and not to God: and I would not that you should have fellowship with demons.

20   You cannot drink the cup of the Lord, and the cup of demons: you cannot be partakers of the Lord's table, and of the table of demons. Do we provoke the Lord to jealousy? are we stronger than he?

Conscience and Others
1 Corinthians 10:23-33; 11:1

21   All things are lawful for me, but all things are not expedient: all things are lawful for me, but all things do not build up. Let no man seek his own, but every man another's good.

22   Whatsoever is sold in the meat market, that eat, asking no question for sake of conscience: for *"the earth is the Lord's, and the fulness thereof."*

23   If any of them that do not believe invite you to a feast, and you be disposed to go; whatsoever is set before you, eat, asking no question for sake of conscience. But if any man says unto you, "This is offered in sacrifice unto idols," do not eat for his sake that told it, and for sake of conscience: for *"the earth is the Lord's, and the fulness thereof."* "Conscience," I say, not your own, but of the other: for why is my liberty judged of another man's conscience? For if I by grace be a partaker, why am I evil spoken of for that for which I give thanks?

24   Whether therefore you eat, or drink, or whatsoever you do, do all to the glory of God. Give no offense, neither to the Jews, nor to the Gentiles, nor to the church of God: even as I please all men in all things, not seeking my own profit, but the profit of many, that they may be saved.

> WHATSOEVER YOU DO, DO ALL TO THE GLORY OF GOD.

25   Be imitators of me, even as I also am of Christ.

CHAPTER 84

⁎⁎ <u>SACREDNESS OF THE LORD'S SUPPER</u> ⁎⁎

Head Covering in Worship
1 Corinthians 11:2-16

Now I praise you, brethren, that you remember me in all things, and 1 keep the traditions, as I delivered them to you.

But I would have you know, that the head of every man is Christ; and 2 the head of the woman is the man; and the head of Christ is God. Every man praying or prophesying, having his head covered, dishonors his head.

But every woman that prays or prophesies with her head uncovered 3 dishonors her head: for that is even all one as if she were shaved. For if the woman be not covered, let her also be sheared: but if it be a shame for a woman to be sheared or shaved, let her be covered.

For a man indeed ought not to cover his head, Inasmuch as he is the 4 image and glory of God: but the woman is the glory of the man. For the man is not of the woman; but the woman of the man. Neither was the man created for the woman; but the woman for the man. For this reason ought the woman to have authority on her head because of the angels.

Nevertheless neither is the man without the woman, neither the 5 woman without the man, in the Lord. For as the woman is of the man, even so is the man also by the woman; but all things of God.

Judge in yourselves: is it proper that a woman pray unto God uncov- 6 ered? Does not even nature itself teach you, that, if a man has long hair, it is a shame unto him? But if a woman has long hair, it is a glory to her: for her hair is given her for a covering.

But if any man seems to be contentious, we have no such custom, nei- 7 ther the churches of God.

Lord's Supper Abuses
1 Corinthians 11:17-22

Now in this that I declare unto you I do not praise you, that you come 8 together not for the better, but for the worse. For first of all, when you come

8 together in the church, I hear that there be divisions among you; and I partly believe it. For there must be also factions among you, that they which are approved may be recognized among you.

9 When you come together therefore into one place, this is not to eat the Lord's supper. For in eating every one takes before another his own supper: and one is hungry, and another is drunk. What? have you not houses to eat and to drink in? or despise you the church of God, and shame them that have nothing? What shall I say to you? shall I praise you in this? I do not praise you.

Lord's Supper Purpose
1 Corinthians 11:23-26

10 For I have received of the Lord that which also I delivered unto you, That the Lord Jesus the same night in which he was betrayed took bread: and when he had given thanks, he broke it, and said, "Take, eat: this is my body, which is broken for you: this do in remembrance of me."

> "THIS IS MY BODY, WHICH IS BROKEN FOR YOU: THIS DO IN REMEMBRANCE OF ME."

11 After the same manner also he took the cup, when supper had ended, saying, "This cup is the new testament in my blood: this do, as often as you drink it, in remembrance of me." For as often as you eat this bread, and drink this cup, you do proclaim the Lord's death till he comes.

> "THIS CUP IS THE NEW TESTAMENT IN MY BLOOD: THIS DO, AS OFTEN AS YOU DRINK IT, IN REMEMBRANCE OF ME."

Lord's Supper Worthiness
1 Corinthians 11:27-34

12 Therefore whosoever shall eat this bread, and drink this cup of the Lord, unworthily, shall be guilty of the body and blood of the Lord. But let a man examine himself, and so let him eat of that bread, and drink of that cup. For he that eats and drinks unworthily, eats and drinks judgment to himself, not discerning the Lord's body.

13 For this reason many are weak and sickly among you, and many sleep. For if we would judge ourselves, we should not be judged. But when we are judged, we are disciplined of the Lord, that we should not be condemned with the world.

14 Therefore, my brethren, when you come together to eat, wait one for another. And if any man is hungry, let him eat at home; that you do not come together unto condemnation. And the rest will I set in order when I come.

CHAPTER 85

SPIRITUAL GIFTS

Unity in Diversity
1 Corinthians 12:1-11

Now concerning spiritual gifts, brethren, I would not have you igno- 1
rant. You know that you were Gentiles, carried away unto these dumb idols,
even as you were led. Therefore I give you to understand, that no man
speaking by the Spirit of God calls Jesus accursed: and that no man can say
that Jesus is the Lord, except by the Holy Ghost.

Now there are diversities of gifts, but the same Spirit. And there are 2
differences of administrations, but the same Lord. And there are diversities
of operations, but it is the same God which works all in all.

But the manifestation of the Spirit is given to every man to profit of 3
all. For to one is given by the Spirit the word of wisdom; to another the word
of knowledge by the same Spirit; to another faith by the same Spirit; to
another the gifts of healing by the same Spirit; to another the working of
miracles; to another prophecy; to another discerning of spirits; to another
different kinds of tongues; to another the interpretation of tongues: but all
these works that one and the selfsame Spirit, dividing to every man indi-
vidually as he wills.

Human Body and Holy Spirit
1 Corinthians 12:12-26

For as the body is one, and has many members, and all the members of 4
that one body, being many, are one body: so also is Christ. For by one Spirit are we all baptized into one body, whether we be Jews or Gentiles, whether
we be slave or free; and have been all made to drink into one Spirit.

For the body is not one member, but many. If the foot shall say, 5
"Because I am not the hand, I am not of the body"; is it therefore not of the
body? And if the ear shall say, "Because I am not the eye, I am not of the

5 body"; is it therefore not of the body? If the whole body were an eye, where would be the hearing? If the whole were hearing, where would be the smelling? But now has God set the members every one of them in the body, as it has pleased him. And if they were all one member, where would be the body? But now are they many members, yet but one body.

> GOD SET THE MEMBERS EVERY ONE OF THEM IN THE BODY, AS IT HAS PLEASED HIM.

6 And the eye cannot say unto the hand, "I have no need of you": nor again the head to the feet, "I have no need of you." No, much more those members of the body, which seem to be more feeble, are necessary: and those members of the body, which we think to be less honorable, upon these we bestow more abundant honor; and our unpresentable parts have more abundant modesty.

7 For our presentable parts have no need: but God has tempered the body together, having given more abundant honor to that part which lacked: that there should be no division in the body; but that the members should have the same care one for another. And whether one member suffers, all the members suffer with it; or one member be honored, all the members rejoice with it.

Excellent Way
1 Corinthians 12:27-31

8 Now you are the body of Christ, and members in particular. And God has set some in the church, first apostles, second prophets, third teachers, after that miracles, then gifts of healings, helpers, governments, diversities of tongues. Are all apostles? are all prophets? are all teachers? are all workers of miracles? Have all the gifts of healing? do all speak with tongues? do all interpret?

> NOW YOU ARE THE BODY OF CHRIST, AND MEMBERS IN PARTICULAR.

9 But earnestly desire the best gifts: and yet I show unto you a more excellent way.

Love
1 Corinthians 13:1-13

10 Though I speak with the tongues of men and of angels, and have not love, I am become as sounding brass, or a tinkling cymbal. And though I have the gift of prophecy, and understand all mysteries, and all knowledge; and though I have all faith, so that I could move mountains, and have not love, I am nothing. And though I bestow all my goods to feed the poor, and though I give my body to be burned, and have not love, it profits me nothing.

11 Love is patient, and is kind; love does not envy; love does not boast itself, is not conceited, does not behave itself rudely, does not seek its own, is not easily provoked, thinks no evil; does not rejoice in iniquity, but rejoices

in the truth; bears all things, believes all things, hopes all things, endures 11 all things.

Love never fails: but whether there be prophecies, they shall fail; 12 whether there be tongues, they shall cease; whether there be knowledge, it shall vanish away. For we know in part, and we prophesy in part. But when that which is perfect is come, then that which is in part shall be done away.

When I was a child, I spoke as a child, I understood as a child, I thought as a child: but when I became a man, I put away childish things. For now we see through a mirror, dimly; but then face to face: now I know in part; but 13

> NOW ABIDES FAITH, HOPE, LOVE, THESE THREE; BUT THE GREATEST OF THESE IS LOVE.

then shall I know even as also I am known. And now abides faith, hope, love, these three; but the greatest of these is love.

CHAPTER 86

DIVERSITY OF GIFTS

Prophesy
1 Corinthians 14:1-19

1   Follow the way of love, and desire spiritual gifts, but especially that you may prophesy. For he that speaks in an unknown tongue speaks not unto men, but unto God: for no man understands him; howbeit in the spirit he speaks mysteries. But he that prophesies speaks unto men to edification, and exhortation, and comfort.

2   He that speaks in an unknown tongue builds up himself; but he that prophesies builds up the church. I would that you all spoke with tongues, but rather that you prophesied: for greater is he that prophesies than he that speaks with tongues, unless he interprets, that the church may receive edification.

3   Now, brethren, if I come unto you speaking with tongues, what shall I profit you, unless I shall speak to you either by revelation, or by knowledge, or by prophesying, or by doctrine? And even things without life giving sound, whether pipe or harp, unless they give a distinction in the sounds, how shall it be known what is piped or harped? For if the trumpet gives an uncertain sound, who shall prepare himself to the battle? So likewise you, unless you utter by the tongue words easy to be understood, how shall it be known what is spoken? for you shall speak into the air.

4   There are, it may be, so many kinds of voices in the world, and none of them is without significance. Therefore if I do not know the meaning of the voice, I shall be unto him that speaks a foreigner, and he that speaks shall be a foreigner unto me. Even so you, Inasmuch as you are zealous of spiritual gifts, seek that you may excel to the edification of the church.

5   Therefore let him that speaks in an unknown tongue pray that he may interpret. For if I pray in an unknown tongue, my spirit prays, but my understanding is unfruitful.

What is it then? I will pray with the spirit, and I will pray with the 6
understanding also: I will sing with the spirit, and I will sing with the understanding also. Else when you shall
bless with the spirit, how shall he that
occupies the room of the unskilled say
"Amen" at your giving of thanks, seeing he understands not what you say?

> I WILL PRAY WITH THE SPIRIT,
> AND I WILL PRAY WITH THE
> UNDERSTANDING ALSO.

For you indeed give thanks well, but the other is not edified.

I thank my God, I speak with tongues more than you all: yet in the 7
church I had rather speak five words with my understanding, that by my
voice I might teach others also, than ten thousand words in an unknown
tongue.

Languages
1 Corinthians 14:20-25

Brethren, be not children in understanding: howbeit in malice be you 8
children, but in understanding be mature. In the law it is written, *"With men
of other tongues and other lips will I speak unto this people; and yet for all
that will they not hear me,"* says the Lord. Therefore tongues are for a sign,
not to them that believe, but to them that do not believe: but prophesying
serves not for them that do not believe, but for them which believe.

If therefore the whole church comes together into one place, and all 9
speak with tongues, and there comes in those that are unskilled, or unbelievers, will they not say that you are mad? But if all prophesy, and there
comes in one that does not believe, or one unskilled, he is convinced of all,
he is judged of all: and thus are the secrets of his heart made manifest; and
so falling down on his face he will worship God, and report that God is in
you of a truth.

Meetings
1 Corinthians 14:26-40

How is it then, brethren? when you come together, every one of you 10
has a psalm, has a doctrine, has a tongue, has a revelation, has an interpretation. Let all things be done unto edification. If any man speaks in an
unknown tongue, let it be by two, or at the most by three, and each in turn;
and let one interpret. But if there be no interpreter, let him keep silent in the
church; and let him speak to himself, and to God.

Let the prophets speak two or three, and let the others judge. If any- 11
thing be revealed to another that sits
by, let the first hold his peace. For you
may all prophesy one by one, that all
may learn, and all may be comforted.
And the spirits of the prophets are sub-

> GOD IS NOT THE AUTHOR OF
> CONFUSION, BUT OF PEACE.

ject to the prophets. For God is not the author of confusion, but of peace, as
in all churches of the saints.

12   Let your women keep silent in the churches: for it is not permitted unto them to speak; but they are commanded to be under obedience, as also says the law. And if they will learn anything, let them ask their husbands at home: for it is a shame for women to speak in the church.

13   What? came the word of God out from you? or came it unto you only?

14   If any man thinks himself to be a prophet, or spiritual, let him acknowledge that the things that I write unto you are the commandments of the Lord. But if any man be ignorant, let him be ignorant. Therefore, brethren, earnestly desire to prophesy, and do not forbid to speak with tongues.

15   Let all things be done decently and in order.

CHAPTER 87

Resurrection Mystery

Resurrection of Jesus
1 Corinthians 15:1-11

Moreover, brethren, I declare unto you the gospel which I preached 1 unto you, which also you have received, and on which you stand; by which also you are saved, if you keep in memory what I preached unto you, unless you have believed in vain.

For I delivered unto you first of all that which I also received, how that 2 Christ died for our sins according to the scriptures; and that he was buried, and that he rose again the third day according to the scriptures: and that he was seen of Cephas, then of the twelve. After that, he was seen by more than five hundred brethren at once; of whom the greater part remain unto this present, but some are fallen asleep. After that, he was seen of James; then of all the apostles. And last of all he was seen of me also, as to one born out of due time.

For I am the least of the apostles, that am not worthy to be called an 3 apostle, because I persecuted the church of God. But by the grace of God I am what I am: and his grace which was bestowed upon me was not in vain; but I labored more abundantly than they all: yet not I, but the grace of God which was with me. Therefore whether it were I or they, so we preach, and so you believed.

Resurrection of the Dead
1 Corinthians 15:12-34

Now if Christ be preached that he rose from the dead, how say some 4 among you that there is no resurrection of the dead? But if there be no resurrection of the dead, then is Christ not risen: and if Christ be not risen, then is our preaching in vain, and your faith is also in vain.

Yes, and we are found false witnesses of God; because we have testi- 5 fied of God that he raised up Christ: whom he raised not up, if so be that

5 the dead rise not. For if the dead rise not, then is Christ not raised: and if Christ be not raised, your faith is in vain; you are yet in your sins. Then they also which are fallen asleep in Christ are perished. If in this life only we have hope in Christ, we are of all men most miserable.

6
> AS IN ADAM ALL DIE, EVEN SO IN CHRIST SHALL ALL BE MADE ALIVE.

But now is Christ risen from the dead, and become the first fruits of them that slept. For since by man came death, by man came also the resurrection of the dead. For as in Adam all die, even so in Christ shall all be made alive.

7 But every man in his own turn: Christ the first fruits; afterward they that are Christ's at his coming. Then comes the end, when he shall have delivered up the kingdom to God, even the Father; when he shall have put down all rule and all authority and power.

8 For he must reign, till he has put all enemies under his feet. The last enemy that shall be destroyed is death. For *"he has put all things under his feet."* But when he says "all things are put under him," it is clear that he is excepted, which did put all things under him. And when all things shall be subdued unto him, then shall the Son also himself be subject unto him that put all things under him, that God may be all in all.

> THE LAST ENEMY THAT SHALL BE DESTROYED IS DEATH.

9 Else what shall they do which are baptized for the dead, if the dead rise not at all? why then are they baptized for the dead? And why do we stand in jeopardy every hour? I protest by your boasting which I have in Christ Jesus our Lord, I die daily. If after the manner of men I have fought with beasts at Ephesus, what does it gain me, if the dead rise not? *"let us eat and drink; for to morrow we die."*

10 Be not deceived: evil company corrupts good character. Awake to righteousness, and sin not; for some have not the knowledge of God: I speak this to your shame.

Resurrection Body
1 Corinthians 15:35-49

11 But some man will say, "How are the dead raised up? and with what body do they come?" You fool, that which you sow is not quickened, unless it dies: and that which you sow, you sow not that body that shall be, but just seed, it may chance of wheat, or of some other grain. But God gives it a body as it has pleased him, and to every seed its own body.

12 All flesh is not the same flesh: but there is one kind of flesh of men, another flesh of beasts, another of fishes, and another of birds. There are also celestial bodies, and bodies terrestrial: but the glory of the celestial is one, and the glory of the terrestrial is another. There is one glory of the sun, and another glory of the moon, and another glory of the stars: for one star differs from another star in glory.

So also is the resurrection of the dead. It is sown in corruption; it is 13
raised in incorruption. It is sown in dishonor; it is raised in glory: it is sown
in weakness; it is raised in power. It is sown a natural body; it is raised a
spiritual body. There is a natural body, and there is a spiritual body.

And so it is written, "The first *man* Adam *was made a living soul*"; the 14
last Adam was made a life-giving spirit. Howbeit that was not first which is
spiritual, but that which is natural; and afterward that which is spiritual. The
first *man* is of the earth, earthy: the second *man* is the Lord from heaven.
As is the earthy, such are they also that are earthy: and as is the heavenly,
such are they also that are heavenly. And as we have borne the image of the
earthy, we shall also bear the image of the heavenly.

Second Coming of Christ
1 Corinthians 15:50-58

Now this I say, brethren, that flesh and blood cannot inherit the king- 15
dom of God; neither does corruption
inherit incorruption. Behold, I show
you a mystery; We shall not all sleep,
but we shall all be changed, in a
moment, in the twinkling of an eye, at
the last trumpet: for the trumpet shall
sound, and the dead shall be raised
incorruptible, and we shall be
changed. For this corruptible must put

> IN A MOMENT, IN THE TWIN-
> KLING OF AN EYE, AT THE LAST
> TRUMPET: FOR THE TRUMPET
> SHALL SOUND, AND THE DEAD
> SHALL BE RAISED INCORRUPT-
> IBLE, AND WE SHALL BE
> CHANGED.

on incorruption, and this mortal must put on immortality.

So when this corruptible shall have put on incorruption, and this mor- 16
tal shall have put on immortality, then shall be brought to pass the saying
that is written, "Death is swallowed up in victory." "*O death, where is your
sting? O grave, where is your victory?*"

The sting of death is sin; and the strength of sin is the law. But thanks 17
be to God, which gives us the victory through our Lord Jesus Christ.

Therefore, my beloved brethren, be you steadfast, immoveable, always 18
abounding in the work of the Lord, Inasmuch as you know that your labor
is not in vain in the Lord.

CHAPTER 88

COLLECTION AND CONCLUSION

Collection
1 Corinthians 16:1-4

1   Now concerning the collection for the saints, as I have given directions to the churches of Galatia, even so do you. Upon the first day of the week let every one of you lay aside in store, as God has prospered him, that there be no collections when I come. And when I come, whomsoever you shall approve by your letters, them will I send to bring your gift unto Jerusalem. And if it be fitting that I go also, they shall go with me.

Travel Plans
1 Corinthians 16:5-12

2   Now I will come unto you, when I shall pass through Macedonia: for I do pass through Macedonia. And it may be that I will remain, yes, and winter with you, that you may send me on my journey wherever I go. For I will not see you now on the way; but I trust to stay a while with you, if the Lord permits. But I will stay at Ephesus until Pentecost. For a great door and opportunity is opened unto me, and there are many adversaries.

3   Now if Timothy comes, see that he may be with you without fear: for he works the work of the Lord, as I also do. Let no man therefore despise him: but conduct him forth in peace, that he may come unto me: for I wait for him with the brethren.

4   As concerning our brother Apollos, I greatly desired him to come unto you with the brethren: but his will was not at all to come at this time; but he will come when he shall have the opportune time.

Conclusion
1 Corinthians 16:13-24

5   Watch, stand fast in the faith, be courageous like men, be strong. Let all your things be done with love.

I beseech you, brethren, (you know the household of Stephanas, that 6
it is the first fruits of Achaia, and that they have devoted themselves to the
ministry of the saints), that you submit yourselves unto such, and to everyone that helps with us, and labors. I am glad of the coming of Stephanas and
Fortunatus and Achaicus: for that which was lacking on your part they have
supplied. For they have refreshed my spirit and yours: therefore acknowledge you them that are such.

The churches of Asia greet you. Aquila and Priscilla greet you much 7
in the Lord, with the church that is in their house. All the brethren greet you.
Greet one another with a holy kiss.

The greeting of me Paul with my own hand. If any man does not 8
love the Lord Jesus Christ, let him be accursed: Our Lord comes. The
grace of our Lord Jesus Christ be with you. My love be with you all in
Christ Jesus. Amen.

PART 22

SECOND LETTER TO CORINTHIANS

Continuing his ministry, Paul reminds the people of the many perils and persecutions he himself endured and was delivered from by God through his faithfulness. He instructs them to endure anxieties and struggles, to guard against false prophets, and to turn away from the material things of the world toward the spiritual things of God, for material things deceive and decay, but spiritual things endure forever. Christ did not come to give us rest, Paul proclaims, but to stir the soul to unrest. Trials are proofs of God's care. Through steadfastness and affliction comes the victory. Jesus' death was not for the reconciliation of God to man, but for the reconciliation of man to God.

GOD, WHO COMMANDED THE LIGHT TO SHINE
OUT OF DARKNESS, HAS SHINED IN OUR HEARTS,
TO GIVE THE LIGHT OF THE KNOWLEDGE OF THE
GLORY OF GOD IN THE FACE OF JESUS CHRIST.

(2 CORINTHIANS 4:6)

CHAPTER 89

OBEDIENCE AND FORGIVENESS AT CORINTH

Greeting to Corinthians
2 Corinthians 1:1-2

Paul, an apostle of Jesus Christ by the will of God, and Timothy our 1
brother, unto the church of God which is at Corinth, with all the saints
which are in all Achaia: Grace be to you and peace from God our Father,
and from the Lord Jesus Christ.

Giving Thanks
2 Corinthians 1:3-11

Blessed be God, even the Father of our Lord Jesus Christ, the Father 2
of mercies, and the God of all comfort; who comforts us in all our tribulation, that we may be able to comfort them which are in any trouble, by the
comfort with which we ourselves are comforted of God. For as the sufferings of Christ abound in us, so our consolation also abounds by Christ.

And whether we be afflicted, it is for your consolation and salvation, 3
which is effective in the enduring of the same sufferings which we also suffer: or whether we be comforted, it is for your consolation and salvation.
And our hope of you is steadfast, knowing, that as you are partakers of the
sufferings, so shall you be also of the consolation.

For we would not, brethren, have you ignorant of our trouble which 4
came to us in Asia, that we were crushed beyond measure, above strength,
insomuch that we despaired even of life. But we had the sentence of death
in ourselves, that we should not trust in ourselves, but in God which raised
the dead: who delivered us from so great a death, and does deliver: in whom
we trust that he will yet deliver us; you also helping together by prayer for
us, that for the gift bestowed upon us by the means of many persons thanks
may be given by many on our behalf.

Delay in Coming
2 Corinthians 1:12-24

For our boasting is this, the testimony of our conscience, that in sim- 5
plicity and godly sincerity, not with fleshly wisdom, but by the grace of

5 God, we have had our conduct in the world, and more abundantly toward you. For we write no other things unto you, than what you read or acknowledge; and I trust you shall acknowledge even to the end; as also you have acknowledged us in part, that we are your boasting, even as you also are ours in the day of the Lord Jesus.

6 And in this confidence I was minded to come unto you before, that you might have a second benefit; and to pass by you into Macedonia, and to come again out of Macedonia unto you, and of you to be helped on my way toward Judea. When I therefore was thus minded, did I use lightness? or the things that I purpose, do I purpose according to the flesh, that with me there should be yes yes, and no no?

7 But as God is faithful, our word toward you was not yes and no. For the Son of God, Jesus Christ, who was preached among you by us, even by me and Silas and Timothy, was not yes and no, but in him was yes. For all the promises of God in him are yes, and in him Amen, unto the glory of God by us. Now he which establishes us with you in Christ, and has anointed us, is God; who has also sealed us, and given the guarantee of the Spirit in our hearts.

> ALL THE PROMISES OF GOD IN HIM ARE YES, AND IN HIM AMEN, UNTO THE GLORY OF GOD BY US.

8 Moreover I call God for a witness upon my soul, that to spare you I came not as yet unto Corinth. Not for that we have dominion over your faith, but are helpers of your joy: for by faith you stand.

Forgiveness for One Offender
2 Corinthians 2:1-11

9 But I determined this with myself, that I would not come again to you in heaviness. For if I make you sorry, who is he then that makes me glad, but the same which is made sorry by me? And I wrote this same unto you, lest, when I came, I should have sorrow from them of whom I ought to rejoice; having confidence in you all, that my joy is the joy of you all. For out of much affliction and anguish of heart I wrote unto you with many tears; not that you should be grieved, but that you might know the love which I have more abundantly unto you.

10 But if any have caused grief, he has not grieved me, but in part: that I may not overstate it to you all. Sufficient to such a man is this punishment, which was inflicted of many. So that contrariwise you ought rather to forgive him, and comfort him, lest perhaps such a one should be swallowed up with excessive sorrow. Therefore I ask you that you would confirm your love toward him.

11 For to this end also did I write, that I might know the proof of you, whether you be obedient in all things. To whom you forgive anything, I forgive also: for if I forgave anything, to whom I forgave it, for your sakes I forgave it in the person of Christ; lest Satan should get an advantage of us: for we are not ignorant of his devices.

Triumph in Christ
2 Corinthians 2:12-17

Furthermore, when I came to Troas to preach Christ's gospel, and a 12 door was opened unto me of the Lord, I had no rest in my spirit, because I found not Titus my brother: but taking my leave of them, I went from there into Macedonia.

Now thanks be unto God, which always causes us to triumph in Christ, 13 and makes manifest the fragrance of his knowledge by us in every place. For we are unto God a sweet aroma of Christ, in them that are saved, and in them that perish: to the one we are the fragrance of death unto death; and to the other the fragrance of life unto life. And who is sufficient for these things? For we are not as many, which corrupt the word of God: but as of sincerity, but as of God, in the sight of God speak we in Christ.

CHAPTER 90

MINISTRY AND RECONCILIATION
Ministers of the New Testament
2 Corinthians 3:1-18

1   Do we begin again to commend ourselves? Or need we, as some others, letters of commendation to you, or letters of commendation from you? You are our letter written in our hearts, known and read of all men: Inasmuch as you are manifestly declared to be the letter of Christ ministered by us, written not with ink, but with the Spirit of the living God; not in tablets of stone, but in human tablets of the heart.

2   And such trust have we through Christ toward God: not that we are sufficient of ourselves to think anything as of ourselves; but our sufficiency is of God; who also has made us able ministers of the new testament; not of the letter, but of the spirit: for the letter kills, but the spirit gives life.

3   But if the ministry of death, written and engraved in stones, was glorious, so that the children of Israel could not steadfastly behold the face of Moses for the glory of his countenance; which glory was to be done away: how shall not the ministry of the spirit be rather glorious? For if the ministry of condemnation be glory, much more does the ministry of righteousness exceed in glory. For even that which was made glorious had no glory in this respect, by reason of the glory that excels. For if that which is done away was glorious, much more that which remains is glorious.

4   Seeing then that we have such hope, we use great boldness of speech: and not as Moses, which put a veil over his face, that the children of Israel could not steadfastly look to the end of that which is abolished. But their minds were blinded: for until this day remains the same veil not taken away in the reading of the old testament; which veil is done away in Christ.

5   But even unto this day, when Moses is read, the veil is upon their heart. Nevertheless when it shall turn to the Lord, the veil shall be taken away. Now the Lord is that Spirit: and where the Spirit of the Lord is, there is

liberty. But we all, with unveiled faces beholding as in a mirror the glory of the Lord, are changed into the same image from glory to glory, even as by the Spirit of the Lord. 5

Treasures of the Ministry
2 Corinthians 4:1-18

Therefore seeing we have this ministry, as we have received mercy, we do not lose heart; but have renounced the hidden things of shame, not walking in deception, nor handling the word of God deceitfully; but by manifestation of the truth commending ourselves to every man's conscience in the sight of God. 6

But if our gospel be hidden, it is hidden to them that are lost: in whom the god of this world has blinded the minds of them which do not believe, lest the light of the glorious gospel of Christ, who is the image of God, should shine unto them. For we preach not ourselves, but Christ Jesus the Lord; and ourselves your servants for Jesus' sake. For God, who commanded the light to shine out of darkness, has shined in our hearts, to give the light of the knowledge of the glory of God in the face of Jesus Christ. 7

But we have this treasure in earthen vessels, that the excellence of the power may be of God, and not of us. We are troubled on every side, yet not distressed; we are perplexed, but not in despair; persecuted, but not forsaken; cast down, but not destroyed; always carrying about in the body the dying of the Lord Jesus, that the life also of Jesus might be made manifest in our body. For we which live are always delivered unto death for Jesus' sake, that the life also of Jesus might be made manifest in our mortal flesh. So then death works in us, but life in you. 8

> WE ARE TROUBLED ON EVERY SIDE, YET NOT DISTRESSED; WE ARE PERPLEXED, BUT NOT IN DESPAIR.

We having the same spirit of faith, according as it is written, "*I believed, and therefore have I spoken*"; we also believe, and therefore speak; knowing that he which raised up the Lord Jesus shall raise up us also with Jesus, and shall present us with you. For all things are for your sakes, that the abundant grace might through the thanksgiving of many abound to the glory of God. 9

For which cause we do not lose heart; but though our outward man perishes, yet the inward man is renewed day by day. For our light affliction, which is but for a moment, works for us a far more exceeding and eternal weight of glory; while we look not at the things which are seen, but at the things which are not seen: for the things which are seen are temporal; but the things which are not seen are eternal. 10

> THE THINGS WHICH ARE SEEN ARE TEMPORAL; BUT THE THINGS WHICH ARE NOT SEEN ARE ETERNAL.

Living in the Faith
2 Corinthians 5:1-10

11   For we know that if our earthly house of this tabernacle were dissolved, we have a building of God, a house not made with hands, eternal in the heavens. For in this we groan, earnestly desiring to be clothed upon with our home which is from heaven: if so be that being clothed we shall not be found naked.

12   For we that are in this tabernacle do groan, being burdened: not that we would be unclothed, but clothed upon, that mortality might be swallowed up of life. Now he that has prepared us for the selfsame thing is God, who also has given unto us the guarantee of the Spirit.

13   Therefore we are always confident, knowing that, while we are at home in the body, we are absent from the Lord: (for we walk by faith, not by sight). We are confident, I say, and willing rather to be absent from the body, and to be present with the Lord.

> WE WALK BY FAITH, NOT BY SIGHT.

14   Therefore we labor, that, whether present or absent, we may be accepted of him. For we must all appear before the judgment seat of Christ; that every one may receive the things done in his body, according to that he has done, whether it be good or bad.

Ministry of Reconciliation
2 Corinthians 5:11-21

15   Knowing therefore the fear of the Lord, we persuade men; but we are made known unto God; and I trust also are made known in your consciences. For we commend not ourselves again unto you, but give you occasion to boast on our behalf, that you may have something to answer them which boast in appearance, and not in heart. For whether we be beside ourselves, it is to God: or whether we be of sound mind, it is for your cause.

16   For the love of Christ compels us; because we thus judge, that if one died for all, then were all dead: and that he died for all, that they which live should not henceforth live unto themselves, but unto him which died for them, and rose again.

17   Therefore hereafter we regard no man according to the flesh: yes, though we have known Christ according to the flesh, yet now henceforth we regard him so no longer. Therefore if any man be in Christ, he is a new creation: old things are passed away; behold, all things are become new. And all things are of God, who has reconciled us to himself by Jesus Christ, and has given to us the ministry of reconciliation; that is, that God was in Christ, reconciling the world unto himself, not counting their trespasses unto them; and has committed unto us the word of reconciliation.

> IF ANY MAN BE IN CHRIST, HE IS A NEW CREATION: OLD THINGS ARE PASSED AWAY; BEHOLD, ALL THINGS ARE BECOME NEW.

Now then we are ambassadors for Christ, as though God did appeal to 18
you by us: we urge you in Christ's behalf, be reconciled to God. For he has
made him to be sin for us, who knew no sin; that we might be made the
righteousness of God in him.

Ministry of Patience
2 Corinthians 6:1-10

We then, as workers together with him, urge you also that you receive 19
not the grace of God in vain. (For he says, *"I have heard you in a time
accepted, and in the day of salvation
have I helped you"*: behold, now is the

> BEHOLD, NOW IS THE DAY OF
> SALVATION.

accepted time; behold, now is the day
of salvation.)

Giving no offense in anything, that the ministry be not blamed: but in 20
all things proving ourselves as the ministers of God, in much patience, in
afflictions, in necessities, in distresses, in stripes, in imprisonments, in
tumults, in labors, in sleepless times, in fastings; by purity, by knowledge,
by patience, by kindness, by the Holy Ghost, by love sincere, by the word
of truth, by the power of God, by the armor of righteousness on the right
hand and on the left, by honor and dishonor, by evil report and good report:
as imposters, and yet true; as unknown, and yet well known; as dying, and,
behold, we live; as chastened, and not killed; as sorrowful, yet always rejoicing; as poor, yet making many rich; as having nothing, and yet possessing
all things.

CHAPTER 91

MINISTRY AND REPENTANCE

Temple of the Living God
2 Corinthians 6:11-18; 7:1

1   O you Corinthians, our mouth is open unto you, our heart is enlarged. You are not constrained in us, but you are constrained in your own hearts. Now for a repayment in the same, (I speak as unto my children), be you also enlarged.

2   Be you not unequally yoked together with unbelievers: for what fellowship has righteousness with unrighteousness? and what communion has light with darkness? And what accord has Christ with Belial? or what part has he that believes with an unbeliever? And what agreement has the temple of God with idols? for you are the temple of the living God; as God has said, *"I will dwell in them, and walk in them; and I will be their God, and they shall be my people."*

3   Therefore *"come out from among them, and be you separate,* says the Lord, *and touch not the unclean thing; and I will receive you, and will be a Father unto you, and you shall be my sons and daughters,* says the Lord Almighty."

4   Having therefore these promises, dearly beloved, let us cleanse ourselves from all filthiness of the flesh and spirit, perfecting holiness in the fear of God.

Ministry of Repentance
2 Corinthians 7:2-16

5   Receive us; we have wronged no man, we have corrupted no man, we have exploited no man. I do not speak this to condemn you: for I have said before, that you are in our hearts to die and live with you. Great is my boldness of speech toward you, great is my boasting of you: I am filled with comfort, I am exceedingly joyful in all our tribulation.

For, when we were come into Macedonia, our flesh had no rest, but 6
we were troubled on every side; outside were fightings, inside were fears.
Nevertheless God, that comforts those that are cast down, comforted us by
the coming of Titus; and not by his coming only, but by the consolation with
which he was comforted in you, when he told us your earnest desire, your
mourning, your fervent mind toward me; so that I rejoiced the more. For
though I made you sorry with a letter, I do not repent, though I did repent:
for I perceive that the same letter has made you sorry, though it were but for
a season.

Now I rejoice, not that you were made sorry, but that you sorrowed to 7
repentance: for you were made sorry after a godly manner, that you might
receive harm by us in nothing. For godly sorrow works repentance to salvation not to be repented of: but the
sorrow of the world works death. For
behold this selfsame thing, that you

> GODLY SORROW WORKS REPEN-
> TANCE TO SALVATION.

sorrowed after a godly manner, what
earnestness it produced in you, yes,
what clearing of yourselves, yes, what indignation, yes, what fear, yes, what
strong desire, yes, what zeal, yes, what revenge! In all things you have
proved yourselves to be clear in this matter. Therefore, though I wrote unto
you, I did it not for his cause that had done the wrong, nor for his cause that
suffered wrong, but that our care for you in the sight of God might appear
unto you.

Therefore we were comforted in your comfort: yes, and exceedingly 8
the more joyed we for the joy of Titus, because his spirit was refreshed by
you all. For if I have boasted anything to him of you, I am not ashamed; but
as we spoke all things to you in truth, even so our boasting, which I made
before Titus, is found a truth. And his inward affection is more abundant
toward you, while he remembers the obedience of you all, how with fear
and trembling you received him. I rejoice therefore that I have confidence
in you in all things.

CHAPTER 92

Messengers and Collection

Readiness in Giving
2 Corinthians 8:1-15

1   Moreover, brethren, we cause you to know of the grace of God bestowed on the churches of Macedonia; how that in a great trial of affliction the abundance of their joy and their deep poverty abounded unto the riches of their generosity. For to their ability, I bear witness, yes, and beyond their ability they were willing of themselves; asking us with much urgency that we would receive the gift, and take upon us the fellowship of the ministering to the saints.

2   And this they did, not as we expected, but first gave their own selves to the Lord, and unto us by the will of God. So that we urged Titus, that as he had begun, so he would also finish in you the same grace also. Therefore, as you abound in everything, in faith, and utterance, and knowledge, and in all diligence, and in your love to us, see that you abound in this grace also.

3   I speak not by command, but by occasion of the earnestness of others, and to test the sincerity of your love. For you know the grace of our Lord Jesus Christ, that, though he was rich, yet for your sakes he became poor, that you through his poverty might be rich.

4   And herein I give my advice: for this is expedient for you, who have begun before, not only to do, but also to be willing a year ago. Now therefore perform the doing of it; that as there was a readiness to will, so there may be a performance also out of that which you have. For if there be first a willing mind, it is accepted according to that a man has, and not according to that he has not.

5   For I mean not that other men be eased, and you burdened: but by an equality, that now at this time your abundance may be a supply for their lack, that their abundance also may be a supply for your lack: that there may

be equality: as it is written, *"He that had gathered much had nothing over;* 5 *and he that had gathered little had no lack."*

Messengers of the Church
2 Corinthians 8:16-24

But thanks be to God, which put the same earnest care into the heart 6 of Titus for you. For indeed he accepted the exhortation; but being more earnest, of his own accord he went unto you. And we have sent with him the brother, whose praise is in the gospel throughout all the churches; and not that only, but who was also chosen of the churches to travel with us with this grace, which is administered by us to the glory of the same Lord, and declaration of your ready mind: avoiding this, that no man should blame us in this abundance which is administered by us: providing for honorable things, not only in the sight of the Lord, but also in the sight of men.

And we have sent with them our brother, whom we have oftentimes 7 proved diligent in many things, but now much more diligent, upon the great confidence which I have in you. Whether any do inquire of Titus, he is my partner and fellow helper concerning you: or our brethren be inquired of, they are the messengers of the churches, and the glory of Christ. Therefore show to them, and before the churches, the proof of your love, and of our boasting on your behalf.

Collection for the Saints
2 Corinthians 9:1-15

8

For as concerning the ministering to the saints, it is of no need for me to write to you: for I know the readiness of your mind, for which I boast of you to them of Macedonia, that Achaia was ready a year ago; and your zeal has stirred very many. Yet have I sent the brethren, lest our boasting of you should be in vain in this behalf; that, as I said, you may be ready: lest perhaps if they of Macedonia come with me, and find you unprepared, we (to say nothing of, you) should be ashamed in this same confident boasting. Therefore I thought it necessary to urge the brethren, that they would go ahead unto you, and make up beforehand your generous gift, which you had promised ahead, that the same might be ready, as a matter of generosity, and not as of obligation.

But this I say, He which sows sparingly shall also reap sparingly; and 9 he which sows bountifully shall also reap bountifully. Every man according as he purposes in his heart, so let him give; not grudgingly, or of necessity: for God loves a cheerful giver. And God is able to make all grace abound

> GOD LOVES A CHEERFUL GIVER.

toward you; that you, always having all sufficiency in all things, may abound to every good work: (as it is written, *"He has dispersed abroad; he has given to the poor: his righteousness remains for ever."*

Now he that supplies seed to the sower both supply bread for your food, 10 and multiply your seed sown, and increase the fruits of your righteousness);

10 being enriched in everything to all bountifulness, which causes through us thanksgiving to God.

11   For the administration of this service not only supplies the needs of the saints, but is overflowing also by many thanksgivings unto God; while by the proof of this service they glorify God for your professed obedience unto the gospel of Christ, and for your liberal distribution unto them, and unto all men; and by their prayer for you, which long after you for the exceeding grace of God in you. Thanks be unto God for his indescribable gift.

CHAPTER 93

⊹ TRUE AND FALSE APOSTLES ⊹

Measuring the Ministry
2 Corinthians 10:1-18

Now I Paul myself appeal to you by the meekness and gentleness of 1
Christ, who in presence am humble among you, but being absent am bold
toward you: but I beg you, that I may not be bold when I am present with
that confidence, with which I think to be bold against some, which think of
us as if we walked according to the flesh.

For though we walk in the flesh, we do not war according the flesh: 2
(for the weapons of our warfare are not worldly, but mighty through God to
the pulling down of strongholds); casting down arguments, and every high
thing that exalts itself against the knowledge of God, and bringing into captivity every thought to the obedience of Christ; and having in a readiness to
punish all disobedience, when your obedience is fulfilled.

Do you look on things according to the outward appearance? If any 3
man trusts to himself that he is Christ's, let him of himself think this again,
that, as he is Christ's, even so are we Christ's. For though I should boast
somewhat more of our authority, which the Lord has given us for building
up, and not for your destruction, I should not be ashamed: that I may not
seem as if I would terrify you by letters.

"For his letters," they say, "are weighty and powerful; but his bodily 4
presence is weak, and his speech contemptible." Let such a one think this,
that, such as we are in word by letters when we are absent, such will we be
also in deed when we are present.

For we dare not make ourselves of the number, or compare ourselves 5
with some that commend themselves: but they measuring themselves by
themselves, and comparing themselves among themselves, are not wise.
But we will not boast of things beyond our measure, but according to the

5 measure of the role which God has distributed to us, a measure to reach even unto you.

6 For we do not stretch ourselves beyond our measure, as though we reached not unto you: for we are come as far as to you also in preaching the gospel of Christ: not boasting of things beyond our measure, that is, of other men's labors; but having hope, when your faith is increased, that we shall be enlarged by you according to our role abundantly, to preach the gospel in the regions beyond you, and not to boast in another man's field of things made ready to our hand.

7 But *"he that boasts, let him boast in the Lord."* For it is not he that commends himself that is approved, but whom the Lord commends.

False Apostles
2 Corinthians 11:1-15

8 Would to God you could bear with me a little in my folly: and indeed bear with me. For I am jealous over you with godly jealousy: for I have pledged you to one husband, that I may present you as a chaste virgin to Christ. But I fear, lest by any means, as the serpent deceived Eve through its cunning, so your minds should be corrupted away from the simplicity that is in Christ.

9 For if he that comes preaches another Jesus, whom we have not preached, or if you receive another spirit, which you have not received, or another gospel, which you have not accepted, you might well bear with him.

10 For I suppose I was not a bit inferior to the very special apostles. But though I be unskilled in speech, yet not in knowledge; but we have been thoroughly made manifest among you in all things.

11 Have I committed a sin in humbling myself that you might be exalted, because I have preached to you the gospel of God without cost? I robbed other churches, taking wages of them, to do you service.

12 And when I was present with you, and in need, I was a burden to no man: for that which was lacking to me the brethren which came from Macedonia supplied: and in all things I have kept myself from being burdensome unto you, and so will I keep myself. As the truth of Christ is in me, no man shall stop me of this boasting in the regions of Achaia. Why? because I do not love you? God knows.

> AS THE TRUTH OF CHRIST IS IN ME, NO MAN SHALL STOP ME.

13 But what I do, that I will do, that I may cut off occasion from them which desire occasion; that wherein they boast, they may be found even as we. For such are false apostles, deceitful workers, transforming themselves into the apostles of Christ. And no wonder; for Satan himself is transformed into an angel of light. Therefore it is no great thing if his ministers also be transformed as the ministers of righteousness; whose end shall be according to their works.

Perils to Apostles
2 Corinthians 11:16-33

I say again, Let no man think me a fool; if otherwise, yet as a fool 14
receive me, that I may boast myself a little. That which I speak, I speak it
not according to the Lord, but as it were foolishly, in this confidence of
boasting. Seeing that many boast according to the flesh, I will boast also.
For you tolerate fools gladly, seeing you yourselves are wise. For you tolerate it, if a man brings you into bondage, if a man devours you, if a man takes
of you, if a man exalts himself, if a man strikes you on the face.

I speak as concerning shame, as though we had been weak. Howbeit 15
in whatever anyone is bold, (I speak foolishly), I am bold also. Are they
Hebrews? so am I. Are they Israelites? so am I. Are they the seed of Abraham? so am I.

Are they ministers of Christ? (I speak as a fool) I am more; in labors 16
more abundant, in stripes beyond measure, in prisons more frequently, in
deaths often. Of the Jews five times I received forty stripes less one. Three
times I was beaten with rods, once I was stoned, three times I suffered shipwreck, a night and a day I have been in the deep; in journeyings often, in
perils of waters, in perils of robbers, in perils by my own countrymen, in
perils by the heathen, in perils in the city, in perils in the wilderness, in perils in the sea, in perils among false brethren; in weariness and painfulness,
in sleepless times often, in hunger and thirst, in fastings often, in cold and
nakedness.

Besides those things that are external, that which comes upon me 17
daily, the anxiety for all the churches. Who is weak, and I am not weak?
who is fallen away, and I do not burn?

If I must of necessity boast, I will boast of the things which concern 18
my infirmities. The God and Father of
our Lord Jesus Christ, which is
blessed for evermore, knows that I do
not lie. In Damascus the governor
under Aretas the king guarded the city
of the Damascenes with a garrison,
desirous to apprehend me: and

> THE GOD AND FATHER OF
> OUR LORD JESUS CHRIST,
> WHICH IS BLESSED FOR EVER-
> MORE, KNOWS THAT I DO
> NOT LIE.

through a window in a basket was I let down by the wall, and escaped his
hands.

CHAPTER 94

REVELATIONS AND CONCLUSION

Visions and Revelations
2 Corinthians 12:1-10

1   It is not expedient for me doubtless to boast. I will come to visions and revelations of the Lord.

2   I knew a man in Christ more than fourteen years ago, (whether in the body, I cannot know; or whether out of the body, I cannot know: God knows); such a one caught up to the third heaven. And I knew such a man, (whether in the body, or out of the body, I cannot know: God knows); how that he was caught up into paradise, and heard unspeakable words, which it is not lawful for a man to utter.

3   Of such a one will I boast: yet of myself I will not boast, but in my infirmities. For though I would desire to boast, I shall not be a fool; for I will say the truth: but now I refrain, lest any man should think of me above that which he sees me to be, or that he hears of me.

4   And lest I should be exalted beyond measure through the abundance of the revelations, there was given to me a thorn in the flesh, the messenger of Satan to hit me, lest I should be exalted beyond measure. For this thing I besought the Lord three times, that it might depart from me. And he said unto me, "My grace is sufficient for you: for my strength is made perfect in weakness." Most gladly therefore will I rather boast in my infirmities, that the power of Christ may rest upon me.

5   Therefore I take pleasure in infirmities, in insults, in needs, in persecutions, in distresses for Christ's sake: for when I am weak, then am I strong.

Future Ministry
2 Corinthians 12:11-21

6   I am become a fool in boasting; you have compelled me: for I ought to have been commended of you: for in nothing am I lacking the very special

apostles, though I be nothing. Truly the signs of an apostle were performed 6
among you in all patience, in signs, and wonders, and mighty deeds. For
what is it wherein you were inferior to other churches, except it be that I
myself was not burdensome to you? forgive me this wrong.

Behold, the third time I am ready to come to you; and I will not be 7
burdensome to you: for I seek not yours, but you: for the children ought not
to lay up for the parents, but the parents for the children. And I will very
gladly spend and be spent for you; though the more abundantly I love you,
the less I be loved.

But be it so, I did not burden you: nevertheless, being crafty, I caught 8
you with trickery. Did I make a gain of you by any of them whom I sent unto
you? I urged Titus, and with him I sent a brother. Did Titus make a gain of
you? walked we not in the same spirit? walked we not in the same steps?

Again, think you that we excuse ourselves unto you? we speak before 9
God in Christ: but we do all things, dearly beloved, for your edification. For
I fear, lest, when I come, I shall not find you such as I wish, and that I shall
be found unto you such as you wish not: lest there be debates, envy, wraths,
strifes, backbitings, whisperings, conceits, tumults: and lest, when I come
again, my God will humble me among you, and that I shall mourn for many
which have sinned already, and have not repented of the uncleanness and
fornication and lewdness which they have committed.

Providing Your Own Faith
2 Corinthians 13:1-10

This is the third time I am coming to you. "*In the mouth of two or* 10
three witnesses shall every word be established." I told you before, and
warn you, as if I were present, the second time; and being absent now I
write to them which heretofore have sinned, and to all others, that, if I come
again, I will not spare: since you seek a proof of Christ speaking in me,
which toward you is not weak, but is mighty in you. For though he was crucified through weakness, yet he lives by the power of God. For we also are
weak in him, but we shall live with him by the power of God toward you.

Examine yourselves, whether you be in the faith; test your own selves. 11
Do you not know your own selves, how that Jesus Christ is in you, unless you
be reprobates? But I trust that you shall know that we are not reprobates.

Now I pray to God that you do no evil; not that we should appear 12
approved, but that you should do that which is right, though we be as reprobates. For we can do nothing against
the truth, but for the truth. For we are
glad, when we are weak, and you are
strong: and this also we wish, even
your perfection.

> WE CAN DO NOTHING AGAINST
> THE TRUTH, BUT FOR THE
> TRUTH.

Therefore I write these things being absent, lest being present I should 13
use sharpness, according to the authority which the Lord has given me to
edification, and not to destruction.

Conclusion
2 Corinthians 13:11-14

14   Finally, brethren, farewell. Be perfect, be of good comfort, be of one mind, live in peace; and the God of love and peace shall be with you. Greet one another with a holy kiss.

15   All the saints greet you. The grace of the Lord Jesus Christ, and the love of God, and the communion of the Holy Ghost, be with you all. Amen.

PART 23

LETTER TO GALATIANS

Fundamental to Paul's conversion and teaching was the tenet that men's actions should be governed by the laws of the Spirit and not by the ritualistic laws of man. His stern letter to the Galatians warns them of their continued imposition of their traditional religious customs as a means to salvation and declares their freedom from bondage to man's law through the revelation of Jesus Christ. Adherence to things of the flesh reaps corruption, but adherence to things of the Spirit reaps life everlasting.

> THERE IS NEITHER JEW NOR GREEK, THERE IS NEITHER BOND NOR FREE, THERE IS NEITHER MALE NOR FEMALE: FOR YOU ARE ALL ONE IN CHRIST JESUS. (GALATIANS 3:28)

CHAPTER 95

PERSONAL PROGRESS

Greeting to Galatians
Galatians 1:1-5

1   Paul, an apostle, (not of men, neither by man, but by Jesus Christ, and God the Father, who raised him from the dead); and all the brethren which are with me, unto the churches of Galatia: Grace be to you and peace from God the Father, and from our Lord Jesus Christ, who gave himself for our sins, that he might deliver us from this present evil world, according to the will of God and our Father: to whom be glory for ever and ever. Amen.

One Gospel of Christ
Galatians 1:6-10

2   I marvel that you are so soon turned from him that called you into the grace of Christ unto another gospel: which is not another; but there be some that trouble you, and would pervert the gospel of Christ.

3   But though we, or an angel from heaven, preach any other gospel unto you than that which we have preached unto you, let him be accursed. As we said before, so say I now again, If any man preach any other gospel unto you than that you have received, let him be accursed.

4   For do I now persuade men, or God? or do I seek to please men? for if I yet pleased men, I should not be the servant of Christ.

Apostle by Revelation
Galatians 1:11-24

5   But I assure you, brethren, that the gospel which was preached of me is not according to man. For I neither received it of man, neither was I taught it, but by the revelation of Jesus Christ.

6   For you have heard of my conduct in time past in the Jews' religion, how that beyond measure I persecuted the church of God, and wasted it: and

progressed in the Jews' religion above many my age in my own nation, 6
being more exceedingly zealous of the traditions of my fathers.

But when it pleased God, who separated me from my mother's womb, 7
and called me by his grace, to reveal his Son in me, that I might preach him
among the Gentiles; immediately I conferred not with flesh and blood: neither went I up to Jerusalem to them which were apostles before me; but I
went into Arabia, and returned again unto Damascus.

Then after three years I went up to Jerusalem to see Peter, and stayed 8
with him fifteen days. But others of the apostles I saw none, except James
the Lord's brother. Now the things which I write unto you, behold, before
God, I do not lie.

Afterward I came into the regions of Syria and Cilicia; and was 9
unknown by face unto the churches of
Judea which were in Christ. But they
had heard only, That "he which persecuted us in times past now preaches
the faith which once he destroyed."
And they glorified God in me.

> "HE WHICH PERSECUTED US
> IN TIMES PAST NOW PREACHES
> THE FAITH."

Meeting at Jerusalem
Galatians 2:1-10

Then fourteen years later I went up again to Jerusalem with Barnabas, 10
and took Titus with me also. And I went up by revelation, and communi-
cated unto them that gospel which I preach among the Gentiles, but privately to them which were of reputation, lest by any means I should run, or
had run, in vain.

But neither Titus, who was with me, being a Greek, was compelled to 11
be circumcised: and that because of false brethren secretly brought in, who
came in secretly to spy out our liberty which we have in Christ Jesus, that
they might bring us into bondage: to whom we gave in to subjection, no, not
for an hour; that the truth of the gospel might continue with you.

But of these who seemed to be something, (whatsoever they were, it 12
makes no matter to me: God accepts no man's person): for they who seemed
to be something in conference added nothing to me. But contrariwise, when
they saw that the gospel of the uncircumcision was committed unto me, as
the gospel of the circumcised was unto Peter; (for he that worked effectively
in Peter to the apostleship of the circumcised, the same was mighty in me
toward the Gentiles): and when James, Cephas, and John, who seemed to be
pillars, perceived the grace that was given unto me, they gave to me and
Barnabas the right hand of fellowship; that we should go unto the Gentiles,
and they unto the circumcised. Only they would that we should remember
the poor; the same which I also was eager to do.

Contrast of Peter and Paul
Galatians 2:11-14

But when Peter was come to Antioch, I withstood him to his face, 13
because he was to be blamed. For before that certain came from James, he

13 did eat with the Gentiles: but when they were come, he withdrew and separated himself, fearing them which were of the circumcision. And the other Jews discriminated likewise with him; insomuch that Barnabas also was carried away with their discrimination.

14 But when I saw that they walked not uprightly according to the truth of the gospel, I said unto Peter before them all, "If you, being a Jew, live according to the manner of Gentiles, and not as do the Jews, why do you compel the Gentiles to live as do the Jews?"

Living the Faith of Christ
Galatians 2:15-21

15 "We who are Jews by nature, and not sinners of the Gentiles, knowing that a man is not justified by the works of the law, but by the faith of Jesus Christ, even we have believed in Jesus Christ, that we might be justified by the faith of Christ, and not by the works of the law: for by the works of the law shall no flesh be justified.

> "WE HAVE BELIEVED IN JESUS CHRIST, THAT WE MIGHT BE JUSTIFIED BY THE FAITH OF CHRIST."

16 "But if, while we seek to be justified by Christ, we ourselves also are found sinners, is therefore Christ the minister of sin? God forbid. For if I build again the things which I destroyed, I make myself a transgressor. For I through the law am dead to the law, that I might live unto God.

17 "I am crucified with Christ: nevertheless I live; yet not I, but Christ lives in me: and the life which I now live in the flesh I live by the faith of the Son of God, who loved me, and gave himself for me. I do not set aside the grace of God: for if righteousness comes by the law, then Christ is dead in vain."

CHAPTER 96

JUSTIFICATION BY FAITH

Contrasting Faith and the Law
Galatians 3:1-14

O foolish Galatians, who has bewitched you, that you should not obey 1 the truth, before whose eyes Jesus Christ has been publicly set forth, crucified among you? This only would I learn of you, Did you receive the Spirit by the works of the law, or by the hearing of faith? Are you so foolish? having begun in the Spirit, are you now made perfect by the flesh? Have you suffered so many things in vain? if it be yet in vain.

He therefore that supplies to you the Spirit, and works miracles among 2 you, does he do it by the works of the law, or by the hearing of faith? even as Abraham *"believed God, and it was accounted to him for righteousness."*

Know you therefore that they which are of faith, the same are the chil- 3 dren of Abraham. And the scripture, foreseeing that God would justify the Gentiles through faith, preached before the gospel unto Abraham, saying, *"In you shall all nations be blessed."* So then they which be of faith are blessed with faithful Abraham.

For as many as are of the works of the law are under the curse: for it 4 is written, *"Cursed is everyone that continues not in all things which are written in the book of the law to do them."* But that no man is justified by the law in the sight of God, it is evident: for, *"The just shall live by faith."* And the law is not of faith: but, *"The man that does them shall live in them."*

Christ has redeemed us from the curse of the law, being made a curse 5 for us: for it is written, *"Cursed is everyone that hangs on a tree"*: that the blessing of Abraham might come on the Gentiles through Jesus Christ; that we might receive the promise of the Spirit through faith.

Contrasting Two Promises
Galatians 3:15-29

Brethren, I speak according to the manner of men; Though it be but a 6 man's covenant, yet if it be confirmed, no man annuls, or adds thereto. Now

6   to Abraham and his seed were the promises made. He says not, "And to seeds," as of many; but as of one, "*And to your seed,*" *which is Christ.*

7   And this I say, that the covenant, that was confirmed before of God in Christ, the law, which was four hundred and thirty years later, cannot annul, that it should make the promise of no effect. For if the inheritance be of the law, it is no more of promise: but God gave it to Abraham by promise.

8   For what then serves the law? It was added because of transgressions, till the seed should come to whom the promise was made; and it was ordained by angels in the hand of a mediator. Now a mediator is not a mediator of one, but God is one.

9   Is the law then against the promises of God? God forbid: for if there had been a law given which could have given life, indeed righteousness should have been by the law. But the scripture has concluded all under sin, that the promise by faith of Jesus Christ might be given to them that believe.

10   But before faith came, we were kept under the law, shut up unto the faith which should afterward be revealed. Therefore the law was our tutor to bring us unto Christ, that we might be justified by faith. But after faith is come, we are no longer under a tutor.

11   For you are all the children of God by faith in Christ Jesus. For as many of you as have been baptized into Christ have put on Christ. There is neither Jew nor Greek, there is neither bond nor free, there is neither male nor female: for you are all one in Christ Jesus. And if you be Christ's, then are you Abraham's seed, and heirs according to the promise.

> YOU ARE ALL THE CHILDREN OF GOD BY FAITH IN CHRIST JESUS.

Concern for Galatians
Galatians 4:1-20

12   Now I say, That the heir, as long as he is a child, differs nothing from a servant, though he be master of all; but is under guardians and stewards until the time appointed of the father.

13   Even so we, when we were children, were in bondage under the elements of the world: but when the fulness of the time was come, God sent forth his Son, born of a woman, born under the law, to redeem them that were under the law, that we might receive the adoption of sons.

14   And because you are sons, God has sent forth the Spirit of his Son into your hearts, crying, "Abba, Father." Therefore you are no more a servant, but a son; and if a son, then an heir of God through Christ.

15   Howbeit then, when you knew not God, you did service unto them which by nature are no gods. But now, after you have known God, or rather are known of God, how do you turn again to the weak and beggarly elements, to which you desire again to be in bondage? You observe days, and months, and times, and years. I am afraid for you, lest I have bestowed upon you labor in vain.

Brethren, I urge you, be as I am; for I am as you are: you have not 16
wronged me at all. You know how through infirmity of the flesh I preached
the gospel unto you at the first. And my temptation which was in my flesh
you despised not, nor rejected; but received me as an angel of God, even as
Christ Jesus.

Where is then the blessedness you spoke of? for I bear you witness, 17
that, if it had been possible, you would have plucked out your own eyes, and
have given them to me. Am I therefore become your enemy, because I tell
you the truth?

They zealously make much of you, but not well; yes, they would 18
exclude you, that you might make much of them. But it is good to be zealously made much of always in a good thing, and not only when I am present with you.

My little children, of whom I labor in birth again until Christ be 19
formed in you, I desire to be present with you now, and to change my tone;
for I stand in doubt of you.

Contrasting Two Peoples
Galatians 4:21-31; 5:1

Tell me, you that desire to be under the law, do you not hear the law? 20
For it is written, that Abraham had two sons, the one by a bondwoman, the
other by a free woman. But he who was of the bondwoman was born
according to the flesh; but he of the free woman was by promise.

Which things are an allegory: for these are the two covenants; the one 21
from the mount Sinai, which genders to bondage, which is Hagar. For this
Hagar is mount Sinai in Arabia, and answers to Jerusalem which now is, and
is in bondage with her children.

But the Jerusalem which is above is free, which is the mother of us all. 22
For it is written, *"Rejoice, you barren that bear not; break forth and cry,
you that labor not: for the desolate has many more children than she which
has a husband."*

Now we, brethren, as Isaac was, are the children of promise. But as 23
then he that was born according to the flesh persecuted him that was born
according to the Spirit, even so it is now. Nevertheless what says the scripture? *"Cast out the bondwoman and her son: for the son of the bondwoman
shall not be heir with the son of the free woman."* So then, brethren, we are
not children of the bondwoman, but of the free.

Stand fast therefore in the liberty by which Christ has made us free, 24
and do not be entangled again with the yoke of bondage.

CHAPTER 97

FRUIT OF THE SPIRIT

Christian Freedom
Galatians 5:2-12

1   Behold, I Paul say unto you, that if you be circumcised, Christ shall profit you nothing. For I testify again to every man that is circumcised, that he is a debtor to keep the whole law. Christ is become of no effect unto you, whosoever of you are justified by the law; you are fallen from grace. For we through the Spirit wait for the hope of righteousness by faith. For in Jesus Christ neither circumcision avails anything, nor uncircumcision; but faith which works by love.

2   You did run well; who did hinder you that you should not obey the truth? This persuasion comes not of him that calls you. A little leaven leavens the whole lump.

3   I have confidence in you through the Lord, that you will be not otherwise minded: but he that troubles you shall bear his judgment, whosoever he be. And I, brethren, if I yet preach circumcision, why do I yet suffer persecution? then is the offense of the cross ceased. I wish they were even cut off which trouble you.

Flesh and Spirit
Galatians 5:13-26

4   For, brethren, you have been called unto liberty; only use not liberty for an opportunity to the flesh, but by love serve one another. For all the law is fulfilled in one word, even in this; *"You shall love your neighbor as yourself."* But if you bite and devour one another, take heed that you be not consumed one of another.

5   This I say then, Walk in the Spirit, and you shall not fulfill the lust of the flesh. For the flesh lusts against the Spirit, and the Spirit against the flesh: and these are contrary the one to the other: so that you cannot do

the things that you wish. But if you be led of the Spirit, you are not under 5 the law.

Now the works of the flesh are manifest, which are these; Adultery, 6 fornication, uncleanness, lewdness, idolatry, witchcraft, hatred, discord, jealousies, wrath, strife, dissensions, factions, envy, murders, drunkenness, orgies, and such like: of which I tell you beforehand, as I have also told you in time past, that they which do such things shall not inherit the kingdom of God.

But the fruit of the Spirit is love, joy, peace, patience, gentleness, 7 goodness, faithfulness, meekness, self-control: against such there is no law. And they that are Christ's have crucified the flesh with its passions and lusts. If we live in the Spirit, let us also walk in the Spirit. Let us not be desirous of foolish boasting, provoking one another, envying one another.

Law of Christ
Galatians 6:1-10

Brethren, if a man be overtaken in a fault, you which are spiritual, 8 restore such a one in the spirit of meekness; considering yourself, lest you also be tempted. Bear one another's burdens, and so fulfill the law of Christ. For if a man thinks himself to be something, when he is nothing, he deceives himself.

> BEAR ONE ANOTHER'S BURDENS, AND SO FULFILL THE LAW OF CHRIST.

But let every man test his own work, and then shall he have rejoicing 9 in himself alone, and not in another. For every man shall bear his own burden. Let him that is taught in the word share with him that teaches in all good things.

Be not deceived; God is not mocked: for whatsoever a man sows, that 10 shall he also reap. For he that sows to his flesh shall of the flesh reap corruption; but he that sows to the Spirit shall of the Spirit reap life everlasting.

> WHATSOEVER A MAN SOWS, THAT SHALL HE ALSO REAP.

And let us not be weary in well doing: for in due season we shall reap, 11 if we do not lose heart. As we have therefore opportunity, let us do good unto all men, especially unto them who are of the household of faith.

Conclusion
Galatians 6:11-18

You see how large a letter I have written unto you with my own hand. 12 As many as desire to make a good showing in the flesh, they compel you to be circumcised; only lest they should suffer persecution for the cross of Christ. For neither they themselves who are circumcised keep the law; but desire to have you circumcised, that they may boast in your flesh.

But God forbid that I should boast, except in the cross of our Lord 13 Jesus Christ, by whom the world is crucified unto me, and I unto the world.

13 For in Christ Jesus neither circumcision avails anything, nor uncircumcision, but a new creature. And as many as walk according to this rule, peace be on them, and mercy, and upon the Israel of God.

14   From henceforth let no man trouble me: for I bear in my body the marks of the Lord Jesus.

15   Brethren, the grace of our Lord Jesus Christ be with your spirit. Amen.

PART 24

LETTER TO ROMANS

Intending to visit Rome in the future, Paul writes to the Romans, con-firming his beliefs and describing his convictions for living in accor-dance with the higher laws of Spirit, rather than the lesser laws of man. His letter reminds them that, while a man can be justified in faith without conforming to the deeds of the law, conforming to the law without the deeds of faith cannot justify man in the eyes of God. Therefore one should take care not to judge others by the axioms of his own faith, but rather should let every man prove in his own life what is good in the sight of God. Those who judge others condemn themselves, but those who live in Christ are free from the fear of judgment.

NEITHER DEATH, NOR LIFE, NOR ANGELS, NOR PRINCIPALITIES, NOR POWERS, NOR THINGS PRESENT, NOR THINGS TO COME, NOR HEIGHT, NOR DEPTH, NOR ANY OTHER CREATURE, SHALL BE ABLE TO SEPARATE US FROM THE LOVE OF GOD, WHICH IS IN CHRIST JESUS OUR LORD.
(ROMANS 8:38-39)

CHAPTER 98

SIN AND JUDGMENT

Greeting to Romans
Romans 1:1-7

1   Paul, a servant of Jesus Christ, called to be an apostle, separated unto the gospel of God, (which he had promised before by his prophets in the holy scriptures), concerning his Son Jesus Christ our Lord, which was made of the seed of David according to the flesh; and declared to be the Son of God with power, according to the spirit of holiness, by the resurrection from the dead. By him we have received grace and apostleship, for obedience to the faith among all nations, for his name: among whom are you also the called of Jesus Christ.

2   To all that be in Rome, beloved of God, called to be saints: Grace to you and peace from God our Father, and the Lord Jesus Christ.

Giving Thanks
Romans 1:8-15

3   First, I thank my God through Jesus Christ for you all, that your faith is spoken of throughout the whole world. For God is my witness, whom I serve with my spirit in the gospel of his Son, that without ceasing I make mention of you always in my prayers; making request, if by any means now at last I might have a prosperous journey by the will of God to come unto you.

4   For I long to see you, that I may impart unto you some spiritual gift, to the end you may be established; that is, that I may be strengthened together with you by the mutual faith both of you and me.

5   Now I would not have you unaware, brethren, that many times I intended to come unto you, (but was prevented until now), that I might have some fruit among you also, even as among other Gentiles.

I am obligated both to the Greeks, and to the barbarians; both to the 6 wise, and to the unwise. So, as much as is in me, I am eager to preach the gospel to you that are at Rome also.

Faith of the Gospel
Romans 1:16-17

For I am not ashamed of the gospel of Christ: for it is the power of God unto salvation to everyone that believes; to the Jew first, and also to the Greek. For therein is the righteousness of God revealed from faith to faith: as it is written, *"The just shall live by faith."*

> I AM NOT ASHAMED OF THE GOSPEL OF CHRIST: FOR IT IS THE POWER OF GOD UNTO SALVATION TO EVERYONE THAT BELIEVES.

7

Sin and Guilt of the World
Romans 1:18-32

For the wrath of God is revealed from heaven against all ungodliness 8 and unrighteousness of men, who suppress the truth in unrighteousness; because that which may be known of God is manifest in them; for God has showed it unto them. For the invisible things of him from the creation of the world are clearly seen, being understood by the things that are made, even his eternal power and Godhead; so that they are without excuse: because, when they knew God, they glorified him not as God, neither were thankful; but became futile in their thoughts, and their foolish hearts were darkened.

Professing themselves to be wise, they became fools, and changed the 9 glory of the incorruptible God into an image made like corruptible man, and to birds, and four-footed animals, and creeping things.

Therefore God also gave them up to uncleanness through the lusts of 10 their own hearts, to dishonor their own bodies between themselves: who changed the truth of God into a lie, and worshiped and served the creature more than the Creator, who is blessed for ever. Amen.

For this cause God gave them up unto vile passions: for even their 11 women did change the natural use into that which is against nature: and likewise also the men, leaving the natural use of the woman, burned in their lust one toward another; men with men working that which is shameful, and receiving in themselves that repayment of their error which was fitting.

And even as they did not like to retain God in their knowledge, God 12 gave them over to a reprobate mind, to do those things which are not fitting; being filled with all unrighteousness, fornication, wickedness, covetousness, maliciousness; full of envy, murder, debate, deceit, malignity; whisperers, backbiters, haters of God, insolent, proud, boasters, inventors of evil things, disobedient to parents, without understanding, covenantbreakers, without natural affection, implacable, unmerciful: who knowing the judgment of God, that they which commit such things are deserving of death, not only do the same, but have pleasure in them that do them.

Impartial Judgment of God
Romans 2:1-16

13   Therefore you are inexcusable, O man, whosoever you are that judge: for wherein you judge another, you condemn yourself; for you that judge do the same things. But we are sure that the judgment of God is according to truth against them which commit such things.

> WHEREIN YOU JUDGE ANOTHER, YOU CONDEMN YOURSELF.

14   And do you think this, O man, that judge them which do such things, and do the same, that you shall escape the judgment of God? Or do you despise the riches of his goodness and forbearance and patience; not knowing that the goodness of God leads you to repentance?

15   But after your hardness and unrepentant heart treasure up unto yourself wrath toward the day of wrath and revelation of the righteous judgment of God; who "will render to every man according to his deeds": to them who by patient continuance in well doing seek for glory and honor and immortality, eternal life: but unto them that are contentious, and do not obey the truth, but obey unrighteousness, indignation and wrath, tribulation and anguish, upon every soul of man that does evil, of the Jew first, and also of the Gentile; but glory, honor, and peace, to every man that works good, to the Jew first, and also to the Gentile: for there is no partiality of persons with God.

> THERE IS NO PARTIALITY OF PERSONS WITH GOD.

16   For as many as have sinned without law shall also perish without law: and as many as have sinned in the law shall be judged by the law; (for not the hearers of the law are just before God, but the doers of the law shall be justified.

17   For when the Gentiles, which have not the law, do by nature the things contained in the law, these, having not the law, are a law unto themselves: which show the work of the law written in their hearts, their conscience also bearing witness, and their thoughts the meanwhile accusing or else excusing one another); in the day when God shall judge the secrets of men by Jesus Christ according to my gospel.

Jews and the Law
Romans 2:17-29

18   Behold, you are called a Jew, and rest in the law, and make your boast of God, and know his will, and approve the things that are more excellent, being instructed out of the law; and are confident that you yourself are a guide of the blind, a light of them which are in darkness, an instructor of the foolish, a teacher of babies, which have the form of knowledge and of the truth in the law.

19   You therefore which teach another, do you not teach yourself? you that preach a man should not steal, do you steal? You that say a man should not

commit adultery, do you commit adultery? you that abhor idols, do you 19 commit sacrilege? You that make your boast of the law, through breaking the law dishonor your God? For *"the name of God is blasphemed among the Gentiles through you,"* as it is written.

> YOU THEREFORE WHICH TEACH ANOTHER, DO YOU NOT TEACH YOURSELF?

For circumcision indeed profits, if you keep the law: but if you be a 20 breaker of the law, your circumcision is made uncircumcision. Therefore if the uncircumcision keeps the righteousness of the law, shall not his uncircumcision be counted for circumcision? And shall not uncircumcision which is by nature, if it fulfills the law, judge you, who by the letter and circumcision do transgress the law?

For he is not a Jew, which is one outwardly; neither is that circumci- 21 sion, which is outward in the flesh: but he is a Jew, which is one inwardly; and circumcision is that of the heart, in the spirit, and not in the letter; whose praise is not of men, but of God.

Unrighteous and Righteous
Romans 3:1-20

What advantage then has the Jew? or what profit is there of circumci- 22 sion? Much every way: chiefly, because unto them were committed the oracles of God.

For what if some did not believe? shall their unbelief make the faith- 23 fulness of God without effect? God forbid: yes, let God be true, but every man a liar; as it is written, *"That you might be justified in your sayings, and might overcome when you are judged."*

But if our unrighteousness commends the righteousness of God, what 24 shall we say? Is God unrighteous who takes vengeance? (I speak as a man) God forbid: for then how shall God judge the world? For if the truth of God has more abounded through my lie unto his glory; why yet am I also judged as a sinner? And not rather, (as we be slanderously reported, and as some affirm that we say), "Let us do evil, that good may come"? whose condemnation is just.

What then? are we better than they? No, in no way: for we have before 25 charged both Jews and Gentiles, that they are all under sin; as it is written, *"There is none righteous, no, not one: there is none that understands, there is none that seeks after God.* They are all gone out of the way, they are together become unprofitable; there is none that does good, no, not one." *"Their throat is an open tomb; with their tongues they have used deceit"*; *"the poison of asps is under their lips"*: *"whose mouth is full of cursing and bitterness." "Their feet are swift to shed blood: destruction and misery are in their ways: and the way of peace have they not known"*: *"there is no fear of God before their eyes."*

Now we know that whatsoever things the law says, it says to them who 26 are under the law: that every mouth may be stopped, and all the world may become accountable before God. Therefore by the deeds of the law there shall no flesh be justified in his sight: for by the law is the knowledge of sin.

CHAPTER 99

‥ JUSTIFICATION AND FAITH ‥

Law of Faith
Romans 3:21-31

1 But now the righteousness of God without the law is manifested, being witnessed by the law and the prophets; even the righteousness of God which is by faith of Jesus Christ unto all and upon all them that believe: for there is no difference: for all have sinned, and come short of the glory of God; being justified freely by his grace through the redemption that is in Christ Jesus: whom God has set forth to be a sacrifice through faith in his blood, to declare his righteousness for the remission of sins that are past, through the forbearance of God; to declare, I say, at this time his righteousness: that he might be just, and the justifier of him which believes in Jesus.

2 Where is boasting then? It is excluded. By what law? of works? No: but by the law of faith. Therefore we conclude that a man is justified by faith without the deeds of the law.

3 Is he the God of the Jews only? is he not also of the Gentiles? Yes, of the Gentiles also: seeing it is one God, which shall justify the circumcision by faith, and uncircumcision through faith.

4 Do we then make void the law through faith? God forbid: yes, we establish the law.

Steps of Faith
Romans 4:1-12

5 What shall we say then that Abraham our father, as pertaining to the flesh, has found? For if Abraham were justified by works, he has something to boast; but not before God. For what says the scripture? *"Abraham believed God, and it was counted unto him for righteousness."*

6 Now to him that works is the reward not counted of grace, but of debt. But to him that works not, but believes on him that justifies the ungodly, his faith is counted for righteousness.

Even as David also describes the blessedness of the man, unto whom 7
God counts righteousness without works, saying, *"Blessed are they whose
iniquities are forgiven, and whose sins are covered. Blessed is the man to
whom the Lord will not count sin."*

Comes this blessedness then upon the circumcision only, or upon the 8
uncircumcision also? for we say that *faith was counted to Abraham for righteousness.* How was it then counted? when he was in circumcision, or in
uncircumcision? Not in circumcision, but in uncircumcision. And he
received the sign of circumcision, a seal of the righteousness of the faith
which he had yet being uncircumcised: that he might be the father of all
them that believe, though they be not circumcised; that righteousness might
be counted unto them also: and the father of circumcision to them who are
not of the circumcision only, but who also walk in the steps of that faith of
our father Abraham, which he had being yet uncircumcised.

Promise by Faith
Romans 4:13-25

For the promise, that he should be the heir of the world, was not to 9
Abraham, or to his seed, through the law, but through the righteousness of
faith. For if they which are of the law be heirs, faith is made void, and the
promise made of no effect: because the law works wrath: for where no law
is, there is no transgression.

Therefore it is of faith, that it might be by grace; to the end the prom- 10
ise might be sure to all the seed; not to that only which is of the law, but to
that also which is of the faith of Abraham; who is the father of us all, (as it
is written, *"I have made you a father of many nations,"*) before him whom
he believed, even God, who quickens the dead, and calls those things which
be not as though they were. Who against hope believed in hope, that he
might become the father of many nations, according to that which was spoken, *"So shall your seed be."*

And being not weak in faith, he considered not his own body now 11
dead, when he was about a hundred years old, neither yet the deadness of
Sara's womb. He doubted not at the promise of God through unbelief; but
was strong in faith, giving glory to God; and being fully persuaded that,
what he had promised, he was able also to perform. And therefore *"it was
counted to him for righteousness."*

Now it was not written for his sake alone, that it was counted to him; 12
but for us also, to whom it shall be counted, if we believe on him that raised
up Jesus our Lord from the dead; who was delivered for our offenses, and
was raised again for our justification.

Peace With God
Romans 5:1-11

Therefore being justified by faith, we have peace with God through 13
our Lord Jesus Christ: by whom also we have access by faith into this grace

13 wherein we stand, and rejoice in hope of the glory of God. And not only so, but we boast in tribulations also: knowing that tribulation works patience; and patience, experience; and experience, hope: and hope makes not disappointment; because the love of God is poured in our hearts by the Holy Ghost which is given unto us.

14 For when we were yet without strength, in due time Christ died for the ungodly. For rarely for a righteous man will one die: yet perhaps for a good man someone would even dare to die. But God commends his love toward us, in that, while we were yet sinners, Christ died for us.

> GOD COMMENDS HIS LOVE TOWARD US, IN THAT, WHILE WE WERE YET SINNERS, CHRIST DIED FOR US.

15 Much more then, being now justified by his blood, we shall be saved from wrath through him.

16 For if, when we were enemies, we were reconciled to God by the death of his Son, much more, being reconciled, we shall be saved by his life. And not only that, but we also rejoice in God through our Lord Jesus Christ, by whom we have now received the atonement.

Contrast of Adam and Christ
Romans 5:12-21

17 Therefore, as by one man sin entered into the world, and death by sin; and so death passed upon all men, for all have sinned: (for until the law sin was in the world: but sin is not charged when there is no law. Nevertheless death reigned from Adam to Moses, even over them that had not sinned after the likeness of Adam's transgression, who is the figure of him that was to come.

18 But not as the offense, so also is the free gift. For if through the offense of one many be dead, much more the grace of God, and the gift by grace, which is by one man, Jesus Christ, has abounded unto many. And not as it was by one that sinned, so is the gift: for the judgment was by one to condemnation, but the free gift is of many offenses unto justification. For if by one man's offense death reigned by one; much more they which receive abundance of grace and of the gift of righteousness shall reign in life by one, Jesus Christ).

19 Therefore as by the offense of one judgment came upon all men to condemnation; even so by the righteousness of one the free gift came upon all men unto justification of life. For as by one man's disobedience many were made sinners, so by the obedience of one shall many be made righteous.

> AS BY ONE MAN'S DISOBEDIENCE MANY WERE MADE SINNERS, SO BY THE OBEDIENCE OF ONE SHALL MANY BE MADE RIGHTEOUS.

Moreover the law entered, that the offense might abound. But where 20 sin abounded, grace did much more abound: that as sin has reigned unto death, even so might grace reign through righteousness unto eternal life by Jesus Christ our Lord.

CHAPTER 100

SUBMISSION TO GOD'S WILL
New Life in Christ
Romans 6:1-14

1   What shall we say then? Shall we continue in sin, that grace may abound? God forbid. How shall we, that are dead to sin, live any longer therein? Do you not know, that as many of us as were baptized into Jesus Christ were baptized into his death? Therefore we are buried with him by baptism into death: that like as Christ was raised up from the dead by the glory of the Father, even so we also should walk in newness of life.

2   For if we have been planted together in the likeness of his death, we shall be also in the likeness of his resurrection: knowing this, that our old man is crucified with him, that the body of sin might be destroyed, that henceforth we should not serve sin. For he that is dead is freed from sin.

3   Now if we be dead with Christ, we believe that we shall also live with him: knowing that Christ being raised from the dead dies no more; death has no more dominion over him. For in that he died, he died unto sin once: but in that he lives, he lives unto God. Likewise consider also yourselves to be dead indeed unto sin, but alive unto God through Jesus Christ our Lord.

4   Let not sin therefore reign in your mortal body, that you should obey it in the lusts thereof. Neither yield your members as instruments of unrighteousness unto sin: but yield yourselves unto God, as those that are alive from the dead, and your members as instruments of righteousness unto God. For sin shall not have dominion over you: for you are not under the law, but under grace.

Wages of Sin
Romans 6:15-23

5   What then? shall we sin, because we are not under the law, but under grace? God forbid. Do you not know, that to whom you yield yourselves

servants to obey, his servants you are to whom you obey; whether of sin 5
unto death, or of obedience unto righteousness? But God be thanked, that
you were the servants of sin, but you have obeyed from the heart that form
of doctrine which was delivered you. Being then made free from sin, you
became the servants of righteousness.

I speak after the manner of men because of the infirmity of your flesh: 6
for as you have yielded your members servants to uncleanness and to iniquity unto iniquity; even so now yield your members servants to righteousness unto holiness. For when you were the servants of sin, you were free
from righteousness. What fruit had you then in those things of which you
are now ashamed? for the end of those things is death.

But now being made free from 7
sin, and becoming servants to God, you
have your fruit unto holiness, and the
end everlasting life. For the wages of
sin is death; but the gift of God is eternal life through Jesus Christ our Lord.

> FOR THE WAGES OF SIN IS
> DEATH; BUT THE GIFT OF GOD
> IS ETERNAL LIFE THROUGH
> JESUS CHRIST.

Motions of Sin
Romans 7:1-6

Do you not know, brethren, (for I speak to them that know the law), 8
how that the law has dominion over a man as long as he lives? For the
woman which has a husband is bound by the law to her husband so long as
he lives; but if the husband be dead, she is loosed from the law of her husband. So then if, while her husband lives, she be married to another man,
she shall be called an adulteress: but if her husband be dead, she is free from
that law; so that she is no adulteress, though she be married to another man.

Therefore, my brethren, you also are become dead to the law by the 9
body of Christ; that you should be married to another, even to him who is
raised from the dead, that we should bring forth fruit unto God. For when
we were in the flesh, the motions of sins, which were by the law, did work
in our natures to bring forth fruit unto death. But now we are delivered from
the law, that being dead wherein we were held; that we should serve in newness of spirit, and not in the oldness of the letter.

Law of Sin
Romans 7:7-25

What shall we say then? Is the law sin? God forbid. No, I had not 10
known sin, but by the law: for I had not known lust, except the law had said,
"You shall not covet." But sin, taking opportunity by the commandment,
produced in me all manner of evil desire. For without the law sin was dead.

For I was alive without the law once: but when the commandment 11
came, sin revived, and I died. And the commandment, which was ordained
to life, I found to be unto death. For sin, taking opportunity by the commandment, deceived me, and by it slew me. Therefore the law is holy, and
the commandment holy, and just, and good.

12 Was then that which is good made death unto me? God forbid. But sin, that it might appear sin, working death in me by that which is good; that sin by the commandment might become exceedingly sinful. For we know that the law is spiritual: but I am carnal, sold under sin.

13 For that which I do I know not: for what I would, that do I not; but what I hate, that do I. If then I do that which I would not, I consent unto the law that it is good.

14 Now then it is no more I that do it, but sin that dwells in me. For I know that in me (that is, in my flesh,) dwells no good thing: for to will is present with me; but how to perform that which is good I find not. For the good that I would I do not: but the evil which I would not, that I do. Now if I do that I would not, it is no more I that do it, but sin that dwells in me.

15 I find then a law, that, when I would do good, evil is present with me.

> I DELIGHT IN THE LAW OF GOD ACCORDING TO THE INWARD MAN.

For I delight in the law of God according to the inward man: but I see another law in my members, warring against the law of my mind, and bringing me into captivity to the law of sin which is in my members. O wretched man that I am! who shall deliver me from the body of this death?

16 I thank God through Jesus Christ our Lord. So then with the mind I myself serve the law of God; but with the flesh the law of sin.

CHAPTER 101

SPIRIT'S PRESENCE IN BELIEVERS
Law of the Spirit
Romans 8:1-17

There is therefore now no condemnation to them which are in Christ 1 Jesus, who walk not after the flesh, but according to the Spirit. For the law of the Spirit of life in Christ Jesus has made me free from the law of sin and death.

For what the law could not do, in that it was weak through the flesh, 2 God sending his own Son in the likeness of sinful flesh, and for sin, condemned sin in the flesh: that the righteousness of the law might be fulfilled in us, who walk not after the flesh, but according to the Spirit.

For they that are after the flesh do mind the things of the flesh; but 3 they that are according to the Spirit the things of the Spirit. For to be carnally minded is death; but to be spiritually minded is life and peace. Because the carnal mind is hostility against God: for it is not subject to the law of God, neither indeed can be. So then they that are in the flesh cannot please God.

But you are not in the flesh, but in the Spirit, if so be that the Spirit of 4 God dwells in you. Now if any man has not the Spirit of Christ, he is none of his. And if Christ be in you, the body is dead because of sin; but the Spirit is life because of righteousness. But if the Spirit of him that raised up Jesus from the dead dwells in you, he that raised up Christ from the dead shall also quicken your mortal bodies by his Spirit that dwells in you.

Therefore, brethren, we are debtors, not to the flesh, to live after the 5 flesh. For if you live after the flesh, you shall die: but if you through the Spirit do put to death the deeds of the body, you shall live. For as many as are led by the Spirit of God, they are the sons of God.

For you have not received the spirit of bondage again to fear; but you 6 have received the Spirit of adoption, whereby we cry, "Abba, Father." The

6 Spirit himself bears witness with our spirit, that we are the children of God: and if children, then heirs; heirs of God, and joint-heirs with Christ; if so be that we suffer with him, that we may be also glorified together.

Glory to Be Revealed Intercession
Romans 8:18-30

7   For I consider that the sufferings of this present time are not worthy to be compared with the glory which shall be revealed in us. For the earnest expectation of the creation waits for the manifestation of the sons of God. For the creation was made subject to vanity, not willingly, but by reason of him who has subjected the same in hope, because the creation itself also shall be delivered from the bondage of corruption into the glorious liberty of the children of God.

8   For we know that the whole creation groans and labors in pain together until now. And not only they, but ourselves also, which have the

> WE ARE SAVED BY HOPE: BUT HOPE THAT IS SEEN IS NOT HOPE.

first fruits of the Spirit, even we ourselves groan within ourselves, waiting for the adoption, that is, the redemption of our body. For we are saved by hope: but hope that is seen is not hope: for what a man sees, why does he yet hope for? But if we hope for that we see not, then do we with patience wait for it.

9   Likewise the Spirit also helps our weaknesses: for we know not what we should pray for as we ought: but the Spirit himself makes intercession for us with groanings which cannot be uttered. And he that searches the hearts knows what is the mind of the Spirit, because he makes intercession for the saints according to the will of God.

10   And we know that all things work together for good to them that love God, to them who are the called according to his purpose. For whom he did

> ALL THINGS WORK TOGETHER FOR GOOD TO THEM THAT LOVE GOD.

foreknow, he also did predestine to be conformed to the image of his Son, that he might be the firstborn among many brethren. Moreover whom he did predestine, them he also called: and whom he called, them he also justified: and whom he justified, them he also glorified.

More Than Conquerors
Romans 8:31-39

11   What shall we then say to these things? If God be for us, who can be against us? He that spared not his own Son, but delivered him up for us all, how shall he not with him also freely give us all things? Who shall lay anything to the charge of God's elect? It is God that justifies. Who is he that condemns? It is Christ that died, yes rather, that is risen again, who is even at the right hand of God, who also makes intercession for us.

Who shall separate us from the love of Christ? shall tribulation, or dis- 12 tress, or persecution, or famine, or nakedness, or peril, or sword? As it is written, "For your sake we are killed all the day long; we are accounted as sheep for the slaughter." No, in all these things we are more than con-querors through him that loved us. For I am persuaded, that neither death, nor life, nor angels, nor principalities, nor

> WHO SHALL SEPARATE US FROM THE LOVE OF CHRIST?

powers, nor things present, nor things to come, nor height, nor depth, nor any other creature, shall be able to separate us from the love of God, which is in Christ Jesus our Lord.

CHAPTER 102

⊷ ROLE OF HEART AND MOUTH IN SALVATION ⊷

Chosen People
Romans 9:1-18

1   I say the truth in Christ, I do not lie, my conscience also bearing me witness in the Holy Ghost, that I have great heaviness and continual sorrow in my heart. For I could wish that my own self were accursed from Christ for my brethren, my own people according to the flesh: who are Israelites; to whom pertains the adoption, and the glory, and the covenants, and the giving of the law, and the service of God, and the promises; whose are the fathers, and of whom as concerning the flesh Christ came, who is over all, God blessed for ever. Amen.

2   Not as though the word of God has taken no effect. For they are not all Israel, which are of Israel: neither, because they are the seed of Abraham, are they all children: but, *"In Isaac shall your seed be called."* That is, They which are the children of the flesh, these are not the children of God: but the children of the promise are counted for the seed. For this is the word of promise, *"At this time will I come, and Sarah shall have a son."*

3   And not only this; but when Rebekah also had conceived by one, even by our father Isaac; (for the children being not yet born, neither having done any good or evil, that the purpose of God according to election might stand, not of works, but of him that calls); it was said unto her, *"The older shall serve the younger."* As it is written, *"Jacob have I loved, but Esau have I hated."*

4   What shall we say then? Is there unrighteousness with God? God forbid. For he says to Moses, *"I will have mercy on whom I will have mercy, and I will have compassion on whom I will have compassion."*

5   So then it is not of him that wills, nor of him that runs, but of God that shows mercy. For the scripture says unto Pharaoh, *"Even for this same purpose have I raised you up, that I might show my power in you, and that my*

name might be declared throughout all the earth." Therefore has he mercy 5
on whom he will have mercy, and whom he will he hardens.

Contrary People
Romans 9:19-33

You will say then unto me, "Why does he yet find fault? For who has 6
resisted his will?" No but, O man, who are you that reply against God?
Shall the thing formed say to him that formed it, "Why have you made me
thus?" Has not the potter power over the clay, of the same lump to make one
vessel unto honor, and another unto dishonor?

What if God, willing to show his wrath, and to make his power known, 7
endured with much patience the vessels of wrath fitted to destruction: and
that he might make known the riches of his glory on the vessels of mercy,
which he had long ago prepared unto glory, even us, whom he has called,
not of the Jews only, but also of the Gentiles

As he says also in Hosea, *"I will call them my people, which were not* 8
my people; and her beloved, which was not beloved". *"And it shall come to*
pass, that in the place where it was said unto them, 'You are not my people';
there shall they be called the children of the living God."

Isaiah also cries out concerning Israel, *"Though the number of the* 9
children of Israel be as the sand of the sea, a remnant shall be saved: for he
will finish the work, and cut it short in righteousness: because a short work
will the Lord make upon the earth." And as Isaiah said before, *"Except the*
Lord of hosts had left us a seed, we had been as Sodom, and been made like
Gomorrah."

What shall we say then? That the Gentiles, which followed not after 10
righteousness, have attained to righteousness, even the righteousness which
is of faith. But Israel, which followed after the law of righteousness, has not
attained to the law of righteousness. Why so? Because they sought it not by
faith, but as it were by the works of the law. For they stumbled at that stumbling stone; as it is written, *"Behold, I lay in Zion a stumbling stone and*
rock of offense: and whosoever believes on him shall not be ashamed."

Salvation for All
Romans 10:1-21

Brethren, my heart's desire and prayer to God for Israel is, that they 11
might be saved. For I bear them witness that they have a zeal of God, but
not according to knowledge. For they being ignorant of God's righteousness, and going about to establish their own righteousness, have not sub-
mitted themselves unto the righteousness of God. For Christ is the end of
the law for righteousness to everyone that believes.

For Moses describes the righteousness which is of the law, *"That the* 12
man which does those things shall live by them." But the righteousness
which is of faith speaks in this way, *"Say not in your heart, 'Who shall*
ascend into heaven?'" (that is, to bring Christ down from above): or, "'Who

12 shall descend into the deep?'" (that is, to bring up Christ again from the dead).

13 But what does it say? *"The word is near you, even in your mouth, and in your heart"*: that is, the word of faith, which we preach; that if you shall confess with your mouth the Lord Jesus, and shall believe in your heart that God has raised him from the dead, you shall be saved. For with the heart man believes unto righteousness; and with the mouth confession is made unto salvation.

14 For the scripture says, *"Whosoever believes on him shall not be ashamed."* For there is no difference between the Jew and the Greek: for the same Lord over all is rich unto all that call upon him. For *"whosoever shall call upon the name of the Lord shall be saved."*

15 How then shall they call on him in whom they have not believed? and how shall they believe in him of whom they have not heard? and how shall they hear without a preacher? And how shall they preach, except they be sent? as it is written, *"How beautiful are the feet of them that preach the gospel of peace, and bring glad tidings of good things!"*

> HOW SHALL THEY BELIEVE IN HIM OF WHOM THEY HAVE NOT HEARD?

16 But they have not all obeyed the gospel. For Isaiah says, *"Lord, who has believed our report?"* So then faith comes by hearing, and hearing by the word of God.

17 But I say, Have they not heard? Yes indeed, *"their sound went into all the earth, and their words unto the ends of the world."* But I say, Did not Israel know? First Moses says, *"I will provoke you to jealousy by them that are not a nation, and by a foolish nation I will anger you."*

> FAITH COMES BY HEARING, AND HEARING BY THE WORD OF GOD.

18 But Isaiah is very bold, and says, *"I was found of them that sought me not; I was made manifest unto them that asked not after me."* But to Israel he says, *"All day long I have stretched forth my hands unto a disobedient and contrary people."*

CHAPTER 103

STRUGGLE FOR SALVATION

Salvation for Jews
Romans 11:1-10

I say then, Has God cast away his people? God forbid. For I also am 1
an Israelite, of the seed of Abraham, of the tribe of Benjamin. God has not
cast away his people which he foreknew. Do you not know what the scripture says of Elijah? how he makes intercession to God against Israel, saying, *"Lord, they have killed your prophets, and dug down your altars; and
I alone am left, and they seek my life."* But what says the answer of God unto
him? *"I have reserved to myself seven thousand men, who have not bowed
the knee to the image of Baal."*

Even so then at this present time also there is a remnant according to 2
the election of grace. And if by grace, then is it no more of works: otherwise grace is no more grace. But if it be of works, then is it no more grace:
otherwise work is no more work.

What then? Israel has not obtained that which it seeks for; but the elect 3
has obtained it, and the rest were blinded (according as it is written, *"God
has given them the spirit of slumber, eyes that they should not see, and ears
that they should not hear); unto this day."* And David says, *"Let their table
be made a snare, and a trap, and a stumbling block, and a repayment unto
them: let their eyes be darkened, that they may not see, and bow down their
back always."*

Salvation for Gentiles
Romans 11:11-24

I say then, Have they stumbled that they should fall? God forbid: but 4
rather through their fall salvation is come unto the Gentiles, to provoke them
to jealousy. Now if the fall of them be the riches of the world, and the dimin-
ishing of them the riches of the Gentiles; how much more their fulness?

5   For I speak to you Gentiles, inasmuch as I am the apostle of the Gentiles, I magnify my office: if by any means I may provoke to jealousy them which are my flesh, and might save some of them. For if the casting away of them be the reconciling of the world, what shall the receiving of them be, but life from the dead? For if the first fruit be holy, the lump is also holy: and if the root be holy, so are the branches.

6   And if some of the branches be broken off, and you, being a wild olive tree, were grafted in among them, and with them partake of the root and fatness of the olive tree; do not boast against the branches. But if you boast, you bear not the root, but the root you. You will say then, "The branches were broken off, that I might be grafted in."

7   Granted; because of unbelief they were broken off, and you stand by faith. Be not high-minded, but fear: for if God spared not the natural branches, take heed lest he also does not spare you.

8   Behold therefore the goodness and severity of God: on them which fell, severity; but toward you, goodness, if you continue in his goodness: otherwise you also shall be cut off. And they also, if they do not continue still in unbelief, shall be grafted in: for God is able to graft them in again. For if you were cut out of the olive tree which is wild by nature, and were grafted contrary to nature into a good olive tree: how much more shall these, which be the natural branches, be grafted into their own olive tree?

Salvation in Times Past
Romans 11:25-32

9   For I would not, brethren, that you should be ignorant of this mystery, lest you should be wise in your own conceits; that blindness in part is happened to Israel, until the fulness of the Gentiles has come in. And so all Israel shall be saved: as it is written, *"There shall come out of Zion the Deliverer, and shall turn away ungodliness from Jacob: for this is my covenant unto them, when I shall take away their sins."*

10   As concerning the gospel, they are enemies for your sakes: but as concerning the election, they are beloved for the fathers' sakes. For the gifts and calling of God are without repentance. For as you in times past have not believed God, yet have now obtained mercy through their unbelief: even so have these also now not believed, that through your mercy they also may obtain mercy. For God has concluded them all in unbelief, that he might have mercy upon all.

Unsearchable Ways of God
Romans 11:33-36

11   O the depth of the riches both of the wisdom and knowledge of God! how unsearchable are his judgments, and his ways past finding out! *"For who has known the mind of the Lord? or who has been his counselor? Or who has first given to him, and it shall be repaid unto him again?"* For of him, and through him, and to him, are all things: to whom be glory for ever. Amen.

CHAPTER 104

HUMILITY AND SUBJECTION
New Life in Christ
Romans 12:1-8

I urge you therefore, brethren, by the mercies of God, that you present 1
your bodies a living sacrifice, holy, acceptable unto God, which is your reasonable service. And be not conformed to this world: but be you transformed by the renewing of your mind, that you may test what is that good,
and acceptable, and perfect, will of God.

For I say, through the grace given unto me, to every man that is among 2
you, not to think of himself more highly than he ought to think; but to think
soberly, according as God has dealt to every man the measure of faith. For
as we have many members in one body, and all members have not the same
office: so we, being many, are one body in Christ, and every one members
one of another.

Having then gifts differing according to the grace that is given to us, 3
whether prophecy, let us prophesy according to the proportion of faith; or
ministry, let us wait on our ministering: or he that teaches, on teaching; or
he that exhorts, on exhortation: he that gives, let him do it with generosity;
he that rules, with diligence; he that shows mercy, with cheerfulness.

Christian Way of Life
Romans 12:9-21

Let love be without pretense. Abhor that which is evil; cling to that 4
which is good. Be kindly affectionate one to another with brotherly love; in
honor preferring one another; not lazy in business; fervent in spirit; serving
the Lord; rejoicing in hope; patient in tribulation; continuing urgently in
prayer; distributing to the needs of saints; given to hospitality.

Bless them which persecute you: bless, and curse not. Rejoice with 5
them that do rejoice, and weep with them that weep. Be of the same mind

5 one toward another. Mind not high things, but relate to men of low status. Be not wise in your own conceits. Repay to no man evil for evil. Provide things honorable in the sight of all men. If it be possible, as much as lies in you, live peaceably with all men.

6 Dearly beloved, avenge not yourselves, but rather give room unto wrath: for it is written, *"Vengeance is mine; I will repay,"* says the Lord. Therefore *"if your enemy hungers, feed him; if he thirsts, give him drink: for in so doing you shall heap coals of fire on his head."* Be not overcome of evil, but overcome evil with good.

> BE NOT OVERCOME OF EVIL, BUT OVERCOME EVIL WITH GOOD.

Duties Toward Authorities
Romans 13:1-7

7 Let every soul be subject unto the higher authorities. For there is no authority but of God: the authorities that be are ordained of God. Whosoever therefore resists the authority, resists the ordinance of God: and they that resist shall receive to themselves judgment. For rulers are not a terror to good works, but to the evil. Will you then not be afraid of the authority? do that which is good, and you shall have praise of the same: for it is the servant of God to you for good. But if you do that which is evil, be afraid; for it bears not the sword in vain: for it is the servant of God, an avenger to execute wrath upon him that does evil.

8 Therefore you must of necessity be subject, not only for wrath, but also for the sake of conscience. For this reason you pay tribute also: for they are God's ministers, attending continually upon this very thing. Render therefore to all their due: tribute to whom tribute is due; custom to whom custom; fear to whom fear; honor to whom honor.

Duties Toward One Another
Romans 13:8-10

9 Owe no man anything, but to love one another: for he that loves another has fulfilled the law. For this, *"You shall not commit adultery," "You shall not kill," "You shall not steal," "You shall not bear false witness," "You shall not covet"*; and if there be any other commandment, it is briefly summed up in this saying, namely, *"You shall love your neighbor as yourself."* Love works no harm to his neighbor: therefore love is the fulfillment of the law.

> LET EVERY SOUL BE SUBJECT UNTO THE HIGHER AUTHORITIES. FOR THERE IS NO AUTHORITY BUT OF GOD: THE AUTHORITIES THAT BE ARE ORDAINED OF GOD.

Awaken in the Light
Romans 13:11-14

10 And that, knowing the time, that now it is high time to awake out of sleep: for now is our salvation nearer than when we believed. The night is

far spent, the day is at hand: let us therefore cast off the works of darkness, 10
and let us put on the armor of light. Let us walk decently, as in the day; not
in carousing and drunkenness, not in promiscuity and wantonness, not in
strife and envy. But put on the Lord Jesus Christ, and make no provision for
the flesh, to fulfill the lusts thereof.

CHAPTER 105

..⊹ TRUE NATURE OF CHRISTIANITY ⊹..

God's Accounting
Romans 14:1-12

1   Receive him that is weak in the faith, but not to doubtful disputes. For one believes that he may eat all things: another, who is weak, eats vegetables. Let not him that eats despise him that eats not; and let not him which eats not judge him that eats: for God has received him. Who are you that judge another man's servant? to his own master he stands or falls. Yes, he shall be held up: for God is able to make him stand.

2   One man esteems one day above another: another esteems every day alike. Let every man be fully persuaded in his own mind. He that regards the day, regards it unto the Lord; and he that regards not the day, to the Lord he does not regard it. He that eats, eats to the Lord, for he gives God thanks; and he that eats not, to the Lord he eats not, and gives God thanks.

3   For none of us lives to himself, and no man dies to himself. For whether we live, we live unto the Lord; and whether we die, we die unto the Lord: whether we live therefore, or die, we are the Lord's. For to this end Christ both died, and rose, and revived, that he might be Lord both of the dead and living.

4   But why do you judge your brother? or why do you reject your brother? for we shall all stand before the judgment seat of Christ. For it is written, *"As I live, says the Lord, every knee shall bow to me, and every tongue shall confess to God."* So then every one of us shall give account of himself to God.

God's Kingdom
Romans 14:13-23

5   Let us not therefore judge one another anymore: but judge this instead, that no man put a stumbling block or an obstacle to fall in his brother's way.

I know, and am persuaded by the Lord Jesus, that there is nothing unclean 5
of itself: but to him that considers anything to be unclean, to him it is
unclean. But if your brother be dis-
tressed with your food, now you do not
walk lovingly. Do not destroy him
with your food, for whom Christ died.

> LET US NOT THEREFORE JUDGE
> ONE ANOTHER ANYMORE.

Let not then your good be denounced: for the kingdom of God is not 6
food and drink; but righteousness, and peace, and joy in the Holy Ghost. For
he that in these things serves Christ is acceptable to God, and approved of
men.

Let us therefore pursue the things which make for peace, and things 7
with which one may edify another. For food do not destroy the work of God.
All things indeed are pure; but it is
evil for that man who eats with
offense. It is good neither to eat flesh,
nor to drink wine, nor anything whereby your brother stumbles, or is fallen
away, or is made weak.

> PURSUE THE THINGS WHICH
> MAKE FOR PEACE, AND THINGS
> WITH WHICH ONE MAY EDIFY
> ANOTHER.

Have you faith? have it to yourself before God. Happy is he that con- 8
demns not himself in that thing which he approves. And he that doubts is
condemned if he eats, because he eats not of faith: for whatsoever is not of
faith is sin.

Help of the Weak by the Strong
Romans 15:1-6

We then that are strong ought to bear the failings of the weak, and not 9
to please ourselves. Let every one of us please his neighbor for his good to
edification. For even Christ pleased not himself; but, as it is written, *"The
insults of them that insulted you fell on me."* For whatsoever things were
written before were written for our learning, that we through patience and
comfort of the scriptures might have hope.

Now the God of patience and consolation grant you to be like-minded 10
one toward another according to Christ Jesus: that you may with one mind
and one mouth glorify God, even the Father of our Lord Jesus Christ.

One Gospel
Romans 15:7-13

Therefore receive one another, as Christ also received us to the glory 11
of God. Now I say that Jesus Christ was a servant of the circumcision for
the truth of God, to confirm the promises made unto the fathers: and that
the Gentiles might glorify God for his mercy; as it is written, *"For this
cause I will confess to you among the Gentiles, and sing unto your name."*
And again he says, *"Rejoice, you Gentiles, with his people."* And again,
"Praise the Lord, all you Gentiles; and laud him, all you people."

12   And again, Isaiah says, *"There shall be a root of Jesse, and he that shall rise to reign over the Gentiles; in him shall the Gentiles trust."* May the God of hope fill you with all joy and peace in believing, that you may abound in hope, through the power of the Holy Ghost.

CHAPTER 106

CONNECTION AND CONCLUSION

Minister to the Gentiles
Romans 15:14-21

And I myself also am persuaded of you, my brethren, that you also are 1 full of goodness, filled with all knowledge, able also to admonish one another. Nevertheless, brethren, I have written the more boldly unto you in some points, as putting you in mind, because of the grace that is given to me of God, that I should be the minister of Jesus Christ to the Gentiles, ministering the gospel of God, that the offering up of the Gentiles might be acceptable, being sanctified by the Holy Ghost.

I have therefore of which I may glory through Jesus Christ in those 2 things which pertain to God. For I will not dare to speak of any of those things which Christ has not wrought by me, to make the Gentiles obedient, by word and deed, through mighty signs and wonders, by the power of the Spirit of God; so that from Jerusalem, and round about unto Illyricum, I have fully preached the gospel of Christ.

Yes, so have I striven to preach the gospel, not where Christ was 3 named, lest I should build upon another man's foundation: but as it is written, *"To whom he was not spoken of, they shall see: and they that have not heard shall understand."*

Plan to Come to Rome
Romans 15:22-33

For which cause also I have been much hindered from coming to you. 4 But now having no more place in these parts, and having a great desire these many years to come unto you; whenever I take my journey into Spain, I will come to you: for I trust to see you in my journey, and to be brought on my way toward there by you, if first I be for a little while filled with your company.

5   But now I go unto Jerusalem to minister unto the saints. For it has pleased them of Macedonia and Achaia to make a certain contribution for the poor saints which are at Jerusalem. It has pleased them indeed; and their debtors they are. For if the Gentiles have been made partakers of their spiritual things, their duty is also to minister unto them in material things.

6   When therefore I have performed this, and have sealed to them this fruit, I will come by you into Spain. And I am sure that, when I come unto you, I shall come in the fulness of the blessing of the gospel of Christ.

7   Now I urge you, brethren, for the Lord Jesus Christ's sake, and for the love of the Spirit, that you strive together with me in your prayers to God for me; that I may be delivered from them that do not believe in Judea; and that my service which I have for Jerusalem may be accepted of the saints; that I may come unto you with joy by the will of God, and may with you be refreshed. Now the God of peace be with you all. Amen.

Personal Greetings
Romans 16:1-24

8   I commend unto you Phoebe our sister, which is a servant of the church which is at Cenchrea: that you receive her in the Lord, as becomes saints, and that you assist her in whatsoever business she has need of you: for she has been a helper of many, and of myself also.

9   Greet Priscilla and Aquila my helpers in Christ Jesus: who have for my life risked their own necks: unto whom not only I give thanks, but also all the churches of the Gentiles. Likewise greet the church that is in their house. Greet my beloved Epaenetus, who is the first fruits of Achaia unto Christ.

10   Greet Mary, who bestowed much labor on us. Greet Andronicus and Junia, my relatives, and my fellow prisoners, who are of note among the apostles, who also were in Christ before me.

11   Greet Amplias my beloved in the Lord. Greet Urbane, our helper in Christ, and Stachys my beloved. Greet Apelles approved in Christ. Greet them which are of Aristobulus' household.

12   Greet Herodion my relative. Greet them that be of the household of Narcissus, which are in the Lord. Greet Tryphena and Tryphosa, who labor in the Lord. Greet the beloved Persis, which labored much in the Lord.

13   Greet Rufus chosen in the Lord, and his mother and mine. Greet Asyncritus, Phlegon, Hermas, Patrobas, Hermes, and the brethren which are with them. Greet Philologus, and Julia, Nereus, and his sister, and Olympas, and all the saints which are with them. Greet one another with a holy kiss. The churches of Christ greet you.

14   Now I urge you, brethren, note them which cause divisions and offenses contrary to the doctrine which you have learned; and avoid them. For they that are such serve not our Lord Jesus Christ, but their own appetites; and by good words and flattering speeches deceive the hearts of

the simple-minded. For your obedience is come abroad unto all men. I am 14
glad therefore on your behalf: but yet I would have you wise unto that which
is good, and innocent concerning evil. And the God of peace shall crush
Satan under your feet shortly. The grace of our Lord Jesus Christ be with
you. Amen.

Timothy my fellow worker, and Lucius, and Jason, and Sosipater, my 15
relatives, greet you. I Tertius, who wrote this letter, greet you in the Lord.
Gaius my host, and of the whole church, greets you. Erastus the city treas-
urer of the city greets you, and Quartus a brother. The grace of our Lord
Jesus Christ be with you all. Amen.

Conclusion and Majestic Closing
Romans 16:25-27

Now to him that is of power to establish you according to my gospel, 16
and the preaching of Jesus Christ, according to the revelation of the mystery, which was kept secret since the world began, but now is made manifest, and by the scriptures of the prophets, according to the commandment
of the everlasting God, made known to all nations for the obedience of faith:
to God only wise, be glory through Jesus Christ for ever. Amen.

PART 25

THIRD MISSIONARY JOURNEY COMPLETION

Paul continues his ministry for Christ, concluding his final mission-ary journey and preaching with passion the correct way to Truth and Life, as demonstrated by Jesus. He implores the faithful but weary seekers that although they may waiver and fall from their vigilance, God will uphold and restore those who are faithful to His purpose in the power of His Spirit. Paul is forewarned by those with him and the prophet Agabus of the danger that awaits him in Jerusalem, yet he cannot be dissuaded from his appointed role as the faithful minister of Christ's message. He continues on his journey undaunted. His faith in God is firm.

I HAVE SHOWED YOU ALL THINGS, HOW THAT SO LABORING YOU OUGHT TO SUPPORT THE WEAK, AND TO REMEMBER THE WORDS OF THE LORD JESUS, HOW HE SAID, "IT IS MORE BLESSED TO GIVE THAN TO RECEIVE." (ACTS 20:35)

CHAPTER 107
PROGRESS BEHIND AND PERIL AHEAD
Ephesus to Macedonia to Greece
Acts 20:1-6

And after the uproar was ceased, Paul called unto himself the disci- 1 ples, and embraced them, and departed to go into Macedonia. And when he had gone over those regions, and had given them much encouragement, he came into Greece, and there stayed three months. And when the Jews plotted against him, as he was about to sail into Syria, he decided to return through Macedonia.

And there accompanied him into Asia Sopater of Berea; and of the 2 Thessalonians, Aristarchus and Secundus; and Gaius of Derbe, and Timothy; and of Asia, Tychicus and Trophimus. These going before tarried for us at Troas. And we sailed away from Philippi after the days of unleavened bread, and came unto them at Troas in five days; where we stayed seven days.

Final Visit With Disciples
Acts 20:7-12

And upon the first day of the week, when the disciples came together 3 to break bread, Paul preached unto them, ready to depart the next day; and continued his speech until midnight. And there were many lamps in the upper room, where they were gathered together.

And there sat in a window a certain young man named Eutychus, being 4 fallen into a deep sleep: and as Paul was long preaching, he sunk down with sleep, and fell down from the third story, and was taken up dead. And Paul went down, and fell on him, and embracing him said, "Trouble not yourselves; for his life is in him." When he therefore was come up again, and had broken bread, and eaten, and talked a long while, even till break of day, so he departed. And they brought the young man alive, and were not a little comforted.

Homeward by Land and by Sea
Acts 20:13-16

And we went ahead to a ship, and sailed unto Assos, there intending 5 to take in Paul: for so had he appointed, intending himself to go on foot.

5 And when he met with us at Assos, we took him on board, and came to Mitylene. And we sailed from there, and came the next day opposite Chios; and the next day we arrived at Samos, and tarried at Trogyllium; and the next day we came to Miletus. For Paul had determined to sail by Ephesus, because he would not spend the time in Asia: for he hastened, if it were possible for him, to be at Jerusalem the day of Pentecost.

Paul's Fond Farewell
Acts 20:17-38

6 And from Miletus he sent to Ephesus, and called the elders of the church. And when they were come to him, he said unto them, "You know, from the first day that I came into Asia, after what manner I have been with you at all seasons, serving the Lord with all humility of mind, and with many tears, and temptations, which befell me by the plotting of the Jews: and how I kept back nothing that was profitable unto you, but have showed you, and have taught you publicly, and from house to house, testifying both to the Jews, and also to the Greeks, repentance toward God, and faith toward our Lord Jesus Christ.

7 "And now, behold, I go bound in the spirit unto Jerusalem, not knowing the things that shall befall me there: except that the Holy Ghost witnesses in every city, saying that bonds and tribulations await me. But none of these things move me, neither count I my life dear unto myself, so that I might finish my course with joy, and the ministry, which I have received of the Lord Jesus, to testify the gospel of the grace of God.

8 "And now, behold, I know that you all, among whom I have gone preaching the kingdom of God, shall see my face no more. Therefore I testify to you this day, that I am pure from the blood of all men. For I have not shunned to declare unto you all the purpose of God.

9 "Take heed therefore unto yourselves, and to all the flock, over which the Holy Ghost has made you overseers, to feed the church of God, which he has purchased with his own blood. For I know this, that after my departure shall fierce wolves enter in among you, not sparing the flock. Also of your own selves shall men arise, speaking perverse things, to draw away disciples after them. Therefore watch, and remember, that by the space of three years I ceased not to warn everyone night and day with tears.

10 "And now, brethren, I commend you to God, and to the word of his grace, which is able to build you up, and to give you an inheritance among all them which are sanctified. I have coveted no man's silver, or gold, or apparel. Yes, you yourselves know, that these hands have ministered unto my necessities, and to them that were with me. I have showed you all things, how that so laboring you ought to support the weak, and to remember the words of the Lord Jesus, how he said, 'It is more blessed to give than to receive.'"

> "IT IS MORE BLESSED TO GIVE THAN TO RECEIVE"

And when he had thus spoken, he kneeled down, and prayed with them 11 all. And they all wept greatly, and fell on Paul's neck, and kissed him, sorrowing most of all for the words which he spoke, that they should see his face no more. And they accompanied him unto the ship.

Third Journey Ends
Acts 21:1-9

And it came to pass, that after we were parted from them, and had 12 launched, we came with a straight course unto Coos, and the following day unto Rhodes, and from there unto Patara. And finding a ship sailing over unto Phoenicia, we went aboard, and set forth. Now when we had sighted Cyprus, we left it on the left hand, and sailed into Syria, and landed at Tyre: for there the ship was to unload its cargo.

And finding disciples, we tarried there seven days: who said to Paul 13 through the Spirit, that he should not go up to Jerusalem. And when we had accomplished those days, we departed and went our way; and they all brought us on our way, with wives and children, till we were out of the city: and we kneeled down on the shore, and prayed. And when we had taken our leave one of another, we took a boat; and they returned home again.

And when we had finished our course from Tyre, we came to Ptole- 14 mais, and greeted the brethren, and stayed with them one day. And the next day we that were of Paul's company departed, and came unto Caesarea: and we entered into the house of Philip the evangelist, which was one of the seven; and stayed with him. And the same man had four daughters, virgins, which did prophesy.

Prophecy of Danger Ahead
Acts 21:10-16

And as we tarried there many days, there came down from Judea a cer- 15 tain prophet, named Agabus. And when he was come unto us, he took Paul's belt, and bound his own hands and feet, and said, "Thus says the Holy Ghost, 'So shall the Jews at Jerusalem bind the man that owns this belt, and shall deliver him into the hands of the Gentiles.'"

And when we heard these things, both we, and they of that place, pleaded 16 with him not to go up to Jerusalem. Then Paul answered, "What do you mean to weep and to break my heart? for I am ready not to be bound only, but also to die at Jerusalem for the name of the Lord Jesus." And when he would not be persuaded, we ceased, saying, "The will of the Lord be done."

And after those days we took up our baggage, and went up to 17 Jerusalem. There went with us also certain of the disciples of Caesarea, and brought with them one Mnason of Cyprus, an early disciple, with whom we should lodge.

Paul Visits Jerusalem Elders
Acts 21:17-26

And when we were come to Jerusalem, the brethren received us gladly. 18 And the following day Paul went in with us unto James; and all the elders

18 were present. And when he had greeted them, he declared in detail what things God had wrought among the Gentiles by his ministry.

19 And when they heard it, they glorified the Lord, and said unto him, "You see, brother, how many thousands of Jews there are which believe; and they are all zealous of the law: and they are informed of you, that you teach all the Jews which are among the Gentiles to forsake Moses, saying that they ought not to circumcise their children, neither to walk according to the customs. What is it therefore? the multitude must of necessity come together: for they will hear that you are come.

20 "Do therefore this that we say to you: We have four men which have a vow on them. Take them, and purify yourself with them, and pay their expenses, that they may shave their heads: and all may know that those things, of which they were informed concerning you, are nothing; but that you yourself also walk orderly, and keep the law.

21 "As concerning the Gentiles which believe, we have written and concluded that they observe no such thing, except only that they keep themselves from things offered to idols, and from blood, and from things slaughtered, and from fornication."

22 Then Paul took the men, and the next day purifying himself with them entered into the temple, to signify the accomplishment of the days of purification, when an offering should be offered for every one of them.

PART 26

Paul's Arrest and Trial

Paul continues his journey to Jerusalem, proclaiming the resurrection to people of all faiths under the higher laws of God. This arouses confusion and division throughout Jerusalem as the people argue among themselves for Paul's death. In a series of confrontations with religious authorities, Paul stands alone in his own defense and in the defense of his God. His answers confuse and divide the authorities, who can find no fault with him. Still they hold him prisoner until they can find a cause, imprisoned by the walls of their doubt and ignorance.

> BE OF GOOD CHEER, PAUL: FOR AS YOU HAVE TESTIFIED OF ME IN JERUSALEM, SO MUST YOU BEAR WITNESS ALSO AT ROME. (ACTS 23:11)

CHAPTER 108

ARREST AND DECLARATION

Paul Seized at the Temple
Acts 21:27-36

1   And when the seven days were almost ended, the Jews which were of Asia, when they saw him in the temple, stirred up all the people, and laid hands on him, Crying out, "Men of Israel, help: This is the man, that teaches all men everywhere against the people, and the law, and this place: and further brought Greeks also into the temple, and has polluted this holy place." (For they had seen previously with him in the city Trophimus an Ephesian, whom they supposed that Paul had brought into the temple.)

2   And all the city was moved, and the people ran together: and they took Paul, and dragged him out of the temple: and immediately the doors were shut. And as they went about to kill him, news came unto the commander of the garrison, that all Jerusalem was in an uproar. Who immediately took soldiers and centurions, and ran down unto them: and when they saw the commander and the soldiers, they stopped beating of Paul.

3   Then the commander came near, and took him, and commanded him to be bound with two chains; and inquired who he was, and what he had done. And some cried one thing, some another, among the multitude: and when he could not know the certainty for the tumult, he commanded him to be carried into the barracks. And when he came upon the stairs, so it was, that he was borne of the soldiers because of the violence of the people. For the multitude of the people followed after, crying, "Away with him."

Paul Before the People
Acts 21:37-39

4   And as Paul was to be led into the barracks, he said unto the commander, "May I speak unto you?" Who said, "Can you speak Greek?" "Are not you that Egyptian, which before these days made an uproar, and led out into the wilderness four thousand men that were murderers?" But Paul said,

"I am a man which am a Jew of Tarsus, a city in Cilicia, a citizen of no 4
obscure city: and, I ask of you, permit me to speak unto the people."

Defense: The Earlier Life
Acts 21:40; 22:1-5

And when he had given him permission, Paul stood on the stairs, and 5
beckoned with the hand unto the people. And when there was made a great
silence, he spoke unto them in the Hebrew tongue, saying, "Men, brethren,
and fathers, hear my defense which I make now unto you." (And when they
heard that he spoke in the Hebrew tongue to them, they kept the more silent:
and he said), "I am indeed a man which am a Jew, born in Tarsus, a city in
Cilicia, but brought up in this city at the feet of Gamaliel, and taught
according to the strict manner of the law of the fathers, and was zealous
toward God, as you all are this day.

"And I persecuted this way unto the death, binding and delivering into 6
prisons both men and women. As also the high priest does bear me witness,
and all the council of the elders: from whom also I received letters unto the
brethren, and went to Damascus, to bring them which were there bound
unto Jerusalem, to be punished.

Defense: The Conversion
Acts 22:6-16

"And it came to pass, that, as I made my journey, and was come near 7
unto Damascus about noon, suddenly
there shone from heaven a great light
round about me. And I fell unto the
ground, and heard a voice saying unto
me, 'Saul, Saul, why do you persecute

> "I AM JESUS OF NAZARETH, WHOM YOU PERSECUTE."

me?' And I answered, 'Who are you, Lord?' And he said unto me, 'I am
Jesus of Nazareth, whom you persecute.'

"And they that were with me indeed saw the light, and were afraid; but 8
they did not hear the voice of him that spoke to me. And I said, 'What shall
I do, Lord?' And the Lord said unto me, 'Arise, and go into Damascus; and
there it shall be told you of all things which are appointed for you to do.'
And when I could not see for the glory of that light, being led by the hand
of them that were with me, I came into Damascus.

"And one Ananias, a devout man according to the law, having a good 9
reputation of all the Jews which dwelt there, came unto me, and stood, and
said unto me, 'Brother Saul, receive your sight.' And the same hour I looked
up upon him.

"And he said, 'The God of our
fathers has chosen you, that you should
know his will, and see that Just One,
and should hear the voice of his mouth.
For you shall be his witness unto all

> "ARISE, AND BE BAPTIZED, AND WASH AWAY YOUR SINS, CALLING ON THE NAME OF THE LORD."

men of what you have seen and heard. And now why do you tarry? arise,
and be baptized, and wash away your sins, calling on the name of the Lord.'

Defense: The Calling
Acts 22:17-21

11   "And it came to pass, that, when I was come again to Jerusalem, even while I prayed in the temple, I was in a trance; and saw him saying unto me, 'Make haste, and get quickly out of Jerusalem: for they will not receive your testimony concerning me.' And I said, 'Lord, they know that I imprisoned and beat in every synagogue them that believed on you. And when the blood of your martyr Stephen was shed, I also was standing by, and consenting unto his death, and kept the clothing of them that slew him.'

12   "And he said unto me, 'Depart: for I will send you far from here unto the Gentiles.'"

Paul Is a Roman Citizen!
Acts 22:22-29

13   And they gave him audience unto this word, and then lifted up their voices, and said, "Away with such a fellow from the earth: for it is not fitting that he should live." And as they cried out, and cast off their clothes,

> "AWAY WITH SUCH A FELLOW FROM THE EARTH: FOR IT IS NOT FIT THAT HE SHOULD LIVE."

and threw dust into the air, The commander commanded him to be brought into the barracks, and ordered that he should be examined by scourging; that he might know why they cried so against him. And as they bound him with thongs, Paul said unto the centurion that stood by, "Is it lawful for you to scourge a man that is a Roman, and uncondemned?"

14   When the centurion heard that, he went and told the commander, saying, "Take heed what you do: for this man is a Roman." Then the commander came, and said unto him, "Tell me, are you a Roman?" He said, "Yes." And the commander answered, "With a great sum obtained I this freedom." And Paul said, "But I was free born." Then straightway they departed from him which should have examined him: and the commander also was afraid, after he knew that he was a Roman, and because he had bound him.

CHAPTER 109

⊹ HEARING AND CONFINEMENT ⊹

Paul Before the Council
Acts 22:30; 23:1-11

The next day, because he would have known the certainty of why he 1
was accused of the Jews, he loosed him from his chains, and commanded
the chief priests and all their council to appear, and brought Paul down, and
set him before them.

And Paul, earnestly beholding the council, said, "Men and brethren, I 2
have lived in all good conscience before God until this day." And the high
priest Ananias commanded them that stood by him to strike him on the
mouth.

Then said Paul unto him, "God shall strike you, you whitewashed 3
wall: for you sit to judge me according to the law, and command me to be
struck contrary to the law?" And they that stood by said, "You insult God's
high priest?" Then said Paul, "I knew not, brethren, that he was the high
priest: for it is written, '*You shall not speak evil of the ruler of your people.*'"

But when Paul perceived that the one part were Sadducees, and the 4
other Pharisees, he cried out in the council, "Men and brethren, I am a Pharisee, the son of a Pharisee: of the hope and resurrection of the dead I am
called in question." And when he had so said, there arose a dissension
between the Pharisees and the Sadducees: and the multitude was divided.
For the Sadducees say that there is no resurrection, neither angel, nor spirit: but the Pharisees confess both.

And there arose a great cry: and the scribes that were of the Pharisees' 5
part arose, and protested, saying, "We find no evil in this man: but if a spirit or an angel has spoken to him, let us not fight against God." And when
there arose a great dissension, the commander, fearing lest Paul should have
been pulled in pieces of them, commanded the soldiers to go down, and to
take him by force from among them, and to bring him into the barracks.

6   And the following night the Lord stood by him, and said, "Be of good cheer, Paul: for as you have testified of me in Jerusalem, so must you bear witness also at Rome."

Plot Against Paul's Life
Acts 23:12-22

7   And when it was day, certain of the Jews banded together, and bound themselves under an oath, saying that they would neither eat nor drink till they had killed Paul. And there were more than forty which had made this conspiracy. And they came to the chief priests and elders, and said, "We have bound ourselves under a great oath, that we will eat nothing until we have killed Paul. Now therefore you with the council signify to the commander that he bring him down unto you tomorrow, as though you would inquire something more thoroughly concerning him: and we, before he comes near, are ready to kill him."

8   And when Paul's sister's son heard of their lying in wait, he went and entered into the barracks, and told Paul. Then Paul called one of the centurions unto him, and said, "Bring this young man unto the commander: for he has a certain thing to tell him." So he took him, and brought him to the commander, and said, "Paul the prisoner called me unto him, and asked me to bring this young man unto you, who has something to say unto you." Then the commander took him by the hand, and went with him aside privately, and asked him, "What is that you have to tell me?"

9   And he said, "The Jews have agreed to ask that you would bring down Paul tomorrow into the council, as though they would inquire something of him more thoroughly. But do not you yield unto them: for there lie in wait for him of them more than forty men, which have bound themselves with an oath, that they will neither eat nor drink till they have killed him: and now are they ready, looking for a promise from you."

10   So the commander then let the young man depart, and commanded him, "See you tell no man that you have showed these things to me."

Paul Taken to Caesarea
Acts 23:23-35

11   And he called unto him two centurions, saying, "Make ready two hundred soldiers to go to Caesarea, and horsemen sixty and ten, and spearmen two hundred, at the third hour of the night; and provide them horses, that they may set Paul on, and bring him safely unto Felix the governor."

12   And he wrote a letter after this manner: Claudius Lysias unto the most excellent governor Felix sends greeting.

13   This man was seized by the Jews, and would have been killed by them: then I came with soldiers, and rescued him, having understood that he was a Roman. And when I would have known the reason why they accused him, I brought him forth into their council: whom I perceived to be accused of questions of their law, but to have nothing laid to his charge deserving of

death or of imprisonment. And when it was told me that the Jews laid an 13
ambush for the man, I sent straightway to you, and gave a command to his
accusers also to say before you what they had against him. Farewell.

Then the soldiers, as it was commanded them, took Paul, and brought 14
him by night to Antipatris. The next day they left the horsemen to go with
him, and returned to the barracks: who, when they came to Caesarea, and
delivered the letter to the governor, presented Paul also before him.

And when the governor had read the letter, he asked of what province 15
he was. And when he understood that he was of Cilicia; "I will hear you,"
he said, "when your accusers are also come." And he commanded him to be
kept in Herod's judgment hall.

Jewish Leaders Accuse Paul
Acts 24:1-9

And after five days Ananias the high priest descended with the elders, 16
and with a certain lawyer named Tertullus, who brought charges to the governor against Paul. And when he was called forth, Tertullus began to accuse
him, saying, Seeing that by you we enjoy great peace, and that very worthy
deeds are done unto this nation by your providence, we accept it always, and
in all places, most noble Felix, with all thankfulness. Nevertheless, that I be
not further tedious unto you, I request of you that you would hear us of your
graciousness a few words."

"For we have found this man a pestilent fellow, and a mover of sedi- 17
tion among all the Jews throughout the world, and a ringleader of the sect
of the Nazarenes: who also has gone about to profane the temple: whom we
took, and would have judged according to our law."

"But the commander Lysias came upon us, and with great violence 18
took him away out of our hands, commanding his accusers to come unto
you: by examining of whom yourself may take knowledge of all these
things, of which we accuse him." And the Jews also assented, saying that
these things were so.

Paul Before Roman Governor Felix
Acts 24:10-23

Then Paul, after the governor had beckoned unto him to speak, 19
answered, "Inasmuch as I know that you have been of many years a judge
unto this nation, I do the more cheerfully answer for myself: because that
you may understand, that there are yet but twelve days since I went up to
Jerusalem to worship.

"And they neither found me in the temple disputing with any man, nei- 20
ther stirring up the people, neither in the synagogues, nor in the city: neither can they prove the things of which they now accuse me.

"But this I confess unto you, that after the way which they call a sect, 21
so I worship the God of my fathers, believing all things which are written

21 in the law and in the prophets: and have hope toward God, which they themselves also accept, that there shall be a resurrection of the dead, both of the
just and unjust. And herein do I exert myself, to have always a conscience
void of offense toward God, and toward men.

22   "Now after many years I came to bring donations to my nation, and
offerings. Whereupon certain Jews from Asia found me purified in the temple, neither with multitude, nor with tumult. Who ought to have been here
before you, and bring charges, if they had anything against me. Or else let
these same here say, if they have found any wrongdoing in me, while I stood
before the council, except it be for this one expression, that I cried standing
among them, 'Concerning the resurrection of the dead I am called in question by you this day.'"

23   And when Felix heard these things, having more thorough knowledge
of that way, he adjourned them, and said, "When Lysias the commander
shall come down, I will know the uttermost of your matter." And he commanded a centurion to keep Paul, and to let him have liberty, and that he
should forbid none of his friends to minister or come unto him.

Paul Kept Two Years in Custody
Acts 24:24-27

    And after certain days, when Felix came with his wife Drusilla, which
24 was a Jewess, he sent for Paul, and heard him concerning the faith in Christ.
And as he reasoned of righteousness, self-control, and judgment to come,
Felix trembled, and answered, "Go your way for this time; when I have a
suitable season, I will call for you." He hoped also that money should have
been given him from Paul, that he might loose him: therefore he sent for
him the oftener, and conversed with him.

    But after two years Porcius Festus came into Felix' succession: and
25 Felix, willing to show the Jews a favor, left Paul bound.

CHAPTER 110

DEFENSE AND DECISION

New Governor Festus Examines Paul
Acts 25:1-9

Now when Festus was come into the province, after three days he 1 ascended from Caesarea to Jerusalem. Then the high priest and the leaders of the Jews brought charges to him against Paul, and urged him, and asked for a favor against him, that he would send for him to be in Jerusalem, laying wait on the road to kill him.

But Festus answered, that Paul should be kept at Caesarea, and that he 2 himself would depart shortly for there. "Let them therefore," said he, "which among you are able, go down with me, and accuse this man, if there be any wickedness in him."

And when he had tarried among them more than ten days, he went 3 down unto Caesarea; and the next day sitting on the judgment seat commanded Paul to be brought. And when he was come, the Jews which came down from Jerusalem stood round about, and laid many and serious complaints against Paul, which they could not prove. While he answered for himself, "Neither against the law of the Jews, neither against the temple, nor against Caesar, have I offended anything at all."

But Festus, willing to do the Jews a favor, answered Paul, and said, "Will 4 you go up to Jerusalem, and there be judged of these things before me?"

Paul Appeals to Caesar
Acts 25:10-12

Then Paul said, "I stand at Caesar's judgment seat, where I ought to be 5 judged: to the Jews I have done no wrong, as you very well know. For if I be a wrongdoer, or have committed anything deserving of death, I do not refuse to die: but if there be none of these things of which these accuse me, no man may deliver me unto them. I appeal unto Caesar."

6   Then Festus, when he had conferred with the council, answered, "You have appealed unto Caesar? unto Caesar shall you go."

Festus Recounts Case to the King
Acts 25:13-22

7   And after certain days king Agrippa (II) and Bernice came unto Caesarea to greet Festus. And when they had been there many days, Festus declared Paul's case unto the king, saying, "There is a certain man left in bonds by Felix: about whom, when I was at Jerusalem, the chief priests and the elders of the Jews informed me, desiring to have judgment against him. To whom I answered, 'It is not the manner of the Romans to deliver any man to die, before that he which is accused has the accusers face to face, and has opportunity to answer for himself concerning the crime laid against him.'

8   "Therefore, when they were come here, without any delay the next day I sat on the judgment seat, and commanded the man to be brought forth. Against whom when the accusers stood up, they brought no accusation of such things as I supposed: but had certain questions against him of their own religion, and of one Jesus, which was dead, whom Paul affirmed to be alive.

9   "And because I doubted of such manner of questions, I asked him whether he would go to Jerusalem, and there be judged of these matters. But when Paul had appealed to be reserved unto the hearing of Augustus, I commanded him to be kept till I might send him to Caesar."

10   Then Agrippa said unto Festus, "I would also hear the man myself." "Tomorrow," said he, "you shall hear him."

Paul Before King Agrippa II
Acts 25:23-27

11   And the next day, when Agrippa was come, and Bernice, with great pomp, and was entered into the place of the hearing, with the commanders, and prominent men of the city, at Festus' command Paul was brought forth. And Festus said, "King Agrippa, and all men which are here present with us, you see this man, about whom all the multitude of the Jews have petitioned me, both at Jerusalem, and also here, shouting that he ought not to live any longer.

12   "But when I found that he had committed nothing deserving of death, and that he himself has appealed to Augustus, I have decided to send him. Of whom I have no certain thing to write unto my emperor. Therefore I have brought him forth before you, and especially before you, O king Agrippa, that, after examination closes, I might have something to write. For it seems to me unreasonable to send a prisoner, and not in addition to signify the crimes laid against him."

Defense: The Earlier Life
Acts 26:1-11

13   Then Agrippa said unto Paul, "You are permitted to speak for yourself." Then Paul stretched forth the hand, and answered for himself: "I think

myself happy, king Agrippa, because I shall answer for myself this day 13
before you concerning all the things of which I am accused of the Jews:
especially because I know you to be expert in all customs and controversies
which are among the Jews. Therefore I beg you to hear me patiently.

"My manner of life from my youth, which was at the first among my 14
own nation at Jerusalem, know all the Jews; which knew me from the beginning, if they would testify, that according to the most strict sect of our religion I lived a Pharisee.

"And now I stand and am judged for the hope of the promise made of 15
God unto our fathers: unto which promise our twelve tribes, earnestly serving God day and night, hope to come. For which hope's sake, king Agrippa,
I am accused of the Jews. Why should it be thought a thing incredible with
you, that God should raise the dead?

"I indeed thought with myself, that I ought to do many things contrary 16
to the name of Jesus of Nazareth. Which thing I also did in Jerusalem: and
many of the saints did I shut up in prison, having received authority from
the chief priests; and when they were put to death, I gave my voice against
them. And I punished them often in every synagogue, and compelled them
to blaspheme; and being exceedingly furious against them, I persecuted
them even unto foreign cities.

Defense: The Conversion
Acts 26:12-15

"Whereupon as I went to Damascus with authority and commission 17
from the chief priests, at midday, O king, I saw on the road a light from
heaven, above the brightness of the sun, shining round about me and them
which journeyed with me. And when we were all fallen to the earth, I
heard a voice speaking unto me, and saying in the Hebrew tongue, 'Saul,
Saul, why do you persecute me? it is hard for you to kick against the
prods.' And I said, 'Who are you, Lord?' And he said, 'I am Jesus whom
you persecute.'"

Defense: The Calling
Acts 26:16-18

"'But rise, and stand upon your feet: for I have appeared unto you for 18
this purpose, to make you a minister
and a witness both of these things
which you have seen, and of those
things in which I will reveal unto you;
delivering you from the people, and
from the Gentiles, unto whom now I
send you, to open their eyes, and to
turn them from darkness to light, and

> "RISE, AND STAND UPON YOUR FEET: FOR I HAVE APPEARED UNTO YOU FOR THIS PURPOSE, TO MAKE YOU A MINISTER AND A WITNESS."

from the power of Satan unto God, that they may receive forgiveness of sins,
and inheritance among them which are sanctified by faith that is in me.'"

Defense: Ministry to This Day
Acts 26:19-23

19 "Therefore, O king Agrippa, I was not disobedient unto the heavenly vision: but showed first unto them of Damascus, and at Jerusalem, and throughout all the regions of Judea, and then to the Gentiles, that they should repent and turn to God, and do works worthy for repentance. For these causes the Jews caught me in the temple, and went about to kill me.

20 "Having therefore obtained help of God, I continue unto this day, witnessing both to small and great, saying no other things than those which the prophets and Moses did say should come: that Christ should suffer, and that he should be the first that should rise from the dead, and should show light unto the people, and to the Gentiles."

> "I CONTINUE UNTO THIS DAY, WITNESSING BOTH TO SMALL AND GREAT."

Defense: Ministry of This Day
Acts 26:24-32

21 And as he thus spoke for himself, Festus said with a loud voice, "Paul, you are gone mad; much learning does make you mad." But he said, "I am not mad, most noble Festus; but speak forth the words of truth and reason. For the king knows of these things, before whom also I speak freely: for I am persuaded that none of these things are hidden from him; for this thing was not done in a corner.

22 "King Agrippa, do you believe the prophets? I know that you believe." Then Agrippa said unto Paul, "Almost you persuade me to be a Christian." And Paul said, "I would to God, that not only you, but also all that hear me this day, were both almost, and altogether such as I am, except these bonds."

> "ALMOST YOU PERSUADE ME TO BE A CHRISTIAN."

23 And when he had thus spoken, the king rose up, and the governor, and Bernice, and they that sat with them: and when they were gone aside, they talked between themselves, saying, "This man does nothing deserving of death or of bonds." Then said Agrippa unto Festus, "This man might have been set at liberty, if he had not appealed unto Caesar."

PART 27

PAUL'S VOYAGE TO ROME

It is then the intent of the Romans to transport Paul to Rome by sea where he is to be held awaiting trial. The voyage proves to be a tempestuous one. Yet Paul remains firm in his faith in God, with a clear vision of what lies ahead. With divine wisdom he warns his captors of the turbulent waters that lie ahead. Despite their skepticism, Paul remains steadfast in the underlying calm of his Christ. His faith in God is unwavering amid the stormy seas. The ship capsizes and its crew endures many frightful experiences; however not one of them is lost. Paul's captors witness in many ways the power of God, and their voyage continues peacefully toward the throne of Caesar.

"THERE STOOD BY ME THIS NIGHT THE ANGEL OF GOD, WHOSE I AM, AND WHOM I SERVE, SAYING, 'FEAR NOT, PAUL; YOU MUST BE BROUGHT BEFORE CAESAR: AND, LO, GOD HAS GIVEN YOU ALL THEM THAT SAIL WITH YOU.'" (ACTS 27:23-24)

CHAPTER 111

ROME VOYAGE

Rome Journey Begins as Prisoner
Acts 27:1-12

1   And when it was decided that we should sail into Italy, they delivered Paul and certain other prisoners unto one named Julius, a centurion of Augustus' regiment. And entering into a ship of Adramyttium, we launched, meaning to sail by the coasts of Asia; one Aristarchus, a Macedonian of Thessalonica, being with us.

2   And the next day we landed at Sidon. And Julius courteously treated Paul, and gave him liberty to go unto his friends to refresh himself. And when we had launched from there, we sailed under Cyprus, because the winds were contrary. And when we had sailed over the sea of Cilicia and Pamphylia, we came to Myra, a city of Lycia. And there the centurion found a ship of Alexandria sailing into Italy; and he put us on board. And when we had sailed slowly many days, and with difficulty were come opposite Cnidus, the wind not permitting us, we sailed under Crete, opposite Salmone; and, with difficulty passing it, came unto a place which is called The Fair Havens; near to which was the city of Lasea.

3   Now when much time was spent, and when sailing was now danger-ous, because the Fast was now already past, Paul warned them, and said unto them, "Sirs, I perceive that this voyage will be with harm and much loss, not only of the cargo and ship, but also of our lives."

4   Nevertheless the centurion believed the pilot and the owner of the ship, more than those things which were spoken by Paul. And because the harbor was not suitable to winter in, the majority advised to depart from there also, if by any means they might attain to Phoenix, and there to win-ter; which is a harbor of Crete, and lies toward the southwest and northwest.

Great Storm at Sea
Acts 27:13-38

5   And when the south wind blew softly, supposing that they had obtained their purpose, taking up anchor from there, they sailed close by

Crete. But not long after there arose against it a tempestuous wind, called 5
Euroclydon. And when the ship was caught, and could not head into the
wind, we let it drive. And running
under a certain island which is called

> WHEN THE SHIP WAS CAUGHT,
> AND COULD NOT HEAD INTO
> THE WIND, WE LET IT DRIVE.

Clauda, we had much work to secure
the lifeboat: which when they had
taken it up, they used cables, under-
girding the ship; and, fearing lest they
should fall into the sandbars, struck sail, and so were driven. And we being
exceedingly tossed with a tempest, the next day they lightened the ship.

And the third day we cast out with our own hands the rigging of the 6
ship. And when neither sun nor stars in many days appeared, and no small
tempest lay on us, all hope that we should be saved was then taken away.

But after long abstinence of food Paul stood forth in the midst of 7
them, and said, "Sirs, you should have listened unto me, and not have sailed
from Crete, and to have incurred this harm and loss. And now I urge you to
be of good cheer: for there shall be no loss of any man's life among you, but
of the ship. For there stood by me this night the angel of God, whose I am,
and whom I serve, saying, 'Fear not, Paul; you must be brought before Caesar: and, lo, God has given you all them that sail with you.' Therefore, sirs,
be of good cheer: for I believe God, that it shall be even as it was told me.
Howbeit we must be cast upon a certain island."

But when the fourteenth night was come, as we were driven up and 8
down in Adria, about midnight the sailors deemed that they drew near to
some land; and sounded, and found it twenty fathoms: and when they had
gone a little farther, they sounded again, and found it fifteen fathoms. Then
fearing lest we should have fallen upon rocks, they cast four anchors out of
the stern, and wished for the daylight.

And as the sailors were about to flee out of the ship, when they had let 9
down the lifeboat into the sea, under pretense as though they would have
cast anchors out of the bow, Paul said to the centurion and to the soldiers,
"Unless these stay in the ship, you cannot be saved." Then the soldiers cut
off the ropes of the lifeboat, and let it fall off.

And while the day was coming on, Paul urged them all to take food, 10
saying, "This day is the fourteenth day that you have waited and continued
fasting, having taken nothing. There-
fore I beg you to take some food: for

> "THERE SHALL NOT A HAIR
> FALL FROM THE HEAD OF ANY
> OF YOU."

this is for your health: for there shall
not a hair fall from the head of any of
you." And when he had thus spoken,
he took bread, and gave thanks to God in presence of them all: and when he
had broken it, he began to eat.

Then were they all of good cheer, and they also took some food. And 11
we were in all in the ship two hundred sixty and sixteen souls. And when

11 they had eaten enough, they lightened the ship, and cast out the wheat into the sea.

Shipwreck
Acts 27:39-44

12   And when it was day, they knew not the land: but they discovered a certain bay with a beach, into which they were minded, if it were possible, to thrust in the ship. And when they had loosed the anchors, they committed themselves unto the sea, and loosed the rudder ropes, and hoisted up the mainsail to the wind, and made toward beach. And falling into a place where two seas met, they ran the ship aground; and the bow stuck fast, and remained immoveable, but the stern was broken with the violence of the waves.

13   And the soldiers' plan was to kill the prisoners, lest any of them should swim out, and escape. But the centurion, willing to preserve Paul, kept them from their purpose; and commanded that they which could swim should cast themselves first into the sea, and get to land: and the rest, some on boards, and some on broken pieces of the ship. And so it came to pass, that they all escaped safely to land.

> AND SO IT CAME TO PASS, THAT THEY ALL ESCAPED SAFELY TO LAND.

Winter Waiting on Island of Malta
Acts 28:1-10

14   And when they were escaped, then they knew that the island was called Malta. And the native people showed us unusual kindness: for they kindled a fire, and received us every one, because of the falling rain, and because of the cold.

15   And when Paul had gathered a bundle of sticks, and laid them on the fire, there came a viper out of the heat, and fastened on his hand. And when the natives saw the venomous creature hang on his hand, they said among themselves, "No doubt this man is a murderer, whom, though he has escaped the sea, yet vengeance allows not to live." And he shook off the creature into the fire, and suffered no harm. Howbeit they looked when he should have swollen, or fallen down dead suddenly: but after they had looked a great while, and saw no harm come to him, they changed their minds, and said that he was a god.

16   In the same area were possessions of the chief man of the island, whose name was Publius; who received us, and lodged us three days courteously. And it came to pass, that the father of Publius lay sick of a fever and of a bloody dysentery: to whom Paul entered in, and prayed, and laid his hands on him, and healed him. So when this was done, others also, which had diseases in the island, came, and were healed: who also honored us with many honors; and when we departed, they provided us with such things as were necessary.

> WHEN WE DEPARTED, THEY PROVIDED US WITH SUCH THINGS AS WERE NECESSARY.

Rome Journey Ends as Prisoner
Acts 28:11-16

And after three months we departed in a ship of Alexandria, which had 17
wintered in the island, whose sign was Castor and Pollux. And landing at
Syracuse, we tarried there three days.
And from there we circled around, and | SO WE WENT TOWARD ROME.
came to Rhegium: and after one day
the south wind blew, and we came the next day to Puteoli: where we found
brethren, and were asked to stay with them seven days: and so we went
toward Rome. And from there, when the brethren heard of us, they came to
meet us as far as Appii Forum, and The Three Taverns: whom when Paul
saw, he thanked God, and took courage.

And when we came to Rome, the centurion delivered the prisoners to 18
the captain of the guard: but Paul was permitted to dwell by himself with a
soldier that guarded him.

PART 28

PAUL'S CONFINEMENT IN ROME

Not yet convicted of any crime by his captors, Paul is permitted to preach openly in Rome of his belief in God and how Christ was sent not merely for the salvation of a select few, but for the salvation of all. While all those who hear Paul listen intently, not all believe. For the true message of Christ is intended not for the seeing eye and hearing ear, but for the listening heart.

> THERE CAME MANY TO HIM INTO HIS LODGING;
> TO WHOM HE EXPLAINED AND DECLARED THE
> KINGDOM OF GOD, PERSUADING THEM CON-
> CERNING JESUS. (ACTS 28:23)

CHAPTER 112

CONFINEMENT IN ROME

Paul Under Guard
Acts 28:17-22

And it came to pass, that after three days Paul called the leaders of the 1
Jews together: and when they were come together, he said unto them, "Men
and brethren, though I have committed nothing against the people, or customs of our fathers, yet was I delivered prisoner from Jerusalem into the
hands of the Romans. Who, when they had examined me, would have let me
go, because there was no cause of death in me.

"But when the Jews spoke against it, I was compelled to appeal unto 2
Caesar; not that I had anything to accuse my nation of. For this reason therefore I have called for you, to see you, and to speak with you: because for
the hope of Israel I am bound with this chain."

And they said unto him, "We neither received letters out of Judea con- 3
cerning you, neither any of the brethren that came showed or spoke any evil
of you. But we desire to hear from you what you think: for as concerning
this sect, we know that everywhere it is spoken against."

Paul Delivers Final Sermon
Acts 28:23-29

And when they had appointed him a day, there came many to him into 4
his lodging; to whom he explained and testified of the kingdom of God, persuading them concerning Jesus, both out of the law of Moses, and out of the
prophets, from morning till evening. And some believed the things which
were spoken, and some believed not.

And when they agreed not among themselves, they departed, after 5
Paul had spoken this word, "Well spoke the Holy Ghost by Isaiah the
prophet unto our fathers, saying, '*Go unto this people, and say, "Hearing
you shall hear, and shall not understand; and seeing you shall see, and not*

5 *perceive: for the heart of this people is grown coarse, and their ears are dull of hearing, and their eyes have they closed; lest they should see with their eyes, and hear with their ears, and understand with their hearts, and should be converted, and I should heal them."'*

6 "Be it known therefore unto you, that the salvation of God is sent unto the Gentiles, and that they will hear it." And when he had said these words, the Jews departed, and had great reasoning among themselves.

PART 29

LETTER TO EPHESIANS

In a matchless moment of history, Paul writes from prison to the church of the Ephesians. In a letter written for all mankind, he assures them of their rich heritage in Christ. With loving guidance he encourages all to place their full confidence in God, so that they may be renewed in the spirit of their mind and receive abundantly all that God has prepared for them that love him. He offers rich wisdom regarding the diverse nature of his people, whose qualities reflect in myriad forms the wisdom and nature of God. The opportunity and ability to reconcile with God, he says, are ever present and eternal.

> THERE IS ONE BODY, AND ONE SPIRIT, EVEN AS YOU ARE CALLED IN ONE HOPE OF YOUR CALL-ING; ONE LORD, ONE FAITH, ONE BAPTISM, ONE GOD AND FATHER OF ALL, WHO IS ABOVE ALL, AND THROUGH ALL, AND IN YOU ALL.
>
> (EPHESIANS 4:4-6)

CHAPTER 113

PRECIOUS PROMISE OF UNITY

Greeting to Ephesians
Ephesians 1:1-2

1   Paul, an apostle of Jesus Christ by the will of God, to the saints which are at Ephesus, and to the faithful in Christ Jesus: Grace be to you, and peace, from God our Father, and from the Lord Jesus Christ.

Spirit of Promise
Ephesians 1:3-14

2   Blessed be the God and Father of our Lord Jesus Christ, who has blessed us with all spiritual blessings in heavenly places in Christ: according as he has chosen us in him before the foundation of the world, that we should be holy and without blame before him in love: having predestined us unto the adoption of children by Jesus Christ to himself, according to the good pleasure of his will, to the praise of the glory of his grace, wherein he has made us accepted in the beloved.

3   In whom we have redemption through his blood, the forgiveness of sins, according to the riches of his grace; wherein he has abounded toward us in all wisdom and prudence; having made known unto us the mystery of his will, according to his good pleasure which he has purposed in himself: that in the dispensation of the fulness of times he might gather together in one all things in Christ, both which are in heaven, and which are on earth; even in him.

4   In him also we have obtained an inheritance, being predestined according to the plan of him who works all things according to the purpose of his own will: that we should be to the praise of his glory, who first trusted in Christ.

5   In whom you also trusted, after you heard the word of truth, the gospel of your salvation: in whom also after you believed, you were sealed with

that Holy Spirit of promise, which is the guarantee of our inheritance until 5
the redemption of the purchased possession, unto the praise of his glory.

Spirit of Wisdom
Ephesians 1:15-23

Therefore I also, after I heard of your faith in the Lord Jesus, and love 6
unto all the saints, cease not to give thanks for you, making mention of you
in my prayers; that the God of our Lord Jesus Christ, the Father of glory,
may give unto you the spirit of wisdom and revelation in the knowledge of
him: the eyes of your understanding being enlightened; that you may know
what is the hope of his calling, and what the riches of the glory of his inheritance in the saints, and what is the exceeding greatness of his power toward
us who believe, according to the working of his mighty power, which he
accomplished in Christ, when he raised him from the dead, and seated him
at his own right hand in the heavenly places, far above all principality, and
power, and might, and dominion, and every name that is named, not only in
this world, but also in that which is to come: and has put all things under his
feet, and gave him to be the head over all things to the church, which is his
body, the fulness of him that fills all in all.

Alive in Christ
Ephesians 2:1-10

And you has he quickened, who were dead in trespasses and sins; 7
wherein in time past you walked according to the course of this world,
according to the prince of the power of the air, the spirit that now works in
the children of disobedience: among whom also we all had our conduct in
times past in the lusts of our flesh, fulfilling the desires of the flesh and of
the mind; and were by nature the children of wrath, even as others.

But God, who is rich in mercy, for his great love with which he loved 8
us, even when we were dead in trespasses, has quickened us together with
Christ, (by grace you are saved); and has raised us up together, and made us
sit together in heavenly places in Christ Jesus: that in the ages to come he
might show the exceeding riches of his grace in his kindness toward us
through Christ Jesus.

For by grace are you saved through faith; and that not of your- 9
selves: it is the gift of God: not of works, lest any man should boast. For
we are his workmanship, created in Christ Jesus unto good works, which

> BY GRACE ARE YOU SAVED
> THROUGH FAITH; AND THAT
> NOT OF YOURSELVES: IT IS THE
> GIFT OF GOD.

God has beforehand ordained that we should walk in them.

One in Christ
Ephesians 2:11-22

Therefore remember, that you being in time past Gentiles in the flesh, 10
who are called Uncircumcision by that which is called the Circumcision in

10   the flesh made by hands; that at that time you were without Christ, being

> BY GRACE ARE YOU SAVED
> THROUGH FAITH; AND
> THAT NOT OF YOURSEVES:
> IT IS THE GIFT OF GOD.

aliens from the commonwealth of Israel, and strangers from the covenants of promise, having no hope, and without God in the world: but now in Christ Jesus you who once were far off are made near by the blood of Christ.

11   For he is our peace, who has made both one, and has broken down the middle wall of partition between us; having abolished in his flesh the hostility, even the law of commandments contained in ordinances; to make in himself of two one new man, so making peace; and that he might reconcile both unto God in one body by the cross, having slain the hostility thereby: and came and preached peace to you which were afar off, and to them that were near. For through him we both have access by one Spirit unto the Father.

12   Now therefore you are no more strangers and foreigners, but fellow

> YOU ARE NO MORE STRAN-
> GERS AND FOREIGNERS, BUT
> FELLOW CITIZENS WITH THE
> SAINTS, AND OF THE HOUSE-
> HOLD OF GOD.

citizens with the saints, and of the household of God; and are built upon the foundation of the apostles and prophets, Jesus Christ himself being the chief cornerstone; in whom all the building fitly framed together grows unto a holy temple in the Lord: in

whom you also are built together for a habitation of God through the Spirit.

Mystery of Christ
Ephesians 3:1-13

13   For this cause I Paul, the prisoner of Jesus Christ for you Gentiles, if you have heard of the stewardship of the grace of God which is given me toward you: how that by revelation he made known unto me the mystery; (as I wrote before in few words, whereby, when you read, you may understand my knowledge in the mystery of Christ) which in other ages was not made known unto the sons of men, as it is now revealed unto his holy apostles and prophets by the Spirit; that the Gentiles should be fellow heirs, and of the same body, and partakers of his promise in Christ by the gospel: of which I was made a minister, according to the gift of the grace of God given unto me by the effective working of his power.

14   Unto me, who am less than the least of all saints, is this grace given, that I should preach among the Gentiles the unsearchable riches of Christ; and to make all men see what is the fellowship of the mystery, which from the beginning of the world has been hidden in God, who created all things by Jesus Christ: to the intent that now unto the principalities and powers in heavenly places might be known by the church the manifold wisdom of God, according to the eternal purpose which he purposed in Christ Jesus our Lord: in whom we have boldness and access with confidence by the faith of him.

Therefore I desire that you do not lose heart at my tribulations for you, 15
which is your glory.

Limitless Love
Ephesians 3:14-21

For this reason I bow my knees unto the Father of our Lord Jesus 16
Christ, of whom the whole family in heaven and earth is named, that he
would grant you, according to the
riaches of his glory, to be strengthened
with might by his Spirit in the inner
man; that Christ may dwell in your
hearts by faith; that you, being rooted
and grounded in love, may be able to
comprehend with all saints what is the

> KNOW THE LOVE OF CHRIST,
> WHICH SURPASSES KNOWL-
> EDGE, THAT YOU MIGHT BE
> FILLED WITH ALL THE FULNESS
> OF GOD.

breadth, and length, and depth, and height; and to know the love of Christ,
which surpasses knowledge, that you might be filled with all the fulness
of God.

Now unto him that is able to do exceedingly abundantly above all that 17
we ask or think, according to the power that works in us, unto him be glory
in the church by Christ Jesus throughout all ages, world without end. Amen.

CHAPTER 114

⊷ Worthy in the Unity ⊷

One and All in One
Ephesians 4:1-16

1   I therefore, the prisoner of the Lord, urge that you walk worthy of the calling with which you are called, with all lowliness and meekness, with patience, bearing with one another in love; endeavoring to keep the unity of the Spirit in the bond of peace. There is one body, and one Spirit, even as you are called in one hope of your calling; one Lord, one faith, one baptism, one God and Father of all, who is above all, and through all, and in you all.

2   But unto every one of us is given grace according to the measure of the gift of Christ. Therefore he says, *"When he "ascended," up on high, he led captivity captive, and gave gifts unto men."* (Now that "he ascended," what is it but that he also descended first into the lower parts of the earth? He that descended is the same also that ascended up far above all heavens, that he might fill all things.)

3   And he gave some, apostles; and some, prophets; and some, evangelists; and some, pastors and teachers; for the perfecting of the saints, for the work of the ministry, for the building up of the body of Christ: till we all come in the unity of the faith, and of the knowledge of the Son of God, unto a perfect man, unto the measure of the stature of the fulness of Christ: that we henceforth be no more children, tossed to and fro, and carried about with every wind of doctrine, by the trickery of men, and cunning craftiness, whereby they plot to deceive; but speaking the truth in love, may grow up into him in all things, which is the head, even Christ: from whom the whole body fitly joined together and compacted by that which every ligament supplies, according to the effective working in the measure of every part, makes increase of the body unto the building up of itself in love.

Unsearchable Riches of Christ
Ephesians 4:17-24

4   This I say therefore, and testify in the Lord, that you henceforth walk not as other Gentiles walk, in the vanity of their mind, having the understanding

darkened, being alienated from the life of God through the ignorance that 4
is in them, because of the blindness of their heart: who being past feeling
have given themselves over unto lewdness, to work all uncleanness with
greediness.

But you have not so learned Christ; if so be that you have heard him, 5
and have been taught by him, as the truth is in Jesus: that you put off concerning the former conduct the old man, which is corrupt according to
the deceitful lusts; and be renewed in the spirit of your mind; and that you
put on the new man, which after God is created in righteousness and true
holiness.

Duties of the New Life
Ephesians 4:25-32

Therefore putting away falsehood, *"speak every man truth with his* 6
neighbor": for we are members one of another. *"Be angry, and not sin"*: let
not the sun go down upon your wrath: neither give room to the devil. Let
him that stole steal no more: but rather let him labor, working with his
hands the thing which is good, that he may have to give to him that needs.

Let no evil talk proceed out of your mouth, but that which is good to 7
the use of edification, that it may provide grace unto the hearers. And do not
grieve the Holy Spirit of God, whereby you are sealed unto the day of
redemption.

Let all bitterness, and wrath, and anger, and clamor, and evil speak- 8
ing, be put away from you, with all
malice: and be kind one to another,
tenderhearted, forgiving one another,
even as God for Christ's sake has forgiven you.

> BE KIND ONE TO ANOTHER,
> TENDERHEARTED, FORGIVING
> ONE ANOTHER.

Avoidance
Ephesians 5:1-5

Be therefore imitators of God, as dear children; and walk in love, as 9
Christ also has loved us, and has given himself for us an offering and a sacrifice to God for a sweet-smelling savor.

But fornication, and all uncleanness, or covetousness, let it not be 10
once named among you, as becomes saints; neither filthiness, nor foolish
talking, nor jesting, which are not fitting: but rather giving of thanks. For
this you know, that no whoremonger, nor unclean person, nor covetous man,
who is an idolater, has any inheritance in the kingdom of Christ and of God.

Darkness to the Light
Ephesians 5:6-21

Let no man deceive you with vain words: for because of these things 11
comes the wrath of God upon the children of disobedience. Be not therefore partakers with them. For you were once darkness, but now you are
light in the Lord: walk as children of light: (for the fruit of the Spirit is in

11 all goodness and righteousness and truth); testing what is acceptable unto the Lord.

12   And have no fellowship with the unfruitful works of darkness, but rather expose them. For it is a shame even to speak of those things which are done of them in secret. But all things that are exposed are made manifest by the light: for whatsoever does make manifest is light. Therefore he says, "Awake you that sleep, and arise from the dead, and Christ shall give you light."

13   See then that you walk circumspectly, not as fools, but as wise, redeeming the time, because the days are evil. Therefore be not unwise, but understanding what the will of the Lord is.

14   And be not drunk with wine, wherein is excess; but be filled with the Spirit; speaking to yourselves in psalms and hymns and spiritual songs, singing and making melody in your heart to the Lord; giving thanks always for all things unto God and the Father in the name of our Lord Jesus Christ; submitting yourselves one to another in the fear of God.

Wives and Husbands
Ephesians 5:22-33

15   Wives, submit yourselves unto your own husbands, as unto the Lord. For the husband is the head of the wife, even as Christ is the head of the church: and he is the savior of the body. Therefore as the church is subject unto Christ, so let the wives be to their own husbands in everything.

16   Husbands, love your wives, even as Christ also loved the church, and gave himself for it; that he might sanctify and cleanse it with the washing

> HUSBANDS, LOVE YOUR WIVES, EVEN AS CHRIST ALSO LOVED THE CHURCH, AND GAVE HIMSELF FOR IT.

of water by the word, that he might present it to himself a glorious church, not having spot, or wrinkle, or any such thing; but that it should be holy and without blemish.

17   So ought men to love their wives as their own bodies. He that loves his wife loves himself. For no man ever yet hated his own flesh; but nourishes and cherishes it, even as the Lord the church: for we are members of his body, of his flesh, and of his bones. *"For this cause shall a man leave his father and mother, and shall be joined unto his wife, and they two shall be one flesh."* This is a great mystery: but I speak concerning Christ and the church.

18   Nevertheless let every one of you in particular so love his wife even as himself; and the wife see that she respects her husband.

Children and Parents
Ephesians 6:1-4

19   Children, obey your parents in the Lord: for this is right. *"Honor your father and mother"*; (which is the first commandment with promise); *"that it may be well with you, and you may live long on the earth."*

And, you fathers, do not provoke your children to anger: but bring 20 them up in the training and admonition of the Lord.

Servants and Masters
Ephesians 6:5-9

Servants, be obedient to them that are your masters according to the 21 flesh, with fear and trembling, in singleness of your heart, as unto Christ; not with eyeservice, as men-pleasers; but as the servants of Christ, doing the will of God from the heart; with goodwill doing service, as to the Lord, and not to men: knowing that whatsoever good thing any man does, the same shall he receive of the Lord, whether he be bond or free.

And, you masters, do the same things unto them, forbearing threatening: 22 knowing that your Master also is in heaven; neither is there partiality of persons with him.

Whole Armor of God
Ephesians 6:10-20

Finally, my brethren, be strong in the Lord, and in the power of his 23 might. Put on the whole armor of God, that you may be able to stand against the wiles of the devil. For we wrestle not against flesh and blood, but against principalities, against powers, against the rulers of the darkness of this world, against spiritual wickedness in high places. Therefore take unto you the

> PUT ON THE WHOLE ARMOR OF GOD, THAT YOU MAY BE ABLE TO STAND AGAINST THE WILES OF THE DEVIL.

whole armor of God, that you may be able to withstand in the evil day, and having done all, to stand.

Stand therefore, having your waist girded with truth, and having on 24 the breastplate of righteousness; and your feet shod with the preparation of the gospel of peace; above all, taking the shield of faith, with which you shall be able to quench all the fiery darts of the wicked.

And take the helmet of salvation, and the sword of the Spirit, which is 25 the word of God: praying always with all prayer and supplication in the Spirit, and watching thereto with all perseverance and supplication for all saints; and for me, that utterance may be given unto me, that I may open my

> TAKE THE HELMET OF SALVATION, AND THE SWORD OF THE SPIRIT, WHICH IS THE WORD OF GOD.

mouth boldly, to make known the mystery of the gospel, for which I am an ambassador in bonds: that therein I may speak boldly, as I ought to speak.

Conclusion
Ephesians 6:21-24

But that you also may know my affairs, and how I do, Tychicus, a 26 beloved brother and faithful minister in the Lord, shall make known to you

26 all things: whom I have sent unto you for the same purpose, that you might know our affairs, and that he might comfort your hearts.

27   Peace be to the brethren, and love with faith, from God the Father and the Lord Jesus Christ. Grace be with all them that love our Lord Jesus Christ in sincerity. Amen.

PART 30

LETTER TO PHILIPPIANS

Still held in house bondage in Rome, Paul writes to the people of Philippi, expressing the hope that he will visit them again in the future, for they have been a good and faithful people. In a bolt of benediction he professes, "the Lord is near." He writes to them of his conviction that, while there is hope in life, there is also a gain in death—for to live in the flesh is to follow Christ, but to die is to be present with Christ. He writes that those who are humble in faith will inherit the rich legacy of God's love and will reach the fruition of His promise. To these, God will throw wide the gates of heaven.

> GOD ALSO HAS HIGHLY EXALTED HIM, AND
> GIVEN HIM A NAME WHICH IS ABOVE EVERY
> NAME: THAT AT THE NAME OF JESUS EVERY KNEE
> SHOULD BOW, OF THINGS IN HEAVEN, AND
> THINGS ON EARTH, AND THINGS UNDER THE
> EARTH; AND THAT EVERY TONGUE SHOULD CON-
> FESS THAT JESUS CHRIST IS LORD, TO THE GLORY
> OF GOD THE FATHER.   (PHILIPPIANS 2:9-11)

CHAPTER 115

PERSONAL AND SOCIAL CONDUCT

Greeting to Philippians
Philippians 1:1-2

1   Paul and Timothy, the servants of Jesus Christ, to all the saints in Christ Jesus which are at Philippi, with the bishops and deacons: Grace be unto you, and peace, from God our Father, and from the Lord Jesus Christ.

Giving Thanks
Philippians 1:3-11

2   I thank my God upon every remembrance of you, always in every prayer of mine for you all making request with joy, for your fellowship in the gospel from the first day until now; being confident of this very thing, that he which has begun a good work in you will perform it until the day of Jesus Christ: even as it is right for me to think this of you all, because I have you in my heart; inasmuch as both in my bonds, and in the defense and confirmation of the gospel, you all are partakers of my grace. For God is my witness, how greatly I long after you all in the affection of Jesus Christ.

3   And this I pray, that your love may abound yet more and more in knowledge and in all judgment; That you may approve things that are excellent; that you may be pure and without offense till the day of Christ; being filled with the fruits of righteousness, which are by Jesus Christ, unto the glory and praise of God.

To Live Is Christ
Philippians 1:12-30

4   But I would you should understand, brethren, that the things which happened unto me have fallen out rather unto the furtherance of the gospel; so that my bonds in Christ are manifest in all the palace, and in all other

places; and many of the brethren in the Lord, becoming confident by my 4
bonds, are much more bold to speak the word without fear.

Some indeed preach Christ even
of envy and strife; and some also of
goodwill: the one preach Christ of
contention, not sincerely, supposing to
add affliction to my bonds: but the
other of love, knowing that I am set for the defense of the gospel.

> I AM SET FOR THE DEFENSE OF
> THE GOSPEL.

What then? notwithstanding, every way, whether in pretense, or in 6
truth, Christ is preached; and I therein do rejoice, yes, and will rejoice. For
I know that this shall result in my deliverance through your prayer, and the
supply of the Spirit of Jesus Christ, according to my earnest expectation and
my hope, that in nothing I shall be ashamed, but that with all boldness, as
always, so now also Christ shall be magnified in my body, whether it be by
life, or by death.

For to me to live is Christ, and to die is gain. But if I live in the flesh, 7
this is the fruit of my labor: yet what I
shall choose I know not. For I am in a
dilemma between the two, having a
desire to depart, and to be with Christ;
which is far better: nevertheless to
remain in the flesh is more needful for you.

> TO ME TO LIVE IS CHRIST,
> AND TO DIE IS GAIN.

And having this confidence, I know that I shall remain and continue 8
with you all for your furtherance and joy of faith; that your rejoicing may
be more abundant in Jesus Christ for me by my coming to you again.

Only let your conduct be as it becomes the gospel of Christ: that 9
whether I come and see you, or else be absent, I may hear of your affairs,
that you stand fast in one spirit, with one mind contending together for the
faith of the gospel; and in nothing terrified by your adversaries: which is to
them an evident sign of perdition, but to you of salvation, and that of God.

For unto you it is given in the behalf of Christ, not only to believe on 10
him, but also to suffer for his sake; having the same conflict which you saw
in me, and now hear to be in me.

Above Every Name
Philippians 2:1-11

If there be therefore any consolation in Christ, if any comfort of love, if 11
any fellowship of the Spirit, if any affections and mercies, fulfill my joy, that
you be like-minded, having the same love, being of one accord, of one mind.

Let nothing be done through selfishness or foolish boasting; but in 12
lowliness of mind let each esteem others better than themselves. Look not
every man on his own things, but every man also on the things of others.

Let this mind be in you, which was also in Christ Jesus: who, being in 13
the form of God, thought it not robbery to be equal with God: but made

13 himself of no reputation, and took upon himself the form of a servant, and was made in the likeness of men. And being found in appearance as a man, he humbled himself, and became obedient unto death, even the death of the cross.

14 Therefore God also has highly exalted him, and given him a name which is above every name: that at the name of Jesus every knee should bow, of things in heaven, and things on earth, and things under the earth; and that every tongue should confess that Jesus Christ is Lord, to the glory of God the Father.

> AT THE NAME OF JESUS EVERY KNEE SHOULD BOW, OF THINGS IN HEAVEN, AND THINGS ON EARTH.

Social Conduct
Philippians 2:12-18

15 Therefore, my beloved, as you have always obeyed, not as in my presence only, but now much more in my absence, work out your own salvation with fear and trembling. For it is God which works in you both to will and to do of his good pleasure.

16 Do all things without grumbling and arguing: that you may be blameless and harmless, the sons of God, without fault, in the midst of a crooked and perverse generation, among whom you shine as lights in the world; holding forth the word of life; that I may rejoice in the day of Christ, that I have not run in vain, neither labored in vain.

> SHINE AS LIGHTS IN THE WORLD.

17 Yes, and if I be offered upon the sacrifice and service of your faith, I joy, and rejoice with you all. For the same reason also do you joy, and rejoice with me.

Wishes and Hopes
Philippians 2:19-30

18 But I trust in the Lord Jesus to send Timothy shortly unto you, that I also may be of good comfort, when I know your state. For I have no man like-minded, who will truly care for your state. For all seek their own, not the things which are Jesus Christ's.

19 But you know the proof of him, that, as a son with the father, he has served with me in the gospel. Him therefore I hope to send presently, as soon as I shall see how it will go with me. But I trust in the Lord that I also myself shall come shortly.

20 Yet I supposed it necessary to send to you Epaphroditus, my brother, and companion in labor, and fellow soldier, but your messenger, and he that ministered to my needs. For he longed for you all, and was full of distress, because that you had heard that he had been sick. For indeed he was sick near unto death: but God had mercy on him; and not on him only, but on me also, lest I should have sorrow upon sorrow.

I sent him therefore the more eagerly, that, when you see him again, 21 you may rejoice, and that I may be the less sorrowful. Receive him therefore in the Lord with all gladness; and hold such in honor: because for the work of Christ he was near unto death, not regarding his life, to supply your lack of service toward me.

CHAPTER 116

⁘ EVILDOERS AND VIRTUOUS THOUGHTS ⁘

Faith and Righteousness
Philippians 3:1-11

1   Finally, my brethren, rejoice in the Lord. To write the same things to you, to me indeed is not troublesome, but for you it is safety.

2   Beware of dogs, beware of evil workers, beware of the circumcisers. For we are the circumcision, which worship God in the spirit, and rejoice in Christ Jesus, and have no confidence in the flesh.

3   Though I might also have confidence in the flesh. If any other man thinks that he has whereof he might trust in the flesh, I more: circumcised the eighth day, of the stock of Israel, of the tribe of Benjamin, a Hebrew of the Hebrews; as concerning the law, a Pharisee; concerning zeal, persecuting the church; concerning the righteousness which is in the law, blameless.

4   But what things were gain to me, those I counted loss for Christ. Yes doubtless, and I count all things but loss for the excellence of the knowledge of Christ Jesus my Lord: for whom I have suffered the loss of all things, and do count them but waste, that I may win Christ, and be found in him, not having my own righteousness, which is of the law, but that which is through the faith of Christ, the righteousness which is of God by faith: that I may know him, and the power of his resurrection, and the fellowship of his sufferings, being made conformable unto his death; if by any means I might attain unto the resurrection of the dead.

Toward the Mark
Philippians 3:12-21; 4:1

5   Not as though I had already attained, either were already perfect: but I press on, if that I may apprehend that for which also I am apprehended of Christ Jesus. Brethren, I count not myself to have apprehended: but this one thing I do, forgetting those things which are behind, and reaching forth unto

those things which are before, I press toward the goal for the prize of the   5
high calling of God in Christ Jesus.

Let us therefore, as many as be mature, be thus minded: and if in any-   6
thing you be otherwise minded, God shall reveal even this unto you. Nevertheless, whereto we have already attained, let us walk by the same rule, let
us mind the same thing.

Brethren, be imitators together of me, and note them which walk so as   7
you have us for an example. (For many walk, of whom I have told you often,
and now tell you even weeping, that they are the enemies of the cross of
Christ: whose end is destruction, whose God is their appetite, and whose
glory is in their shame, who mind earthly things.)

For our citizenship is in heaven; from which also we look for the Sav-   8
ior, the Lord Jesus Christ: who shall change our lowly body, that it may be
fashioned like unto his glorious body, according to the working whereby he
is able even to subdue all things unto himself.

Therefore, my brethren dearly beloved and longed for, my joy and   9
crown, so stand fast in the Lord, my dearly beloved.

Precious Promise of Peace
Philippians 4:2-9

I plead with Euodias, and plead with Syntyche, that they be of the   10
same mind in the Lord. And I urge you also, true companion, help those
women which labored with me in the gospel, with Clement also, and with
others my fellow laborers, whose names are in the book of life.

Rejoice in the Lord always: and   11
again I say, Rejoice. Let your moderation be known unto all men. The Lord   THE PEACE OF GOD, WHICH
is at hand. Be anxious for nothing; but   SURPASSES ALL UNDERSTAND-
in everything by prayer and supplica-   ING, SHALL KEEP YOUR HEARTS
tion with thanksgiving let your   AND MINDS THROUGH CHRIST.
requests be made known unto God.
And the peace of God, which surpasses all understanding, shall keep your hearts and minds through Christ Jesus.

Finally, brethren, whatsoever things are true, whatsoever things are   12
noble, whatsoever things are just,
whatsoever things are pure, whatsoev-   THE GOD OF PEACE SHALL BE
er things are lovely, whatsoever things   WITH YOU.
are of good report; if there be any
virtue, and if there be any praise, think
on these things. Those things, which you have both learned, and received,
and heard, and seen in me, do: and the God of peace shall be with you.

Thank You
Philippians 4:10-20

But I rejoiced in the Lord greatly, that now at the last your concern of   13
me has flourished again; wherein you were also concerned, but you lacked

13 opportunity. Not that I speak in respect of need: for I have learned, in whatsoever state I am, therewith to be content. I know both how to be in need, and I know how to abound: everywhere and in all things I am instructed both to be full and to be hungry, both to abound and to suffer need. I can do all things through Christ which strengthens me. Nevertheless you have done well, that you did share with my affliction.

> I CAN DO ALL THINGS THROUGH CHRIST WHICH STRENGTHENS ME.

14 Now you Philippians know also, that in the beginning of the gospel, when I departed from Macedonia, no church shared with me as concerning giving and receiving, but you only. For even in Thessalonica you sent once and again unto my necessities. Not because I seek a gift: but I seek fruit that may increase to your credit. But I have all, and increase: I am full, having received of Epaphroditus the things which were sent from you, a fragrance of a sweet smell, a sacrifice acceptable, well pleasing to God. But my God shall supply all your need according to his riches in glory by Christ Jesus.

> GOD SHALL SUPPLY ALL YOUR NEED ACCORDING TO HIS RICHES IN GLORY BY CHRIST.

15 Now unto God and our Father be glory for ever and ever. Amen.

Conclusion
Philippians 4:21-23

16 Greet every saint in Christ Jesus. The brethren which are with me greet you. All the saints greet you, especially they that are of Caesar's household.

17 The grace of our Lord Jesus Christ be with you all. Amen.

PART 31

LETTER TO COLOSSIANS

Although Paul had never visited the city of Colosse in the past, he writes to the Colossians, having received word in prison of their struggle against the influence of outsiders who would place ritualistic codes of outward worship above those of inward intent. To Paul, the Christian life was not found in doctrines or creeds, but in gaining a newness of mind as demonstrated in the practical application of God's law. Those who seek to find grace in the eyes of God through human doctrines, he states, do not fully understand the nature of Christ.

> Beware lest any man capture you through philosophy and empty deceit, according to the tradition of men, according to the rudiments of the world, and not according to Christ. (Colossians 2:8)

CHAPTER 117

Preeminence of Christ

Greeting to Colossians
Colossians 1:1-2

1   Paul, an apostle of Jesus Christ by the will of God, and Timothy our brother, to the saints and faithful brethren in Christ which are at Colosse: Grace be unto you, and peace, from God our Father and the Lord Jesus Christ.

Giving Thanks
Colossians 1:3-8

2   We give thanks to God and the Father of our Lord Jesus Christ, praying always for you, since we heard of your faith in Christ Jesus, and of the love which you have to all the saints, for the hope which is laid up for you in heaven, of which you heard before in the word of the truth of the gospel; which is come unto you, as it is in all the world; and brings forth fruit, as it does also in you, since the day you heard of it, and knew the grace of God in truth: as you also learned of Epaphras our dear fellow servant, who is for you a faithful minister of Christ; who also declared unto us your love in the Spirit.

All Things in Christ
Colossians 1:9-20

3   For this cause we also, since the day we heard it, do not cease to pray for you, and to desire that you might be filled with the knowledge of his will in all wisdom and spiritual understanding; that you might walk worthy of the Lord unto all pleasing, being fruitful in every good work, and increasing in the knowledge of God; strengthened with all might, according to his glorious power, unto all endurance and patience with joyfulness; giving thanks unto the Father, which has made us worthy to be partakers of the inheritance of the saints in light: who has delivered us from the power of

darkness, and has brought us into the kingdom of his dear Son: in whom we 3
have redemption through his blood, even the forgiveness of sins.

He is the image of the invisible God, the firstborn of every creature: 4
for by him were all things created, that
are in heaven, and that are on earth,
visible and invisible, whether they be
thrones, or dominions, or principalities, or powers: all things were created
by him, and for him. And he is before
all things, and by him all things exist.

> FOR BY HIM WERE ALL THINGS CREATED, THAT ARE IN HEAVEN, AND THAT ARE ON EARTH, VISIBLE AND INVISIBLE.

And he is the head of the body, the church: who is the beginning, the 5
firstborn from the dead; that in all things he might have the preeminence.
For it pleased the Father that in him should all fulness dwell; and, having
made peace through the blood of his cross, by him to reconcile all things
unto himself; by him, I say, whether they be things on earth, or things in
heaven.

Gospel Ministry
Colossians 1:21-29

And you, that were once alienated and enemies in your mind by 6
wicked works, yet now has he reconciled in the body of his flesh through
death, to present you holy and blameless and faultless in his sight: if you
continue in the faith grounded and settled, and be not moved away from the
hope of the gospel, which you have heard, and which was preached to every
creature which is under heaven; of which I Paul am made a minister.

I now rejoice in my sufferings for you, and fill up that which is lack- 7
ing of the afflictions of Christ in my flesh for his body's sake, which is the
church: of which I am made a minister, according to the stewardship of God
which is given to me for you, to fulfill the word of God; even the mystery
which has been hidden from ages and from generations, but now is made
known to his saints: to whom God would make known what is the riches of
the glory of this mystery among the Gentiles; which is Christ in you, the
hope of glory.

Him we preach, warning every man, and teaching every man in all 8
wisdom; that we may present every man perfect in Christ Jesus: to which I
also labor, striving according to his working, which works in me mightily.

Knowledge and Wisdom
Colossians 2:1-5

For I would that you knew what great conflict I have for you, and for 9
them at Laodicea, and for as many as have not seen my face in the flesh;
that their hearts might be encouraged, being knit together in love, and unto
all riches of the full assurance of understanding, to the knowledge of the
mystery of God, and of the Father, and of Christ; in whom are hidden all the
treasures of wisdom and knowledge.

10 And this I say, lest any man should beguile you with enticing words. For though I be absent in the flesh, yet am I with you in the spirit, rejoicing and beholding your order, and the steadfastness of your faith in Christ.

Philosophy and Ordinances
Colossians 2:6-19

11 As you have therefore received Christ Jesus the Lord, so walk in him: rooted and built up in him, and established in the faith, as you have been taught, abounding therein with thanksgiving.

12 Beware lest any man capture you through philosophy and empty deceit, according to the tradition of men, according to the rudiments of the world, and not according to Christ.

13 For in him dwells all the fulness of the Godhead bodily. And you are complete in him, which is the head of all principality and power: in whom also you are circumcised with the circumcision made without hands, in putting off the body of the sins of the flesh by the circumcision of Christ: buried with him in baptism, wherein also you are risen with him through the faith of the working of God, who has raised him from the dead.

> YOU ARE COMPLETE IN HIM, WHICH IS THE HEAD OF ALL PRINCIPALITY AND POWER.

14 And you, being dead in your sins and the uncircumcision of your flesh, has he quickened together with him, having forgiven you all trespasses; blotting out the handwriting of ordinances that was against us, which was contrary to us, and took it out of the way, nailing it to his cross; and having disarmed principalities and powers, he made a show of them openly, triumphing over them in it.

15 Let no man therefore judge you in food, or in drink, or in respect of a festival, or of the new moon, or of the sabbath days: which are a shadow of things to come; but the substance is of Christ.

16 Let no man beguile you of your reward in a voluntary humility and worshiping of angels, intruding into those things which he has not seen, falsely puffed up by his fleshly mind, and not holding the Head, from which all the body by joints and ligaments having nourishment ministered, and joined together, increases with the increase of God.

Renewal
Colossians 2:20-23

17 Therefore if you be dead with Christ from the rudiments of the world, why, as though living in the world, are you subject to ordinances, ("touch not; taste not; handle not"; which all are to perish with the using); according to the commandments and doctrines of men? Which things have indeed a show of wisdom in self-imposed worship, and humility, and neglect of the body; not in any honor to the satisfying of the flesh.

CHAPTER 118

⸱⸱BEHAVIOR IN CHRIST'S NAME⸱⸱

New Life in Christ
Colossians 3:1-17

If you then be risen with Christ, seek those things which are above, 1
where Christ sits on the right hand of God. Set your affection on things
above, not on things on the earth. For you are dead, and your life is hidden
with Christ in God. When Christ, who is our life, shall appear, then shall
you also appear with him in glory.

Put to death therefore your natures which are upon the earth; fornica- 2
tion, uncleanness, inordinate passion, evil desire, and covetousness, which
is idolatry: for which things' sake the wrath of God comes on the children
of disobedience: in which you also walked sometimes, when you lived in
them.

But now you also put off all these; anger, wrath, malice, slander, filthy 3
language out of your mouth. Lie not one to another, seeing that you have
put off the old man with his deeds; and have put on the new man, which is
renewed in knowledge after the image of him that created him: where there
is neither Greek nor Jew, circumcision nor uncircumcision, barbarian,
Scythian, bond nor free: but Christ is all, and in all.

Put on therefore, as the elect of God, holy and beloved, a heart of com- 4
passion, kindness, humbleness of mind, meekness, patience; bearing with
one another, and forgiving one another, if any man has a quarrel against
another: even as Christ forgave you, so also do you.

And above all these things put on love, which is the bond of perfect- 5
ness. And let the peace of God rule in your hearts, to which also you are
called in one body; and be thankful.

Let the word of Christ dwell in you richly in all wisdom; teaching and 6
admonishing one another in psalms and hymns and spiritual songs, singing
with grace in your hearts to the Lord. And whatsoever you do in word or

6 deed, do all in the name of the Lord Jesus, giving thanks to God and the Father by him.

Duties of the New Life
Colossians 3:18-25; 4:1

7 Wives, submit yourselves unto your own husbands, as it is fitting in the Lord.

8 Husbands, love your wives, and be not bitter toward them.

9 Children, obey your parents in all things: for this is well pleasing unto the Lord.

10 Fathers, provoke not your children to anger, lest they be discouraged.

11 Servants, obey in all things your masters according to the flesh; not with eyeservice, as men-pleasers; but in singleness of heart, fearing God. And whatsoever you do, do it heartily, as to the Lord, and not unto men; knowing that of the Lord you shall receive the reward of the inheritance: for you serve the Lord Christ.

> WHATSOEVER YOU DO, DO IT HEARTILY, AS TO THE LORD, AND NOT UNTO MEN.

12 But he that does wrong shall receive for the wrong which he has done: and there is no partiality of persons.

13 Masters, give unto your servants that which is just and equal; knowing that you also have a Master in heaven.

Redeeming the Time
Colossians 4:2-6

14 Continue in prayer, and watch in the same with thanksgiving; with praying also for us, that God would open unto us a door of utterance, to speak the mystery of Christ, for which I am also in bonds: that I may make it clear, as I ought to speak.

15 Walk in wisdom toward them that are outside, redeeming the time. Let your speech be always with grace, seasoned with salt, that you may know how you ought to answer every man.

> LET YOUR SPEECH BE ALWAYS WITH GRACE.

Final Greetings
Colossians 4:7-17

16 All my state shall Tychicus declare unto you, who is a beloved brother, and a faithful minister and fellow servant in the Lord: whom I have sent unto you for the same purpose, that he might know your circumstances, and comfort your hearts; with Onesimus, a faithful and beloved brother, who is one of you. They shall make known unto you all things which are done here.

17 Aristarchus my fellow prisoner greets you, and Marcus, sister's son to Barnabas, (concerning whom you received commandments: if he comes

unto you, receive him); and Jesus, which is called Justus, who are of the cir- 17
cumcision. These only are my fellow workers unto the kingdom of God,
which have been a comfort unto me.

Epaphras, who is one of you, a servant of Christ, greets you, always 18
laboring fervently for you in prayers, that you may stand perfect and complete in all the will of God. For I bear him witness, that he has a great zeal
for you, and them that are in Laodicea, and them in Hierapolis.

Luke, the beloved physician, and Demas, greet you. Greet the brethren 19
which are in Laodicea, and Nymphas, and the church which is in his house.

And when this letter is read among you, cause that it be read also in 20
the church of the Laodiceans; and that you likewise read the letter from
Laodicea.

And say to Archippus, "Take heed to the ministry which you have 21
received in the Lord, that you fulfill it."

Conclusion
Colossians 4:18

The greeting by the hand of me, Paul. Remember my bonds. Grace be 22
with you. Amen.

PART 32

LETTER TO PHILEMON

In a personal plea on behalf of his faithful follower and messenger, Onesimus, Paul writes to his friend, Philemon, asking him to forgive Onesimus. Onesimus had been a servant of Philemon's, but had stolen his goods and fled. He asks him to take Onesimus back graciously, not as a servant, but as a brother in Christ. This he asks Philemon to do willingly and of a free spirit. In a significant example of Christian faith, Paul offers to repay Onesimus' debts in return for Philemon's forgiveness, thus replacing Onesimus' servitude for man with his service for Christ.

> WITHOUT YOUR CONSENT WOULD I DO NOTH-
> ING; THAT YOUR GOOD DEED SHOULD NOT BE AS
> IT WERE OF NECESSITY, BUT WILLINGLY.
>
> (PHILEMON 1:14)

CHAPTER 119

CHRISTIAN MERCY

Greeting to Philemon
Philemon 1:1-3

1 Paul, a prisoner of Jesus Christ, and Timothy our brother, unto Philemon our dearly beloved, and fellow laborer, and to our beloved Apphia, and Archippus our fellow soldier, and to the church in your house: Grace to you, and peace, from God our Father and the Lord Jesus Christ.

Giving Thanks
Philemon 1:4-7

2 I thank my God, making mention of you always in my prayers, hearing of your love and faith, which you have toward the Lord Jesus, and toward all saints; that the sharing of your faith may become effective by the acknowledging of every good thing which is in you in Christ Jesus. For we have great joy and consolation in your love, because the hearts of the saints are refreshed by you, brother.

Plea for Onesimus
Philemon 1:8-22

3 Therefore, though I might be bold enough in Christ to order you that which is fitting, yet for love's sake I rather appeal to you, being such a one as Paul the aged, and now also a prisoner of Jesus Christ. I appeal to you for my son Onesimus, whom I have begotten in my bonds: which in time past was to you unprofitable, but now profitable to you and to me: whom I have sent back: you therefore receive him, that is, my own heart: whom I would have retained with me, that in your behalf he might have ministered unto me in the bonds of the gospel. But without your consent would I do nothing; that your good deed should not be as it were of necessity, but willingly.

4 For perhaps he therefore departed for a season, that you should receive him for ever; not now as a servant, but above a servant, a brother beloved,

4 especially to me, but how much more unto you, both in the flesh, and in the Lord?

5   If you count me therefore a partner, receive him as myself. If he has wronged you, or owes you anything, put that on my account. I Paul have written it with my own hand, I will repay it: albeit I do not say to you how you owe unto me even your own self besides. Yes, brother, let me have joy of you in the Lord: refresh my heart in the Lord.

6   Having confidence in your obedience I wrote unto you, knowing that you will also do more than I say. But in addition prepare me also a lodging: for I trust that through your prayers I shall be given unto you.

Conclusion
Philemon 1:23-25

7   There greet you Epaphras, my fellow prisoner in Christ Jesus; Marcus, Aristarchus, Demas, Lucas, my fellow laborers.

8   The grace of our Lord Jesus Christ be with your spirit. Amen.

PART 33

ACTS OF APOSTLES COMPLETION

This brief interlude concludes the written Acts of the Apostles, as Paul preaches openly in Rome while under house arrest. Afforded his own accommodations and personal freedom, he continues writing letters of encouragement and spiritual guidance to his fellow disciples. However, Paul's peaceful ministry for two years belies the tragedy of his eventual execution at the hands of the Roman Empire. While it may appear inconsequential, this short passage is significant in that it represents a closure of the Acts of the Apostles and the conclusion of the recorded history in the Bible.

434

PAUL DWELT TWO WHOLE YEARS IN HIS OWN
RENTED HOUSE, AND RECEIVED ALL THAT CAME
IN UNTO HIM.   (ACTS 28:30)

CHAPTER 120

COMPLETION OF HISTORICAL RECORD

Paul Continues Gospel at Rome
Acts 28:30-31

1   And Paul dwelt two whole years in his own rented house, and received all that came in unto him, preaching the kingdom of God, and teaching those things which concern the Lord Jesus Christ, with all confidence, no man forbidding him.

PART 34

FIRST LETTER TO TIMOTHY

Paul's letter to Timothy, one of his youngest followers, was written during his confinement in Rome. Knowing that Timothy was facing many challenges in the church at Ephesus, Paul provides guidance on matters of doctrine for the church concerning appropriate behavior for women, elders, and widows, and their treatment in terms of personal respect and the law. He emphasizes the importance of faith through works, not simply through words, for many of those who profess to be faithful in the church are easily swayed by riches, extravagance, and godless chatter. These become hypocrites through their own words.

436

> GOD WAS MANIFESTED IN THE FLESH, JUSTIFIED
> IN THE SPIRIT, SEEN OF ANGELS, PREACHED UNTO
> THE GENTILES, BELIEVED ON IN THE WORLD,
> RECEIVED UP INTO GLORY.   (1 TIMOTHY 3:16)

CHAPTER 121

DOCTRINE AND REASON

Greeting to Timothy
1 Timothy 1:1-2

1 Paul, an apostle of Jesus Christ by the commandment of God our Savior, and Lord Jesus Christ, which is our hope; unto Timothy, my true son in the faith: Grace, mercy, and peace, from God our Father and Jesus Christ our Lord.

False and Sound Doctrine
1 Timothy 1:3-11

2 As I urged you to remain there at Ephesus, when I went into Macedonia, that you might order some that they teach no other doctrine, neither give heed to fables and endless genealogies, which promote controversies, rather than godly edification which is in faith: so do.

3 Now the purpose of the instruction is love out of a pure heart, and of a good conscience, and of faith sincere: from which some having swerved have turned aside unto empty babbling; desiring to be teachers of the law; understanding neither what they say, nor of what they affirm.

4 But we know that the law is good, if a man uses it lawfully; knowing this, that the law is not made for a righteous man, but for the lawless and disobedient, for the ungodly and for sinners, for the unholy and profane, for murderers of fathers and murderers of mothers, for manslayers, for whoremongers, for them that defile themselves with mankind, for kidnappers, for liars, for perjurers, and if there be any other thing that is contrary to sound doctrine; according to the glorious gospel of the blessed God, which was committed to my trust.

Saving Sinners
1 Timothy 1:12-20

5 And I thank Christ Jesus our Lord, who has strengthened me, for he counted me faithful, putting me into the ministry; who was before a

blasphemer, and a persecutor, and injurious: but I obtained mercy, because 5
I did it ignorantly in unbelief. And the grace of our Lord was exceedingly
abundant with faith and love which is in Christ Jesus.

This is a faithful saying, and worthy of all acceptance, that Christ 6
Jesus came into the world to save sin-
ners; of whom I am chief. Howbeit for
this cause I obtained mercy, that in me
first Jesus Christ might show forth all
patience, for a pattern to them which
should hereafter believe on him to life everlasting. Now unto the King eternal, immortal, invisible, the only wise God, be honor and glory for ever and
ever. Amen.

> JESUS CAME INTO THE WORLD
> TO SAVE SINNERS.

This charge I commit unto you, son Timothy, according to the prophe- 7
cies which went before on you, that you by them might war a good warfare;
holding faith, and a good conscience; which some having put away concerning faith have made shipwreck: of whom is Hymenaeus and Alexander;
whom I have delivered unto Satan, that they may learn not to blaspheme.

Doctrine and Prayer
1 Timothy 2:1-7

I urge therefore, that, first of all, supplications, prayers, intercessions, 8
and giving of thanks, be made for all men; for kings, and for all that are in
authority; that we may lead a quiet and peaceable life in all godliness and
dignity. For this is good and acceptable in the sight of God our Savior; who
will have all men to be saved, and to come unto the knowledge of the truth.

For there is one God, and one
mediator between God and men, the
man Christ Jesus; who gave himself a
ransom for all, to be testified in due
time. To which I am ordained a
preacher, and an apostle, (I speak the truth in Christ, and do not lie); a
teacher of the Gentiles in faith and truth.

> THERE IS ONE GOD, AND ONE
> MEDIATOR BETWEEN GOD
> AND MEN.

Women and Men
1 Timothy 2:8-15

I will therefore that men pray everywhere, lifting up holy hands, with- 10
out anger and quarreling.

In like manner also, that women adorn themselves in modest apparel, 11
with decency and propriety; not with braided hair, or gold, or pearls, or costly
array; but (which becomes women professing godliness) with good works.

Let the woman learn in silence with all submission. But I do not per- 12
mit a woman to teach, nor to have authority over the man, but to be in
silence.

For Adam was first formed, then Eve. And Adam was not deceived, 13
but the woman being deceived was in the transgression. Nevertheless she

13 shall be saved through childbearing, if they continue in faith and love and holiness with decency.

Bishops
1 Timothy 3:1-7

14 This is a faithful saying, If a man desires the office of a bishop, he desires a good work. A bishop then must be blameless, the husband of one wife, vigilant, sober-minded, of good behavior, given to hospitality, apt to teach; not given to wine, not violent, not greedy of dishonest gain; but patient, not a brawler, not covetous; one that rules well his own house, having his children in subjection with all gravity; (for if a man knows not how to rule his own house, how shall he take care of the church of God?) not a novice, lest being lifted up with conceit he fall into the condemnation of the devil. Moreover he must have a good reputation of them which are outside; lest he fall into disgrace and the snare of the devil.

> THIS IS A TRUE SAYING, IF A MAN DESIRES THE OFFICE OF A BISHOP, HE DESIRES A GOOD WORK.

Deacons
1 Timothy 3:8-13

15 Likewise must the deacons be serious, not double-tongued, not given to much wine, not greedy of dishonest gain; holding the mystery of the faith in a pure conscience. And let these also first be tested; then let them use the office of a deacon, being found blameless.

16 Even so must their wives be serious, not slanderers, temperate, faithful in all things.

17 Let the deacons be the husbands of one wife, managing their children and their own houses well. For they that have used the office of a deacon well gain to themselves a good standing, and great boldness in the faith which is in Christ Jesus.

Mystery of Godliness
1 Timothy 3:14-16

18 These things write I unto you, hoping to come unto you shortly: but if I tarry long, that you may know how you ought to behave yourself in the house of God, which is the church of the living God, the pillar and ground of the truth.

19 And without controversy great is the mystery of godliness: God was manifested in the flesh, justified in the Spirit, seen of angels, preached unto the Gentiles, believed on in the world, received up into glory.

CHAPTER 122

PEACEFUL LIVING

False Teachings
1 Timothy 4:1-5

Now the Spirit speaks expressly, that in the latter times some shall 1
depart from the faith, giving heed to seducing spirits, and doctrines of
demons; speaking lies in hypocrisy; having their conscience seared with a
hot iron; forbidding to marry, and teaching to abstain from foods, which
God has created to be received with thanksgiving of them which believe and
know the truth.

For every creature of God is good, and nothing to be refused, if it be 2
received with thanksgiving: for it is sanctified by the word of God and
prayer.

Good Ministry
1 Timothy 4:6-16

If you put the brethren in remembrance of these things, you shall be a 3
good minister of Jesus Christ, nourished up in the words of faith and of
good doctrine, which you have attained. But refuse profane and old wives'
fables, and exercise yourself rather unto godliness. For bodily exercise profits little: but godliness is profitable unto all things, having promise of the
life that now is, and of that which is to come.

This is a faithful saying and worthy of all acceptance. For this purpose 4
we both labor and suffer disgrace, because we trust in the living God, who
is the Savior of all men, especially of those that believe.

These things command and teach. Let no man despise your youth; but 5
be an example of the believers, in word, in conduct, in love, in spirit, in faith,
in purity. Till I come, give attention to reading, to exhortation, to doctrine.
Do not neglect the gift that is in you, which was given you by prophecy, with
the laying on of the hands of the elders.

6   Meditate upon these things; give yourself wholly to them; that your progress may appear to all. Take heed unto yourself, and unto the doctrine; continue in them: for in doing this you shall both save yourself, and them that hear you.

Elders and Widows
1 Timothy 5:1-16

7   Rebuke not an older man, but appeal to him as a father; and the younger men as brethren; the older women as mothers; the younger as sisters, with all purity.

8   Honor widows that are widows indeed. But if any widow has children or grandchildren, let them learn first to show piety at home, and to repay their parents: for that is good and acceptable before God.

9   Now she that is a widow indeed, and alone, trusts in God, and continues in supplications and prayers night and day. But she that lives in pleasure is dead while she lives.

10   And these things give in instruction, that they may be blameless. But if anyone provides not for his own, and especially for those of his own household, he has denied the faith, and is worse than an unbeliever.

11   Let not a widow be taken into the number under sixty years old, having been the wife of one man, well reported of for good works; if she has brought up children, if she has lodged strangers, if she has washed the saints' feet, if she has relieved the afflicted, if she has diligently followed every good work.

12   But the younger widows refuse: for when they have begun to grow restless against Christ, they will marry; having condemnation, because they have cast off their first faith. And in addition they learn to be idle, wandering about from house to house; and not only idle, but tattlers also and busybodies, speaking things which they ought not.

13   I will therefore that the younger women marry, bear children, guide the house, give no occasion to the adversary to speak slanderously. For some are already turned aside after Satan. If any man or woman that believes has widows, let them relieve them, and let not the church be burdened; that it may relieve them that are widows indeed.

Double Honor
1 Timothy 5:17-20

14   Let the elders that rule well be counted worthy of double honor, especially they who labor in the word and doctrine. For the scripture says, "*You shall not muzzle the ox that treads out the grain.*" And, "The laborer is worthy of his wages."

15   Against an elder do not receive an accusation, except before two or three witnesses. Them that sin rebuke before all, that others also may fear.

Personal Partiality
1 Timothy 5:21-25

I call upon you before God, and the Lord Jesus Christ, and the 16 elect angels, that you observe these things without preferring one before another, doing nothing by partiality.

Lay hands hastily on no man, neither be partaker of other men's sins: keep yourself pure. 17

> KEEP YOURSELF PURE.

Drink not only water, but use a little wine for your stomach's sake 18 and your frequent infirmities.

Some men's sins are obvious beforehand, going ahead to judgment; 19 and some men they follow later. Likewise also the good works of some are obvious beforehand; and they that are otherwise cannot be hidden.

Servants and Masters
1 Timothy 6:1-2

Let as many servants as are under the yoke count their own masters 20 worthy of all honor, that the name of God and his doctrine be not blasphemed. And they that have believing masters, let them not despise them, because they are brethren; but rather do them service, because they are faithful and beloved, partakers of the benefit. These things teach and urge.

CHAPTER 123

·⊶———— CHRISTIAN'S WALK ————⊷·

True Wealth
1 Timothy 6:3-10

1   If any man teaches otherwise, and does not consent to wholesome words, even the words of our Lord Jesus Christ, and to the doctrine which is according to godliness; he is conceited, knowing nothing, but doting about controversies and disputes over words, of which comes envy, strife, insults, evil suspicions, perverse endless wrangling of men of corrupt minds, and destitute of the truth, supposing that gain is godliness: from such withdraw yourself.

2   But godliness with contentment is great gain. For we brought nothing into this world, and it is certain we can carry nothing out. And having food and clothing let us be content with that.

3   But they that would be rich fall into temptation and a snare, and into many foolish and harmful lusts, which drown men in destruction and perdition. For the love of money is the root of all evil: which while some coveted after, they have wandered from the faith, and pierced themselves through with many sorrows.

Good Fight of Faith
1 Timothy 6:11-16

4   But you, O man of God, flee these things; and follow after righteousness, godliness, faith, love, patience, meekness. Fight the good fight of faith, lay hold on eternal life, to which you are also called, and have professed a good profession before many witnesses.

5   I give you charge in the sight of God, who quickens all things, and before Christ Jesus, who before Pontius Pilate witnessed a good confession; that you keep this commandment without spot, faultless, until the appearing of our Lord Jesus Christ: which in his times he shall show, who is the

blessed and only Potentate, the King of kings, and Lord of lords; who only 5
has immortality, dwelling in the light which no man can approach unto;
whom no man has seen, nor can see: to whom be honor and power everlasting. Amen.

Good Works and the Rich
1 Timothy 6:17-19

Charge them that are rich in this world, that they be not high-minded, 6
nor trust in uncertain riches, but in the
living God, who gives us richly all
things to enjoy; that they do good, that
they be rich in good works, ready to
distribute, willing to share; laying up
in store for themselves a good founda-
tion toward the time to come, that they may lay hold on eternal life.

> BE NOT HIGH-MINDED, NOR
> TRUST IN UNCERTAIN RICHES,
> BUT IN THE LIVING GOD.

Conclusion
1 Timothy 6:20-21

O Timothy, keep that which is committed to your trust, avoiding pro- 7
fane and empty babblings, and contradictions of knowledge falsely so
called: which some professing have wandered concerning the faith. Grace
be with you. Amen.

PART 35

LETTER TO TITUS

Paul pauses to write a letter to Titus, a close companion and one of his senior followers, on how to deal with matters of the church in Crete. He instructs Titus on how to rebuke ungodliness among the people, the qualifications for a Christian life, and how important inspired doctrine is to the body of Christ. He encourages Titus to do what is right and good and to teach the same in his church. Paul wants Titus to not only know God's grace, but to give it.

WE SHOULD LIVE SENSIBLY, RIGHTEOUSLY, AND
GODLY, IN THIS PRESENT WORLD; LOOKING FOR
THAT BLESSED HOPE, AND THE GLORIOUS APPEAR-
ING OF THE GREAT GOD AND OUR SAVIOR JESUS
CHRIST; WHO GAVE HIMSELF FOR US.

(TITUS 2:12-13)

CHAPTER 124

ENCOURAGEMENT IN CHRIST

Greeting to Titus
Titus 1:1-4

Paul, a servant of God, and an apostle of Jesus Christ, according to the 1
faith of God's elect, and the acknowledging of the truth which is after godliness; in hope of eternal life, which God, that cannot lie, promised before
the world began; but has in due times manifested his word through preaching, which is committed unto me according to the commandment of God
our Savior; to Titus, my own son after the common faith: Grace, mercy, and
peace, from God the Father and the Lord Jesus Christ our Savior.

Elders and Bishops
Titus 1:5-9

For this reason I left you in Crete, that you should set in order the 2
things that are lacking, and ordain elders in every city, as I had appointed
you: if any be blameless, the husband of one wife, having faithful children
not accused of loose living or disobedience.

For a bishop must be blameless, as the steward of God; not self-willed, 3
not soon angry, not given to wine, not violent, not given to dishonest gain;
but a lover of hospitality, a lover of good men, sober-minded, just, holy,
temperate; holding fast the faithful word as he has been taught, that he may
be able by sound doctrine both to instruct and to refute the opponents.

True of the Cretans
Titus 1:10-16

For there are many unruly and empty talkers and deceivers, especially 4
they of the circumcision: whose mouths must be stopped, who unsettle
whole households, teaching things which they ought not, for dishonest
gain's sake.

5   One of themselves, even a prophet of their own, said, "The Cretans are always liars, evil beasts, lazy gluttons." This witness is true. Therefore rebuke them sharply, that they may be sound in the faith; not giving heed to Jewish fables, and commands of men, that turn from the truth.

6   Unto the pure all things are pure: but unto them that are defiled and unbelieving is nothing pure; but even their mind and conscience is defiled. They profess that they know God; but in works they deny him, being abominable, and disobedient, and unto every good work reprobate.

> UNTO THE PURE ALL THINGS ARE PURE.

Sound Doctrine
Titus 2:1-15

7   But speak you the things which become sound doctrine: that the older men be temperate, serious, sensible, sound in faith, in love, in patience.

8   The aged women likewise, that they be in behavior as becomes holiness, not false accusers, not given to much wine, teachers of good things; that they may teach the young women to be temperate, to love their husbands, to love their children, to be discreet, chaste, homemakers, good, obedient to their own husbands, that the word of God be not blasphemed.

9   Young men likewise encourage to be self-controlled.

10   In all things showing yourself a pattern of good works: in doctrine showing integrity, seriousness, sincerity, sound speech, that cannot be condemned; that he that is of the opposition may be ashamed, having no evil thing to say of you.

11   Urge servants to be obedient unto their own masters, and to please them well in all things; not answering again; not stealing, but showing all good fidelity; that they may adorn the doctrine of God our Savior in all things.

12   For the grace of God that brings salvation has appeared to all men, teaching us that, denying ungodliness and worldly lusts, we should live sensibly, righteously, and godly, in this present world; looking for that blessed hope, and the glorious appearing of the great God and our Savior Jesus Christ; who gave himself for us, that he might redeem us from all iniquity, and purify unto himself a peculiar people, zealous of good works.

> THE GRACE OF GOD THAT BRINGS SALVATION HAS APPEARED TO ALL MEN.

13   These things speak, and encourage, and rebuke with all authority. Let no man disregard you.

Doing What Is Good
Titus 3:1-11

14   Put them in mind to be subject to principalities and authorities, to obey magistrates, to be ready to every good work, to speak evil of no man, to be no quarrelers, but gentle, showing all meekness unto all men.

For we ourselves also were once foolish, disobedient, deceived, 15 serving various lusts and pleasures, living in malice and envy, hateful, and hating one another.

But after that the kindness and love of God our Savior toward man 16 appeared, not by works of righteousness which we have done, but according to his mercy he saved us, by the washing of regeneration, and renewing of the Holy Ghost; which he poured on us abundantly through

> HE SAVED US, BY THE WASHING OF REGENERATION, AND RENEWING OF THE HOLY GHOST.

Jesus Christ our Savior; that being justified by his grace, we should be made heirs according to the hope of eternal life.

This is a faithful saying, and these things I insist that you affirm con- 17 stantly, that they which have believed in God might be careful to maintain good works. These things are good and profitable unto men.

But avoid foolish disputes, and genealogies, and contentions, and 18 quarrels about the law; for they are unprofitable and futile. A man that is a heretic after the first and second admonition reject; knowing that he that is such is corrupt, and sins, being condemned of himself.

Conclusion
Titus 3:12-15

When I shall send Artemas unto you, or Tychicus, be diligent to come 19 unto me to Nicopolis: for I have determined there to winter. Bring Zenas the lawyer and Apollos on their journey diligently, that nothing be lacking unto them. And let ours also learn to maintain good works for necessary uses, that they be not unfruitful.

All that are with me greet you. Greet them that love us in the faith. 20 Grace be with you all. Amen.

PART 36

SECOND LETTER TO TIMOTHY

At the writing of this letter, Paul is held prisoner in Rome with little hope for release. Deserted by most of his friends and followers, he stands before the Roman council alone in his own defense—with only his God at his side. Knowing that he faces almost certain death, he implores Timothy, who is one of his strongest hopes, to endure in his faith with sound doctrine. Paul is satisfied that he himself has fought the good fight. He has kept the faith. He has finished his course with righteousness and honor.

CONTINUE IN THE THINGS WHICH YOU HAVE
LEARNED AND HAVE BEEN ASSURED OF.

(2 TIMOTHY 3:14)

CHAPTER 125

MINISTER'S WALK

Greeting to Timothy
2 Timothy 1:1-2

Paul, an apostle of Jesus Christ by the will of God, according to the 1
promise of life which is in Christ Jesus, to Timothy, my dearly beloved son:
Grace, mercy, and peace, from God the Father and Christ Jesus our Lord.

Apostle and Teacher of Gentiles
2 Timothy 1:3-18

I thank God, whom I serve from my forefathers with pure conscience, 2
that without ceasing I have remembrance of you in my prayers night and
day; greatly desiring to see you, being mindful of your tears, that I may be
filled with joy; when I call to remembrance the sincere faith that is in you,
which dwelt first in your grandmother Lois, and your mother Eunice; and I
am persuaded that is in you also.

Therefore I put you in remembrance that you stir up the gift of God, 3
which is in you by the putting on of my hands. For God has not given us the
spirit of fear; but of power, and of love, and of a sound mind.

Be not therefore ashamed of the testimony of our Lord, nor of me his 4
prisoner: but be partaker of the afflictions of the gospel according to the
power of God; who has saved us, and called us with a holy calling, not
according to our works, but according to his own purpose and grace, which
was given us in Christ Jesus before the world began, but is now made manifest by the appearing of our Savior Jesus Christ, who has abolished death,
and has brought life and immortality to light through the gospel: to which I
am appointed a preacher, and an apostle, and a teacher of the Gentiles. For
which cause I also suffer these things: nevertheless I am not ashamed: for I
know whom I have believed, and am persuaded that he is able to keep that
which I have committed unto him toward that day.

5   Hold fast the pattern of sound words, which you have heard of me, in faith and love which is in Christ Jesus. That good thing which was committed unto you keep by the Holy Ghost which dwells in us.

6   This you know, that all they which are in Asia have turned away from me; of whom are Phygellus and Hermogenes.

7   The Lord give mercy unto the household of Onesiphorus; for he often refreshed me, and was not ashamed of my chain: but, when he was in Rome, he sought me out very diligently, and found me. The Lord grant unto him that he may find mercy of the Lord in that day: and in how many things he ministered unto me at Ephesus, you know very well.

Grace of Christ
2 Timothy 2:1-13

8   You therefore, my son, be strong in the grace that is in Christ Jesus. And the things that you have heard of me among many witnesses, the same commit you to faithful men, who shall be able to teach others also.

9   You therefore endure hardship, as a good soldier of Jesus Christ. No man that wars entangles himself with the affairs of this life; that he may please him who has chosen him to be a soldier.

10   And if a man also competes for masteries, yet is he not crowned, except he competes lawfully. The farmer that labors must be first partaker of the fruits. Consider what I say; and the Lord will give you understanding in all things.

11   Remember that Jesus Christ of the seed of David was raised from the dead according to my gospel: for which I suffer trouble, as an evildoer, even unto bonds; but the word of God is not bound. Therefore I endure all things for the elect's sakes, that they may also obtain the salvation which is in Christ Jesus with eternal glory.

12   It is a faithful saying: for if we be dead with him, we shall also live with him: if we endure, we shall also reign with him: if we deny him, he also will deny us: if we believe not, yet he abides faithful: he cannot deny himself.

Personal Conduct
2 Timothy 2:14-26

13   Of these things put them in remembrance, charging them before the Lord that they do not dispute about words to no profit, but to the undermining of the hearers. Strive to show yourself approved unto God, a workman that needs not to be ashamed, rightly dividing the word of truth.

14   But shun profane and empty babblings: for they will increase unto more ungodliness. And their word will eat as does a cancer: of whom is Hymenaeus and Philetus; who concerning the truth have wandered, saying that the resurrection is past already; and overthrow the faith of some. Nevertheless the foundation of God stands sure, having this seal, "*The Lord*

knows them that are his." And, "Let everyone that names the name of Christ 14 depart from iniquity."

But in a great house there are not only vessels of gold and of silver, 15 but also of wood and of clay; and some to honor, and some to dishonor. If a man therefore purges himself from these, he shall be a vessel unto honor, sanctified, and useful for the master's use, and prepared unto every good work.

Flee also youthful lusts: but follow righteousness, faith, love, peace, 16 with them that call on the Lord out of a pure heart. But foolish and uneducated speculations avoid, knowing that they do gender quarrels.

> CALL ON THE LORD OUT OF A PURE HEART.

And the servant of the Lord must not quarrel; but be gentle unto all 17 men, able to teach, patient, in meekness instructing those that oppose themselves; if God perhaps will give them repentance to the acknowledging of the truth; and that they may recover themselves out of the snare of the devil, who are taken captive by him at his will.

CHAPTER 126

Paul's Farewell to Timothy

Perils of the Last Days
2 Timothy 3:1-9

1   This know also, that in the last days perilous times shall come. For men shall be lovers of their own selves, lovers of money, boasters, arrogant, slanderers, disobedient to parents, unthankful, unholy, without natural affection, irreconcilable, false accusers, without self-control, fierce, despisers of those that are good, treacherous, reckless, conceited, lovers of pleasures more than lovers of God; having a form of godliness, but denying the power thereof: from such turn away.

2   For of this sort are they which creep into households, and lead captive simple women burdoned with sins, led away with various lusts, ever learning, and never able to come to the knowledge of the truth.

3   Now as Jannes and Jambres withstood Moses, so do these also resist the truth: men of corrupt minds, reprobate concerning the faith. But they shall proceed no further: for their folly shall be evident unto all men, as theirs also was.

Scripture
2 Timothy 3:10-17

4   But you have fully known my doctrine, manner of life, purpose, faith, patience, love, endurance, persecutions, afflictions, which came unto me at Antioch, at Iconium, at Lystra; what persecutions I endured: but out of them all the Lord delivered me.

5   Yes, and all that will live godly in Christ Jesus shall suffer persecution. But evil men and seducers shall grow worse and worse, deceiving, and being deceived.

6   But continue in the things which you have learned and have been assured of, knowing of whom you have learned them; and that from a childhood you

have known the holy scriptures, which are able to make you wise unto sal- 6
vation through faith which is in Christ Jesus.

All scripture is given by inspiration of God, and is profitable for doc- 7
trine, for reproof, for correction, for
instruction in righteousness: that the | ALL SCRIPTURE IS GIVEN BY
man of God may be complete, thor- | INSPIRATION OF GOD.
oughly equipped unto all good works.

As an Evangelist
2 Timothy 4:1-8

I charge you therefore before God, and the Lord Jesus Christ, who 8
shall judge the quick and the dead at his appearing and his kingdom; preach
the word; be persistent in season, out of season; convince, rebuke, encourage with all patience and doctrine.

For the time will come when they will not endure sound doctrine; but 9
according to their own lusts shall they heap to themselves teachers, having
itching ears; and they shall turn away their ears from the truth, and shall be
turned unto fables. But watch in all things, endure afflictions, do the work
of an evangelist, make full proof of your ministry.

For I am now ready to be offered, and the time of my departure is at 10
hand. I have fought a good fight, I
have finished my course, I have kept | I HAVE FOUGHT A GOOD
the faith: henceforth there is laid up | FIGHT, I HAVE FINISHED MY
for me a crown of righteousness, | COURSE, I HAVE KEPT THE
which the Lord, the righteous judge, | FAITH.
shall give me at that day: and not to
me only, but unto all them also that long for his appearing.

Personal Instructions
2 Timothy 4:9-18

Do your diligence to come shortly unto me: for Demas has forsaken 11
me, having loved this present world, and is departed unto Thessalonica;
Crescens to Galatia, Titus unto Dalmatia.

Only Luke is with me. Take Mark, and bring him with you: for he is 12
helpful to me for the ministry. And Tychicus have I sent to Ephesus. The
cloak that I left at Troas with Carpus, when you come, bring with you, and
the books, but especially the parchments.

Alexander the coppersmith did me much harm: the Lord will repay 13
him according to his works: of whom you beware also; for he has greatly
withstood our words.

At my first defense no man stood with me, but all men forsook me: I 14
pray God that it may not be laid to their blame. Notwithstanding the Lord
stood with me, and strengthened me; that by me the preaching might be
fully known, and that all the Gentiles might hear: and I was delivered out of
the mouth of the lion. And the Lord shall deliver me from every evil work,

14 and will preserve me unto his heavenly kingdom: to whom be glory for ever and ever. Amen.

Conclusion
2 Timothy 4:19-22

15   Greet Priscilla and Aquila, and the household of Onesiphorus. Erastus stayed at Corinth: but Trophimus have I left at Miletus sick. Do your diligence to come before winter. Eubulus greets you, and Pudens, and Linus, and Claudia, and all the brethren.

16   The Lord Jesus Christ be with your spirit. Grace be with you. Amen.

PART 37

LETTER TO HEBREWS

This exquisite letter by Paul is written to believers of all faiths. Paul instructs those who follow Christ to be on guard against getting caught up in works without faith and thereby falling astray. Works alone will not assure us a place in heaven. He points to the lives of many great people of the Bible, reiterating their faith in God. The one thing we must do, Paul insists, is to have faith, for faith is "the substance of things hoped for and the evidence of things not seen." Paul wants all to realize that faith in Jesus Christ is supreme over all other means and is the only true measure of our sincerity. This clarion call to faith is one of the most memorable letters written by Paul and was the last of his letters.

> THROUGH FAITH WE UNDERSTAND THAT THE
> WORLDS WERE FRAMED BY THE WORD OF GOD,
> SO THAT THINGS WHICH ARE SEEN WERE NOT
> MADE OF THINGS WHICH DO APPEAR.
>
> (HEBREWS 11:3)

CHAPTER 127

INTRODUCTION OF THE CHRIST

Greeting to Hebrews
Hebrews 1:1-4

1   God, who at many times and in various ways spoke in time past unto the fathers by the prophets, has in these last days spoken unto us by his Son, whom he has appointed heir of all things, by whom also he made the worlds; who being the brightness of his glory, and the express image of his person, and upholding all things by the word of his power, when he had by himself purged our sins, sat down on the right hand of the Majesty on high; being made so much better than the angels, as he has by inheritance obtained a more excellent name than they.

Christ and Angels
Hebrews 1:5-14

2   For unto which of the angels said he at any time, *"You are my Son, this day have I begotten you"*? And again, *"I will be to him a Father, and he shall be to me a Son"*? And again, when he brings in the first begotten into the world, he says, *"And let all the angels of God worship him."* And of the angels he says, *"Who makes his angels spirits, and his ministers a flame of fire."*

3   But unto the Son he says, *"Your throne, O God, is for ever and ever: a scepter of righteousness is the scepter of your kingdom. You have loved righteousness, and hated iniquity; therefore God, even your God, has anointed you with the oil of gladness above your companions."*

4   And, *"You, Lord, in the beginning have laid the foundation of the earth; and the heavens are the works of your hands: they shall perish; but you remain; and they all shall grow old as does a garment; and as a cloak shall you fold them up, and they shall be changed: but you are the same, and your years shall not fail."*

5   But to which of the angels said he at any time, *"Sit on my right hand, until I make your enemies your footstool"*? Are they not all ministering spirits, sent forth to minister for them who shall be heirs of salvation?

God's Great Plan of Salvation
Hebrews 2:1-4

Therefore we ought to give the more earnest attention to the things 6 which we have heard, lest at any time we should let them drift away. For if the word spoken by angels was steadfast, and every transgression and disobedience received a just repayment of reward; how shall we escape, if we neglect such great salvation; which at the first began to be spoken by the Lord, and was confirmed unto us by them that heard him; God also bearing them witness, both with signs and wonders, and with various miracles, and gifts of the Holy Ghost, according to his own will?

> WE OUGHT TO GIVE THE MORE EARNEST ATTENTION TO THE THINGS WHICH WE HAVE HEARD.

Christ's Part in God's Plan
Hebrews 2:5-18

For unto the angels has he not put in subjection the world to come, of 7 which we speak. But one in a certain place testified, saying, *"What is man, that you are mindful of him? or the son of man, that you visit him? You made him a little lower than the angels; you crowned him with glory and honor, and did set him over the works of your hands: you have put all things in subjection under his feet."* For in that he put all in subjection under him, he left nothing that is not put under him. But now we do not see yet all things put under him.

> BUT NOW WE DO NOT SEE YET ALL THINGS PUT UNDER HIM.

But we see Jesus, who *was made a little lower than the angels* for the 8 suffering of death, *crowned with glory and honor;* that he by the grace of God should taste death for every man.

For it became him, for whom are all things, and by whom are all 9 things, in bringing many sons unto glory, to make the captain of their salvation perfect through sufferings.

For both he that sanctifies and they who are sanctified are all of one: 10 for which cause he is not ashamed to call them brethren, saying, *"I will declare your name unto my brethren, in the midst of the church will I sing praise unto you."* And again, *"I will put my trust in him.* And again, *Behold I and the children which God has given me."*

Inasmuch then as the children are partakers of flesh and blood, he also 11 himself likewise took part of the same; that through death he might destroy him that had the power of death, that is, the devil; and deliver them who through fear of death were all their lifetime subject to bondage. For surely he took not on himself the nature of angels; but he took on himself the seed of Abraham.

Therefore in all things it behooved him to be made like unto his brethren, 12 that he might be a merciful and faithful high priest in things pertaining to

12 God, to make reconciliation for the sins of the people. For in that he himself has suffered being tempted, he is able to help them that are tempted.

Christ Greater Than Moses
Hebrews 3:1-6

13 Therefore, holy brethren, partakers of the heavenly calling, consider the Apostle and High Priest of our profession, Christ Jesus; who was faithful to him that appointed him, as also Moses was faithful in all his house.

14

> HE THAT BUILT ALL THINGS IS GOD.

For this man was counted worthy of more glory than Moses, inasmuch as he who has built the house has more honor than the house. For every house is built by some man; but he that built all things is God.

15 And Moses indeed was faithful in all his house, as a servant, for a testimony of those things which were to be spoken afterward; but Christ as a son over his own house; whose house are we, if we hold fast the confidence and the rejoicing of the hope firm unto the end.

God's People and Unbelief
Hebrews 3:7-19

16 Therefore (as the Holy Ghost says, "*Today if you will hear his voice, harden not your hearts, as in the rebellion, in the day of temptation in the wilderness: when your fathers tempted me, tested me, and saw my works forty years. Therefore I was grieved with that generation, and said, 'They do always go astray in their heart; and they have not known my ways.' So I swore in my wrath, 'They shall not enter into my rest.'"*)

17 Take heed, brethren, lest there be in any of you an evil heart of unbelief, in departing from the living God. But encourage one another daily, while it is called "*Today*"; lest any of you be hardened through the deceitfulness of sin.

18 For we are made partakers of Christ, if we hold the beginning of our

> WE ARE MADE PARTAKERS OF CHRIST.

confidence steadfast unto the end; while it is said, "*Today if you will hear his voice, harden not your hearts, as in the rebellion.*"

19 For some, when they had heard, did provoke: howbeit not all that came out of Egypt by Moses. But with whom *was he grieved forty years*? was it not with them that had sinned, whose carcasses fell in the wilderness? And to whom *swore he that they should not enter into his rest*, but to them that believed not? So we see that they could not enter in because of unbelief.

God's Promise of Rest
Hebrews 4:1-13

20 Let us therefore fear, lest, a promise being left us of entering into his rest, any of you should seem to come short of it. For unto us was the gospel

preached, as well as unto them: but the word preached did not profit them, 20
not being mixed with faith in them that heard it.

For we which have believed do enter into rest, as he said, "*As I have* 21
*sworn in my wrath, 'if they shall enter
into my rest' ''*: although the works
were finished from the foundation of
the world. For he spoke in a certain
place of the seventh day in this way,

> WE WHICH HAVE BELIEVED
> DO ENTER INTO REST.

"*and God did rest the seventh day from all his works.*" And in this place
again, "*If they shall enter into my rest.*"

Seeing therefore it remains that some must enter therein, and they to 22
whom it was first preached entered not in because of unbelief: again, he
appoints a certain day, saying in David, "*Today,*" after so long a time; as it
is said, "*Today if you will hear his voice, harden not your hearts.*"

For if Joshua had given them rest, then would he not afterward have 23
spoken of another day. There remains therefore a rest to the people of God.
For he that is entered into his rest, he also has ceased from his own works,
as God did from his.

Let us labor therefore to enter into that rest, lest any man fall accord- 24
ing to the same example of unbelief.

For the word of God is quick, and powerful, and sharper than any two- 25
edged sword, piercing even to the
dividing asunder of soul and spirit,
and of the joints and marrow, and is a
discerner of the thoughts and intents
of the heart. Neither is there any creature that is not manifest in his sight:

> THE WORD OF GOD IS QUICK,
> AND POWERFUL, AND SHARPER
> THAN ANY TWO-EDGED SWORD.

but all things are naked and opened unto the eyes of him with whom we
have to give account.

CHAPTER 128

Improvement From God
Great High Priest
Hebrews 4:14-16

1   Seeing then that we have a great high priest, that is passed into the heavens, Jesus the Son of God, let us hold fast our profession. For we have not a high priest which cannot be touched with the feeling of our weaknesses; but was in all points tempted like as we are, yet without sin.

2   Let us therefore come boldly unto the throne of grace, that we may obtain mercy, and find grace to help in time of need.

A Priest Forever
Hebrews 5:1-10

3   For every high priest taken from among men is ordained for men in things pertaining to God, that he may offer both gifts and sacrifices for sins: who can have compassion on the ignorant, and on them that are going astray; for he himself also is beset with weakness.

4   And by reason of this he must, as for the people, so also for himself, to offer sacrifice for sins. And no man takes this honor unto himself, but he that is called of God, as was Aaron.

5   So also Christ glorified not himself to be made a high priest; but he that said unto him, *"You are my Son, today have I begotten you."* As he says also in another place, *"You are a priest for ever after the order of Melchizedek."*

6   Who in the days of his flesh, when he had offered up prayers and supplications with loud crying and tears unto him that was able to save him from death, and was heard in that he feared; though he were a Son, yet he learned obedience by the things which he suffered; and being made perfect, he became the author of eternal salvation unto all them that obey him; called of God a high priest *"after the order of Melchizedek."*

Learn and Discern
Hebrews 5:11-14

Of whom we have many things to say, and hard to be uttered, seeing 7
you are dull of hearing. For when for the time you ought to be teachers, you
have need that one teach you again which be the first principles of the oracles of God; and are become such as have need of milk, and not of solid
food.

For everyone that uses milk is unskilled in the word of righteousness: 8
for he is a baby. But solid food belongs to them that are of full age, even
those who by reason of use have their senses trained to discern both good
and evil.

Perfection of Faith
Hebrews 6:1-12

Therefore leaving the principles of the doctrine of Christ, let us go on 9
unto perfection; not laying again the foundation of repentance from dead
works, and of faith toward God, of the doctrine of baptisms, and of laying
on of hands, and of resurrection of the dead, and of eternal judgment. And
this will we do, if God permits.

For it is impossible for those who were once enlightened, and have 10
tasted of the heavenly gift, and were made partakers of the Holy Ghost, and
have tasted the good word of God, and the powers of the world to come, if
they shall fall away, to renew them again unto repentance; seeing they crucify to themselves the Son of God again, and put him to public shame.

For the earth which drinks in the rain that comes often upon it, and 11
brings forth herbs useful for them by whom it is cultivated, receives blessing from God: but that which bears thorns and thistles is rejected, and is
near unto cursing; whose end is to be burned.

But, beloved, we are persuaded better things of you, and things that 12
accompany salvation, though we thus speak. For God is not unrighteous to
forget your work and labor of love, which you have showed toward his
name, in that you have ministered to the saints, and do minister.

And we desire that every one of you do show the same diligence to the 13
full assurance of hope unto the end: that you be not lazy, but imitators of
them who through faith and patience inherit the promises.

CHAPTER 129

PROMISES

God's Promise to Abraham
Hebrews 6:13-20

1   For when God made promise to Abraham, because he could swear by no greater, *he swore by himself*, saying, "*Surely blessing I will bless you, and multiplying I will multiply you.*" And so, after he had patiently endured, he obtained the promise.

2   For men indeed swear by the greater: and an oath for confirmation is to them an end of all strife. Wherein God, willing more abundantly to show unto the heirs of promise the immutability of his purpose, confirmed it by an oath: that by two immutable things, in which it was impossible for God to lie, we might have a strong consolation, who have fled for refuge to lay hold upon the hope set before us. That hope we have as an anchor of the soul, both sure and steadfast, and which enters into that within the veil; where the forerunner is for us entered, even Jesus, made a high priest for ever after the order of Melchizedek.

Priest Melchizedek
Hebrews 7:1-28

3   For this *Melchizedek, king of Salem, priest of the most high God, who met Abraham returning from the slaughter of the kings, and blessed him*; to whom also *Abraham gave a tenth part of all*; first being by interpretation "King of righteousness," and after that also *King of Salem*, which is, "King of peace"; without father, without mother, without descent, having neither beginning of days, nor end of life; but made like unto the Son of God; remains a priest continually.

4   Now consider how great this man was, unto whom even the patriarch Abraham gave the tenth of the spoils.

And indeed they that are of the sons of Levi, who receive the office of 5
the priesthood, have a commandment to take tithes of the people according
to the law, that is, of their brethren, though they come out of the loins of
Abraham: but he whose genealogy is not traced from them received tithes
of Abraham, and blessed him that had the promises.

And without all contradiction the less is blessed of the better. And here 6
men that die receive tithes; but there
he receives them, of whom it is witnessed that he lives. And as I may so
say, Levi also, who receives tithes,

> THE LESS IS BLESSED OF THE
> BETTER.

paid tithes through Abraham. For he was yet in the loins of his father, when
Melchizedek met him.

If therefore perfection were by the Levitical priesthood, (for under it 7
the people received the law), what further need was there that another priest
should rise after the order of Melchizedek, and not be called after the order
of Aaron?

For the priesthood being changed, there is made of necessity a change 8
also of the law. For he of whom these things are spoken pertains to another
tribe, of which no man gave attendance at the altar. For it is evident that our
Lord sprang out of Judah; of which tribe Moses spoke nothing concerning
priesthood.

And it is yet far more evident: for that after the likeness of 9
Melchizedek there arises another priest, who is made, not after the law of a
carnal commandment, but after the power of an endless life. For he testifies,
"You are a priest for ever after the order of Melchizedek."

For there is indeed an annulling of the previous commandment for the 10
weakness and unprofitableness thereof. For the law made nothing perfect,
but the bringing in of a better hope did; by which we draw near unto God.

And inasmuch as not without an oath he was made priest: (for those 11
priests were made without an oath; but this with an oath by him that said
unto him, *"The Lord swore and will not repent, 'You are a priest for ever
after the order of Melchizedek'"*): by so much was Jesus made a guarantee
of a better testament.

And there truly were many priests, because they were not allowed to 12
continue by reason of death: but this man, because he continues always, has
an unchangeable priesthood. Therefore he is able also to save them to the
uttermost that come unto God by him, seeing he always lives to make intercession for them.

For such a high priest became us, who is holy, harmless, undefiled, sep- 13
arate from sinners, and made higher than the heavens; who needs not daily, as
those high priests, to offer up sacrifices, first for his own sins, and then for
the people's: for this he did once, when he offered up himself. For the law
makes men high priests which have weakness; but the word of the oath,
which was since the law, makes the Son, who is made perfect for evermore.

CHAPTER 130

COVENANT

New and Better Covenant
Hebrews 8:1-13

1   Now of the things which we have spoken this is the main point: We have such a high priest, who is seated on the right hand of the throne of the Majesty in the heavens; a minister of the sanctuary, and of the true tabernacle, which the Lord set up, and not man.

2   But now he has obtained a more excellent ministry, inasmuch as he is also the mediator of a better covenant, which was established upon better promises. For every high priest is ordained to offer gifts and sacrifices: therefore it is of necessity that this man have something also to offer. For if he were on earth, he should not be a priest, seeing that there are priests that offer gifts according to the law: who serve unto the copy and shadow of heavenly things, as Moses was admonished of God when he was about to make the tabernacle: for, *"See,"* says he, *"that you make all things according to the pattern shown to you on the mountain."*

3   For if that first covenant had been faultless, then should no place have been sought for the second.

4   For finding fault with them, he says, *"Behold, the days come, says the Lord, when I will make a new covenant with the house of Israel and with the house of Judah: not according to the covenant that I made with their fathers in the day when I took them by the hand to lead them out of the land of Egypt; because they continued not in my covenant, and I regarded them not, says the Lord. For this is the covenant that I will make with the house of Israel after those days, says the Lord; I will put my laws into their mind, and write them in their hearts: and I will be to them a God, and they shall be to me a people: and they shall not teach every man his neighbor, and every man his brother, saying, 'Know the Lord': for all shall know me, from the*

least to the greatest. For I will be merciful to their unrighteousness, and 4
their sins and their iniquities will I remember no more."

In that he says, "*A new covenant,*" he has made the first old. Now that 5
which decays and grows old is ready to vanish away.

Earthly Sanctuary
Hebrews 9:1-10

Then indeed the first covenant had also ordinances of divine service, 6
and a worldly sanctuary. For there was a tabernacle made; the first, wherein was the lampstand, and the table, and the showbread; which is called the
sanctuary. And beyond the second veil, the tabernacle which is called the
Holiest of all; which had the golden censer, and the ark of the covenant
overlaid round about with gold, wherein was the golden pot that had manna,
and Aaron's rod that budded, and the tablets of the covenant; and over it the
cherubim of glory shadowing the mercy seat; of which we cannot now
speak in detail.

Now when these things were thus ordained, the priests went always 7
into the first tabernacle, accomplishing the service of God. But into the
second went the high priest alone once every year, not without blood, which
he offered for himself, and for the sins of the people: the Holy Ghost this
signifying, that the way into the holiest of all was not yet made manifest,
while the first tabernacle was yet standing. This was an example for the
time then present, in which were offered both gifts and sacrifices, that could
not make him that did the service perfect, as pertaining to the conscience;
which stood only in foods and drinks, and various washings, and carnal
ordinances, imposed on them until the time of reformation.

CHAPTER 131

Faith as the Way of Life

Heavenly Sanctuary
Hebrews 9:11-22

1   But Christ being come a high priest of good things to come, by a greater and more perfect tabernacle, not made with hands, that is to say, not of this creation; neither by the blood of goats and calves, but by his own blood he entered in once into the holy place, having obtained eternal redemption for us.

2   For if the blood of bulls and of goats, and the ashes of a heifer sprinkling the unclean, sanctifies to the purification of the flesh: how much more shall the blood of Christ, who through the eternal Spirit offered himself without blemish to God, cleanse your conscience from dead works to serve the living God?

3   And for this reason he is the mediator of the new testament, that by means of death, for the redemption of the transgressions that were under the first testament, they which are called might receive the promise of eternal inheritance. For where a testament is, there must also of necessity be the death of the testator. For a testament is of force after men are dead: otherwise it is of no strength at all while the testator lives. Hence neither the first testament was put into effect without blood.

4   For when Moses had spoken every precept to all the people according to the law, he took the blood of calves and of goats, with water, and scarlet wool, and hyssop, and sprinkled both the book, and all the people, saying, *"This is the blood of the testament which God has commanded unto you."*

5   Moreover he sprinkled with blood both the tabernacle, and all the vessels of the ministry. And almost all things are by the law purified with blood; and without shedding of blood is no remission.

Patterns of Things
Hebrews 9:23-28

It was therefore necessary that the copies of things in the heavens 6 should be purified with these; but the heavenly things themselves with better sacrifices than these.

For Christ is not entered into the holy places made with hands, which 7 are the symbols of the true; but into heaven itself, now to appear in the presence of God for us: nor that he should offer himself often, as the high priest enters into the holy place every year with blood of others; for then must he often have suffered since the foundation of the world: but now once in the end of the world has he appeared to put away sin by the sacrifice of himself.

And as it is appointed unto men once to die, but after this the judgment: so Christ was once offered to bear the sins of many; and unto them that look for him shall he appear the second time without sin unto salvation. 8

> IT IS APPOINTED UNTO MEN ONCE TO DIE, BUT AFTER THIS THE JUDGMENT.

Offerings and One Offering
Hebrews 10:1-18

For the law having a shadow of good things to come, and not the very 9 image of the things, can never with those sacrifices which they offered year by year continually make those who approach perfect. For then would they not have ceased to be offered? because the worshipers once purified should have had no more consciousness of sins. But in those sacrifices there is a remembrance again made of sins every year. For it is not possible that the blood of bulls and of goats should take away sins.

Therefore when he came into the world, he said, "*Sacrifice and offer-* 10 *ing you would not, but a body have you prepared me: in burnt offerings and sacrifices for sin you have had no pleasure. Then said I, 'Lo, I come (in the volume of the book it is written of me), to do your will, O God.'*" Above when he said, "*Sacrifice and offering and burnt offerings and offering for sin you would not, neither had pleasure therein*"; which are offered by the law; then he said, "*Lo, I come to do your will, O God.*" He takes away the first, that he may establish the second. By which will we are sanctified through the offering of the body of Jesus Christ once for all.

And every priest stands daily ministering and offering repeatedly the 11 same sacrifices, which can never take away sins: but this man, after he had offered one sacrifice for sins for ever, sat down on the right hand of God; from henceforth waiting till his enemies be made his footstool. For by one offering he has perfected for ever them that are sanctified.

Whereof the Holy Ghost also is a witness to us: for after that he had 12 said before, "*This is the covenant that I will make with them after those*

12 *days, says the Lord, I will put my laws into their hearts, and in their minds will I write them; and their sins and iniquities will I remember no more."* Now where remission of these is, there is no more offering for sin.

Profession of Faith
Hebrews 10:19-25

13   Having therefore, brethren, boldness to enter into the holiest by the blood of Jesus, by a new and living way, which he has consecrated for us, through the veil, that is to say, his flesh; and having a high priest over the house of God; let us draw near with a true heart in full assurance of faith, having our hearts sprinkled from an evil conscience, and our bodies washed with pure water.

14   Let us hold fast the profession of our faith without wavering; (for he is faithful that promised); and let us

> LET US HOLD FAST THE PRO-
> FESSION OF OUR FAITH WITH-
> OUT WAVERING.

consider one another to arouse unto love and to good works: not forsaking the assembling of ourselves together, as the manner of some is; but encouraging one another: and so much the more, as you see the day approaching.

Spirit of Grace
Hebrews 10:26-39

15   For if we sin willfully after we have received the knowledge of the truth, there remains no more sacrifice for sins, but a certain fearful expectation of judgment and fiery indignation, which shall devour the adversaries.

16   He that rejected Moses' law died without mercy under two or three witnesses: of how much worse punishment, suppose you, shall he be thought worthy, who has trampled under foot the Son of God, and has counted the blood of the covenant, with which he was sanctified, an unholy thing, and has done outrage unto the Spirit of grace? For we know him that has said, *"Vengeance belongs unto me, I will repay,"* says the Lord. And again, *"The Lord shall judge his people."* It is a fearful thing to fall into the hands of the living God.

17   But call to remembrance the former days, in which, after you were enlightened, you endured a great struggle of sufferings; partly, while you were made a spectacle both by insults and persecutions; and partly, while you became companions of them that were so treated. For you had compassion of me in my bonds, and took joyfully the seizure of your goods, knowing in yourselves that you have in heaven a better and an enduring substance.

18   Therefore do not cast away your confidence, which has great repayment of reward. For you have need of endurance, that, after you have done the will of God, you might receive the promise. *"For yet a little while, and he that shall come will come, and will not delay. Now the just shall live by faith: but if any man draws back, my soul shall have no pleasure in him."*

19   But we are not of them who draw back unto perdition; but of them that believe to the saving of the soul.

CHAPTER 132

FAITH

Faith
Hebrews 11:1-40

Now faith is the substance of things hoped for, the evidence of things 1
not seen. For by it the elders obtained a good testimony.

Through faith we understand that the worlds were framed by the word 2
of God, so that things which are seen were not made of things which do
appear.

By faith Abel offered unto God a more excellent sacrifice than Cain, 3
by which he obtained witness that he was righteous, God testifying of his
gifts: and by it he being dead yet speaks.

By faith Enoch was translated that he should not see death; "*and was* 4
not found, because God had translated him": for before his translation he
had this testimony, *that he pleased God*. But without faith it is impossible
to please him: for he that comes to God must believe that he is, and that he
is a rewarder of them that diligently seek him.

By faith Noah, being warned of God of things not seen as yet, moved 5
with fear, prepared an ark to the saving of his household; by which he condemned the world, and became heir of the righteousness which is by faith.

By faith Abraham, when he was called to go out into a place which he 6
should afterward receive for an inheritance, obeyed; and he went out, not
knowing where he went. By faith he dwelt in the land of promise, as in a
foreign country, dwelling in tabernacles with Isaac and Jacob, the heirs with
him of the same promise: for he looked for a city which has foundations,
whose builder and maker is God.

Through faith also Sarah herself received strength to conceive seed, 7
and was delivered of a child when she was past the age, because she judged
him faithful who had promised. Therefore sprang there even of one, and

7　him as good as dead, as many as the stars of the sky in multitude, and as the sand which is by the seashore innumerable.

8　　These all died in faith, not having received the promises, but having seen them far ahead, and were persuaded of them, and embraced them, and confessed that they were strangers and pilgrims on the earth. For they that say such things declare plainly that they seek a country. And truly, if they had been mindful of that country from which they came out, they might have had opportunity to have returned. But now they desire a better country, that is, a heavenly one: therefore God is not ashamed to be called their God: for he has prepared for them a city.

9　　By faith Abraham, when he was tested, offered up Isaac: and he that had received the promises offered up his only begotten son, of whom it was said, *"That in Isaac shall your seed be called"*: reasoning that God was able to raise him up, even from the dead; from which also he received him in a manner of speaking.

10　　By faith Isaac blessed Jacob and Esau concerning things to come. By faith Jacob, when he was dying, blessed both the sons of Joseph; and *worshiped, leaning upon the top of his staff.* By faith Joseph, when he died, made mention of the departure of the children of Israel; and gave instructions concerning his bones.

11　　By faith Moses, when he was born, was hidden three months by his parents, because they saw he was a beautiful child; and they were not afraid of the king's command. By faith Moses, when he was come of age, refused to be called the son of Pharaoh's daughter; choosing rather to suffer hardship with the people of God, than to enjoy the pleasures of sin for a season; esteeming the scorn of Christ greater riches than the treasures in Egypt: for he had respect unto the repayment of the reward.

12　　By faith he forsook Egypt, not fearing the wrath of the king: for he endured, as seeing him who is invisible. Through faith he kept the passover, and the sprinkling of blood, lest he that destroyed the firstborn should touch them.

13　　By faith they passed through the Red sea as by dry land: which the Egyptians attempting to do were drowned. By faith the walls of Jericho fell down, after they were encircled about seven days.

14　　By faith the harlot Rahab did not perish with them that did not believe, when she had received the spies with peace.

15　　And what shall I more say? for the time would fail me to tell of Gideon, and of Barak, and of Samson, and of Jephthah; of David also, and Samuel, and of the prophets: who through faith subdued kingdoms, worked righteousness, obtained promises, stopped the mouths of lions, quenched the violence of fire, escaped the edge of the sword, out of weakness were made strong, grown valiant in battle, turned to flight the armies of the foreigners.

Women received their dead raised to life again: and others were tor- 16
tured, not accepting deliverance; that they might obtain a better resurrection: and others had trial of cruel mockings and scourgings, yes, moreover
of bonds and imprisonment. They were stoned, they were sawn in two, were
tempted, were slain with the sword: they wandered about in sheepskins and
goatskins; being destitute, persecuted, tormented; (of whom the world was
not worthy): they wandered in deserts, and in mountains, and in dens and
caves of the earth.

And these all, having obtained a good blessing through faith, did not 17
receive the promise: God having provided some better thing for us, that they
apart from us should not be made perfect.

CHAPTER 133

DESCRIPTION OF THE CHRIST

Author and Finisher
Hebrews 12:1-13

1   Therefore seeing we also are surrounded with so great a cloud of witnesses, let us lay aside every weight, and the sin which does so easily entangle us, and let us run with perseverance the race that is set before us, looking unto Jesus the author and finisher of our faith; who for the joy that was set before him endured the cross, despising the shame, and is seated at the right hand of the throne of God.

2   For consider him that endured such hostility of sinners against himself, lest you be wearied and discouraged in your minds.

3   You have not yet resisted unto shedding blood, striving against sin. And you have forgotten the encouragement which speaks unto you as unto children, "*My son, do not disregard the disciplining of the Lord, nor discouraged when you are corrected by him: for whom the Lord loves he disciplines, and punishes every son whom he receives.*"

4   If you endure disciplining, God deals with you as with sons; for what son is he whom the father does not discipline? But if you be without disciplining, of which all are partakers, then are you illegitimate, and not sons.

5   Furthermore we have had fathers of our flesh which corrected us, and we gave them reverence: shall we not much rather be in subjection unto the Father of spirits, and live? For they indeed for a few days disciplined us according to their own pleasure; but he for our profit, that we might be partakers of his holiness.

6   Now no disciplining for the present seems to be joyful, but painful: nevertheless afterward it yields the peaceful fruit of righteousness unto them which are trained thereby.

Therefore lift up the hands which hang down, and the feeble knees; 7
and make straight paths for your feet, lest that which is lame be turned
away; but let it rather be healed.

Grace of God
Hebrews 12:14-17

Pursue peace with all men, and holiness, without which no man shall 8
see the Lord: looking diligently lest any man fail of the grace of God; lest
any root of bitterness springing up trouble you, and thereby many be
defiled; lest there be any immoral person, or profane person, as Esau, who
for one morsel of food sold his birthright. For you know how that afterward,
when he would have inherited the blessing, he was rejected: for he found no
place of repentance, though he sought it earnestly with tears.

Mediator of New Covenant
Hebrews 12:18-29

For you are not come unto the mountain that might be touched, and 9
that burned with fire, nor unto blackness, and darkness, and tempest, and
the sound of a trumpet, and the voice of words; which voice they that heard
begged that the word should not be spoken to them anymore: (for they could
not endure that which was commanded, *"and if so much as an animal touches the mountain, it shall be stoned, or thrust through with an arrow"*: and
so terrible was the sight, that Moses said, *"I exceedingly fear and tremble"*):
but you are come unto mountain Zion, and unto the city of the living God,
the heavenly Jerusalem, and to an innumerable company of angels, to the
joyful assembly and church of the firstborn, which are written in heaven,
and to God the Judge of all, and to the spirits of just men made perfect, and
to Jesus the mediator of the new covenant, and to the blood of sprinkling,
that speaks better things than that of Abel.

See that you do not refuse him that speaks. For if they did not escape 10
who refused him that spoke on earth, much more shall we not escape, if we
turn away from him that speaks from heaven: whose voice then shook the
earth: but now he has promised, saying, *"Yet once more I do not shake the
earth only, but also heaven."* And this word, *"Yet once more,"* signifies the
removing of those things that are shaken, as of things that are made, that
those things which cannot be shaken may remain.

Therefore we receiving a kingdom which cannot be shaken, let us be 11
thankful, whereby we may serve God acceptably with reverence and godly
fear: for our God is a consuming fire.

CHAPTER 134

GOD'S PLEASURE

How to Please God
Hebrews 13:1-19

1   Let brotherly love continue. Be not forgetful to entertain strangers: for thereby some have entertained angels unawares.

2   Remember them that are in bonds, as bound with them; and them which suffer adversity, as being yourselves also in the body. Marriage is honorable in all, and the bed undefiled: but fornicators and adulterers God will judge.

3   Let your conduct be without covetousness; and be content with such things as you have: for he has said, *"I will never leave you, nor forsake you."* So that we may boldly say, *"The Lord is my helper, and I will not fear what man shall do unto me."*

4   Remember them which have the rule over you, who have spoken unto you the word of God: whose faith imitate, considering the outcome of their conduct. Jesus Christ the same yesterday, and today, and for ever.

5   Be not carried about with various and strange doctrines. For it is a good thing that the heart be established with grace; not with foods, which have not profited them that have been occupied therein. We have an altar, from which they have no right to eat which serve the tabernacle.

6   For the bodies of those animals, whose blood is brought into the sanctuary by the high priest for sin, are burned outside the camp. Therefore Jesus also, that he might sanctify the people with his own blood, suffered outside the gate. Let us go forth therefore unto him outside the camp, bearing his reproach. For here have we no continuing city, but we seek one to come.

7   By him therefore let us offer the sacrifice of praise to God continually, that is, the fruit of our lips giving thanks to his name. But to do good and to share do not forget: for with such sacrifices God is well pleased.

Obey them that have the rule over you, and submit yourselves: for they 8
watch over for your souls, as they that must give account, that they may do
it with joy, and not with grief: for that is unprofitable for you.

Pray for us: for we trust we have a good conscience, in all things will- 9
ing to live honorably. But I urge you the more to do this, that I may be
restored to you the sooner.

Conclusion
Hebrews 13:20-25

Now the God of peace, that brought again from the dead our Lord 10
Jesus, that great shepherd of the sheep, through the blood of the everlasting
covenant, make you complete in every good work to do his will, working in
you that which is well pleasing in his sight, through Jesus Christ; to whom
be glory for ever and ever. Amen.

And I appeal to you, brethren, bear with the word of encouragement: 11
for I have written a letter unto you in few words. Know that our brother Timothy is set free; with whom, if he comes shortly, I will see you.

Greet all them that have the rule over you, and all the saints. They of 12
Italy greet you.

Grace be with you all. Amen.

PART 38

FIRST LETTER FROM PETER

After Paul's death, other followers of Christ assume the legacy of his faith and continue his ministry, as evidenced by the many letters written by the disciples that follow. Here Peter writes to the Christians who have been scattered throughout the Roman province of Asia Minor to encourage them during a time of persecution and suffering. He is exhorting them to be holy, as Christ is Holy. He warns that their suffering is not over and that persecution looms. However they are to keep hope alive for the second coming of Christ. They are to treasure the gospel that is within them and to be courageous, knowing that they are the ones who are called and will inherit a blessing.

CHRIST ALSO HAS SUFFERED ONCE FOR SINS, THE
JUST FOR THE UNJUST, THAT HE MIGHT BRING US
TO GOD, BEING PUT TO DEATH IN THE FLESH,
BUT QUICKENED BY THE SPIRIT.   (1 PETER 3:18)

CHAPTER 135

LIVING AND LIFE

Greeting From Peter
1 Peter 1:1-2

Peter, an apostle of Jesus Christ, to the strangers scattered throughout 1
Pontus, Galatia, Cappadocia, Asia, and Bithynia, elect according to the
foreknowledge of God the Father, through sanctification of the Spirit, unto
obedience and sprinkling of the blood of Jesus Christ: Grace unto you, and
peace, be multiplied.

Living Hope
1 Peter 1:3-12

Blessed be the God and Father of our Lord Jesus Christ, which accord- 2
ing to his abundant mercy has begotten us again unto a living hope by the
resurrection of Jesus Christ from the dead, to an inheritance incorruptible,
and undefiled, and that does not fade away, reserved in heaven for you, who
are kept by the power of God through faith unto salvation ready to be
revealed in the last time.

In this you greatly rejoice, though now for a season, if need be, you 3
are in sadness through many trials: that the genuineness of your faith, being
much more precious than of gold that perishes, though it be refined with
fire, might be found unto praise and honor and glory at the revelation of
Jesus Christ: whom having not seen, you love; in whom, though now you
do not see him, yet believing, you rejoice with joy beyond words and full of
glory: receiving the goal of your faith, even the salvation of your souls.

Of which salvation the prophets have inquired and searched dili- 4
gently, who prophesied of the grace that was to come unto you: searching
what, or what manner of time the Spirit of Christ which was in them did
signify, when it testified beforehand the sufferings of Christ, and the
glory that was to follow. Unto whom it was revealed, that not unto themselves, but unto us they did minister the things, which are now reported

4   unto you by them that have preached the gospel unto you with the Holy
Ghost sent down from heaven; which things the angels desire to look into.

Holy Living
1 Peter 1:13-25

5   Therefore prepare your minds, be self-controlled, and hope to the end
for the grace that is to be brought unto
you at the revelation of Jesus Christ;
as obedient children, not conforming
yourselves according to the former
desires in your ignorance: but as he
which has called you is holy, so be
you holy in all manner of conduct; because it is written, *"Be you holy; for
I am holy."*

> AS HE WHICH HAS CALLED
> YOU IS HOLY, SO BE YOU HOLY
> IN ALL MANNER OF CONDUCT.

6   And if you call on the Father, who without partiality of persons judges
according to every man's work, pass the time of your dwelling here in fear:
inasmuch as you know that you were not redeemed with corruptible things,
as silver and gold, from your empty way of life received by tradition from
your fathers; but with the precious blood of Christ, as of a lamb without
blemish and without defect. He indeed was foreordained before the foundation of the world, but was revealed in these last times for you, who by him
do believe in God, that raised him up from the dead, and gave him glory;
that your faith and hope might be in God.

7   Seeing you have purified your souls in obeying the truth through the
Spirit unto sincere love of the brethren,
see that you love one another with a
pure heart fervently: being born again,
not of corruptible seed, but of incor-
ruptible, by the word of God, which lives and abides for ever.

> LOVE ONE ANOTHER WITH A
> PURE HEART FERVENTLY.

8   For *"all flesh is as grass, and all the glory of man as the flower of
grass. The grass withers, and the flower thereof falls away: but the word of
the Lord endures for ever."* And this is the word which by the gospel is
preached unto you.

Living Stones
1 Peter 2:1-10

9   Therefore laying aside all malice, and all deceit, and hypocrisies, and
envies, and all evil speakings, as newborn babies, desire the pure milk of
the word, that you may grow thereby: if so be you have tasted that the Lord
is gracious.

10   To whom coming, as unto a living stone, rejected indeed of men, but
chosen of God, and precious, you also, as living stones, are built up a spiritual house, a holy priesthood, to offer up spiritual sacrifices, acceptable to
God by Jesus Christ. Therefore also it is contained in the scripture, *"Behold,
I lay in Zion a chief cornerstone, elect, precious: and he that believes on
him shall not be put to shame."*

Unto you therefore which believe, he is precious: but unto them which 11
be disobedient, *"the stone which the builders rejected, the same is made the
head of the cornerstone,"* and *"a stone of stumbling, and a rock of offense,"*
even to them which stumble at the word, being disobedient: to which also
they were appointed.

But you are *a chosen generation, a royal priesthood, a holy nation, a* 12
precious people; that you should show forth the praises of him who has
called you out of darkness into his marvelous light: which in time past were
not a people, but are now the people of God: which had not obtained mercy,
but now have obtained mercy.

CHAPTER 136

Suffering and Life

Ordinances of Man
1 Peter 2:11-17

1   Dearly beloved, I appeal to you as foreigners and exiles, abstain from fleshly desires, which war against the soul; having your behavior honorable among the Gentiles: that, whereas they speak against you as evildoers, they may by your good works, which they shall behold, glorify God in the day of visitation.

2   Submit yourselves to every ordinance of man for the Lord's sake: whether it be to the king, as supreme; or unto governors, as unto them that are sent by him for the punishment of evildoers, and for the praise of them that do well. For so is the will of God, that with well doing you may put to silence the ignorance of foolish men: as free, and not using your liberty for a cover-up of maliciousness, but as the servants of God. Honor all men. Love the brotherhood. Fear God. Honor the king.

Christ's Suffering an Example
1 Peter 2:18-25

3   Servants, be subject to your masters with all respect; not only to the good and gentle, but also to the harsh. For this is praiseworthy, if a man for conscience toward God endures grief, suffering unjustly. For what credit is it, if, when you be beaten for your faults, you shall take it patiently? but if, when you do right, and suffer for it, you take it patiently, this is acceptable with God.

4   For even to this were you called: because Christ also suffered for us, leaving us an example, that you should follow his steps: "*who did no sin, neither was deceit found in his mouth*": who, when he was insulted, insulted not in return; when he suffered, he threatened not; but committed himself to him that judges righteously: who his own self bore our sins in his own body on the cross, that we, being dead to sins, should live unto righteousness: by

whose wounds you were healed. For you were as sheep going astray; but are 4
now returned unto the Shepherd and Bishop of your souls.

Wives and Husbands
1 Peter 3:1-7

Likewise, you wives, be in submission to your own husbands; that, if 5
any obey not the word, they also may without the word be won by the conduct of the wives; while they behold your pure conduct coupled with reverence. Whose adorning let it not be that outward adorning of braiding the
hair, and of wearing of gold, or of putting on of apparel; but let it be the hidden man of the heart, in that which is not corruptible, even the beauty of a
meek and quiet spirit, which is in the sight of God of great value.

For after this manner in the old time the holy women also, who trusted 6
in God, adorned themselves, being in subjection unto their own husbands:
even as Sarah obeyed Abraham, calling him lord: whose daughters you are,
as long as you do well, and are not afraid with any alarm.

Likewise, you husbands, dwell with them according to understanding, 7
giving honor unto the wife, as unto the weaker partner, and as being heirs
together of the grace of life; that your prayers be not hindered.

Doing Good and Seeking Peace
1 Peter 3:8-12

Finally, be you all of one mind, having compassion one of another, 8
love as brethren, be tenderhearted, be courteous: not rendering evil for evil,
or insult for insult: but on the contrary blessing; knowing that you are for
this called, that you may inherit a blessing.

For *"he that will love life, and see good days, let him refrain his tongue* 9
from evil, and his lips that they speak no deceit: let him turn away from evil,
and do good; let him seek peace, and pursue it. For the eyes of the Lord are
over the righteous, and his ears are open unto their prayers: but the face of
the Lord is against them that do evil."

CHAPTER 137

SUFFERING AND LIVING

Suffering
1 Peter 3:13-22

1   And who is he that will harm you, if you be imitators of that which is good? But and if you suffer for righteousness' sake, blessed are you: "*and be not afraid of their threats, neither be troubled*"; but *sanctify the Lord God* in your hearts: and be ready always to give an answer to every man that asks you a reason of the hope that is in you with meekness and reverence: having a good conscience; that, whereas they speak evil of you, as of evil-doers, they may be ashamed that falsely accuse your good conduct in Christ. For it is better, if the will of God be so, that you suffer for well doing, than for evil doing.

2   For Christ also has suffered once for sins, the just for the unjust, that he might bring us to God, being put to death in the flesh, but quickened by the Spirit: by which also he went and preached unto the spirits in prison; which long ago were disobedient, when once the patience of God waited in the days of Noah, while the ark was being prepared, in which few, that is, eight souls were preserved through water.

3   The same symbol to which even baptism does also now saves us (not the washing away of the filth of the flesh, but the answer of a good conscience toward God), by the resurrection of Jesus Christ: who is gone into heaven, and is on the right hand of God; angels and authorities and powers being made subject unto him.

Having Love to the End
1 Peter 4:1-11

4   Inasmuch then as Christ has suffered for us in the flesh, arm yourselves likewise with the same mind: for he that has suffered in the flesh has ceased from sin; that he no longer should live the rest of his time in the flesh to the passions of men, but to the will of God.

For the time up to now of our life may suffice us to have done the will 5
of the Gentiles, when we walked in lewdness, lusts, excess of wine, orgies,
carousing, and abominable idolatries: wherein they think it strange that you
run not with them to the same excess of loose living, speaking evil of you:
who shall give account to him that is ready to judge the quick and the dead.
For this reason was the gospel preached also to them that are dead, that they
might be judged according to men in the flesh, but live according to God in
the spirit.

But the end of all things is at hand: be you therefore of sound mind, 6
and alert unto prayer. And above all things have fervent love among yourselves: for *"love shall cover the multitude of sins."*

Use hospitality one to another without grumbling. As every man has 7
received the gift, even so serve the same one to another, as good stewards
of the varied grace of God.

If any man speaks, let him speak as the oracles of God; if any man 8
serves, let him do it as of the ability
which God gives: that God in all
things may be glorified through Jesus
Christ, to whom be praise and dominion for ever and ever. Amen.

> IF ANY MAN MINISTER, LET
> HIM DO IT AS OF THE ABILITY
> WHICH GOD GIVETH.

Fiery Trial of a Christian
1 Peter 4:12-19

Beloved, do not think it strange concerning the fiery trial which is to 9
prove you, as though some strange thing happened unto you: but rejoice, inasmuch as you are partakers of Christ's sufferings; that, when his glory shall
be revealed, you may be glad also with exceeding joy. If you be insulted for
the name of Christ, blessed are you; for the spirit of glory and of God rests
upon you: on their part he is evil spoken of, but on your part he is glorified.

But let none of you suffer as a murderer, or as a thief, or as an evil- 10
doer, or as a busybody in other men's matters. Yet if any man suffers as a
Christian, let him not be ashamed; but let him glorify God on this behalf.

For the time is come that judgment must begin with the household of 11
God: and if it first begins with us, what shall the end be of them that do not
obey the gospel of God? And *"if the righteous scarcely be saved, where
shall the ungodly and the sinner appear?"*

Therefore let them that suffer according to the will of God commit the 12
keeping of their souls to him in well doing, as unto a faithful Creator.

Elders Feeding the Flock
1 Peter 5:1-4

The elders which are among you I appeal, who am also an elder, and 13
a witness of the sufferings of Christ, and also a partaker of the glory that
shall be revealed. Shepherd the flock of God which is among you, taking
the oversight thereof, not by compulsion, but willingly; not for dishonest

13 gain, but of a ready mind; neither as being domineering over God's entrusted, but being examples to the flock. And when the chief Shepherd shall appear, you shall receive a crown of glory that does not fade away.

Younger Submitting in Humility
1 Peter 5:5-11

14 Likewise, you younger, submit yourselves unto the elders. Yes, all of you be subject one to another, and be clothed with humility: for "*God resists the proud, and gives grace to the humble.*"

15 Humble yourselves therefore under the mighty hand of God, that he may exalt you in due time: casting all your care upon him; for he cares for you.

16 Be self-controlled, be vigilant; because your adversary the devil, as a roaring lion, walks about, seeking whom he may devour: whom resist steadfast in the faith, knowing that the same sufferings are experienced by your brethren that are in the world.

17 But the God of all grace, who has called us unto his eternal glory by Christ Jesus, after you have suffered a while, shall make you complete, establish, strengthen, settle you. To him be glory and dominion for ever and ever. Amen.

Conclusion
1 Peter 5:12-14

18 By Silas, a faithful brother unto you, as I regard, I have written briefly, encouraging, and testifying that this is the true grace of God in which you stand.

19 The church that is at Babylon, chosen together with you, greets you; and so does Mark my son.

20 Greet one another with a kiss of love. Peace be with you all that are in Christ Jesus. Amen.

PART 39

SECOND LETTER FROM PETER

Again Peter writes to the Christians who have faced many trials. During this second letter, he addresses the issues of false teachers among them. He warns against deception, which comes in many forms, and advises them to mature in the truth of God, which comes in only one form, that of Christ. Peter urges them to be aware of the personal responsibilities they have as believers and to take solace that "exceedingly great and precious promises" are given to us as children of God. He is sure that God's righteousness will be revealed at the second coming of Christ and that the ungodly will receive due judgment. Those who are diligent in the spirit of Christ will never fall.

THE DAY OF THE LORD WILL COME AS A THIEF IN
THE NIGHT; IN WHICH THE HEAVENS SHALL PASS
AWAY WITH A GREAT NOISE, AND THE ELEMENTS
SHALL MELT WITH FERVENT HEAT, THE EARTH
ALSO AND THE WORKS THAT ARE THEREIN SHALL
BE BURNED UP.   (2 PETER 3:10)

CHAPTER 138

REMEMBERING

Greeting From Peter
2 Peter 1:1-4

1   Simon Peter, a servant and an apostle of Jesus Christ, to them that have
obtained the same precious faith with us through the righteousness of God
and our Savior Jesus Christ. Grace and peace be multiplied unto you
through the knowledge of God, and of Jesus our Lord, according as his
divine power has given unto us all things that pertain unto life and godliness, through the knowledge of him that has called us to glory and virtue:
by which are given unto us exceedingly great and precious promises: that
by these you might be partakers of the divine nature, having escaped the
corruption that is in the world through lust.

Adding to Your Faith
2 Peter 1:5-11

2   And besides this, giving all diligence, add to your faith virtue; and to
virtue knowledge; and to knowledge self-control; and to self-control perseverance; and to perseverance godliness; and to godliness brotherly kindness;
and to brotherly kindness love. For if these things be in you, and abound,
they make you that you shall neither be barren nor unfruitful in the knowledge of our Lord Jesus Christ. But he that lacks these things is blind, and
cannot see very far, and has forgotten that he was cleansed from his old sins.

3   Therefore then, brethren, give diligence to make your calling and election sure: for if you do these things, you shall never fall: for so an entrance
shall be provided unto you abundantly into the everlasting kingdom of our
Lord and Savior Jesus Christ.

Remembrance
2 Peter 1:12-15

4   Therefore I will not be negligent to put you always in remembrance of
these things, though you know them, and be established in the present truth.

Yes, I think it right, as long as I am in this tabernacle, to stir you up by put- 4
ting you in remembrance; knowing that shortly I must put off this my tabernacle, even as our Lord Jesus Christ has showed me. Moreover I will
endeavor that you may be able after my decease to have these things always
in remembrance.

Eyewitnesses
2 Peter 1:16-21

For we have not followed cunningly devised fables, when we made 5
known unto you the power and coming of our Lord Jesus Christ, but were
eyewitnesses of his majesty. For he received from God the Father honor and
glory, when there came such a voice to him from the magnificent glory,
"This is my beloved Son, in whom I am well pleased." And this voice which
came from heaven we heard, when we were with him in the holy mountain.

We have also a more sure word of prophecy; to which you do well that 6
take heed, as unto a light that shines in
a dark place, until the day dawns, and
the morning star arises in your hearts:
knowing this first, that no prophecy of
the scripture is of any private interpre-

NO PROPHECY OF THE SCRIP-
TURE IS OF ANY PRIVATE
INTERPRETATION.

tation. For the prophecy did not come in old time by the will of man: but
holy men of God spoke as they were moved by the Holy Ghost.

CHAPTER 139

ACKNOWLEDGING

False Prophets and Teachers
2 Peter 2:1-22

1   But there were false prophets also among the people, even as there shall be false teachers among you, who secretly shall bring in destructive heresies, even denying the Lord that redeemed them, and bring upon themselves swift destruction. And many shall follow their pernicious ways; by reason of whom the way of truth shall be discredited. And through covetousness shall they with deceptive words make exploitation of you: whose condemnation now from a long time lingers not, and their destruction slumbers not.

2   For if God did not spare the angels that sinned, but cast them down to hell, and delivered them into chains of darkness, to be reserved unto judgment; and did not spare the old world, but saved Noah the eighth person, a preacher of righteousness, bringing in the flood upon the world of the ungodly; and turning the cities of Sodom and Gomorrah into ashes condemned them with total destruction, making them an example unto those that afterward to should live ungodly; and delivered righteous Lot, oppressed with the filthy conduct of the wicked: (for that righteous man dwelling among them, in seeing and hearing, tormented his righteous soul from day to day with their unlawful deeds); the Lord knows how to deliver the godly out of temptations, and to reserve the unjust unto the day of judgment to be punished: but especially them that walk according to the flesh in the lust of uncleanness, and despise authority. Presumptuous are they, arrogant, they are not afraid to speak evil of celestial beings.

3   Whereas angels, which are greater in power and might, do not bring slanderous accusation against them before the Lord. But these, as natural brute beasts, made to be taken and destroyed, speak evil of the things that they do not understand; and shall utterly perish in their own corruption; and

shall receive the wages of unrighteousness, as they that count it pleasure to 3 carouse in the daytime. Spots they are and blemishes, amusing themselves with their own deceptions while they feast with you; having eyes full of adultery, and that cannot cease from sin; enticing unstable souls: a heart they have trained with covetous practices; accursed children: which have forsaken the right way, and are gone astray, following the way of Balaam the son of Beor, who loved the wages of unrighteousness; but was rebuked for his iniquity: the dumb donkey speaking with man's voice restrained the madness of the prophet.

These are wells without water, clouds that are carried with a tempest; 4 to whom the mist of darkness is reserved for ever. For when they speak great swelling words of vanity, they entice through the lusts of the flesh, through much wantonness, those that were barely escaped from them who live in error. While they promise them liberty, they themselves are the servants of corruption: for of whom a man is overcome, of the same is he brought in bondage.

For if after they have escaped the defilements of the world through the 5 knowledge of the Lord and Savior Jesus Christ, they are again entangled therein, and overcome, the latter end is worse with them than the beginning. For it had been better for them not to have known the way of righteousness, than, after they have known it, to turn from the holy commandment delivered unto them. But it is happened unto them according to the true proverb, *"The dog is turned to his own vomit again"*; and "the sow that was washed to her wallowing in the mire."

The Day of the Lord
2 Peter 3:1-13

This second letter, beloved, I now write unto you; in both which I stir 6 up your sincere minds by way of remembrance: that you may be mindful of the words which were spoken long ago by the holy prophets, and of the command of us the apostles of the Lord and Savior: knowing this first, that there shall come in the last days scoffers, walking according to their own lusts, and saying, "Where is the promise of his coming? for since the fathers fell asleep, all things continue as they were from the beginning of the creation."

For this they willingly are forgetful of, that by the word of God the 7 heavens were of old, and the earth standing out of the water and in the water: whereby the world that then was, being overflowed with water, perished: but the heavens and the earth, which are now, by the same word are kept in store, reserved unto fire toward the day of judgment and destruction of ungodly men.

But, beloved, be not ignorant of this one thing, that one day is with 8 the Lord as a thousand years, and a thousand years as one day. The Lord is not slow concerning his promise, as some men count slowness; but is patient toward us, not willing that any should perish, but that all should come to repentance.

9   But the day of the Lord will come as a thief in the night; in which the heavens shall pass away with a great noise, and the elements shall melt with fervent heat, the earth also and the works that are therein shall be burned up.

10   Seeing then that all these things shall be dissolved, what manner of persons ought you to be in all holy conduct and godliness, looking for and hastening unto the coming of the day of God, wherein the heavens being on fire shall be dissolved, and the elements shall melt with fervent heat?

> ACCORDING TO HIS PROMISE, LOOK FOR NEW HEAVENS AND A NEW EARTH, WHEREIN DWELLS RIGHTEOUSNESS.

Nevertheless we, according to his promise, look for new heavens and a new earth, wherein dwells righteousness.

Beloved Brother Paul
2 Peter 3:14-16

11   Therefore, beloved, seeing that you look for such things, be diligent that you may be found of him in peace, without blemish, and blameless. And consider that the patience of our Lord is salvation; even as our beloved brother Paul also according to the wisdom given unto him has written unto you; as also in all his letters, speaking in them of these things; in which are some things hard to be understood, which they that are uneducated and unstable misinterpret, as they do also the other scriptures, unto their own destruction.

Conclusion
2 Peter 3:17-18

12   You therefore, beloved, seeing you know these things beforehand, beware lest you also, being led away with the error of the wicked, fall from your own steadfastness.

13   But grow in grace, and in the knowledge of our Lord and Savior Jesus Christ. To him be glory both now and for ever. Amen.

PART 40

Letter From Jude

In a bold declaration of things good and bad to come, Jude, the brother of Jesus, writes a scathing letter of rebuke and reprobation to those who distort and subvert the Word of God. Oblivious to the result of their evil ways, they will be judged and convicted by their own actions and will be fairly dealt with by the archangel of His presence. Those who would walk with Christ in the hereafter must follow his ways here on earth.

> REMEMBER THE WORDS WHICH WERE SPOKEN
> BEFORE OF THE APOSTLES OF OUR LORD JESUS
> CHRIST; HOW THAT THEY TOLD YOU THERE
> SHOULD BE MOCKERS IN THE LAST TIME, WHO
> SHOULD WALK ACCORDING TO THEIR OWN
> UNGODLY LUSTS.   (JUDE 1:17-18)

CHAPTER 140

ADVANCING AND AVOIDING

Greeting From Jude
Jude 1:1-2

1   Jude, the servant of Jesus Christ, and brother of James, to them that are sanctified by God the Father, and preserved in Jesus Christ, and called: Mercy unto you, and peace, and love, be multiplied.

Contending for the Faith
Jude 1:3-16

2   Beloved, when I gave all diligence to write unto you of the common salvation, it was needful for me to write unto you, and appeal to you that you should earnestly contend for the faith which was once delivered unto the saints. For there were certain men who crept in secretly, who were long ago designated for this condemnation, ungodly men, turning the grace of our God into lewdness, and denying the only Lord God, and our Lord Jesus Christ.

3   I will therefore put you in remembrance, though you once knew this, how that the Lord, having saved the people out of the land of Egypt, afterward destroyed them that did not believe. And the angels which did not keep their first domain, but left their own habitation, he has reserved in everlasting chains under darkness unto the judgment of the great day. Even as Sodom and Gomorrah, and the cities about them in like manner, giving themselves over to sexual immorality, and going after strange flesh, are set forth for an example, suffering the vengeance of eternal fire.

4   Likewise also these filthy dreamers defile the flesh, reject authority, and speak evil of dignitaries. Yet Michael the archangel, when contending with the devil he disputed about the body of Moses, dared not bring against him a slanderous accusation, but said, "The Lord rebuke you."

But these speak evil of those things which they know not: but what 5 they know naturally, as brute beasts, in those things they corrupt themselves. Woe unto them! for they have gone in the way of Cain, and ran greedily after the error of Balaam for reward, and perished in the rebellion of Korah.

These are blemishes in your feasts of love, when they feast with you, 6 feeding themselves without fear: clouds they are without water, carried about of winds; trees whose fruit withers, without fruit, twice dead, plucked up by the roots; raging waves of the sea, foaming out their own shame; wandering stars, to whom is reserved the blackness of darkness for ever.

And Enoch also, the seventh from Adam, prophesied of these, saying, 7 "Behold, the Lord comes with ten thousands of his saints, to execute judgment upon all, and to convict all that are ungodly among them of all their ungodly deeds which they have ungodly committed, and of all their harsh speeches which ungodly sinners have spoken against him."

These are murmurers, complainers, walking after their own lusts; and 8 their mouth speaks great swelling words, having men's persons in admiration because of advantage.

Keeping in the Love of God
Jude 1:17-23

But, beloved, remember the words which were spoken before of the 9 apostles of our Lord Jesus Christ; how that they told you there would be mockers in the last time, who would walk according to their own ungodly lusts. These be they who cause divisions, sensual, having not the Spirit.

But you, beloved, building up yourselves on your most holy faith, 10 praying in the Holy Ghost, keep yourselves in the love of God, looking for the mercy of our Lord Jesus Christ unto eternal life.

And of some have compassion, making a difference: and others save 11 with fear, pulling them out of the fire; hating even the garment stained by the flesh.

Conclusion
Jude 1:24-25

Now unto him that is able to keep you from falling, and to present you 12 faultless before the presence of his glory with exceeding joy, to the only wise God our Savior, be glory and majesty, dominion and power, both now and ever. Amen.

PART 41

FIRST LETTER FROM JOHN

This letter, authored by John the son of Zebedee, was written in an attempt to warn the people against false teachings and to reassure believers that God's love is above the things of this world. John writes, "...greater is He that is in you, than He that is in the world.? During this time, there are those who are teaching that Christ could not have come in human form. John wants to make sure that fellow Christians do not fall prey to such belief. He instructs them to walk in the light, to abide in Christ's love, and to love their brothers. The consummate life, he says, is one lived in righteousness and truth.

THERE ARE THREE THAT BEAR WITNESS IN HEAV-
EN, THE FATHER, THE WORD, AND THE HOLY
GHOST: AND THESE THREE ARE ONE. AND THERE
ARE THREE THAT BEAR WITNESS ON EARTH, THE
SPIRIT, AND THE WATER, AND THE BLOOD: AND
THESE THREE AGREE IN ONE.   (1 JOHN 5:7-8)

CHAPTER 141

TRUE AND TRUTH

Greeting From John
1 John 1:1-4

That which was from the beginning, which we have heard, which we 1
have seen with our eyes, which we have looked upon, and our hands have
handled, of the Word of life; (for the life was made visible, and we have seen
it, and bear witness, and declare unto you that eternal life, which was with
the Father, and was made visible unto us); that which we have seen and
heard we declare unto you, that you also may have fellowship with us: and
truly our fellowship is with the Father, and with his Son Jesus Christ. And
these things we write unto you, that your joy may be full.

God the Light
1 John 1:5-10

This then is the message which we have heard of him, and declare unto 2
you, that God is light, and in him is no darkness at all. If we say that we have
fellowship with him, and walk in darkness, we lie, and do not the truth: but
if we walk in the light, as he is in the light, we have fellowship one with
another, and the blood of Jesus Christ his Son cleanses us from all sin.

If we say that we have no sin, we deceive ourselves, and the truth is 3
not in us. If we confess our sins, he is faithful and just to forgive us our sins,
and to cleanse us from all unrighteousness. If we say that we have not
sinned, we make him a liar, and his word is not in us.

Christ the Advocate
1 John 2:1-6

My little children, these things I write unto you, that you not sin. And 4
if any man sins, we have an advocate with the Father, Jesus Christ the righteous: and he is the atonement for our sins: and not for ours only, but also
for the sins of the whole world.

5　　And hereby we do know that we know him, if we keep his commandments. He that says, "I know him," and does not keep his commandments, is a liar, and the truth is not in him. But whoever keeps his word, in him truly is the love of God perfected: hereby we know that we are in him. He that says he abides in him ought himself also so to walk, even as he walked.

True Light
1 John 2:7-17

6　　Brethren, I write no new command unto you, but an old command which you had from the beginning. The old command is the word which you have heard from the beginning. Again, a new command I write unto you, which thing is true in him and in you: because the darkness is past, and the true light now shines.

> THE DARKNESS IS PAST, AND THE TRUE LIGHT NOW SHINES.

7　　He that says he is in the light, and hates his brother, is in darkness even until now. He that loves his brother abides in the light, and there is no occasion of stumbling in him. But he that hates his brother is in darkness, and walks in darkness, and knows not where he goes, because that darkness has blinded his eyes.

8　　I write unto you, little children, because your sins are forgiven you for his name's sake. I write unto you, fathers, because you have known him that is from the beginning. I write unto you, young men, because you have overcome the wicked one. I write unto you, little children, because you have known the Father.

9　　I have written unto you, fathers, because you have known him that is from the beginning. I have written unto you, young men, because you are strong, and the word of God abides in you, and you have overcome the wicked one.

10　　Love not the world, neither the things that are in the world. If any man loves the world, the love of the Father is not in him. For all that is in the world, the lust of the flesh, and the lust of the eyes, and the pride of life, is not of the Father, but is of the world. And the world passes away, and the lust thereof: but he that does the will of God abides for ever.

> THE WORLD PASSES AWAY, AND THE LUST THEREOF: BUT HE THAT DOES THE WILL OF GOD ABIDES FOR EVER.

Antichrists
1 John 2:18-29

11　　Little children, it is the last hour: and as you have heard that antichrist shall come, even now are there many antichrists; whereby we know that it is the last hour. they went out from us, but they were not of us; for if they had been of us, they would no doubt have continued with us: but they went out, that they might be made obvious that they all were not of us.

But you have an anointing from the Holy One, and you know all 12
things. I have not written unto you because you do not know the truth, but
because you know it, and that no lie is
of the truth. Who is a liar but he that

> HE THAT ACKNOWLEDGES
> THE SON HAS THE FATHER
> ALSO.

denies that Jesus is the Christ? He is
antichrist, that denies the Father and
the Son. Whosoever denies the Son,
the same has not the Father: (but) he that acknowledges the Son has the
Father also.

Let that therefore abide in you, which you have heard from the begin- 13
ning. If that which you have heard from the beginning shall remain in you,
you also shall continue in the Son, and in the Father. And this is the promise that he has promised us, even eternal life.

These things have I written unto you concerning them that seduce you. 14
But the anointing which you have received of him abides in you, and you
need not that any man teach you: but as the same anointing teaches you of
all things, and is truth, and is no lie, and even as it has taught you, you shall
abide in him.

And now, little children, abide in him; that, when he shall appear, we 15
may have confidence, and not be ashamed before him at his coming. If you
know that he is righteous, you know that everyone that does righteousness
is born of him.

CHAPTER 142

GOD AND LOVE

Children of God
1 John 3:1-10

1   Behold, what manner of love the Father has bestowed upon us, that we should be called the children of God: therefore the world does not know us, because it did not know him. Beloved, now are we the children of God, and it does not yet appear what we shall be: but we know that, when he shall appear, we shall be like him; for we shall see him as he is. And every man that has this hope in him purifies himself, even as he is pure.

2   Whosoever commits sin transgresses also the law: for sin is the transgression of the law. And you know that he was made visible to take away our sins; and in him is no sin. Whosoever abides in him does not sin: whosoever sins has not seen him, neither known him.

3   Little children, let no man deceive you: he that does righteousness is righteous, even as he is righteous. He that commits sin is of the devil; for the devil sins from the beginning. For this purpose the Son of God was made visible, that he might destroy the works of the devil.

4   Whosoever is born of God does not commit sin; for his seed remains in him: and he cannot sin, because he is born of God. In this the children of God are revealed, and the children of the devil: whosoever does not righteousness is not of God, neither he that does not love his brother.

Loving One Another
1 John 3:11-24

5   For this is the message that you heard from the beginning, that we should love one another. Not as Cain, who was of that wicked one, and slew his brother. And why did he murder him? Because his own works were evil, and his brother's righteous.

Marvel not, my brethren, if the world hates you. We know that we have 6
passed from death unto life, because we love the brethren. He that does not
love his brother abides in death. Whosoever hates his brother is a murderer:
and you know that no murderer has eternal life abiding in him.

Hereby we perceive the love of God, because he laid down his life for 7
us: and we ought to lay down our lives for the brethren. But whoever has
this world's goods, and sees his brother have need, and shuts up his heart of
compassion from him, how does the love of God dwell in him? My little
children, let us not love in word, neither in tongue; but in deed and in truth.

And hereby we know that we are of the truth, and shall assure our 8
hearts before him. For if our heart condemns us, God is greater than our
heart, and knows all things.

Beloved, if our heart condemns us not, then we have confidence 9
toward God. And whatsoever we ask, we receive of him, because we keep
his commandments, and do those things that are pleasing in his sight.

And this is his commandment, That we should believe on the name of 10
his Son Jesus Christ, and love one
another, as he gave us commandment.
And he that keeps his commandments
dwells in him, and he in him. And
hereby we know that he abides in us,
by the Spirit which he has given us.

> BELIEVE ON THE NAME OF HIS
> SON JESUS CHRIST, AND LOVE
> ONE ANOTHER, AS HE GAVE US
> COMMANDMENT.

True and False Spirits
1 John 4:1-6

Beloved, believe not every spirit, but test the spirits whether they are 11
of God: because many false prophets are gone out into the world.

Hereby you know the Spirit of God: Every spirit that confesses that 12
Jesus Christ is come in the flesh is of God: and every spirit that does not
confess that Jesus Christ is come in the flesh is not of God: and this is that
spirit of antichrist, of which you have heard that it should come; and even
now already is it in the world.

You are of God, little children, and have overcome them: because 13
greater is he that is in you, than he that
is in the world. They are of the world:
therefore they speak of the world, and
the world hears them. We are of God:
he that knows God hears us; he that is

> GREATER IS HE THAT IS IN
> YOU, THAN HE THAT IS IN THE
> WORLD.

not of God does not hear us. Hereby do we know the spirit of truth, and the
spirit of error.

Perfect Love
1 John 4:7-21

Beloved, let us love one another: for love is of God; and everyone that 14
loves is born of God, and knows God. He that does not love does not know

14 God; for God is love. in this was revealed the love of God toward us, because God sent his only begotten Son into the world, that we might live through him. Herein is love, not that we loved God, but that he loved us, and sent his Son to be the atonement for our sins.

15 Beloved, if God so loved us, we ought also to love one another. No man has seen God at any time. If we love one another, God dwells in us, and his love is perfected in us.

16 Hereby we know that we dwell in him, and he in us, because he has given us of his Spirit. And we have seen and do testify that the Father sent the Son to be the Savior of the world. Whosoever shall confess that Jesus is the Son of God, God dwells in him, and he in God.

17 And we have known and believed the love that God has to us. God is love; and he that dwells in love dwells in God, and God in him. Herein is our love made perfect, that we may have boldness in the day of judgment: because as he is, so are we in this world. There is no fear in love; but perfect love casts out fear: because fear has torment. He that fears is not made perfect in love.

> GOD IS LOVE; AND HE THAT DWELLS IN LOVE DWELLS IN GOD, AND GOD IN HIM.

18 We love him, because he first loved us.

19 If a man says, "I love God," and hates his brother, he is a liar: for he that does not love his brother whom he has seen, how can he love God whom he has not seen? And this commandment we have from him, That he who loves God loves his brother also.

CHAPTER 143

Overcoming

Victory
1 John 5:1-5

Whosoever believes that Jesus is the Christ is born of God: and every- 1
one that loves him that begot loves him also that is begotten of him. By this
we know that we love the children of God, when we love God, and keep his
commandments. For this is the love of God, that we keep his commandments: and his commandments are not burdensome. For whatsoever is born
of God overcomes the world: and this is the victory that overcomes the
world, even our faith. Who is he that overcomes the world, but he that
believes that Jesus is the Son of God?

Eternal Life in the Son
1 John 5:6-12

This is he that came by water and blood, even Jesus Christ; not by 2
water only, but by water and blood. And it is the Spirit that bears witness,
because the Spirit is truth.

For there are three that bear witness in heaven, the Father, the Word, 3
and the Holy Ghost: and these three are one. And there are three that bear
witness on earth, the Spirit, and the water, and the blood: and these three
agree in one.

If we receive the witness of men, the witness of God is greater: for this 4
is the witness of God which he has testified of his Son. He that believes on
the Son of God has the witness in himself: he that does not believe God has
made him a liar; because he does not believe the testimony that God gave
of his Son. And this is the testimony, that God has given to us eternal life,
and this life is in his Son. He that has the Son has life; and he that does not
have the Son of God does not have life.

Conclusion
1 John 5:13-21

5   These things I have written unto you that believe on the name of the Son of God; that you may know that you have eternal life, and that you may believe on the name of the Son of God.

6   And this is the confidence that we have in him, that, if we ask anything according to his will, he hears us: and if we know that he hears us, whatsoever we ask, we know that we have the petitions that we desired of him.

7   If any man sees his brother sin a sin which is not unto death, he shall ask, and he shall give him life for them that sin not unto death. There is a sin unto death: I do not say that he shall pray for it. All unrighteousness is sin: and there is a sin not unto death.

8   We know that whosoever is born of God does not sin; but he that is begotten of God protects himself, and that wicked one does not touch him. And we know that we are of God, and the whole world lies in the power of the evil one. And we know that the Son of God is come, and has given us an understanding, that we may know him that is true, and we are in him that is true, even in his Son Jesus Christ. This is the true God, and eternal life.

9   Little children, keep yourselves from idols. Amen.

PART 42

SECOND LETTER FROM JOHN

In this brief letter, John writes to the "elect lady" and her children, meaning the church and its congregation. He wants to ensure that those who receive and support the traveling evangelists use discernment, for some are false teachers. He warns that those who do not believe that Jesus came in the flesh are deceivers and antichrists. He invites Christians to walk in obedient love. Truth, he says, advocates love.

> MANY DECEIVERS ARE ENTERED INTO THE
> WORLD, WHO DO NOT CONFESS THAT JESUS
> CHRIST IS COME IN THE FLESH. THIS IS A
> DECEIVER AND AN ANTICHRIST.   (2 JOHN 1:7)

CHAPTER 144

PERSEVERING

Greeting to the Elect Lady
2 John 1:1-3

1   The elder unto the elect lady and her children, whom I love in the truth; and not I only, but also all they that have known the truth; for the truth's sake, which dwells in us, and shall be with us for ever.

2   Grace be with you, mercy, and peace, from God the Father, and from the Lord Jesus Christ, the Son of the Father, in truth and love.

Loving One Another
2 John 1:4-11

3   I rejoiced greatly that I found your children walking in truth, as we have received a commandment from the Father. And now I ask you, lady, not as though I wrote a new commandment unto you, but that which we had from the beginning, that we love one another. And this is love, that we walk according to his commandments. This is the commandment, That, as you have heard from the beginning, you should walk in it.

4   For many deceivers are entered into the world, who do not confess that Jesus Christ is come in the flesh. This is a deceiver and an antichrist. Look to yourselves, that we do not lose those things which we have worked for, but that we receive a full reward. Whosoever transgresses, and does not abide in the doctrine of Christ, does not have God. He that abides in the doctrine of Christ, he has both the Father and the Son.

5   If there comes anyone unto you, and does not bring this doctrine, do not receive him into your house, neither bid him Godspeed: for he that bids him Godspeed is partaker of his evil deeds.

Conclusion
2 John 1:12-13

Having many things to write unto you, I would not write with paper 6
and ink: but I trust to come unto you, and speak face to face, that our joy
may be full.

The children of your elect sister greet you. Amen. 7

PART 43

THIRD LETTER FROM JOHN

John writes to his good friend Gaius, commending him for his hospitality to the evangelists who travel through the Roman province of Asia Minor. He is overjoyed with Gaius' faithfulness in supporting the missionaries. He rebukes the acts of Diotrephes, the self-assertive church leader who refuses to help the missionaries and has rebelled against John's leadership. He praises Demetrius, who is a model church member, using him as an example that all should follow.

> BELOVED, I PRAY ABOVE ALL THINGS THAT YOU
> MAY PROSPER AND BE IN HEALTH, EVEN AS YOUR
> SOUL PROSPERS. (3 JOHN 1:2)

CHAPTER 145

ADVISING

Greeting to Gaius
3 John 1:1-4

The elder unto the beloved Gaius, whom I love in the truth. Beloved, 1
I pray above all things that you may prosper and be in health, even as your
soul prospers.

For I rejoiced greatly, when the brethren came and testified of the truth 2
that is in you, even as you walk in the truth. I have no greater joy than to
hear that my children walk in truth.

Treatment of Strangers
3 John 1:5-12

Beloved, you do faithfully whatsoever you do to the brethren, and to 3
strangers; which have borne witness of your love before the church: whom
if you send forward on their journey after a godly manner, you shall do well:
because that for his name's sake they went forth, taking nothing of the Gentiles. We therefore ought to receive such, that we might be fellow helpers to
the truth.

I wrote unto the church: but Diotrephes, who loves to have the pre- 4
eminence among them, does not receive us. Therefore, if I come, I will
remember his deeds which he does, gossiping against us with malicious
words: and not content with that, neither does he himself receive the
brethren, and forbids them that would, and casts them out of the church.

Beloved, do not imitate that which is evil, but that which is good. He 5
that does good is of God: but he that does evil has not seen God.

Demetrius has good testimony of all men, and of the truth itself: yes, 6
and we also bear witness; and you know that our witness is true.

Conclusion
3 John 1:13-14

7   I had many things to write, but I will not with ink and pen write unto you: but I trust I shall shortly see you, and we shall speak face to face. Peace be to you. Our friends greet you. Greet the friends by name.

PART 44

REVELATION

The words of Revelation are mighty in message and meaning. They have both intrigued and confounded readers of the Scriptures throughout history. Given to John in a revelation from Jesus Christ, they offer a ringing account of his vision of things to come. In metaphor and parable they unfold spiritual mysteries for future ages. The revelation of John foresees a new world, a different world, of promise and hope, a world in which we are united in the hope and presence of Him who is both the beginning and the end, the Alpha and Omega. The many faces of evil, in their varied and hideous forms, fall in final defeat before the angels of God's presence. In this moment of time, time is no more, for time passes into eternity. We are left with the assurance that Christ will abide with us forever, even as we abide in Him.

> BLESSED IS HE THAT READS, AND THEY THAT
> HEAR THE WORDS OF THIS PROPHECY, AND KEEP
> THOSE THINGS WHICH ARE WRITTEN IN IT: FOR
> THE TIME IS AT HAND. (REVELATION 1:3)

CHAPTER 146

REVELATION OF JESUS CHRIST

Opening: Introduction
Revelation 1:1-3

1   The Revelation of Jesus Christ, which God gave unto him, to show unto his servants things which must shortly come to pass; and he sent and signified it by his angel unto his servant John: who bore witness of the word of God, and of the testimony of Jesus Christ, and of all things that he saw.

2   Blessed is he that reads, and they that hear the words of this prophecy, and keep those things which are written in it: for the time is at hand.

Opening: Greeting to Churches
Revelation 1:4-8

3   John to the seven churches which are in Asia: Grace be unto you, and peace, from him which is, and which was, and which is to come; and from the seven Spirits which are before his throne; and from Jesus Christ, who is the faithful witness, and the first begotten of the dead, and the ruler of the kings of the earth. Unto him that loved us, and washed us from our sins in his own blood, and has made us kings and priests unto God and his Father; to him be glory and dominion for ever and ever. Amen.

4   *Behold, he comes with clouds*; and every eye shall see him, and they also which pierced him: and all peoples of the earth shall mourn because of him. Even so, Amen.

5   "I am Alpha and Omega, the beginning and the ending," says the Lord, "which is, and which was, and which is to come, the Almighty."

The Great Voice
Revelation 1:9-16

6   I John, who also am your brother, and companion in tribulation, and in the kingdom and patient endurance of Jesus Christ, was on the island that

is called Patmos, because of the word of God, and because of the testimony 6
of Jesus Christ.

I was in the Spirit on the Lord's day, and heard behind me a great 7
voice, as of a trumpet, saying, "I am Alpha and Omega, the first and the
last": and, "What you see, write in a book, and send it unto the seven
churches which are in Asia; unto Ephesus, and unto Smyrna, and unto Pergamos, and unto Thyatira, and unto Sardis, and unto Philadelphia, and unto
Laodicea."

And I turned to see the voice that spoke with me. And being turned, I 8
saw seven golden lampstands; and in the midst of the seven lampstands one
like unto the Son of man, clothed with a garment down to the feet, and
wrapped about the chest with a golden band.

His head and his hair were white like wool, as white as snow; and his 9
eyes were as a flame of fire; and his feet like unto fine brass, as if they
glowed in a furnace; and his voice as the sound of many waters. And he had
in his right hand seven stars: and out of his mouth went a sharp two-edged
sword: and his countenance was as the sun shines in its strength.

The Great Assignment
Revelation 1:17-20

And when I saw him, I fell at his feet as dead. And he laid his right 10
hand upon me, saying unto me, "Fear not; I am the first and the last: I am
he that lives, and was dead; and, behold, I am alive for evermore, Amen; and
have the keys of Hades and of death.

"Write the things which you have seen, and the things which are, and 11
the things which shall be hereafter; the mystery of the seven stars which you
saw in my right hand, and the seven golden lampstands. The seven stars are
the angels of the seven churches: and the seven lampstands which you saw
are the seven churches."

CHAPTER 147

MESSAGES TO SEVEN CHURCHES

Ephesus—The Loveless Church
Revelation 2:1-7

1   "Unto the angel of the church of Ephesus write; 'These things says he that holds the seven stars in his right hand, who walks in the midst of the seven golden lampstands; "I know your works, and your labor, and your perseverance, and how you cannot bear them which are evil: and you have tested them which say they are apostles, and are not, and have found them liars: and have borne, and have perseverance, and for my name's sake have labored, and have not become weary.

2   "Nevertheless I have something against you, because you have left your first love. Remember therefore from where you are fallen, and repent, and do the first works; or else I will come unto you quickly, and will remove your lampstand out of its place, unless you repent. But this you have, that you hate the deeds of the Nicolaitans, which I also hate.

3   "He that has an ear, let him hear what the Spirit says unto the churches; to him that overcomes will I give to eat of the tree of life, which is in the midst of the paradise of God." '

Smyrna—The Persecuted Church
Revelation 2:8-11

4   "And unto the angel of the church in Smyrna write; 'These things says the first and the last, which was dead, and is alive; "I know your works, and tribulation, and poverty, (but you are rich) and I know the slander of them which say they are Jews, and are not, but are the synagogue of Satan. Fear none of those things which you shall suffer: behold, the devil shall cast some of you into prison, that you may be tested; and you shall have tribulation ten days: be faithful unto death, and I will give you a crown of life.

"He that has an ear, let him hear what the Spirit says unto the churches; 5 he that overcomes shall not be hurt of the second death." '

Pergamum—The Compromising Church
Revelation 2:12-17

"And to the angel of the church in Pergamos write; 'These things says 6 he which has the sharp sword with two edges; "I know your works, and where you dwell, even where Satan's throne is: and you hold fast my name, and have not denied my faith, even in those days in which Antipas was my faithful martyr, who was slain among you, where Satan dwells.

"But I have a few things against you, because you have there them that 7 hold the doctrine of Balaam, who taught Balak to cast a stumbling block before the children of Israel, to eat things sacrificed unto idols, and to commit sexual immorality. So have you also them that hold the doctrine of the Nicolaitans, which thing I hate. Repent; or else I will come unto you quickly, and will fight against them with the sword of my mouth.

"He that has an ear, let him hear what the Spirit says unto the churches; 8 to him that overcomes will I give to eat of the hidden manna, and will give him a white stone, and on the stone a new name written, which no man knows except he that receives it." '

Thyatira—The Corrupt Church
Revelation 2:18-29

"And unto the angel of the church in Thyatira write; 'These things says 9 the Son of God, who has his eyes like unto a flame of fire, and his feet are like fine brass; "I know your works, and love, and service, and faith, and your perseverance, and your works; and the last to be more than the first.

"Notwithstanding I have a few things against you, because you permit 10 that woman Jezebel, which calls herself a prophetess, to teach and to seduce my servants to commit sexual immorality, and to eat things sacrificed unto idols. And I gave her time to repent of her immorality; and she did not repent.

"Behold, I will cast her into a bed, and them that commit adultery 11 with her into great tribulation, unless they repent of their deeds. And I will kill her children with death; and all the churches shall know that I am he which searches the minds and hearts: and I will give unto every one of you according to your works.

"But unto you I say, and unto the rest in Thyatira, as many as do not 12 have this doctrine, and which have not known the depths of Satan, as they speak; I will put upon you no other burden. But that which you have already hold fast till I come.

"And he that overcomes, and keeps my works unto the end, to him will 13 I give authority over the nations: and 'he shall rule them with a rod of iron;

13 as the vessels of a potter shall they be broken to pieces': even as I received of my Father. And I will give him the morning star.

14 "He that has an ear, let him hear what the Spirit says unto the churches." '

Sardis—The Dead Church
Revelation 3:1-6

15 "And unto the angel of the church in Sardis write; 'These things says he that has the seven Spirits of God, and the seven stars; "I know your works, that you have a name that you are alive, and are dead. Be watchful, and strengthen the things which remain, that are about to die: for I have not found your works complete before God. Remember therefore how you have received and heard, and hold fast, and repent. If therefore you shall not watch, I will come on you as a thief, and you shall not know what hour I will come upon you.

16 "You have a few names even in Sardis which have not defiled their garments; and they shall walk with me in white: for they are worthy. He that overcomes, the same shall be clothed in white clothing; and I will not blot out his name out of the book of life, but I will confess his name before my Father, and before his angels.

17 "He that has an ear, let him hear what the Spirit says unto the churches." '

Philadelphia—The Faithful Church
Revelation 3:7-13

18 "And to the angel of the church in Philadelphia write; 'These things says he that is holy, "he that is true, he that has the key of David, he that opens, and no man shuts; and shuts, and no man opens; I know your works: behold, I have set before you an open door, and no man can shut it: for you have a little strength, and have kept my word, and have not denied my name.

19 "Behold, I will make them of the synagogue of Satan, which say they are Jews, and are not, but do lie; behold, I will make them to come and worship before your feet, and to know that I have loved you. Because you have kept the word of my patience, I also will keep you from the hour of temptation, which shall come upon all the world, to test them that dwell upon the earth.

20 "Behold, I come quickly: hold that fast which you have, that no man take your crown. He that overcomes will I make a pillar in the temple of my God, and he shall go no more out: and I will write upon he the name of my God, and the name of the city of my God, which is new Jerusalem, which comes down out of heaven from my God: and I will write upon he my new name.

21 "He that has an ear, let him hear what the Spirit says unto the churches." '

Laodicea—The Lukewarm Church
Revelation 3:14-22

"And unto the angel of the church of the Laodiceans write; 'These 22 things says the Amen, the faithful and true witness, the beginning of the creation of God; "I know your works, that you are neither cold nor hot: I would you were cold or hot.

"So then because you are lukewarm, and neither cold nor hot, I will 23 spew you out of my mouth. Because you say, 'I am rich, and increased with wealth, and have need of nothing'; and do not know that you are wretched, and pitiful, and poor, and blind, and naked: I advise you to buy of me gold refined in the fire, that you may be rich; and white clothing, that you may be clothed, and that the shame of your nakedness does not appear; and anoint your eyes with eye salve, that you may see. As many as I love, I correct and discipline: be earnest therefore, and repent.

"Behold, I stand at the door, and knock: if any man hears my voice, 24 and opens the door, I will come in to him, and will eat with him, and he with me. To him that overcomes I will grant to sit with me on my throne, even as I also overcame, and am seated with my Father on his throne.

> TO HIM THAT OVERCOMES I WILL GRANT TO SIT WITH ME ON MY THRONE.

"He that has an ear, let him hear what the Spirit says unto the 25 churches." ' "

CHAPTER 148

THINGS WHICH SHALL BE HEREAFTER

Interlude—Door Opened in Heaven
Revelation 4:1-11

1   After this I looked, and, behold, a door was opened in heaven: and the first voice which I heard was as it were of a trumpet speaking with me; which said, "Come up here, and I will show you things which must be hereafter." And immediately I was in the spirit: and, behold, a throne was set in heaven, and one sat on the throne.

2   And he that sat was to look upon like a jasper and a sardine stone: and there was a rainbow round about the throne, in sight like unto an emerald. And round about the throne were four and twenty seats: and upon the seats I saw four and twenty elders sitting, dressed in white clothing; and they had on their heads crowns of gold. And out of the throne proceeded lightnings and thunderings and voices: and there were seven lamps of fire burning before the throne, which are the seven Spirits of God.

3   And before the throne there was a sea of glass like unto crystal: and in the midst of the throne, and round about the throne, were four living creatures full of eyes before and behind. And the first living creature was like a lion, and the second living creature like a calf, and the third living creature had a face as a man, and the fourth living creature was like a flying eagle. And the four living creatures had each of them six wings about him; and they were full of eyes within: and they do not rest day and night, saying, "Holy, holy, holy, Lord God Almighty, which was, and is, and is to come."

4   And when those living creatures give glory and honor and thanks to him that sits on the throne, who lives for ever and ever, the four and twenty elders fall down before him that sits on the throne, and worship him that lives for ever and ever, and cast their crowns before the throne, saying, "You are worthy, O Lord, to receive glory and honor and power: for you have created all things, and for your pleasure they are and were created."

Interlude—Scroll With Seven Seals
Revelation 5:1-14

And I saw in the right hand of him that sat on the throne a scroll writ- 5 ten within and on the back side, sealed with seven seals. And I saw a strong angel proclaiming with a loud voice, "Who is worthy to open the scroll, and to break the seals of it?" And no man in heaven, nor on earth, neither under the earth, was able to open the scroll, neither to look upon it.

> I SAW IN THE RIGHT HAND OF HIM THAT SAT ON THE THRONE A SCROLL WRITTEN WITHIN AND ON THE BACK SIDE, SEALED WITH SEVEN SEALS.

And I wept much, because no man was found worthy to open and to 6 read the scroll, neither to look upon it. And one of the elders said unto me, "Do not weep: behold, the Lion of the tribe of Judah, the Root of David, has prevailed to open the scroll, and to break the seven seals of it."

And I beheld, and, lo, in the midst of the throne and of the four living 7 creatures, and in the midst of the elders, stood a Lamb as if it had been slain, having seven horns and seven eyes, which are the seven Spirits of God sent forth into all the earth. And he came and took the scroll out of the right hand of him that sat upon the throne.

And when he had taken the scroll, the four living creatures and four 8 and twenty elders fell down before the Lamb, having every one of them harps, and golden vials full of incense, which are the prayers of saints. And they sang a new song, saying, "You are worthy to take the scroll, and to open the seals of it: for you were slain, and have redeemed us to God by your blood out of every tribe, and tongue, and people, and nation; and have made us unto our God kings and priests: and we shall reign on the earth."

And I beheld, and I heard the voice of many angels round about the 9 throne and the living creatures and the elders: and the number of them was ten thousand times ten thousand, and thousands of thousands; saying with a loud voice, "Worthy is the Lamb that was slain to receive power, and riches, and wisdom, and strength, and honor, and glory, and blessing."

And every creature which is in heaven, and on the earth, and under the 10 earth, and such as are in the sea, and all that are in them, heard I saying, "Blessing, and honor, and glory, and power, be unto him that sits upon the throne, and unto the Lamb for ever and ever." And the four living creatures said, Amen. And the four and twenty elders fell down and worshiped him that lives for ever and ever.

CHAPTER 149

SEVEN SEALS JUDGMENTS

Seal 1: White Horse—Conquest
Revelation 6:1-2

1 And I saw when the Lamb opened one of the seals, and I heard, as if it were the noise of thunder, one of the four living creatures saying, "Come and see." And I saw, and behold a white horse: and he that sat on it had a bow; and a crown was given unto him: and he went forth conquering, and to conquer.

Seal 2: Red Horse—War
Revelation 6:3-4

2 And when he had opened the second seal, I heard the second living creature say, "Come and see." And there went out another horse that was red: and power was given to him that sat on it to take peace from the earth, and that they should kill one another: and there was given unto him a great sword.

Seal 3: Black Horse—Famine
Revelation 6:5-6

3 And when he had opened the third seal, I heard the third living creature say, "Come and see." And I beheld, and lo a black horse; and he that sat on it had a pair of scales in his hand. And I heard a voice in the midst of the four living creatures say, "A measure of wheat for a silver coin, and three measures of barley for a silver coin; and see you do not damage the oil and the wine."

Seal 4: Pale Horse—Death
Revelation 6:7-8

4 And when he had opened the fourth seal, I heard the voice of the fourth living creature say, "Come and see." And I looked, and behold a pale horse: and his name that sat on it was Death, and Hades followed with him.

And power was given unto them over the fourth part of the earth, to kill with 4
sword, and with hunger, and with pestilence, and with the wild animals of
the earth.

Seal 5: White Robes—Martyrs
Revelation 6:9-11

And when he had opened the fifth seal, I saw under the altar the souls
of them that were slain for the word of God, and for the testimony which 5
they held: and they cried with a loud voice, saying, "How long, O Lord, holy
and true, do you not judge and avenge our blood on them that dwell on the
earth?" And white robes were given unto every one of them; and it was said
unto them, that they should rest yet for a little season, until their fellow servants also and their brethren, that should be killed as they were, should be
fulfilled.

Seal 6: Cosmic Storms—Wrath
Revelation 6:12-17

And I beheld when he had opened the sixth seal, and, lo, there was a 6
great earthquake; and the sun became black as sackcloth of hair, and the
moon became as blood; and the stars of heaven fell unto the earth, even as
a fig tree drops its unripe figs, when it is shaken of a mighty wind. And the
sky receded as a scroll when it is rolled together; and every mountain and
island was moved out of its place.

And the kings of the earth, and the great men, and the rich men, and 7
the commanders, and the mighty men, and every bondman, and every free
man, hid themselves in the caves and in the rocks of the mountains; and said
to the mountains and rocks, Fall on us, and hide us from the face of him that
sits on the throne, and from the wrath of the Lamb: "for the great day of his
wrath is come; and who shall be able to stand?"

Pause: Servants of God Sealed
Revelation 7:1-8

And after these things I saw four angels standing on the four corners 8
of the earth, holding the four winds of the earth, that the wind should not
blow on the earth, nor on the sea, nor on any tree.

And I saw another angel ascending from the east, having the seal of 9
the living God: and he cried with a loud voice to the four angels, to whom
it was given to harm the earth and the sea, saying, "Do not harm the earth,
neither the sea, nor the trees, till we have sealed the servants of our God
upon their foreheads."

And I heard the number of them which were sealed: and there were 10
sealed a hundred and forty and four thousand of all the tribes of the children of Israel. Of the tribe of Judah were sealed twelve thousand. Of the
tribe of Reuben were sealed twelve thousand. Of the tribe of Gad were
sealed twelve thousand. Of the tribe of Asher were sealed twelve thousand.

10   Of the tribe of Naphtali were sealed twelve thousand. Of the tribe of Manasseh were sealed twelve thousand. Of the tribe of Simeon were sealed twelve thousand. Of the tribe of Levi were sealed twelve thousand. Of the tribe of Issachar were sealed twelve thousand. Of the tribe of Zebulun were sealed twelve thousand. Of the tribe of Joseph were sealed twelve thousand. Of the tribe of Benjamin were sealed twelve thousand.

Pause: Multitude in White Robes
Revelation 7:9-17

11   After this I beheld, and, lo, a great multitude, which no man could number, of all nations, and tribes, and peoples, and tongues, stood before the throne, and before the Lamb, dressed with white robes, and palm branches in their hands; and cried with a loud voice, saying, "Salvation to our God which sits upon the throne, and unto the Lamb."

12   And all the angels stood round about the throne, and about the elders and the four living creatures, and fell before the throne on their faces, and worshiped God, saying, "Amen: Blessing, and glory, and wisdom, and thanksgiving, and honor, and power, and might, be unto our God for ever and ever. Amen."

13   And one of the elders answered, saying unto me, "What are these which are arrayed in white robes? and from where have they come?" And I said unto him, "Sir, you know." And he said to me, "These are they which came out of great tribulation, and have washed their robes, and made them white in the blood of the Lamb.

14   "Therefore are they before the throne of God, and serve him day and night in his temple: and he that sits on the throne shall dwell among them.

> THEY SHALL HUNGER NO MORE, NEITHER THIRST ANYMORE; NEITHER SHALL THE SUN BEAT UPON THEM, NOR ANY BURNING HEAT.

They shall hunger no more, neither thirst anymore; neither shall the sun beat upon them, nor any burning heat. For the Lamb which is in the midst of the throne shall shepherd them, and shall lead them unto living fountains of waters: and God shall wipe away all tears from their eyes."

Seal 7: Silence, Seven Trumpets
Revelation 8:1-5

15   And when he had opened the seventh seal, there was silence in heaven about the space of half an hour. And I saw the seven angels which stood before God; and to them were given seven trumpets.

16   And another angel came and stood at the altar, having a golden censer; and there was given unto him much incense, that he should offer it with the prayers of all saints upon the golden altar which was before the throne. And the smoke of the incense, which came with the prayers of the saints, ascended up before God out of the angel's hand.

And the angel took the censer, and filled it with fire of the altar, and 17 cast it into the earth: and there were noises, and thunderings, and lightnings, and an earthquake.

CHAPTER 150

SEVEN TRUMPETS JUDGMENTS

Trumpet 1: Hail, Fire, and Blood
Revelation 8:6-7

1   And the seven angels which had the seven trumpets prepared themselves to sound.

2   The first angel sounded, and there followed hail and fire mingled with blood, and they were cast upon the earth: and the third part of trees was burned up, and all green grass was burned up.

Trumpet 2: Sea Struck
Revelation 8:8-9

3   And the second angel sounded, and as it were a great mountain burning with fire was cast into the sea: and the third part of the sea became blood; and the third part of the creatures which were in the sea, and had life, died; and the third part of the ships were destroyed.

Trumpet 3: Waters Struck
Revelation 8:10-11

4   And the third angel sounded, and there fell a great star from heaven, burning as it were a torch, and it fell upon the third part of the rivers, and upon the fountains of waters; and the name of the star is called Wormwood: and the third part of the waters became wormwood; and many men died of the waters, because they were made bitter.

Trumpet 4: Light Struck
Revelation 8:12-13

5   And the fourth angel sounded, and the third part of the sun was struck, and the third part of the moon, and the third part of the stars; that as the third part of them was darkened, and the day did not shine for a third part of it, and the night likewise.

And I beheld, and heard an angel flying through the midst of heaven, 6 saying with a loud voice, "Woe, woe, woe, to the inhabitants of the earth by reason of the other voices of the trumpet of the three angels, which are yet to sound!"

Trumpet 5: The Bottomless Pit
Revelation 9:1-12

And the fifth angel sounded, and I saw a star fall from heaven unto the 7 earth: and to him was given the key of the bottomless pit. And he opened the bottomless pit; and there arose a smoke out of the pit, as the smoke of a great furnace; and the sun and the air were darkened by reason of the smoke of the pit.

> AND I SAW A STAR FALL FROM HEAVEN UNTO THE EARTH.

And there came out of the smoke locusts upon the earth: and unto 8 them was given power, as the scorpions of the earth have power. And it was commanded them that they should not harm the grass of the earth, neither any green thing, neither any tree; but only those men which did not have the seal of God upon their foreheads.

And to them it was given that they should not kill them, but that they 9 should be tormented five months: and their torment was as the torment of a scorpion, when it strikes a man. And in those days shall men seek death, and shall not find it; and shall desire to die, and death shall flee from them.

And the shapes of the locusts were like unto horses prepared unto bat- 10 tle; and on their heads were as it were crowns like gold, and their faces were as the faces of men. And they had hair as the hair of women, and their teeth were as the teeth of lions.

And they had breastplates, as it were breastplates of iron; and the 11 sound of their wings was as the sound of chariots of many horses running into battle. And they had tails like unto scorpions, and there were stings in their tails: and their power was to hurt men five months.

And they had a king over them, which is the angel of the bottomless 12 pit, whose name in the Hebrew tongue is Abaddon, but in the Greek tongue has his name Apollyon.

One woe is past; and, behold, there comes two woes more hereafter. 13

Trumpet 6: The Destroying Angels
Revelation 9:13-21

And the sixth angel sounded, and I heard a voice from the four horns 14 of the golden altar which is before God, saying to the sixth angel which had the trumpet, "Release the four angels which are bound at the great river Euphrates." And the four angels were released, which were prepared for an hour, and a day, and a month, and a year, to slay the third part of men. And the number of the army of the horsemen were two hundred million: and I heard the number of them.

15   And thus I saw the horses in the vision, and them that sat on them, having breastplates of fiery red, and of sapphire blue, and brimstone yellow: and the heads of the horses were as the heads of lions; and out of their mouths poured fiery red and smoke and brimstone yellow. By these three was the third part of men killed, by the fiery red, and by the smoke, and by the brimstone yellow, which poured out of their mouths. For their power is in their mouth, and in their tails: for their tails were like unto serpents, and had heads, and with them they do injure.

16   And the rest of mankind which were not killed by these plagues still did not repent of the works of their hands, that they should not worship demons, and idols of gold, and silver, and brass, and stone, and of wood: which neither can see, nor hear, nor walk: neither did they repent of their murders, nor of their sorceries, nor of their sexual immorality, nor of their thefts.

Interlude—The Little Scroll
Revelation 10:1-11

17   And I saw another mighty angel come down from heaven, clothed with a cloud: and a rainbow was upon his head, and his face was as it were the sun, and his feet as pillars of fire: and he had in his hand a little scroll open: and he set his right foot upon the sea, and his left foot on the land, and cried with a loud voice, as when a lion roars: and when he had cried, seven thunders uttered their voices.

18   And when the seven thunders had uttered their voices, I was about to write: and I heard a voice from heaven saying unto me, "Seal up those things which the seven thunders uttered, and do not write them."

19   And the angel which I saw stand upon the sea and upon the land lifted up his hand to heaven, and swore by him that lives for ever and ever, who created heaven, and the things that therein are, and the earth, and the things that therein are, and the sea, and the things which are therein, that there should be time no longer: but in the days of the voice of the seventh angel, when he shall begin to sound, the mystery of God should be finished, as he has declared to his servants the prophets.

20   And the voice which I heard from heaven spoke unto me again, and said, "Go and take the little scroll which is open in the hand of the angel which stands upon the sea and upon the land."

21   And I went unto the angel, and said unto him, "Give me the little scroll." And he said unto me, "Take it, and eat it up; and it shall make your belly bitter, but it shall be in your mouth sweet as honey." And I took the little scroll out of the angel's hand, and ate it up; and it was in my mouth sweet as honey: and as soon as I had eaten it, my belly was bitter.

22   And he said unto me, "You must prophesy again about many peoples, and nations, and tongues, and kings."

Interlude—The Two Witnesses
Revelation 11:1-14

And there was given me a reed like unto a measuring rod: and the 23
angel stood, saying, "Rise, and measure the temple of God, and the altar,
and them that worship therein. But the court which is outside the temple
leave out, and do not measure it; for it is given unto the Gentiles: and the
holy city shall they trample underfoot forty and two months. And I will give
power unto my two witnesses, and they shall prophesy a thousand two hundred and sixty days, clothed in sackcloth."

These are the two olive trees, and the two lampstands standing before 24
the God of the earth. And if any man will harm them, fire proceeds out of
their mouths, and devours their enemies: and if any man will harm them, he
must in this manner be killed. These have power to shut the sky, that it cannot rain in the days of their prophecy: and have power over waters to turn
them to blood, and to strike the earth with all plagues, as often as they will.

And when they shall have finished their testimony, the beast that 25
ascends out of the bottomless pit shall make war against them, and shall
overcome them, and kill them. And their dead bodies shall lie in the street
of the great city, which spiritually is called Sodom and Egypt, where also
our Lord was crucified.

And they of the peoples and tribes and tongues and nations shall see 26
their dead bodies three and a half days, and shall not allow their dead bodies to be put in graves. And they that dwell upon the earth shall rejoice over
them, and make merry, and shall send gifts one to another; because these
two prophets tormented them that dwell on the earth.

And after three and a half days the breath of life from God entered into 27
them, and they stood upon their feet; and great fear fell upon them which
saw them. And they heard a great voice from heaven saying unto them,
"Come up here." And they ascended up to heaven in a cloud; and their enemies saw them.

And the same hour was there a great earthquake, and the tenth part of 28
the city fell, and in the earthquake were killed of men seven thousand: and
the survivors were terrified, and gave glory to the God of heaven.

The second woe is past; and, behold, the third woe comes quickly. 29

Trumpet 7: The Kingdom Proclaimed
Revelation 11:15-19

And the seventh angel sounded; and there were great voices in heaven, 30
saying, "The kingdom of this world is become the kingdom of our Lord, and
of his Christ; and he shall reign for ever and ever."

And the four and twenty elders, which sat before God on their thrones, 31
fell upon their faces, and worshiped God, saying, "We give you thanks, O
Lord God Almighty, which are, and were, and are to come; because you
have taken to yourself your great power, and have reigned. And the nations

31 were angry, and your wrath is come, and the time of the dead, that they should be judged, and that you should give reward unto your servants the prophets, and to the saints, and them that fear your name, small and great; and should destroy them which destroy the earth."

32   And the temple of God was opened in heaven, and there was seen in his temple the ark of his covenant: and there were lightnings, and noises, and thunderings, and an earthquake, and great hailstorm.

CHAPTER 151

Mystic Signs

Sign 1: The Woman and Dragon
Revelation 12:1-6

And there appeared a great sign in heaven; a woman clothed with the 1 sun, and the moon under her feet, and upon her head a crown of twelve stars: and she being with child cried out, laboring in birth, and anguished to give birth.

And there appeared another sign in heaven; and behold a great red 2 dragon, having seven heads and ten horns, and seven crowns upon his heads. And his tail drew the third part of the stars of heaven, and did cast them to the earth: and the dragon stood before the woman which was about to give birth, to devour her child as soon as it was born.

And she brought forth a male child, who was to rule all nations with a 3 rod of iron: and her child was caught up unto God, and to his throne. And the woman fled into the wilderness, where she has a place prepared of God, that they should feed her there a thousand two hundred and sixty days.

Satan—Cast Out of Heaven
Revelation 12:7-12

And there was war in heaven: Michael and his angels fought against 4 the dragon; and the dragon fought and his angels, and did not prevail; neither was their place found any longer in heaven. And the great dragon was cast out, that old serpent, called the Devil, and Satan, which deceives the whole world: he was cast out to the earth, and his angels were cast out with him.

And I heard a loud voice saying in heaven, "Now is come salvation, 5 and power, and the kingdom of our God, and the power of his Christ: for the accuser of our brethren is cast down, which accused them before our God day and night. And they overcame him by the blood of the Lamb, and by the

5 word of their testimony; and they did not love their lives unto the death. Therefore rejoice, you heavens, and you that dwell in them. Woe to the inhabitants of the earth and of the sea! for the devil is come down unto you, having great wrath, because he knows that he has but a short time."

Satan—Cast to the Earth
Revelation 12:13-17

6 And when the dragon saw that he was cast unto the earth, he persecuted the woman which brought forth the male child. And to the woman were given two wings of a great eagle, that she might fly into the wilderness, into her place, where she is nourished for a time, and times, and half a time, from the presence of the serpent.

7 And the serpent spewed out of his mouth water as a flood after the woman, that he might cause her to be carried away of the flood. And the earth helped the woman, and the earth opened its mouth, and swallowed up the flood which the dragon spewed out of his mouth.

8 And the dragon was furious with the woman, and went to make war with the rest of her offspring, which keep the commandments of God, and have the testimony of Jesus Christ.

Sign 2: Beast From the Sea
Revelation 13:1-10

9 And I stood upon the sand of the sea, and saw a beast rise up out of the sea, having seven heads and ten horns, and upon his horns ten crowns, and upon his heads the name of blasphemy.

10 And the beast which I saw was like unto a leopard, and his feet were as the feet of a bear, and his mouth as the mouth of a lion: and the dragon gave him his authority, and his throne, and great authority. And I saw one of his heads as if it were wounded to death; and his deadly wound was healed: and all the world followed with wonder the beast. And they worshiped the dragon which gave authority unto the beast: and they worshiped the beast, saying, "Who is like unto the beast? who is able to make war against him?"

11 And there was given unto him a mouth speaking haughty things and blasphemies; and authority was given unto him to continue forty and two months. And he opened his mouth in blasphemy against God, to blaspheme his name, and his dwelling place, and them that dwell in heaven.

12 And it was given unto him to make war against the saints, and to overcome them: and authority was given him over all tribes, and tongues, and nations. And all that dwell upon the earth shall worship him, whose names are not written in the book of life of the Lamb slain from the foundation of the world.

13 If any man has an ear, let him hear.

He that leads into captivity shall go into captivity: he that kills with 14 the sword must be killed with the sword. Here is the endurance and the faith of the saints.

Sign 3: Beast From the Earth
Revelation 13:11-18

And I beheld another beast coming up out of the earth; and he had two 15 horns like a lamb, and he spoke as a dragon. And he exercises all the authority of the first beast before him, and causes the earth and them which dwell therein to worship the first beast, whose deadly wound was healed.

And he performs great signs, so that he makes fire come down from 16 heaven on the earth in the sight of men, and deceives them that dwell on the earth by the means of those miracles which he had power to do in the sight of the beast; saying to them that dwell on the earth, that they should make an image to the beast, which had the wound by a sword, and did live.

And he had power to give breath unto the image of the beast, that the 17 image of the beast should both speak, and cause that as many as would not worship the image of the beast should be killed. And he causes all, both small and great, rich and poor, free and bond, to receive a mark on their right hands, or on their foreheads: and that no man might buy or sell, except he that had the mark, or the name of the beast, or the number of his name.

Here is wisdom. Let him that has understanding calculate the number 18 of the beast: for it is the number of a man; and his number is Six hundred sixty and six.

Sign 4: The Redeemed With the Lamb
Revelation 14:1-5

And I looked, and, lo, a Lamb stood on the mount Zion, and with 19 him a hundred forty and four thousand, having his Father's name written on their foreheads. And I heard a voice from heaven, as the sound of many waters, and as the sound of a great thunder: and I heard the sound of harpers harping with their harps: and they sang as it were a new song before the throne, and before the four living creatures, and the elders: and no man could learn that song but the hundred and forty and four thousand, which were redeemed from the earth.

These are they which were not defiled with women; for they are vir- 20 gins. These are they which follow the Lamb wherever he goes. These were redeemed from among men, being the first fruits unto God and to the Lamb. And in their mouth was found no deceit: for they are without fault before the throne of God.

Sign 5: The Everlasting Gospel
Revelation 14:6-7

And I saw another angel fly in the midst of heaven, having the ever- 21 lasting gospel to proclaim unto them that dwell on the earth, and to every

21 nation, and tribe, and tongue, and people, saying with a loud voice, "Fear God, and give glory to him; for the hour of his judgment is come: and worship him that made heaven, and earth, and the sea, and the fountains of waters."

Proclamation—The Doom of Babylon
Revelation 14:8

22   And there followed another angel, saying, "Babylon is fallen, is fallen, that great city, because she made all nations drink of the wine of the wrath of her immoral passion."

Proclamation—The Mark of the Beast
Revelation 14:9-13

23   And the third angel followed them, saying with a loud voice, "If any man worships the beast and its image, and receives its mark on his forehead, or on his hand, the same shall drink of the wine of the wrath of God, which is poured out without dilution into the cup of his indignation; and he shall be tormented with fire and brimstone in the presence of the holy angels, and in the presence of the Lamb: and the smoke of their torment ascends up for ever and ever: and they have no rest day nor night, who worships the beast and its image, and whosoever receives the mark of its name."

24   Here is the endurance of the saints: here are they that keep the commandments of God, and the faith of Jesus.

25   And I heard a voice from heaven saying unto me, "Write, 'Blessed are the dead which die in the Lord from henceforth' ": "Yes," says the Spirit, "that they may rest from their labors; and their works do follow them."

Sign 6: The Harvest of the Earth
Revelation 14:14-16

26   And I looked, and behold a white cloud, and upon the cloud one sat like unto the Son of man, having on his head a golden crown, and in his hand a sharp sickle. And another angel came out of the temple, crying with a loud voice to him that sat on the cloud, "Thrust in your sickle, and reap: for the time is come for you to reap; for the harvest of the earth is ripe."

> I LOOKED, AND BEHOLD A WHITE CLOUD, AND UPON THE CLOUD ONE SAT LIKE UNTO THE SON OF MAN.

27   And he that sat on the cloud thrust in his sickle on the earth; and the earth was reaped.

Reaping—The Grapes of Wrath
Revelation 14:17-20

28   And another angel came out of the temple which is in heaven, he also having a sharp sickle. And another angel came out from the altar, which had power over fire; and cried with a loud cry to him that had the sharp sickle, saying, "Thrust in your sharp sickle, and gather the clusters of the vine of the earth; for its grapes are fully ripe."

And the angel thrust in his sickle into the earth, and gathered the vine 29 of the earth, and cast it into the great winepress of the wrath of God. And the winepress was trampled outside the city, and blood came out of the winepress, even up to the horses' bridles, by the distance of about two hundred miles.

Sign 7: The Seven Last Plagues
Revelation 15:1-8

And I saw another sign in heaven, great and astonishing, seven angels 30 having the seven last plagues; for in them is filled up the wrath of God.

And I saw as it were a sea of glass mingled with fire: and them that 31 had gotten the victory over the beast, and over its image, and over its mark, and over the number of its name, stand on the sea of glass, having the harps of God. And they sang the song of Moses the servant of God, and the song of the Lamb, saying, "Great and marvelous are your works, Lord God Almighty; just and true are your ways, you King of saints. Who shall not fear you, O Lord, and glorify your name? for you only are holy: for all nations shall come and worship before you; for your judgments have been revealed."

And after that I looked, and, behold, the temple of the tabernacle of the 32 testimony in heaven was opened: and the seven angels came out of the temple, having the seven plagues, dressed in pure and white linen, and having their breasts wrapped with golden bands.

And one of the four living creatures gave unto the seven angels seven 33 golden vials full of the wrath of God, who lives for ever and ever. And the temple was filled with smoke from the glory of God, and from his power; and no man was able to enter into the temple, till the seven plagues of the seven angels were completed.

CHAPTER 152

Seven Vials Judgments

Vial 1: Sores On Beast's Followers
Revelation 16:1-2

1   And I heard a great voice out of the temple saying to the seven angels, "Go your ways, and pour out the vials of the wrath of God upon the earth."

2   And the first went, and poured out his vial upon the earth; and there fell a foul and grievous sore upon the men which had the mark of the beast, and upon them which worshiped its image.

Vial 2: Death in the Sea
Revelation 16:3

3   And the second angel poured out his vial upon the sea; and it became as the blood of a dead man: and every living thing died in the sea.

Vial 3: Waters Become Blood
Revelation 16:4-7

4   And the third angel poured out his vial upon the rivers and fountains of waters; and they became blood.

5   And I heard the angel of the waters say, "You are righteous, O Lord, which are, and were, and shall be, because you have judged thus. For they have shed the blood of saints and prophets, and you have given them blood to drink; for they deserve it."

6   And I heard another out of the altar say, "Even so, Lord God Almighty, true and righteous are your judgments."

Vial 4: Blasphemers Scorched
Revelation 16:8-9

7   And the fourth angel poured out his vial upon the sun; and power was given unto him to scorch men with fire. And men were scorched with great

heat, and blasphemed the name of God, which has power over these 7
plagues: and they did not repent to give him glory.

Vial 5: Darkness and Pain
Revelation 16:10-11

And the fifth angel poured out his vial upon the throne of the beast; 8
and his kingdom was full of darkness; and they gnawed their tongues in
agony, and blasphemed the God of heaven because of their pains and their
sores, and did not repent of their deeds.

Vial 6: Euphrates Dried Up
Revelation 16:12-16

And the sixth angel poured out his vial upon the great river Euphrates; 9
and the water thereof was dried up, that the way of the kings of the east
might be prepared. And I saw three unclean spirits like frogs come out of
the mouth of the dragon, and out of the mouth of the beast, and out of the
mouth of the false prophet. For they are the spirits of demons, performing
signs, which go forth unto the kings of the earth and of the whole world, to
gather them to the battle of that great day of God Almighty.

"Behold, I come as a thief. Blessed is he that watches, and keeps his 10
clothing, lest he walk naked, and they see his shame." And he gathered them
together into a place called in the Hebrew tongue Armageddon.

Vial 7: Great Stones of Hail
Revelation 16:17-21

And the seventh angel poured out his vial into the air; and there came 11
a great voice out of the temple of heaven, from the throne, saying, "It is
done." And there were noises, and thunders, and lightnings; and there was
a great earthquake, such as was not since men were upon the earth, so
mighty an earthquake, and so great.

And the great city was divided into three parts, and the cities of the 12
nations fell: and great Babylon came in remembrance before God, to give
unto her the cup of the wine of the fierceness of his wrath. And every island
fled away, and the mountains were not found. And there fell upon men a
great hail out of heaven, every hailstone about the weight of a hundred
pounds: and men blasphemed God because of the plague of the hail; for the
plague thereof was exceedingly great.

CHAPTER 153

CHRIST PREVAILS OVER ANTICHRIST

Babylon—The Great Mystery
Revelation 17:1-6

1 And there came one of the seven angels which had the seven vials, and talked with me, saying unto me, "Come here; I will show unto you the judgment of the great harlot that sits upon many waters: with whom the kings of the earth have committed immorality, and the inhabitants of the earth have been made drunk with the wine of her immorality."

2 So he carried me away in the spirit into the wilderness: and I saw a woman sit upon a scarlet-colored beast, full of names of blasphemy, having seven heads and ten horns. And the woman was arrayed in purple and scarlet color, and adorned with gold and precious stones and pearls, having a golden cup in her hand full of abominations and filthiness of her fornication: and upon her forehead was a name written, MYSTERY, BABYLON THE GREAT, THE MOTHER OF HARLOTS AND ABOMINATIONS OF THE EARTH.

3 And I saw the woman drunk with the blood of the saints, and with the blood of the martyrs of Jesus: and when I saw her, I wondered with great wonder.

Babylon—The Mystery Explained
Revelation 17:7-18

4 And the angel said unto me, "Why did you marvel? I will tell you the mystery of the woman, and of the beast that carries her, which has the seven heads and ten horns. The beast that you saw was, and is not; and shall ascend out of the bottomless pit, and go into perdition: and they that dwell on the earth shall wonder, whose names were not written in the book of life from the foundation of the world, when they behold the beast that was, and is not, and yet is.

"And here is the mind which has wisdom. The seven heads are seven 5 mountains, on which the woman sits. And there are seven kings: five are fallen, and one is, and the other is not yet come; and when he comes, he must continue a short time. And the beast that was, and is not, even it is the eighth, and is of the seven, and goes into perdition.

"And the ten horns which you saw are ten kings, which have received 6 no kingdom as yet; but receive power as kings for one hour with the beast. These have one mind, and shall give their power and authority unto the beast. These shall make war with the Lamb, and the Lamb shall overcome

> HE IS LORD OF LORDS, AND KING OF KINGS: AND THEY THAT ARE WITH HIM ARE CALLED, AND CHOSEN, AND FAITHFUL.

them: for he is Lord of lords, and King of kings: and they that are with him are called, and chosen, and faithful."

And he says unto me, "The waters which you saw, where the harlot 7 sits, are peoples, and multitudes, and nations, and tongues. And the ten horns which you saw upon the beast, these shall hate the harlot, and shall make her desolate and naked, and shall eat her flesh, and burn her with fire. For God has put in their hearts to fulfill his purpose, and to agree, and give their kingdom unto the beast, until the words of God shall be fulfilled.

"And the woman which you saw is that great city, which reigns over 8 the kings of the earth."

Babylon—The Great Fall
Revelation 18:1-8

And after these things I saw another angel come down from heaven, 9 having great authority; and the earth was illuminated with his splendor. And he cried mightily with a strong voice, saying, "Babylon the great is fallen, is fallen, and is become the dwelling place of demons, and the prison of every foul spirit, and a cage of every unclean and hated bird. For all nations have drunk of the wine of the wrath of her immoral passion, and the kings of the earth have committed immorality with her, and the merchants of the earth are grown rich through the abundance of her luxury."

And I heard another voice from heaven, saying, "Come out of her, my 10 people, that you be not partakers of her sins, and that you receive not of her plagues. For her sins have reached unto heaven, and God has remembered her iniquities. Render to her even as she rendered to you, and render unto her double according to her works: in the cup which she has filled fill to her double. How much she has glorified herself, and lived luxuriously, so much torment and sorrow give her: for she says in her heart, 'I sit a queen, and am no widow, and shall see no sorrow.' Therefore shall her plagues come in one day, death, and mourning, and famine; and she shall be utterly burned with fire: for strong is the Lord God who judges her.

Babylon—World Laments the Fall
Revelation 18:9-20

"And the kings of the earth, who have committed immorality and lived 11 luxuriously with her, shall weep for her, and lament for her, when they shall

11 see the smoke of her burning, standing far off for the fear of her torment, saying, 'Alas, alas, that great city Babylon, that mighty city! for in one hour is your judgment comes.'

12 "And the merchants of the earth shall weep and mourn over her; for no man buys their merchandise anymore: the merchandise of gold, and silver, and precious stones, and of pearls, and fine linen, and purple, and silk, and scarlet, and all scented wood, and all kinds of objects of ivory, and all kinds of objects of most precious wood, and of brass, and iron, and marble, and cinnamon, and incense, and ointments, and frankincense, and wine, and oil, and fine flour, and wheat, and cattle, and sheep, and horses, and chariots, and slaves, and souls of men.

13 "And the fruits that your soul lusted after are departed from you, and all things which were dainty and splendid are departed from you, and you shall find them no more at all. The merchants of these things, which were made rich by her, shall stand far off for the fear of her torment, weeping and wailing, and saying, 'Alas, alas, that great city, that was clothed in fine linen, and purple, and scarlet, and adorned with gold, and precious stones, and pearls!

14 " 'For in one hour such great riches is come to nothing.' And every shipmaster, and all the company in ships, and sailors, and as many as trade by sea, stood far off, and cried out when they saw the smoke of her burning, saying, 'What city is like unto this great city!'

15 "And they threw dust on their heads, and cried out, weeping and wailing, saying, 'Alas, alas, that great city, in which were made rich all that had ships in the sea by reason of her wealth! for in one hour is she made desolate.' Rejoice over her, O heaven, and you saints and apostles and prophets; for God has avenged you on her."

Babylon—The Fall Is Final
Revelation 18:21-24

16 And a mighty angel took up a stone like a great millstone, and cast it into the sea, saying, "Thus with violence shall that great city Babylon be thrown down, and shall be found no more at all.

17 "And the sound of harpers, and musicians, and of pipers, and trumpeters, shall be heard no more at all in you; and no craftsman, of whatsoever craft he be, shall be found anymore in you; and the sound of a millstone shall be heard no more at all in you; and the light of a lamp shall shine no more at all in you; and the sound of the bridegroom and of the bride shall be heard no more at all in you: for your merchants were the great men of the earth; for by your sorceries were all nations deceived.

18 "And in her was found the blood of prophets, and of saints, and of all that were slain upon the earth."

Heavenly Praise of God
Revelation 19:1-10

19 And after these things I heard a great voice of many people in heaven, saying, "Alleluia; Salvation, and glory, and honor, and power, unto the Lord

our God: for true and righteous are his judgments: for he has judged the 19 great harlot, which did corrupt the earth with her immorality, and has avenged the blood of his servants at her hand."

And again they said, "Alleluia. And her smoke rose up for ever and 20 ever." And the four and twenty elders and the four living creatures fell down and worshiped God that sat on the throne, saying, "Amen; Alleluia."

And a voice came out of the throne, saying, "Praise our God, all you 21 his servants, and you that fear him, both small and great."

And I heard as it were the voice of a great multitude, and as the sound 22 of many waters, and as the sound of mighty thunderings, saying, "Alleluia: for the Lord God omnipotent reigns. Let us be glad and rejoice, and give honor to him: for the marriage of the Lamb is come, and his bride has made herself ready." And to her was granted that she should be arrayed in fine linen, clean and white: for the fine linen is the righteousness of saints.

And he said unto me, "Write, 'Blessed are they which are called unto 23 the marriage supper of the Lamb.'" And he said unto me, "These are the true sayings of God." And I fell at his feet to worship him. And he said unto me, "See you do it not: I am your fellow servant, and of your brethren that have the testimony of Jesus: worship God: for the testimony of Jesus is the spirit of prophecy."

A White Horse and Faithful Rider
Revelation 19:11-21

And I saw heaven opened, and behold a white horse; and he that sat 24 upon it was called Faithful and True, and in righteousness he does judge and make war. His eyes were as a flame of fire, and on his head were many crowns; and he had a name written, that no man knew, except he himself. And he was dressed with a robe dipped in blood: and his name is called The Word of God.

> I SAW HEAVEN OPENED, AND BEHOLD A WHITE HORSE; AND HE THAT SAT UPON IT WAS CALLED FAITHFUL AND TRUE.

And he has on his robe and on his thigh a name written, KING OF 25 KINGS, AND LORD OF LORDS. And the armies which were in heaven followed him upon white horses, clothed in fine linen, white and clean. And out of his mouth goes a sharp sword, that with it he should strike the

> KING OF KINGS, AND LORD OF LORDS

nations: and he shall rule them with a rod of iron: and he treads the winepress of the fierceness and wrath of Almighty God.

And I saw an angel standing in the sun; and he cried with a loud 26 voice, saying to all the birds that fly in the midst of heaven, "Come and gather yourselves together unto the supper of the great God; that you may eat the flesh of kings, and the flesh of captains, and the flesh of mighty men,

26 and the flesh of horses, and of them that sit on them, and the flesh of all men, both free and bond, both small and great."

27   And I saw the beast, and the kings of the earth, and their armies, gathered together to make war against him that sat on the horse, and against his army. And the beast was captured, and with it the false prophet that performed signs before it, with which it deceived them that had received the mark of the beast, and them that worshiped its image. These both were cast alive into a lake of fire burning with brimstone. And the rest were slain with the sword of him that sat upon the horse, which sword proceeded out of his mouth: and all the birds were filled with their flesh.

CHAPTER 154

CHRIST PREVAILS OVER SATAN

Satan Bound One Thousand Years
Revelation 20:1-3

And I saw an angel come down from heaven, having the key of the 1
bottomless pit and a great chain in his hand. And he seized the dragon, that
old serpent, which is the Devil, and Satan, and bound him for a thousand
years, and cast him into the bottomless pit, and locked him up, and set a seal
upon him, that he should deceive the nations no more, till the thousand
years should be finished: and after that he must be released a little season.

The First Resurrection
Revelation 20:4-6

And I saw thrones, and they sat upon them, and judgment was given 2
unto them: and I saw the souls of them that were beheaded for the witness
of Jesus, and for the word of God, and which had not worshiped the beast,
neither his image, neither had received his mark upon their foreheads, or on
their hands; and they lived and reigned with Christ a thousand years.

But the rest of the dead did not live again until the thousand years were 3
finished. This is the first resurrection. Blessed and holy is he that has part
in the first resurrection: on such the second death has no power, but they
shall be priests of God and of Christ, and shall reign with him a thousand
years.

The Final Defeat of Satan
Revelation 20:7-10

And when the thousand years are expired, Satan shall be released out 4
of his prison, and shall go out to deceive the nations which are in the four
corners of the earth, Gog and Magog, to gather them together to battle: the
number of whom is as the sand of the sea.

5 And they went up on the breadth of the earth, and encircled the camp of the saints, and the beloved city: and fire came down from God out of heaven, and devoured them. And the devil that deceived them was cast into the lake of fire and brimstone, where the beast and the false prophet are, and shall be tormented day and night for ever and ever.

The Final Judgment
Revelation 20:11-15

6 And I saw a great white throne, and him that sat on it, from whose presence the earth and the heaven fled away; and there was found no place for them. And I saw the dead, small and great, stand before God; and the books were opened: and another book was opened, which is the book of life: and the dead were judged out of those things which were written in the books, according to their works.

7 And the sea gave up the dead which were in it; and death and Hades delivered up the dead which were in them: and they were judged every man according to their works. And death and Hades were cast into the lake of fire. This is the second death.

8 And whosoever was not found written in the book of life was cast into the lake of fire.

CHAPTER 155

A New Heaven and a New Earth

A New Heaven and Earth
Revelation 21:1-8

And I saw a new heaven and a new earth: for the first heaven and the ¹ first earth were passed away; and there was no more sea.

And I John saw the holy city, new Jerusalem, coming down from God ² out of heaven, prepared as a bride adorned for her husband. And I heard a great voice out of heaven saying, "Behold, the tabernacle of God is with men, and he will dwell with them, and they shall be his people, and God himself shall be with them, and be their God. And God shall wipe away all tears from their eyes; and there shall be no more death, neither sorrow, nor crying, neither shall there be any more pain: for the former things are passed away."

And he that sat upon the throne said, "Behold, I make all things new." ³ And he said unto me, "Write: for these words are true and faithful."

And he said unto me, "It is done. I am Alpha and Omega, the ⁴ beginning and the end. I will give unto him that is thirsty of the fountain of the water of life freely. He that overcomes shall inherit all things; and I will be his God, and he shall be my son.

"But the fearful, and unbelieving, and the abominable, and mur- ⁵ derers, and whoremongers, and sorcerers, and idolaters, and all liars, shall have their part in the lake which burns with fire and brimstone: which is the second death."

A New Jerusalem
Revelation 21:9-27

And there came unto me one of the seven angels which had the seven ⁶ vials full of the seven last plagues, and talked with me, saying, "Come here, I will show you the bride, the Lamb's wife."

7　　　And he carried me away in the spirit to a great and high mountain, and showed me that great city, the holy Jerusalem, descending out of heaven from God, having the glory of God: and its light was like unto a stone most precious, even like a jasper stone, clear as crystal; and had a wall great and high, and had twelve gates, and at the gates twelve angels, and names written thereon, which are the names of the twelve tribes of the children of Israel: on the east three gates; on the north three gates; on the south three gates; and on the west three gates. And the wall of the city had twelve foundations, and in them the names of the twelve apostles of the Lamb.

8　　　And he that talked with me had a golden reed to measure the city, and the gates thereof, and the wall thereof. And the city lies perfectly square, and the length is as large as the breadth: and he measured the city with the reed, about one thousand five hundred miles. The length and the breadth and the height of it are equal. And he measured the wall thereof, two hundred and sixteen feet, according to the measure of a man, that is, of the angel. And the building of the wall of it was of jasper: and the city was pure gold, like unto clear glass.

9　　　And the foundations of the wall of the city were adorned with all kinds of precious stones. The first foundation was jasper; the second, sapphire; the third, a chalcedony; the fourth, an emerald; the fifth, sardonyx; the sixth, sardius; the seventh, chrysolite; the eighth, beryl; the ninth, a topaz; the tenth, a chrysoprasus; the eleventh, a jacinth; the twelfth, an amethyst. And the twelve gates were twelve pearls; every individual gate was of one pearl: and the street of the city was pure gold, as it were transparent glass.

10

> THE CITY HAD NO NEED OF THE SUN, NEITHER OF THE MOON, TO SHINE IN IT: FOR THE GLORY OF GOD DID ILLUMINATE IT.

And I saw no temple therein: for the Lord God Almighty and the Lamb are the temple of it. And the city had no need of the sun, neither of the moon, to shine upon it: for the glory of God did illuminate it, and the Lamb is the light thereof.

11　　　And the nations of them which are saved shall walk in the light of it: and the kings of the earth do bring their glory and honor into it. And the gates of it shall not be shut at all by day: for there shall be no night there. And they shall bring the glory and honor of the nations into it.

12　　　And there shall in no way enter into it anything that defiles, neither whatsoever works abomination, or makes a lie: but they which are written in the Lamb's book of life.

A Pure River of Water, Tree of Life
Revelation 22:1-5

13　　　And he showed me a pure river of water of life, clear as crystal, flowing out of the throne of God and of the Lamb. In the middle of the street of the city, and on either side of the river, was there the tree of life, which bore twelve kinds of fruits, and yielded its fruit every month: and the leaves of the tree were for the healing of the nations.

And there shall be no more curse: but the throne of God and of the 14 Lamb shall be in it; and his servants shall serve him: and they shall see his face; and his name shall be on their foreheads. And there shall be no night there; and they need no lamp, neither light of the sun; for the Lord God gives them light: and they shall reign for ever and ever.

CHAPTER 156

CONCLUSION

"Behold, I Come Quickly"
Revelation 22:6-11

1   And he said unto me, "These sayings are faithful and true": and the Lord God of the holy prophets sent his angel to show unto his servants the things which must shortly be done. "Behold, I come quickly: blessed is he that keeps the sayings of the prophecy of this book."

2   And I John saw these things, and heard them. And when I had heard and seen, I fell down to worship before the feet of the angel which showed me these things. Then he said unto me, "See that you do not that: for I am your fellow servant, and of your brethren the prophets, and of them which keep the sayings of this book: worship God."

3   And he said unto me, "Do not seal the sayings of the prophecy of this book: for the time is at hand. He that is unjust, let him be unjust still: and he which is filthy, let him be filthy still: and he that is righteous, let him be righteous still: and he that is holy, let him be holy still.

"I Am the Alpha and Omega"
Revelation 22:12-17

4   "And, behold, I come quickly; and my reward is with me, to give every man according as his work shall be. I am Alpha and Omega, the beginning and the end, the first and the last."

5   Blessed are they that do his commandments, that they may have the right to the tree of life, and may enter in through the gates into the city. For outside are dogs, and sorcerers, and whoremongers, and murderers, and idolaters, and whosoever loves and practices a lie.

6   "I Jesus have sent my angel to testify unto you these things in the churches. I am the root and the offspring of David, and the bright and morning star."

And the Spirit and the bride say, "Come." And let him that hears say, 7
"Come." And let him that is thirsty come. And whosoever will, let him take
the water of life freely.

Conclusion
Revelation 22:18-21

For I testify unto every man that hears the words of the prophecy of 8
this book, If any man shall add unto these things, God shall add unto him
the plagues that are written in this book: and if any man shall take away
from the words of the book of this prophecy, God shall take away his part
out of the book of life, and out of the holy city, and from the things which
are written in this book.

He which testifies these things says, "Surely I come quickly." Amen. 9
Even so, come, Lord Jesus.

The grace of our Lord Jesus Christ be with you all. Amen.   10

And so these words written two thousand years ago are written here again, not that they should be read and forgotten, or that they should be thought of as merely beautiful scripture intended for others in earlier times, but that they might be used as instruction for the nourishment and reclamation of the soul for all generations, now and for all time.

About the Compiler

Developed more by Providence than by plan, this book represents the culmination of a spiritual journey by the compiler, Charles Roller, that took him through a quarter century of study and searching.

Born in Tulsa, Oklahoma, at the beginning of the Great Depression, he spent his younger years without a father. Between the ages of six and eleven he was raised by his grandparents on a farm near Vinita, Oklahoma, as his mother was unable to work and care for the young boy. The King James Bible that lay on end table in the living room of his grandparents' house was one of the few books they had in the house. During this time was his first remembrance of the Scriptures, for at the church in their town where two railroads crossed in the middle, the preacher talked of the book of Jesus and told the congregation that not everyone believed that Jesus was the Son of God. Young Charles wondered how this could be. So he took his grandparents Bible, big in his small hands, and began to read. It was filled with many words, and he knew but a few. This was his first venture into the book that was to become a central part of his life, summoning a deep calling that would remain with him throughout his years.

Eventually he and his mother reunited and returned to Tulsa, where he attended public schools. He went on to attend Northeastern State University in Oklahoma, where he worked his way through college at part-time jobs. He received a BS Degree in Business Administration in 1954, and in doing so became the first in his family to receive a college degree. As an adult he attended a variety of Protestant churches and in time came to develop an abiding love of the Scripture. He retained a silent yearning to understand more and would often awaken at night with a deep sense that he had not yet done what he was put here to do—yet knew that he should.

Over the years, his longing to understand more of the New Testament became focused on the fragmented compilation of the Bible and the beautiful but archaic language used by the King James Version. Studying a single event carefully across many pages would sometimes cause him to lose track of the story. One day he tried to locate a passage of Scripture that he had been reading the previous evening, but was unable to find it again. The story of unequal wages paid to workers in the field was one he wanted to reread. Frustrated in his search, he asked a friend to help him sort through the myriad of biblical accounts of the event.

This rather ordinary episode turned into the seed of an extraordinary idea that would occupy the next twenty-five years of Charles' life. He realized he needed a book for someone like himself—an ordinary person looking for a Bible that would lift the story of Jesus out of the darkness of ancient translations and into the light of today.

Searching through the shelves of libraries and bookstores for such a book, but finding none, he set out to compile his own personal edition of the New Testament based on his grandparents' beloved King James text, as it remains today the most beautiful and purest English translation of the bible ever written. His work would tell the story of the life of Christ chronologically, in one single thread of events, blending the many accounts of Jesus' life into one story that all could easily read and understand. It would tell an uninterrupted story of the life of Christ, from his birth through his death and resurrection, and continuing through the works of his followers. Above all else, it would be a Bible compiled *by* a layperson *for* the layperson, built on the work of the religious scholars who had come before, yet unencumbered by the outdated language of the early theologians.

To accomplish this, he first called a friend and asked if she would consent to cut up the King James New Testament and paste it back together again in order. She was horrified. And so Charles labor began, in a small rented apartment in 1976 with a pair of scissors and a commitment himself and his Maker. Over the years, others joined in the endeavor, each adding their time, treasure, and their sense of the Scripture. The collective effort of ministers, learned religious professionals, and everyday seekers of Truth added immensely to the result. With every precious detail of the King James text intact, it was molded into a form that those of all ages and backgrounds could apply to their own lives and from which those who had wandered from the bible might gather fresh meaning.

With care and precision the many separate accounts of Jesus' journey given in the King James, Gospels were blended into one single interwoven story that would allow the reader witness the chronological unfolding of events much the same as the disciples had done so many years before. Christian editors and religious advisors edited the work for accuracy and suitability for today's reader. The last half of the New Testament, containing the Acts and Letters, followed in a blended continuum of the first, undergoing the same careful attention. As the work came to fruition, the unique new presentation of this ageless story would astonish even those who had been closely involved.

After a quarter-century of arduous labor requiring the review of over 400 Bibles, references, and biblical studies, there lay before them a spiritual compilation of immense proportion. Charles had believed in his vision of the Scripture as a child and had never wavered from that belief. We share with you here the result of his quest—*the Bible he searched for but could not find.*

It is my hope that as Jesus' words of faith and hope begin their journey from these pages to each heart, they will fulfill the heart's insatiable desire for truth. To each of your questions, His timeless answer awaits.

Timeline

THE JOURNEY OF CHRIST
AND
THE JOURNEY OF THE APOSTLES

Timeline

———————————— The Journey of Christ ————————————

Year	10(BC)	0	10	20	30	40	50

BIRTH AND CHILDHOOD
- 6 BC The Angel's Announcement to Mary
- 5 BC The Birth of Jesus Christ
- 5 BC The Angel's News to Shepherds
- 4 BC Wise Men Come From the East
- 8 Jesus in the Temple (Age 12)

PUBLIC PREPARATION
- 25 Jesus Baptized (Age 30)
- 25 Temptation by the Devil
- 25 First Disciples
- 25 Water Made Wine Miracle
- 25 *'You Must Be Born Again'*
- 25 The Woman at the Well

MIRACLES IN GALILEE
- 26 First Healing Scenes
- 26 *'I Will Make You Fishers of Men'*
- 26 Twelve Ordained as Apostles

THE SERMON ON THE MOUNT
- 26 Blessings
- 26 *'Love Your Enemies'*
- 26 The Lord's Prayer
- 26 The Golden Rule

PURPOSE AND PARABLES
- 26 Parable of the Sower
- 26 Calming Wind and Sea
- 26 Apostles Sent Forth
- 26 John the Baptist Beheaded

EARLY REVELATIONS
- 27 Feeding Four Thousand
- 27 God's Plan for Redemption
- 27 The Transfiguration
- 27 Children Greatest in Kingdom
- 27 Brotherly Correction and Unity

DOCTRINES OF TRUTH
- 28 *'My Doctrine Is Not Mine'*
- 28 Adulterous Woman Forgiven
- 28 *'You Shall Know the Truth'*
- 28 *'I Am the Good Shepherd'*
- 28 Parable of the Good Samaritan

SERVING AND SERVITUDE
- 28 Gateway to the Kingdom
- 28 Parable of the Prodigal Son
- 28 Law and the Prophets
- 28 Duties of a Servant
- 28 *'I Am the Resurrection'*

(• Event — • *'Quotation'* — • **Letter** (themes) — • **Book**)

Year 10(BC)	0	10	20	30	40	50

FINAL JOURNEY
- 29 Marriage and Divorce
- 29 Blessing Little Children
- 29 Parable of the Laborers
- 29 Healing Blind Bartimaeus

LAST SUPPER
- 29 The Triumphal Entry
- 29 End Times Described
- 29 The Last Supper
- 29 The Precious Promises
- 29 Intercessory Prayer

BETRAYAL, TRIAL, AND DEATH
- 29 Judas Betrays Jesus
- 29 The Jewish Trial of Jesus
- 29 The Roman Trial of Jesus
- 29 The Crucifixion of Jesus
- 29 Jesus Provides for His Mother

RESURRECTION AND ASCENSION
- 29 The Resurrection of Jesus
- 29 *'Receive the Holy Ghost'*
- 29 The Great Commission
- 29 The Ascension of Jesus

--------- Historical Events ---------

ROMAN RULERS
- 37 BC – AD 14 Caesar Augustus
- AD 11 – 37 Tiberius Caesar

JEWISH RULERS
- 37 BC – 4 BC Herod (king of all Palestine)
- 4 BC – AD 6 Herod Archelaus (ruler of Judea and Samaria)
- 4 BC – AD 39 Herod Antipas (ruler of Galilee and Perea)
- 4 BC – AD 34 Philip II Herod (ruler of Iturea and Trachonitis)

ROMAN GOVERNORS
- AD 6 – 26 Four Governors (Judea and Samaria)
- AD 26 – 36 Pontius Pilate (Judea and Samaria)

JEWISH HIGH PRIESTS
- AD 6 – 15 Annas
- AD 18 – 36 Caiaphas
- 20 BC – AD 62 Building of Jerusalem Temple
- 4 BC Death of Herod
- AD 6 Herod Archelaus (ruler of Judea and Samaria) removed

The Journey of Apostles

Year	25	30	40	50	60	70	80	90	100

EMERGENCE OF THE APOSTLES (29 – 34)
- 29 Arrival of the Holy Ghost
- 29 Peter's Address to the Crowd
  - 33 Martyrdom of Stephen
  - 33 Persecution of the Congregations

CONVERSION OF BELIEVERS (35 – 45)
- 35 Conversion of the Persecutor Saul (Paul)
- 37 Peter's Conversion of a Gentile
- 37 Peter's Report to Jerusalem Assembly
  - 44 *Letter from James* (a brother of Jesus)
    (partiality / faith and works / hearers and doers / the tongue)
  - 44 Martyrdom of an Apostle (James)
  - 44 Death of Herod (Agrippa I)

FIRST MISSIONARY JOURNEY (46 – 48)
- 47 Seven New Congregations
- 48 Council of Jerusalem Decision

SECOND MISSIONARY JOURNEY (48 – 52)
- 49 New Churches in Greece
  - 50 *First Letter to Thessalonians*
    (second coming of Christ)
  - 50 *Second Letter to Thessalonians*
    (before the second coming)

THIRD MISSIONARY JOURNEY (53 – 58)
- 55 *Gospel of Mark*
- 56 *First Letter to Corinthians*
  (the Lord's supper / love / resurrection)
- 56 *Second Letter to Corinthians*
  (eternal things / transformation / reconciliation)
- 57 *Letter to Galatians*
  (justification by faith / fruit of the Spirit / God's plan)
- 58 *Letter to Romans*
  (sin and salvation / forgiveness / predestination)

PAUL'S ARREST AND TRIAL (59 – 62)
- 60 Appeal to Caesar as Roman citizen
- 60 *Gospel of Matthew*
- 61 Paul Before King Agrippa II (the king)

PAUL'S CONFINEMENT IN ROME (62 – 64)
- 62 *Letter to Ephesians*
  (unity in Christ / spiritual strength / limitless love)
- 62 *Letter to Philippians*
  (gratitude / preexistence / virtuous thoughts)
- 62 *Letter to Colossians*
  (false teachers / forgiveness / limitless living)
- 62 *Letter to Philemon*
- 62 *Gospel of Luke*

Year 45   50   60   70   80   90   100   110   120

ACTS OF THE APOSTLES COMPLETION

- 65 *Acts of the Apostles*
- 65 *First Letter to Timothy*
  (contrary doctrine / good ministry / eternal life)
- 65 *Letter to Titus*
  (false teachers / sound doctrine / faith-grace)
- 65 *Second Letter to Timothy*
  (scriptures guide / leading / ending / farewell)
- 66 *Letter to Hebrews*
  (faith / foreshadowing / superior Christ)
- 66 *First Letter from Peter*
  (hope / holiness / true grace / persecution)
- 66 *Second Letter from Peter*
  (false teachers / in the last days / farewell)
- 67 *Letter from Jude* (a Brother of Jesus)
  (faith / false teachers / in the last days)
- 68 Apostles Peter and Paul are executed
- 85 *Gospel of John*
- 90 *First Letter from John*
  (love / light / antichrists)
- 90 *Second Letter from John*
  (loving all / deceivers)
- 90 *Third Letter from John*
- 95 *Revelation*
  (letters / judgment / renewal)

———————————— Historical Events ————————————

ROMAN RULERS
- 11 – 37 Tiberius Caesar
- 37 – 41 Caligula
- 41 – 54 Claudius
- 54 – 68 Nero
- 69 – 79 Vespasian
- 79 – 81 Titus
- 81 – 96 Domitian

JEWISH RULERS
- 4 BC – AD 39 Herod Antipas
- 41 – 44 Herod Agrippa I
- 53 – 93 Herod Agrippa II (the king)

ROMAN GOVERNORS
- 52 – 60 Felix
- 60 – 62 Festus
- 64 Burning of Rome
- 66 – 70 Roman-Jewish War
- 70 Destruction of Jerusalem

Research and References

In addition to the research and study of numerous textbooks, publications, and works of a similar nature, the following books were reviewed in preparation for the compilation of this book. The background and insight gleaned from this research effort was of immense value, as each scholar and author brought unique contributions in the form of guidance, inspiration, and fulfillment to the compilation of *The Seamless Bible*.

Bibles:

Eight Translation New Testament. Tyndale House Publishers, Inc., 1974.

KJV/NKJV Parallel Reference Bible. Thomas Nelson, Inc., 1991.

New American Standard Bible New Testament, 6th Edition. Lockman Foundation, 1963.

Reese Chronological Bible. Reese. Bethany House Publishers, 1980.

The Guidepost Parallel Bible. Guideposts, 1983.

The Greek New Testament, 3rd Edition. United Bible Societies, 1975.

The Holy Bible, King James Version. American Bible Society, n.d.

The Interlinear Greek-English New Testament. Zondervan Publishing House, 1887.

The NIV/KJV Parallel Bible. Thomas Nelson Publishers, 1991.

The Narrated Bible (NIV). F. LaGard Smith. Harvest House Publishers, 1984.

The People's New Testament With Explanatory Notes. Christian Publishing Company, 1891.

The Ryrie Study Bible New Testament. Ryrie. Moody Bible Institute, 1976.

The Student's Bible, 79th Edition. Nave & Nave, Abingdon Press, 1907.

Tyndale House Publishers Bible, 2nd Edition. Tyndale House Publishers, 1534. (A modern-spelling edition and with an introduction by David Daniell, Yale University Press, 1995).

Harmonies:

A Harmony of the Four Gospels. Daniel. Baker House, 1986.

A Harmony of the Gospels, 12th Edition. Kerr. Flemming H. Revell Company, 1903, 1924.

A Harmony of the Gospels for Historical Study, 3rd Edition. Stevens & Burton. Scribner's, 1904.

A Harmony of the Gospels for Students of the Life of Christ. Robertson. Harper & Row, 1922.

The Gospels Interwoven: Reference Edition. Zarley. Victor Books, 1987.

The Life of Christ in Stereo, 2nd Edition. Cheney, Western Baptist Press, 1971.

Concordances and Word Studies:

An Expository Dictionary of New Testament Word. Vine. F.W. Revelle, 1939, 1952.

Bible Student's English-Greek Concordance. Gall. Baker Book House, 1863, 1953.

New Testament Words in Today's Language. Detzler. Victor Books, 1986.

The Bible Word-Book. Wright. MacMillan Company, 1884.

The Book of New Testament Word Studies. Partridge. Barbour and Company, 1987.

The Language of the King James Bible. Elliott. Doubleday & Company, Inc., 1967.

Word Meanings in the New Testament. Earle. Baker House, Inc., 1986.

Wuest's Word Studies of the Greek New Testament. Wuest. Eerdmans Publishing Co., 1973.

Young's Analytical Concordance to the Bible. Young. MacDonald Publishing, 1880.

Dictionaries

A Dictionary of Contemporary Usage. Evans. Random House, Inc., 1957.

New Standard Bible Dictionary, 3rd Edition. Funk and Wagnalls Company, 1936.

Webster's New International Dictionary, 2nd Edition. G.C. Merriam Co., 1934.

Webster's New World Bible Dictionary. Simon & Schuster, Inc., 1986.

Webster's Third New International Dictionary. Merriam-Webster, Inc., 1961.

Other Sources

A General Introduction to the Bible. Geisler & Nix. Moody Press, 1968.

A General Introduction to the Bible (From Ancient Tablets to Modern Translations). Ewert. Zondervan Publishing House, 1983, 1990.

A New Testament History, 5th Edition. Floyd Filson. Westminster Press, n.d.

A Survey of the New Testament, 3rd Edition. Robert Gundry. Zondervan Publishing House, 1994.

Baker's Bible Handbook. Shaw. 1984, edited by W. Elwell. Baker Book House, 1986.

Cowman Hand Book of the Bible. Demarey. Cowman Publishing Co., 1964.

Handbook to the Gospels. John Wijngaards. Servant Books, 1979.

The New Testament Comes Alive. Oral Roberts. Parthenon Press, 1984.

The Interpreters Bible. Abingdon Press, 1952.

The Life and Work of Florus Josephus. John Winston Company, 1957.

The Making of the Old and the New Testaments. Mallory Beattie. Exposition Press, 1953.

The New Testament—A Critical Introduction. Freed. Wadswoth Publishing Co., 1990.

New Testament Introduction. Fiensy. College Press Publishing Company, 1994.

New Testament Survey, Revised. Tenney. Eerdmans Publishing Company, 1985.

The New Testament Speaks. Barker Laney Michaels. Harper and Row Publishers, 1969.

The Bible as History, 2nd Edition. Keller. William Morrow and Co., 1956, 1961.

The Heart of the New Testament. Hester. Broadman Press, 1950, 1963.

Understanding the New Testament, 2nd Edition. Kee & Young & Froehlich. Prentice-Hall, 1957, 1965.

Books of Interest

A History of God. Karen Armstrong. Knopf, 1993.

Book of Mercies. Frantz. Bobbs-Merrill Company, 1952.

Idioms in the Bible Explained / Key to the Original Gospels. Lamsa. HarperSanFran, 1931.

In the Steps of the Master. Morton. Methuen & Co., 1934, 1937, 1962.

Jesus the Son of Man. Gibran. Knopf, 1928, 1956, 1973.

Science and Health With Key to the Scriptures. Mary Baker Eddy, (Boston: The Writings of Mary Baker Eddy)1875-1934 (Phraseology and spiritual interpretations used in *The Seamless Bible* commentaries.)

The Four Gospels & Acts of the Apostles. Richard Roberts. n.p., 1992.

The 100: A Ranking of the Most Influential Persons in History. Hart. Hart Publishing, 1978.

The Dead Sea Scrolls and the Bible. Charles Pfeiffer. Baker House Company, 1969.

The Innocents Abroad. Mark Twain. 1869 (*Reader's Digest* edition, 1990).

The Life and Times of Jesus the Messiah. Edersheim. MacDonald Publishing, 1886.

The Life of Jesus Christ. James Stalker (1848-1927). Zondervan Publishing House, 1983.

The Miracle of Language. Lederer. Pocket Books, 1991.

The Mother Tongue (And How It Got That Way). Bryson. W. Morrow & Co., 1990.

The Original Jesus. Tom Wright. Lion Publishing, 1996.

The Story of Civilization: Part III Caesar and Christ. Durant. Simon & Schuster, 1944.

"The Story of Jesus," Reader's Digest. Reader's Digest Association, 1993.

The Story of Stories. Hinkley. NavPress, 1991.

Today's Handbook of Bible Characters. Blaiklock. Bethany House Publishers, 1979.

What the Bible Really Says. Manfred Barthel. Quill, 1980, 1983.

Index of Topics

Additional copies of this book and other
book titles from DESTINY IMAGE are
available at your local bookstore.

For a bookstore near you, call **1-800-722-6774**

Send a request for a catalog to:

Destiny Image® Publishers, Inc.
P.O. Box 310
Shippensburg, PA 17257-0310

*"Speaking to the Purposes of God for This
Generation and for the Generations to Come"*

**For a complete list of our titles,
visit us at www.destinyimage.com**